Moral Matters

Moral Matters

second edition

Jan Narveson

broadview press

Canadian Cataloguing in Publication Data

Narveson, Jan, 1936-
  Moral matters

2nd ed.

ISBN 1-55111-212-4

1. Social ethics.   2. Social problems.   I. Title.

HM216.N38 1999   303.3'.72   C99-930542-5

The publisher has made every attempt to locate the authors of the copyrighted material or their heirs and assigns, and would be grateful for information that would allow correction og any errors or omissions in subsequent editions of the work.

BROADVIEW PRESS, LTD.
is an independent, international publishing house, incorporated in 1985

North America
Post Office Box 1243, Peterborough, Ontario, Canada K9J 7H5
3576 California Road, Orchard Park, New York, USA 14127
TEL: (705) 743-8990; FAX (705) 743-8353; E-MAIL: 75322.44@compuserve.com

United Kingdom and Europe
Turpin Distribution Services, Ltd.,
Blackhorse Rd., Letchworth, Hertfordshire, SO6 EHN
TEL: (1462) 672555; FAX: (1462) 480947; E-MAIL: turpin@rsc.org

Australia
St. Clair Press, Post Office Box 287, Rozelle, NSW 2039
TEL: (612) 818-1942; FAX: (612) 418-1923

www.broadviewpress.com

Broadview Press gratefully acknowledges the financial support of the
Book Publishing Industry Development Program, Government of Canada.

Printed in Canada

Contents

Preface

The essays in the first edition of this book were the "result of reflection stimulated by classroom experience of rather more than twenty years, by reading and discussion with colleagues near and far, and by the experience of more decades of life experience than I like to admit." The stimulus for this second edition includes response to the first, as well as several more years of all of the above. All of this—I said—"has firmed up my perception of the proper point of view for dealing with moral matters, even though my results often differ from the views of other philosophers and of media moralists." The experience of those further years has also suggested the need for emphasizing what was not sufficiently emphasized previously, as well as a few modest alterations—for the better, I hope.

I also said, in the introduction to that first edition, that "These essays may strike some readers as polemical." That has proven to be quite true, even though I then went on to say, "There is no intention here of simply surveying the views in the field and leaving the reader with no indication of which view has the weight of reason on its side. The reader must decide that in any case, of course; my purpose is to assemble what seem to me the most compelling arguments. Those who don't concur will, I trust, be stimulated to find out what is wrong with them, and to do better."

There is room for reasonable differences on moral matters; that is a point that I hope emerges intact. Indeed, the scope for reasonable difference is in considerable part what informs the point of view of these essays. Nevertheless, as I explained in the first edition, I do not make a great effort here to represent the views of others; my purpose is to develop what seems to me the truth of the matter at hand, the views of others being noted briefly or by implication. Instead, I refer the reader to the huge and often excellent array of anthologies, well filled with competently written articles by those of differing views. While I hope to have anticipated much of what they say, there is no substitute for listening to them say it for themselves.

The point of view that unifies this book lends itself to succinct description. Morals, I point out, are supposed to be *for everybody*—they concern, as St. Thomas Aquinas says, the "common good." They are not confined to some segment of the populace, but must somehow reach to all. There are different ways of trying to do this, but most of them are at fault in neglecting one obvious fact: that the "all" to whom morality reaches are, each of them, moral *agents*, people who must and do make their own decisions about things, and who marshal their own cognitive resources in making them. But then, we come up against the fact that people *vary*; they have their own greatly differing interests and priorities. Despite this diversity, morals must stem from our interests, for there is nothing else to go by: appeals to magic or authority are useless and obfuscating in moral matters and readily subject to the charge of merely amounting to an attempt to promote the interests of their advocates, likely against those of the rest of us. An instructive example is afforded by St. Thomas Aquinas, himself a monk: despite his powerful perception of the universality of morals, Aquinas could support the persecution of heretics. It is distressing, and food for thought, that this can happen. But happen it does, and we must learn from the fact.

Morality, in short, needs to take account of our differences, and a morality for all must support and promote the diverse interests of the agents whose actions it purports to direct. For this reason, the *prima facie* rule, I hold, is always that an individual is to be allowed to act as he or she sees fit. If we are to override this freedom, we need good reasons for doing so. And those reasons, to be credible, must be good from the point of view *of the agent*, the very person of whom we are asking a change in conduct. Such reasons, I believe, can be discerned, sometimes readily, sometimes not. This book is an attempt to bring out those reasons, while arguing that competing accounts do not pass muster.

The general idea is that life should be as free as possible for all of us—and yet, in seeming paradox, that is itself the ground of our duties. I am far from the first to have proposed this. This book falls squarely within a classic tradition of moral philosophy that includes Mill, Kant, Hobbes, and, in some respects, the ancients. Perhaps it is in the nature of moral subjects that so much more of the truth about them is to be found in long-ago writers. However, little reference to those writers will be found here—not because they are unimportant but quite the opposite: they are much too interesting for the brief treatment I would have to confine myself to here.

The first chapter briefly explains this viewpoint, after which we plunge into specific issues. Not too specific, though: these are mostly matters of perennial rather than passing interest. I hope the selection is found of interest, and affords ample scope for reflection, especially on the innumerable issues not broached in this book.

An operational note to the reader is in order at this point. This book stems from notes for a course on moral issues that I have taught many times at the University of Waterloo. Recent versions of that course have employed two anthologies: my own *Moral Issues* and Eldon Soifer's *Ethical Issues*.[1] However, there are many other excellent collections on these matters, all of them containing plenty of articles opposed in one way or another to the views defended here. The worst way to defend a belief is to close one's eyes to all alternatives. My own views have been formulated in reaction to a vast literature arrayed mostly (but not entirely) on, as it were, the "other" side(s) of these controversial matters. Reading some of those materials is urged. However, in no case is it required in order to understand the essays in this book.

It remains only to express my thanks to the hundreds of students, the several teaching assistants, and the many colleagues far and wide with whom I have discussed these subjects over the years. If they have benefited from and enjoyed those exchanges as much as I have, they are fortunate indeed.

And finally, to add a stylistic caveat: I have, in the main, eschewed the currently "politically correct" fashion of seeking gender-neutrality in language at all costs, whereby one's writing must bear the clumsy burden either of innumerable "s/he," "he/she," and "she or he" constructions or of countless hypothetical Johns and Susans, Sams and Samanthas.

Chapter One

Moral Issues
and Moral Theory

The Subject Matter of This Inquiry

Until about thirty years ago, courses in ethics were devoted almost exclusively to the study of moral *theory*, in a very rarefied sense of the term "theory", that is,theories *about* morality, about the *concepts* of right and wrong, good and bad, and so on. This book, however, stems from a course concerned with what philosophers call "normative", "substantive", or, broadly, "applied" ethics: with views about which sorts of acts *are* right or wrong, *which* moral rules to follow, *which* moral principles we should actually have. In this book, we will be looking at a number of fairly specific areas of life in regard to which there has been and still is considerable controversy. Even the perennial ones are live issues in the minds of many people.

We will not look much into the history of ethical theory. Yet we will find in every case that issues of moral theory do crop up, demanding an idea of what morality is for—what it is all about—if we are to have any resolution. For some time now, philosophers have been aware that no rigid separation can be maintained between the high-level, "meta-ethical" theory to which philosophy, it was previously thought, should be exclusively devoted and the actual questions of what is right or wrong, that we face in our daily lives. But lately there has been a tendency to go to an opposite extreme and suppose that we can reflect on "practice" without doing "theory" at all. That is a theoretical stance that I roundly reject. Our involvement in particular issues will get us, willy-nilly, into theoretical questions that cannot be swept under the proverbial carpet. The appropriate response is to accept the need to look at theory and do the best we can with our limited encounter.

This work aims to be a reasoned inquiry into moral matters. We want to know what reasons there might be to think that this or that sort of act is right or wrong. Many of the answers suggested and argued for will, I am sure, be quite familiar to the reader. They will, I hope, have the "feel of rightness" about them. They will, in the jargon of recent philosophy, agree with "our intuitions." Others may not; some may even seem quite radical. But in all cases, I hope to show that there are good reasons for the views in question: that, indeed, is the purpose of this whole inquiry. We are not here simply to confirm your or my antecedent prejudices, or what we have learned at our mother's knee—nor, like refractory children, simply to deny them. We must, as Aristotle says, "value the truth above our friends"—and this includes the case where our "friends" are pet beliefs, or our mothers, or our fellow members of the various tribes we live among or stem from. They, too, one hopes, will prefer the truth to their own previous views, should those conflict.

So we can hardly help but try to come up with general ideas about morality as we attempt to come to grips with moral matters. We do so starting from, and keeping our focus on, the real world of action rather than on general theories that various philosophers have proposed. Still, as I say, theorizing is inevitable. We all have theories, whatever we call them, and so the only question is whether they can be supported. Thus, the rest of this introduction does what we mostly won't do thereafter: namely, sketch a general conception of what morals are all about.

What Is Morality About?

The specific connotations of the terms 'morals' and 'morality' are important here. There are issues of a kind that could reasonably be called "ethical" whose resolution lies quite beyond the limits of this course. That is one main reason why we need an introduction, to explain what we are and are not going to be inquiring into.

To start with, morality is not about vanilla versus chocolate—nor even about Prokofiev versus Rachmaninoff, or Homer versus Virgil. Those are matters of *taste*, however "high-brow" the latter may be. Matters of taste, though, go far beyond food or literature.

People have preferences for ways of life as well as for books and dishes. Even when the varying involvements are at that level, amounting even to different "philosophies of life," morality is still not about that. So what is the difference?

Briefly, matters of taste concern those that are *up to you*, as in the old saying: "there's no disputing about taste." That saying is plainly false in one clear sense: after all, people do dispute about such things, and frequently. But while we may dispute, there is notorious difficulty settling any such disputes. Establishing that my taste is superior to yours—except, of course, in my own mind!—is no easy matter. And when, as so often, we do not come to agreement on that level, then what? That is where there is room for *morals*, which purport to offer principles and rules that can be used to over-rule or set aside the deliverances of taste. Morals say to *all*, "Do this! Don't do that!" and "This is recommended, that is discouraged." They cannot do that reasonably if they are nothing but further expressions of taste. Indeed, for this purpose the view strongly rec-ommends itself that people simply have no business imposing their tastes on others. We can recommend, we can criticize, and we do, certainly, "dispute"—but that's all. What we choose in such areas is our own business.

We must realize, however, that the very claim that the items listed are "matters of taste," and that such matters have no author-ity over those who do not share them is itself a *moral* one. That people ought to be allowed to make their own decisions about mat-ters of taste is a moral conclusion, not an aesthetic one. In fact, taste is a fine example of an area about which there are and have long been moral issues. The example of pornography, for instance, comes to mind: moral criticism of pornography must not amount to mere assertions of taste. Thus we need to try to explain the dif-ference.

Subjectivity

It is an important view, popular over at least twenty-three centuries, that morals are "subjective" in a sense implying that they are *mere-ly* a "matter of opinion," there being no such thing as moral *knowl-edge*, nothing about which we can be really correct or incorrect. A pure subjectivist view would have it that for Jones to think that x is wrong is merely for Jones to be "against" x—nothing more. That view assimilates matters of morals to matters of taste.

But the subjectivist view embodies a fallacy, a greatly mistaken inference from an important enough truth. Morality is about action and decision, and therefore about subjective states—feelings, desires, interests. People do have sharply opposed opinions on moral questions; despite this, it doesn't follow that morals is just a matter of feelings or opinions, beyond the reach of rational improvement, any more than a similar conclusion would follow about geology, despite the sharp differences of view often held by different geologists.

In fact, the case is just the opposite of what subjectivism holds. When we have an opinion about morals, it isn't just an opinion about what we, in particular, are to do. It is also an opinion about what *everybody else* should do. When we think murder is wrong, we think that *no one* ought to murder *anyone*. When we think that Colgate is the "right" brand of toothpaste, on the other hand, we do not think that everybody must agree and heap censure upon all who don't choose the same brand.

That moral matters aren't just matters of how we feel, of what feelings we actually have, may be seen from looking at a pure case of feeling. Consider the claims (1) that I have a headache, and (2) that you don't. Do we "disagree"? Clearly not. Yet one who thinks that abortion is wrong *disagrees* with one who thinks that it is not wrong.

Do they, perhaps, only "disagree" in attitude? This idea was seriously advanced at one time.[1] But whatever one might think of its logic, one thing is clear: insofar as disagreements in attitude are just that—differences in attitude—they are incapable of rational resolution. If we are to get anywhere by rational methods, we must examine the bearing of facts, accessible to the familiar methods of evidence and scientific reasoning, relevant to the matter in question. And if resolution or at least progress is possible, then moral "attitudes," as such, don't constitute enough of the story about morality to be fundamental.

Politics and Morals

Nor are morals a matter of who has more votes. That's a political method of settling things, and is itself morally controversial; whether a given issue is one that ought to be settled by voting is itself a moral question. Whether the fact that a majority *thinks* X to be morally right is logically enough to show that X *is* morally right is a conceptual question about morals. And the answer is flatly negative. We can never simply identify what is wrong with what is merely *thought* to be wrong. It is not a part of the very meaning of morals that whatever the majority approves is right, whatever it disapproves wrong. It is, on the other hand, part of the very meaning of morals that attitudes require justification beyond themselves, that mere feelings aren't enough.

Law and Morals

Morality and immorality are also not the same as legality and illegality. A law requiring or forbidding us to do something may itself be either morally justified or not. There can be, and surely have been, unjust or immoral laws. What to do about them is, again, a moral question, and not one that can be answered simply by reiterating that the law in question "is the law." (Chapter 14 considers this question.)

Legislatures pass laws. But they cannot "pass" morals. Legislators must consider, among other things, whether proposed laws are morally acceptable. One does not determine this just by noting that enough other legislators will vote for a law to ensure passage, nor even that it would be very popular with the electorate, for they could all be acting immorally—and not infrequently have.

Morals are Public

What we are talking about here are rules or principles—directives intended for people generally. They are *public* guides to behaviour. What, then, is a "public rule of action" of the kind exemplified by moral rules?

First, it *applies to* everyone in the public in question: it tells everybody in that public what to do or not do, in one way or another. It is easy to misunderstand this point. Might there not be rules about the treatment of children, or of the disabled, or pregnant women, and so on? Of course there can be such rules. But even in those cases, where only some are directly involved, everyone else is involved indirectly—indirectly, and very importantly. It is of the essence of moral rules that *all* people are called on to reprove those who do wrong, to approve and encourage those who do right, and to teach whomever one can which way is right and which not. These secondary or indirect activities of *reinforcement* of the primary rules are in fact what make rules moral. By contrast, the typical individual need say or do nothing at all regarding, say, optimal strategies at poker or the management of shoe stores.

Second, these rules of action are intended to *overrule* particular individuals when they wish to do otherwise. If I want to do something, but that thing, as it turns out, would be wrong, then I ought not to do it. Here we have a large part of the idea of morals: it is to be a set of rules for action having *authority* over everybody in the group whose morality it is intended to be.

Now, there may also be cases where I want to do something but realize that it would be silly or too expensive. If so, that, too, implies a reason for me not to do it. But it implies a different sort of reason from the moral type. It may not matter to the public what I do, or it may be none of their business. The moral rule may be, "So go ahead, dummy!" Morals may leave the decision up to you, but that doesn't mean there is no further question whether you should do it. Of course there is, but it goes beyond the limited realm of morals into the much wider one of how to live one's life.

The question of morals, we may say, is always of this type: When is someone not to be allowed to do what he or she might prefer? More loosely, when is someone to be discouraged from doing that? When must one yield to some rule that supposedly holds for everybody? When would some action (or inaction) be what one *ought* to do, whether one likes it or not? And when would it be desirable, advisable, or sensible to do or refrain from some such act?

Custom vs. Morality

Our inquiry concerns what the public rules of action should be. But in every human community, we will find an accepted set of moral rules, a prevailing morality. What those rules actually are in a given community is a matter for empirical investigation: anthropologists make it their business to gather facts about such things. But we must make a distinction between moralities in that sense and what we may call "ideal" morality—the set of rules that there *ought* to be, even if it does not quite, or at all, exist here and now. We might find that there is some generally accepted view about what we ought to do that is, nevertheless, untenable or even irrational. Then what do we do?

What we should do about that is itself an interesting moral question. Do I just act on my own preferred view of what's right, or do I go along with the prevailing rule, even if I think my own to be better? How much may we do, and how much ought we to do, to try to change the current practice, if we think it wrong? That is another interesting subject that we will not discuss in detail in this book, though we will say something about it in relation to the analogous subject of obedience to the law in Chapter 14.

What, you may ask, does 'should' mean when we say that some moral rule of our society "should be" different from what it currently is? We can put the answer in terms of *reasons*: the claim is that there is a *good reason* for the public to have a rule of the proposed type. Of course, that leads us to the next, very fundamental question: what constitutes a good reason for action? Plainly, if we are going to have a reasoned inquiry, we must have some idea about that. We will discuss it often when we look at particular issues.

In one sense, the question of what constitutes good reasons for action is the question of what life is all about. However, an interesting feature of morals is that we can discern reasonable moral rules even though we do not claim to know how to answer that ultimate question. We can identify reasons for action for any given individual without actually having the answer to the question just asked: the reasons for action for a given agent are whatever considerations that agent actually accepts as recommending an action over its alternatives. Our reasons for action are based on our *interests*—or more precisely, on our understanding of them. If we can be shown that our understanding is in error, then we shall perhaps come to regret what we have done on its basis. But until then, the agent must act on what he believes.

Now we must recall the central feature of morality, one that it is impossible to emphasize too strongly: namely, that it applies to *everyone*—not just me or you, not just us and our friends, or people with the same religion or the same interests in music, or persons of the same sex, but *all* of us. The importance of this will become very clear as we proceed. In case after case, we will have occasion to reject some proposed rule on the ground that it could not be reasonable to require certain people to follow it. It fails to be universal.

Universality has been a much discussed and, I think, much misunderstood subject in moral philosophy. When the great German philosopher, Immanuel Kant, tells us that the fundamental principle of morals is "Act only on maxims that you could will to be universal law," he effectively points to a defining feature of morals. Morality consists of rules for all; if it is impossible for everyone to act successfully on a given rule, then that rule is *ipso facto* ineligible for the role of *moral* rule.

We can go further. What matters for morals is that the rules are individually reasonable for people to accept and to follow, so long as others do, too. No proposed moral rule that fails to be thus reasonable can be accepted by everyone. It is unreasonable to expect people to follow rules that have no basis in *their* interests, *their* reasons. Moral rules, then, have to be framed with a view to advancing the interests of all, insofar as their interests can all be advanced. Of course, this requires that their interests not be inescapably in conflict. Some interests are intrinsically impossible to advance without someone else's being thwarted—Smith's interest in making Jones miserable, for instance. Such interests can't be condoned by a reasonable morality: sadism, and certain sorts of "elitism," as in typical forms of racism, will necessarily fail to qualify. By contrast, consider competitive game-playing. Both sides can't win, but both do agree to be bound by specific rules, and both prefer playing, despite the chance of losing, to not playing at all. That provides, in fact, a paradigm of how conflicts of interest may be resolved in a rational way.

The Challenge of Moral Relativism

Moral questions, we have seen, concern rules for a group, especially for a group whose members are more or less thrown together, such as by the chance of being born to people who already live in it. But how large a group? Is there, and should there be, group variability?

This question brings up the familiar theoretical subject of *relativism*. There is certainly some level at which different cultures, especially, have different moral beliefs and rules. But it is unclear, and the subject of much discussion, whether the variation is of fundamental significance. Is morality essentially relative? Or is the variation a matter of relative detail against an underlying structure that is the same for all?

At the limit, it might be held that the idea of a common morality for all people is a mirage. That view has, I believe, been shown after centuries of discussion to be flatly untenable and based on misunderstandings. Pronouncements to the effect that something cannot be done tend to be short-sighted: they look at the difficulties in the way, but fail to consider the larger benefits of solution. In the case of morality, those potential benefits are enormous. The absence of morality applying to individuals within a group would make life perfectly miserable for everyone. That is the reply to what we may call *individual* relativism, the view that morality is only valid for the individual whose morality it is. But the same can hold of groups. When different groups come in contact with each other, the absence of a solution to problems encountered as a result of those contacts, the problems of juxtaposed societies that can and do have relations with each other, means, in effect, a worse life for people in both groups. No common morality means no solution to those problems. If we know what's good for us, we will *find* solutions to them, rather than throwing up our hands and declaring that it can't be done. In the realm of the practical, solutions are generally achievable—but not without effort.

Whether the fact of cultural variability implies any criticism of our own culture or our own rules is a related question that, practically speaking, is very important. The moral issues we will discuss here at least have to do with our own "group," and that group I take to comprise at least all people living in the technologically advanced world. Whether we can learn something from, say, the Inuit or the Bantu is a reasonable and open question. In turn, whether we are doing the right thing to or about such groups is another, and not only a "reasonable" one but, in the case of mixed modern societies such as that of the Americans and Canadians most likely to see this book, one to which finding answers is a pressing matter. Yet it is hardly easy or obvious.

Meanwhile, we may make an observation about moral relativism that might do much to dispel any tendency the idea may have to captivate the fancy of the reader. Societies contain members who deal with each other in various ways, who "interact." When societies do not interact, as was often true of various pairs or sets of them in times past, then the question of the need for a common morality in their intersocietal relations is moot, for there were none. In that case, moral relativism will look perfectly possible. But as soon as the members of different groups start to have dealings with each other, the situation becomes similar, and in the end identical, to what obtains between one individual and another within the same community. In the modern world, we talk, quite reasonably, of the "global community." When global community is a fact, global morality becomes a necessity.

Moral Rules and Moral Inquiry: How to Proceed?

Moral theory asks what a moral rule is and what, if anything, would "validate" or "confirm" such a rule. To the first, there is a plausible general answer, in two parts—two, because the expression 'moral rule' has, as we have already seen, two different, though related, senses. First there is the sense in which a moral rule is an actual feature of the social life of some group of people. Second is the sense in which a rule is being proposed or advocated as an improvement over what we have or, alternatively, is claimed to be a good rule that we are fortunate to have.

Regarding the first sense, we may say that a rule within a certain group is one of its *moral* rules when

(1) Members of the group typically criticize each other for deviating from the rule in question, and/or praise each other for conforming to it. The people they feel they can do this to are at least, in principle, all members of their own society (though there might also be rules of etiquette, say, that restrict the occasions or linguistic form of such criticism); but it will hardly be surprising if they attempt to do so regarding non-members as well. Most members of most cultural groups are probably not cultural relativists!

(2) When individuals thus praise or blame each other, they suppose that they are *justified*. They assume that the rule they invoke has some basis, making it a reasonable rule to follow, so that it's not just an arbitrary imposition. (That is, it must not be *just* arbitrary. In cases where it may seem so, there may be a need for an arbitrary rule regarding the matter at hand—deciding things by lot, for instance. Or there may be a reason why we should follow *some* rule or other, even when it is arbitrary just *which* rule we have—driving on the right, for instance.) They may well not be able to state that justification, however. They will, rather, have an obscure sense of rightness: an "intuition," as moral philosophers have come to call it.

Many philosophers seem to have come to the conclusion that these intuitions are actually all there is to morals—the very stuff or essence of the subject. That idea will come in for occasional comment in the rest of this book. It is, I think, a mistake, but an understandable one. Most of us are like this regarding arithmetic, too: we don't know *why* 2+2=4, but we are very sure that this is true. However, going on to suggest that there actually isn't any further reason why this is so is quite another matter, and would make arithmetic a mysterious and undiscussable subject. To say that about morals would make them, too, fundamentally undiscussable subjects—but with much more serious practical consequences than saying it about arithmetic.

The informality of morals is one of the main points that distinguish them from law. Law is bound up with an institution in which certain specified persons make written rules; the same or other specified persons then administer them, by publishing them, judging disputed cases under them, and administering punishments to those who don't conform. By contrast, moral rules are not made by anyone in particular, are not written up anywhere "officially," and are administered by everybody, not just by certain people with a legal mandate to do so. De facto morality is an informal social phenomenon: we are all involved in morals, whatever else.

The second feature confronts us with the need for a decent answer to the question of justification. A moral rule must not be arbitrary—it must have reason behind it. Yet some particular rules of some group might well be thought to be arbitrary and unreasonable, and that criticism might be plausible, too.

This point brings up the need for a second sense of "moral rule": that in which a certain sentence formulates a possible rule for a certain group, or for all of humankind in general, and that proposal is claimed to *be* reasonable, to be the very rule we ought all to accept and live by. This sense is given the tag "ideal" morality: morality as it ought to be. The choice of 'ideal' here is not ideal, either, for it suggests an unattainable state of affairs, whereas a proposed moral rule, claimed to be better than what we now have, might be perfectly "attainable." For example, in North American society, attitudes towards unmarried couples living together have changed enormously. Neither the old attitude nor the new is Utopian, but the new one can reasonably be regarded as much better.

At any rate, both parts of morals are essential—the generality despite informality, and the implicit claim to reasonableness—and perhaps they are all we need.

The Meaning of "Moral"

What, then, does one mean by saying that some act is morally wrong? We have distinguished, in effect, three components:

(1) One professes to disapprove of anyone's doing it, and therefore implies that one disapproves of doing it oneself.

(2) One thinks that everybody else should also disapprove and refrain from it—in short, that there ought to be (if there isn't already) a social rule against it.

(3) One thinks that there is a good reason why (2) should be the case—a good reason from the point of view of everybody, not just oneself. (It could be claimed that this good reason is "absolute," having nothing to do with points of view. But then, if a reason is absolute, it must be so from everyone's point of view, properly understood. Those who claim to disbelieve it must, on this view, be irrational or at least confused.)

The notion of there being a moral rule against or in favour of this or that is quite vague. The above characterization of having a social rule adopted, after all, would only be literally realized if absolutely everyone in the community agreed about it. Yet such a degree of agreement is doubtless all but non-existent. How many does it take, then, to say that there is "a community rule"? This is like asking how many hairs it takes to make a beard: a lot, obviously, but no precise number. As a working definition, we could say that a community, C, has a rule, R, if a "great majority" of the people in C adopt and reinforce R. For many purposes, including ours, precise answers to this question do not matter, for we are interested mainly in the justificatory question, not the factual question of exactly what our society's morals currently are.

Moral Issues

This book is about moral matters, many of which are in at least some respects controversial. They are, as we say, *issues*, moral issues in our and many other communities. But to say that there are moral *issues* in a society is to say that these are matters on which there is no consensus, not even a clear majority view, regarding the specific point in question, and thus that there really is no such thing as "the current view" on those matters.

Notice, by the way, that my characterization of the meaning of 'moral' does not require that there be *actual* consensus on the actions in question, but only that it would be *reasonable* (because there *is* reason) for everyone to accept the rule in question: to believe that x is wrong is to believe that disapproval of x would get a rational consensus if all addressed themselves to it clearly, which, of course, they most likely will not. This makes it clear enough why there can be moral issues in a community, unsettled matters regarding the status of certain sorts of general conduct, including the human community at large.Even when there clearly is a consensus on some point, condition (2), that everyone else should disapprove, provides for the legitimacy of criticism. No matter how well received the moral rule may be, we can ask whether we ought to have it or not. And, of course, there is room to ask what the reason for the rule is, even if it seems perfectly obvious that it is a good one. Many of the rules proposed as we go along will, I hope, be of that kind: obvious, but still worth knowing their basis.

Inquiring into the basis of a moral rule is especially important in disputed cases. We all agree that killing innocent normal adults is wrong, and people aren't greatly concerned to discern why. But we do not all agree that abortion is wrong, even though abortion is a sort of killing, and those killed are certainly not guilty of anything. Nor is there complete agreement on whether a parent may put to death an incurably suffering child who is severely mentally handicapped.[2] Clearly we can only get to the bottom of the abortion issue if we know *why* killing is wrong, not just *that* it is. (Chapter Eight takes up this particular issue.)

Moral Rules and Their Application

All explanations of morality in terms of systems of *rules* or general principles encounter the need for a distinction between the general and abstract judgements embodied in the rules and the concrete and particular judgements that we must make in daily life. When one asks, "Ought I to do this?," the action one contemplates may be the subject of some general rule, such as a rule against lying. Suppose you are thinking of telling someone an untruth. However, the act being considered has another feature, too: it would, let us say, spare the feelings of the host at the party you have just been to. No, you didn't enjoy the party very much, but do you have to *say* that to the people who went to so much trouble to put it on? We should not lie, true; but neither should we wound or offend. In this case, we must choose between these two rules, for here they conflict: to tell the truth in this case is to offend. Which is one to do? Most of us think that one should tell a "white lie." We are probably right about that.

The sort of moral judging embodied in general rules is said to be *prima facie* (literally, "first face"). Prima facie judgements *describe* actions in a certain way and then declare that, *insofar as* they are of *that* description, they are to be done or to be avoided. But this leaves room for the possibility that in a particular situation where an act of that description could be performed, that act would turn out to have other features, other descriptions, that would bring it under another and contrary rule. What, then, is the moral agent to do? Clearly, she must decide which of the different rules that apparently apply is the "weightier" one in the circumstances and act accordingly. When we say that a particular act is right or wrong, we are making an *overall* judgement, not just a prima facie judgement. To do that involves taking account of the action in all its complexity—or at any rate, as much of its complexity as we can manage to grasp, finite beings that we are.[3]

Some theorists, and some ordinary people, would like to believe that some general rules always hold, without qualification. Depending on which rules they single out for that status, these people often strike others as rigid, hidebound, perhaps unfeeling. Be warned: philosophers have come to appreciate that there probably are no rules at all that can plausibly be held in that wholly inflexible manner. But it is crucial to realize that giving up on rigid principles does not mean giving up on principles altogether. Plenty of actual lies *are* wrong, even though the fact that an act is a lie does not wholly settle the question of whether it is wrong, taking all things into account. Which rules there are makes a big difference, even if none of them can be maintained with absolute strictness.

Moral Inquiry: Approaches

So how are we to proceed on these disputed issues? Current writing on these matters tends to distinguish two allegedly contrasting general approaches: "foundationalist" and "anti-foundationalist."

(1) The **foundationalist** approach holds that we should identify the small number of fundamental, underlying truths in the area and then carefully deduce their implications for the issue at hand; our results, if properly arrived at, will give us the truth of the matter. In this sense, the foundationalist's moral theory is like mathematics, especially Euclidean geometry. In the case of morals, this approach would try to identify the basic moral principles and then carefully apply them to particular issues.

(2) The **anti-foundationalist** (also known as the "neo-intuitionist") approach, on the other hand, denies that there are any fundamental principles in the field and holds that we must piece

together the truth from many different sources. We are always, as it were, flying by the seat of our pants. In particular, we will always take what is currently *believed* as our starting point. Presumably, reflection might make us change a pre-existing belief, for instance, by showing that it conflicts with another of our pre-existing beliefs to which we find ourselves even more attached. Still, the sheer fact that we hold those beliefs is supposed to count in their favour, even if we have no idea why we hold them.

My own view is rather contrary to typical current philosophical practice in favouring a version of the foundationalist approach. The trouble with the other approach is that it seems mushy: we are told nothing about what makes a given bit of information a piece of "evidence" for or against a moral rule, nor what it means for a rule to be a moral rule. Indeed, it isn't even clear whether evidence is relevant at all. It is as if we expose ourselves to facts and other people's opinions and just let them bounce around, without controls, regarding whatever emerges as somehow "justified." That seems an absurd picture of justification: "Here, you are to do so-and-so, because I think you should, even though I have no idea why!" Anti-foundationalists will, no doubt, deny that this is an accurate picture of their view. The question in my mind is whether their view can really be sustained without, in effect, moving in the direction of the view proposed here.

Perhaps a sort of compromise is possible. We must agree with the anti-foundationalists that systematic study of anything emerges out of a background of unsystematic experience and that results supposedly confirmed in our systematic study that conflicted totally with that background would be meaningless, unrecognizable, and thus rejected. But it doesn't follow that systematic study could not show us what underlies our background experience, making it more intelligible and prompting us to rely on the carefully reasoned results of systematic inquiry in preference to the chaotic inputs of unorganized experience.

Meanwhile, we may lay down a few points about moral inquiry. If we are seriously inquiring into something we must

1. suppose that there is a truth to be discovered on the matter;
2. presume that some possible facts are relevant to it, others not;
3. think through the problem and discern what kind of information is relevant, what not;

4. determine what the relevant facts actually are;
5. discern what follows, and then let our opinions be guided by those results, rather than by sheer feeling. If we are reluctant to accept those results, then we need to figure out where we went wrong. Until we do so, our reluctance is not justified.

This is not to say that we should ignore what others have to say. The path of reason is refutation, not exclusion from the mind. No matter what our view may be, we can agree that it is a good thing to have rival views available, as illustrated in the anthologies of readings on these matters, which include many conflicting views. However, we must treat them as *views*, reasoned workings-out of proposed solutions, not simply as expressions of attitudes that happen to be held by those people. We must consider those views and try to see what is to be said for or against them.

Logic: Moral Argumentation

In this book we will always ask *why* we are supposed to think that such-and-such is right or wrong, as the view we are considering holds. The proponent of a particular moral stance must give us an **argument**, that is:

> a set of statements (called *premises*) put forward *as supporting* some other statements (the *conclusions* drawn from the first set).

The premises are claimed to be truths of some kind (just what that means will be considered a few paragraphs below). Premises need not even be verbal: one may invoke non-verbal presentations instead of verbally articulated premises by presenting a picture or pointing to something in real life. Still, words are pretty central in arguments, for arguments in the sense relevant to these discussions are social affairs, and language is a social institution, a vehicle for communication. Our conclusions are in words, and if we try to go straight from pictures or other presented non-verbal happenings to words, there is much room for misinterpretation. Language is not inherently precise, but it is capable of being made more so when that is needed.

Once we have assembled our premises, and identified the proposed conclusion(s), we are then in a position to ask two questions:

(1) *Validity*. Do the premises really support the conclusions? To determine this, we ask whether the conclusions could be false

even if the premises were true. If so, then those premises aren't enough to do the job at hand, and the argument must be changed or abandoned. One way to change it would be to admit that the conclusions *could* be false even if the premises are true, but that they are *very unlikely* to be false, given true premises. We should then have to inquire into the state of the evidence for this weaker claim. It has not been proved, but still *some* reason has been given in support of it. The question is: how much is enough, and why is it enough? When the conclusions *cannot* be false if the premises are true, that problem doesn't arise. That is the feature of argument known as "validity": a valid argument is one in which the premises, *if* true, really do require the truth of the conclusion.

(2) *Soundness*. If the argument is valid *and* its premises are true, then the argument is said to be "sound"; with such an argument, the conclusion is *proven*. But when are the premises true?

Here it becomes important to distinguish different kinds of premises. Philosophers have divided them into a variety of types, of which we will distinguish three.

First, there are *factual* claims. Such claims purport to describe the world, and can, hopefully, be established by suitable investigation. Science and common-sense experience are our sources here. Sometimes we can lead our interlocutor to the relevant area and just point out the facts—or he can lead us there and show us that they aren't as we claimed. At other times, we will appeal to the currently published results of scientific work. And sometimes we must admit that we just don't have enough evidence. In that case, of course, our conclusions are going to be weakened to the extent that evidence is lacking—and what to do about that may become a matter of serious moral importance.

Second, there are sometimes statements intended to be true "by definition"; here we appeal to the very meaning of the terms employed. A bachelor is unmarried: we don't have to examine bachelors to know this but merely need to know the meaning of the word. Sometimes we do use words in non-normal senses, and in those cases we must take care to explain how we are using them. There is no point in using words in a way that differs arbitrarily from the uses of those we hope to persuade. That will cause only confusion—which may be intended, of course, but in any serious inquiry, our purpose is truth, not persuasion for its own sake.

Other premises may be *a priori*—conceptual truths, such as those in mathematics. It is rare, but by no means impossible, for such things to loom large in moral arguments. Proof for such claims is a matter of conceptual argument of the appropriate kind. Most of us, if the claim is highly technical, will have to depend on the pronouncements of those knowledgeable in such matters—if the experts are agreed. And if they are not, we do well not to depend on the claim in question.

Finally, however, there will be claims of *value*: that something is right or wrong, good or bad, just or unjust, beautiful or ugly, virtuous or vicious, and so on. In the twentieth century especially, philosophers (and others) have become very concerned about claims of these kinds. How do we go about "confirming" or "verifying" such judgements? Plainly, it is crucial to have a good understanding of this matter, for it is immensely plausible to think that no argument whose conclusion is evaluative can be devoid of evaluative premises. If it is claimed that facts "support" values in question, then an explanation is needed. Sometimes the explanation is that what has been claimed as "fact" is, after all, a value in disguise. And sometimes, the fact is a fact *about someone's values*. Whether Picasso is a great artist is debatable, but we can at least establish, sometimes, that Jones *thinks* he is.

The present essays are about morals in particular, not values in general. There is serious question as to what truth consists of in the case of evaluative assertions. In the special case of morals, we may propose something that some may at first find rather disconcerting: namely, that what really matters is whether the premises in question are *accepted* by all concerned. For if they are, then our argument, if it passes the first test, will at any rate convince *them*. That proposal may sound outrageous to some, and they may be somewhat mollified if we go to on to suggest that what is accepted should be *reasonably* accepted. But that won't get us very far in many cases. Should we say that Smith's preference for Bordeaux over sherry is "reasonable"? If we do, what could we mean? What does reason have to do with taste in wines?

We can answer that a value is held "reasonably" by person A when A holds it without doing so on the basis of some detectable factual mistake or lack of logic and has actually thought about the matter, at least a little. And that is enough because of two crucial things. First, morality is *practical*: it intends to issue in actions and in decisions whether to do some action or approve of its being done. As Aristotle pointed out, we act on our values, and we do this whether they are reasoned or not. In arguments, we are reasoning about action: we are trying, on the basis of articulate speech, to influence action. If we can show someone that his action is unreasonable, fine: that will influence the individual's behaviour, or at least reconcile that person to the sorts of reactions to his behaviour that reason indicates to be appropriate. But otherwise, we can make no criticism that will be relevant from his point of view; we will then have failed to influence his actions. And if influence is what matters, then our failure matters.

The leading methodological idea of this book is suggested by the very idea, the definition, of morals: *informally reinforced rules that are to be the same for all in the group whose morals they are intended to be*. Rational action is action directed by one's values—the things one prefers—in light of one's information about the likely effects of one's actions. A *reasonable* moral rule is one that is reasonable *for* all those who are subject to it. When we tell someone that his behaviour is wrong, we intend to affect the individual's actions. Our saying that will do so only if we can connect those "wrong" values with the rule that would declare what is done to be wrong. In that case, the person cannot deny that the judgement is relevant, and that it is grounded, for it is that person's grounds, plus various facts about the world that in turn he cannot reasonably deny, that support the judgement in question. This, then, is our aim in using moral language.

Someone may, on further consideration, decide that he was mistaken in accepting some premise. If so, that will reopen the argument. It will, however, leave the person in a poor position to complain about his treatment in the meantime, for after all, did that person not accept it then? One could suggest that we have something like "absolute" truth when all parties accept premises that they would never change their minds about, no matter how much new evidence they consider or how carefully they scrutinize it. This ideal is doubtless a remote one, but that need not detain us here. Getting to principles that are well based in the actually held values of all concerned, where those values are not likely to change in relevant ways so far as we can see, is a lot, and for almost all purposes, enough.

Putting Argument in Perspective

Arguments that fail on the first score depicted above are *invalid*. Arguments failing in the second way are *unsound*. It is extremely important to bear in mind that an argument can be either invalid or unsound, that is, it can fail one or both of tests (1) and (2), *even though its conclusion is true*. A bad argument fails to *prove* its conclusion, but its badness does not prove that its conclusion is false; truth is not the same as proof. Failure of an argument shows that one set of alleged reasons does not establish its conclusion. If those are also the *only* reasons we had for believing it, then its effect will be to undermine that conclusion. Our belief is shown, at least for the time being, to be unreasonable. In moral argument, unlike some other areas of life, this is important, for if you have an admittedly unreasonable moral belief, then you are in a pretty weak position to be proposing to control people's actions on the basis of it, should they happen to disagree. Yet such control, as pointed out, is the very essence of the matter. Conclusions affecting only yourself, on the other hand, are your business—whether reasonable or not. Morality, as we will see, consists in considerable part of making room for precisely such conclusions. We think, or at any rate I will argue that we should think, that people may not be compelled to do anything other than what they like to do, in the case where what they like to do is sufficiently isolated from others that it has no adverse effect on those others. Bad moral arguments undermine the authority of the arguer to deprive people of their freedom of action.

Unreasonableness isn't the same as falsehood: unreasonable beliefs could be true. In order to show that the conclusion of our bad argument is actually false, we would need another argument, one that has the denial of that conclusion as its conclusion, and this other argument, in turn, would have to be a good one: its premises must be both true and such as to imply its conclusion. Often, of course, we will have neither. We won't be able to show decisively that a conclusion is false, nor yet that some other is true. We shall then have to try to decide whether, on the whole, the evidence favours one more than another. We will have to do more homework before we can be secure in our beliefs. Not many beliefs, in fact, will be totally secure. But many of them will be reasonably secure: they will be well supported by wide experience, and they fit well with the rest of what we know. If we can't do "better," we may still do well enough for all practical purposes; and practice is our subject, after all.

Why Argument?

It may occur to the reader to ask why these beliefs have to be supported by argument at all. Why not just suppose that there are some "fundamental moral truths" that we can know by a kind of "perception," like the colour of the sky? The belief in question would then admit of no argument—one either sees it or one doesn't! The answer is as before. If we can find a belief that everybody accepts without argument, fine. But what if we can't? What if people disagree in action, some feeling free to stamp out contrary opinions by force rather than reason—reason being, they suppose, not available? And what if, as is frequently the case, the "everybody" who agree is not quite everybody, but only everybody except some few who will suffer greatly at the hands of the many who agree? That, I think, shows the crucial weakness of what has been called "intuition" in morals. Those who proceed this way are in the position of saying: "Admittedly I have no *reason* for believing that this is right; nevertheless, I am morally entitled to force you to act this way!" If you don't think that an acceptable way to proceed, then my point is made: arguments are indispensable in morals, even though they aren't in many other areas of life.

A cautionary note is in order. I am not assuming that real people, in the course of their lives, normally go about producing arguments. Arguments, in general, occur when people are challenged, either by others or by themselves in a reflective moment. Philosophers are always arguing because they are always trying to improve their (and our) systems of belief. Even so, the method of inquiry by argument is not based on a distortion of real life. Instead, it scrutinizes real life more carefully than, perhaps, we normally do.

An Important Example: Theological Ethics

In the past it seems to have been almost universally supposed—at least in European-derived-cultures—that there was an important connection between morality and *religion*: namely, that morality *depends* on religion. This view in effect holds that if there were no god or gods, then nothing would be morally right or wrong. A simple formulation would be that to be right is to be approved by God; to be wrong is to be disapproved by that personage. This religious view is still held, it seems, by many people today. It is a useful example, for despite its popularity, it is provably untenable. It is worth a brief detour here to see why.

If we ask the theological theorist of ethics *why* the word of God is what makes an act right or wrong, we are likely to be met at first with a reaction of hostility or silence: who are we to question the ways of the Divinity? But what is meant is this: what is it *about* God that makes his word so authoritative in this area? To this, two answers, or variants of them, are (and as far as I can see are the only two that could be) given: (1) It will be said that God is supremely powerful—"omnipotent."(2) It will be said that God is supremely Good.

The first answer invites the following response: Look, surely you don't believe that might makes right? On this view, morals could be just *anything*: suppose God decides he doesn't like the look of people with white skin, so he declares that everyone is to torture people with white skin. No serious religious person will allow this. To make the "omnipotence" answer relevant, he will have to make it much subtler. For example, he might point out that God has, after all, created everything, and therefore created the whole of whatever makes morality a possible subject.

Of course, if we don't think there is any truth to theology, we won't accept that premise. However, we can table that. For what matters here is that it is a way of retreating from the image of God as a kind of whimsical despot and moving towards one that could reconcile that omnipotence with the kind of thing morality really is. For instance, it may be that various facts about people are what make morality true; the theologian is merely contending that those facts were, ultimately, created by a deity. Provided we all agreed which facts were relevant, we could then table the subject of whether a deity did actually create the world containing them.

(2) The answer that God is good is, at first sight, much more promising. At second sight, however, it is seen to be *too* promising. For what could the theological moralist *mean* when he says that God is "good"? For one thing, he must have meant that he is *morally* good—we don't expect moral truth to be based on the will of an infinitely great basketball player or violinist. Only an infinitely just person, a morally good one, could possibly qualify.

Very well, but then the question arises, what are we saying about someone when we say that he is just or morally good? Of course there are various answers that have been given to that—we will be exploring one general sort of answer to it in the pages of this book (which I think to be the right answers). But the point is that if we can answer that independently of any knowledge of God, then we demonstrate that morality is, as philosophers put it, "logically prior" to theology, rather than the other way around, as theological ethics would have it.

And what if we can't answer it? Alas, in that case the term 'God' turns out to be meaningless. For to be God is to be an omnipotent and perfectly good being; but now one of those two defining features would be without meaning!

The result is straightforward: referring to the supposed will of God in moral matters is *pointless*. God will, *necessarily*, be in favour of whatever is right, and so those who believe in God will believe that whatever they think is right is also approved by God. But its being so will do nothing at all to explain what *makes* it right, and therefore nothing at all to help us understand what is right. Theology is necessarily a fifth wheel in morals: it can do no useful work.

It can, however, do a great deal to make moral discussion intractable, for to hold that morality depends on God is to make it unfathomable and undiscussable. All too often, unfortunately, this goes along with resorting to plastic bombs and machine guns. This is another reason why moral theory and moral application or practice cannot really be separated. Moral theory matters because morals matter; we can't adequately discuss moral matters without any understanding of what morality is.

Tolerance and Liberalism

Suppose that your view about a certain practical matter is unsupported, but mine is no better. Then what? Should we say, "To each his own"? Interestingly enough, when it's a *moral* matter, we can't do that, for there is a problem: what these beliefs are about, remember, is what *everyone* is to do. It is therefore not possible to "tolerate" two opposing views in morals. A given act cannot be both okay and not okay from this perspective. We cannot say, "Jones thinks that everyone ought to do x, and I think that no one ought to do x, and neither of us has proved his case; *therefore*, I should 'tolerate' Jones' view." What could it mean for me to do this? Am I going to believe that everyone should do x on Mondays, Wednesdays, and Fridays, and avoid it on Tuesdays, Thursdays, and Saturdays (and perhaps do nothing on Sunday? That makes no sense. I may say that Jones is entitled to his belief, and me to mine—but if the "resolution" of our disagreement is that people may do x *if they please*, then this is not *toleration* of Jones's view, but *rejection*. For his view, remember, is that everyone ought to do it. It is also a rejection of mine, if mine was that no one ought to do x. It is, instead, a new view: the view that the situation in which those who please may go ahead and do x and those who don't please may go ahead and refrain from doing x is to be accepted *by everybody*, including both Jones and me.

In other cases, though, the alternative of toleration may be unacceptable. If x is murder, then there is a set of people—the proposed victims—who, very reasonably, do *not* agree that people should be able to do this just as they please. We have to find out what can be tolerated and what not. Murder is a good example of what cannot be; there are others.

What we must say, then, is this: if nobody's view about what everyone ought to do or ought not to do is any better than anybody else's, then people may do what they like in that respect. For instance, if it is not established that no one may perform abortions, then we must allow anyone who wants one to get one and anyone competent to perform them to do so upon arranging that with the client in question. But to say that is to take a real moral stand rather than just refraining from having one. It is to accept that people have, in general, the right to do what they want in the absence of publicly good reason for denying that right.

In short, tolerance, the liberal option, is itself the expression of a proposed uniformity: the social rule that each may do as he or she likes, using his or her own judgement about the matter. Views that people "may do what they like" are not, when acceptable, merely vague expressions of a wishy-washy refusal to address the issue. The view that somebody may do as she likes is the view that we *may not prevent* her from doing so. A moral view to the effect that someone may not do something must be supported by reasons that are good ones from everybody's point of view. Morals do not consist of one group ganging up on another; instead, it is the whole group, the group of all of us, finding that there are good reasons for each of us to accept a rule of the type in question. In cases where we differ, if some of us are to be justified in preventing the others from acting as they prefer in their own cases, we need to find a reason in terms not only of our own preferences, but of *theirs* as well. That's a lot more difficult.

Reason and Tolerance

So why is tolerance, or liberalism in the above sense, the indicated social rule in cases where there is not sufficient reason to have any other social rule? The answer has much to do with the nature of reasons. We are, of course, talking about *practical* reasons here, that is, reasons for doing or not doing something. But whose reasons are those? The answer to this is that individuals are the only beings that can reason in an articulate manner, and their conclusions are *their* reasons for acting—what get *them* into action. Reasons are essentially individual.

If we are to justify imposing uniformities of behaviour, we have to appeal to facts about people in respect of which they are uniform, facts about *all* people that give us all good reason to support these rules, which purport to override individual reasons to the contrary.[4] In the end, the support for a moral rule to be applied to your action has to come from *you*. Where people's reasons differ and there is no such uniformity about people to support restrictions on the behaviour of individuals, we always have reason to be allowed to do what we want. What a given individual wants is what life is about, so far as that individual is concerned.

Weighed against this principle of preferring to be allowed to do what we want might be a preference that others be made to do what we want, too—and thus, not allowed to do as *they* want. Looked at from the point of view of the others, of course, this is not a desirable policy. Suppose we have no reason that makes sense to them why they shouldn't be allowed to act on their own interests and values? If so, then how can my preferences regarding their action have any rational weight with them? The sheer desire of mine that others do this or that is clearly not a reasonable basis for their action, and thus not for general action. And they in turn, we may be sure, have plenty of preferences for suppressing our own freedom to do what we want.

Consider the rule against murder, for instance. Everybody normally has the strongest reasons to want not to be killed. The murderer doesn't want to die, any more than his victim does. Given this configuration of preferences, what is to be done? It is extremely plausible to suggest that anyone's reasons for not wanting to be killed far outweigh their reasons for wanting to kill others. The conflict of interest between killer and victim is total: there is no compromise.

But a murderer will get no benefit from his act if others then proceed to make *him* the victim. Yet, as Thomas Hobbes so long ago pointed out, anyone has the capacity to kill anyone else.[5] Thus all, including even murderers themselves, have reasons to support a rule against murder. There is a common interest that makes the rule against killing a rational rule. Those who murder people go against a rule that they themselves agree to be reasonable.

Can we imagine someone of whom this is not true? In cases of suicide and euthanasia, persons do think they have reason to want to die, and even to be killed by others. In a duel, both killer and victim agree to a competition from which only one emerges alive. Those special cases are so far from normal that they set the case for normally forbidding murder in a particularly clear light. The rule against murder is a rule against the killing of *involuntary* victims. Determining when an act is voluntary is not always easy, to be sure; but it is a highly relevant difference when we understand morality to be a set of rules of our own making, rather than deliverances from on high.

Are there any other grounds for exception? Does anyone think his reasons for being free to kill others outweigh his own reasons for not wanting to be killed by them? Such a person can have no objection to *our* killing *him*. If the rest of us forbid murder, and propose to execute those who do murder someone, they can have no reasonable objection. That was the moral of Hobbes's "State of Nature": insofar as there are no agreed rules, anything goes, and no one can effectively complain about anything.

Moral liberalism, then, is certainly not the view that "anything goes." It is, rather, the view that freedom is the presumptive rule. Making it into a rule involves recognizing an obligation to let people do as they see fit, unless and until some reason in terms of everyone's interests (including the agent's own interests) defeats this. There often are such reasons, as we will see.

A Note about 'Right' and 'Wrong'

What is in question when we ask whether a certain action is *wrong* is, I think, reasonably clear. For an act to be wrong is for there to be good reason to discourage or even to prevent people from doing it, blaming and perhaps punishing those who do it: we are to avoid doing it. But when we ask whether a certain action is *right*, things are not quite so clear. The term 'right' turns out to be importantly ambiguous. Specifically, we need to distinguish two senses of the term, which I'll call the "strong" and the "weak" senses.

Strong: sometimes, the word 'right' has the sense of "morally required" or "obligatory." Such an action is one that you positively ought to do, that you must do, that it is your *duty* to do. You are to be blamed, perhaps punished, if you do *not* do it.

Weak: Many actions that we'd hesitate to say are wrong, and if we must choose would want to say are "right," are nevertheless surely not right in our "strong" sense. In these cases, what we're really saying when we say they're right is that they are "all right," or "okay"—morally *permitted*, but not required. For these you get neither praise nor blame. In an important category of cases, such as heroism or charity, you get praise for doing them, but no blame for not doing them.

There is a neat way to define both of these in terms of the one notion of being wrong. We can capture the strong sense by specifying that it is wrong *not* to do the action so called: omission is wrong. In its weak sense, however, 'right' means merely that the act is not wrong—neither wrong to do nor wrong not to do. Weakly right actions are up to you—you may do as you like, so far as morals are concerned.

Moral vocabulary is not easy to pin down. The word 'right', for instance, is also used to mean that the act is *either* strongly *or* weakly right: if an act is positively required, after all, it must at least be permitted. To complicate life still further, we sometimes employ the term "right" to signify admirable actions, which are by no means morally indifferent, but which people should nevertheless be left free to decide for themselves whether to do or not. The heroic or the extraordinarily benevolent may think in their own consciences that they are "merely doing their duty," but we certainly have no business insisting that anyone fulfil such a "duty." Instead, we should be grateful and show our respect and admiration for those who do such things. Their actions, we might say, are the most truly "right" of all: the actions that we as people in general are most enthusiastic about.

In the following inquiries on moral issues, we will mainly be asking whether some or other kind of behaviour is wrong. If the answer is that it is not wrong, then the indicated moral rule is that people may do it or not as they please, without fear of punishment, preventive actions, or even serious criticism. For example, when some people say that suicide is right, what they mean is that it isn't wrong. Very few people have ever supposed that suicide is *generally required* (though many have thought that it was on certain occasions and for certain persons). But the main question to be addressed is whether suicide is generally *wrong*: is there some generally operative reason why we should regard suicide as disreputable, deplorable, and to be forbidden?

If we want to know whether some act is right in the strong sense, we are asking whether there is any reason to forbid the *non-doing* of the action in question. Are we, for instance, to be allowed to omit to help feed the hungry? A negative answer amounts to holding that feeding the hungry is *obligatory*, i.e., that it is right in our strong sense.

So our apparently myopic focus on wrongness won't deprive us of the main categories of right and wrong action. Concentrating on right and wrong, however, may well leave in the background considerations of virtue and vice, and thus of good and bad *character*. Nor will we be mainly concerned with moral *value* or moral *ideals*. This calls for explanation, since I in no way mean to denigrate or deny the usefulness of those concepts.

Right and Wrong, Good and Bad

Here we should take a moment to consider, though briefly, a pervasive distinction of great importance to the whole field. On the one hand, we sometimes say not that an act was right or wrong, but that it would be a *good or a bad thing to do*; or that it would produce good or bad results; or, quite often, that it was done from good or bad motives, that one who does or would do such things is admirable or despicable, a good person or a bad one. On the other hand, we often ask whether an act is right or wrong, as discussed in the preceding. What, then, is the connection between these two parts of the moral vocabulary—the good/bad/better/worse part and the right/wrong/obligatory/forbidden part?

If we look at the writings of professional philosophers, one could easily get the impression that there is some kind of basic conflict between these two sets of concepts. Philosophers have long distinguished two schools of thought on moral matters. "Deontologists" are said to hold that whether an act is right or wrong is quite independent of any considerations of good and bad consequences. Others, the "teleologists" (also called "consequentialists"), are said to hold the opposite: that whether an act is right or wrong *must* depend on its consequences for good or bad, better or worse.

If these were indeed two "sides," as they are so often said to be, then the choice between them would be difficult indeed, for we can easily see that both have a point. How, asks the teleologist, could there be any meaningful, sensible criticisms of conduct having nothing to do with whether we produce good or bad results? We all want to live the best life we can, to be happy rather than miserable; how can this ever be irrelevant in practical matters?

But then, deontologists can point out that whether an act is right or wrong isn't always simply settled by seeing whether it's good or bad in certain obvious, specifiable respects, and certainly not by seeing only whether it actually does succeed in producing certain specific good or bad consequences. The decision about an act's morality cannot await anything so uncertain.

But this supposed general division into two camps is seriously muddled. The teleologists are said to hold that the way to decide whether something is right or wrong is by looking at "the consequences." But consequences from whose point of view? *To whom* do they matter? The trouble is that consequentialism is characterized as if there is a single way of appraising consequences that is the *same for everyone*. And this simply isn't so. People are different: what counts for one person is frequently of no interest to another. If we all had literally the same values, the same set of preferences, then we could just be "consequentialists," no doubt; for of course each of us is concerned about results. But it is not so. I am concerned about some results, you are concerned about others, and so on.

Talk about "consequences" in moral matters suggests a high level of agreement about which ones are good and which not. To counter this, we need to appreciate that relevant agreement about consequences is not at hand if we only agree about the *general* descriptions of those consequences. Hunger, for instance, may be agreed to be an evil, and satisfying it a good—to those who are hungry or well-fed. Yet well-fed people in place X may have no concern at all for the very hungry people over in place Y. To have genuine agreement relevant to practice, the *particular* states of affairs favoured by one party must be the same ones as those favoured by the other; and moreover, they must be favoured to the same degree, so that they constitute motives sufficient to stimulate acceptance of the same actions. Real disagreement on such things is masked by semantics when it is blandly "agreed" that, say, hunger is evil. Jones and Smith may agree that the "best man should win," but if they disagree over which man that is or what constitutes being "best," disagreement about who gets the prize will persist.

When we are fully aware of the point just made, then we also see that the characteristic condition of people is divergence, not agreement, concerning the merits, the goodness or badness, of particular consequences. And when we do not agree in that sense, then the question of what uniform rule *all* are to follow cannot even be intelligibly answered in terms of general appeals to "consequences."

Those who think it can probably think that people who agree about generalities (like the badness of hunger) yet disagree about particulars (such as whether Ms. Brown should do anything to alleviate Mr. Black's hunger) are thereby showing themselves to be unreasonable or to be not looking at things from "the moral point of view." But that is question-begging.

Consider, especially, the moral view known as *utilitarianism*, according to which the morally right action is the one that produces the greatest net utility or benefit for all. On this view, a given "amount" of benefit for you should count the same as a like amount for me. But quite apart from the obviously enormous difficulty of making the required measurements, it is plainly questionable whether the most rational resolution of our disagreements is one that ignores our individual differences in the way that the utilitarian's supposedly uniform measure does. The act claimed to maximize general utility may be totally awful for some people. To say that they are being unreasonable in objecting to that is absurd.

If the utilitarian says that individuals *ought* not to care who they are or what they want in particular, there is a large problem awaiting them. We are, after all, dealing with people, not with pure ideal types or computer-generated models of what we think people should be like. Individual people do not attach equal weight to the "equal interests" of all persons, counting themselves as just one more person along with the rest. If a philosopher comes along and tells them that they *ought* to do so, those individual people will ask *why* they ought to. Whatever the answer to that, it should be realized, it can't be a "consequentialist" one. "You should adopt utilitarianism, because if you do that will produce more general utility!" is not going to convince anyone not already convinced of the truth of utilitarianism.

Yet each individual is, indeed, concerned about consequences: about how good or bad things would be if she or someone or everyone did this rather than that. Which consequences will be accounted "good" ones, and how good, are highly variable matters from one person to another. This helps to explain why it is not obvious that just because something is "bad," then it is also *wrong*, or that if it is "good," then it is *right*. Right and wrong have to do with how I should treat *you*, and you *me*; good and bad, on the other hand, have to do with how attractive various things are to someone contemplating them with a possible view to choosing among them. It is wrong for you not to pay your voluntarily-incurred debts, even though you think the uses to which the payee will put the money are bad ones. It is wrong for you to murder Smith even though you and many others think his life quite worthless. It is wrong for me to hold up a bank to finance a chamber music concert, even though I can hardly imagine a better use for anyone's money. And so on. So consequentialists have to explain to us why we should use *their* favoured schedule of consequences instead of *ours*—when these differ greatly. Adopting principles that don't depend on spurious agreement on consequences is clearly the recommended course.

The point is still clearer when we talk not in terms of right and wrong, as such, but in terms of whether people *have a right* to do something. For clearly we can have a *right* to do something that turns out to be not very *good* for us, such as the right to listen to bad music—to take an example close to this writer's heart. And clearly people can do what has good effects from quite deplorable motives. And so on. Thus, the idea that there is *one* view in the field called "consequentialism" by means of which right and wrong can be determined is fundamentally baseless.

Meanwhile, those philosophers who proclaim that right and wrong have nothing to do with consequences, right actions being so in virtue of their "form" as distinct from their "consequences," face a different conceptual problem that, so far as I can see, is completely insuperable. Their view requires that the "form" of an act should be specifiable independent of any considerations of consequences, and yet plausibly relevant to morality when so specified. But reviewing any selection of perfectly obvious examples shows that this is not so. Suppose I promise you that I'll do something. Can I keep any promise *without producing any results*? Or consider murder. How can Mr. A murder Mr. B without producing the *consequence* that Mr.

B is dead? The idea of a "pure form of murder" that leaves no one actually dead is nonsense. Yet any actual murder will consist of performing some action, such as pulling a trigger or plunging a knife into a chest, such that *as a consequence* the victim dies. But anyone who thinks that pulling a trigger is wrong *apart from its consequences* has a very bizarre view of morality.[6]

In short, the alleged contrast between "deontology" and "consequentialism" is fundamentally untenable. There is a tendency for writers on ethics to classify the basic views in the field into these two camps. It should be sobering to appreciate that both views, as they are usually depicted, are fundamentally wrong—at least if what is wanted is to depict views about which reasonable people may differ.

Having a Right vs. Being Right

Before leaving these general discussions, it will be useful to identify one more concept that will often enough be employed in what follows: the concept of right as in "*having* a right," the nominal rather than adjectival form of the word. What is the relation between an act's *being* right or wrong, on the one hand, and someone's *having* or not having *a right*, on the other? The answer is this. When you have a right to do something, the situation is that other people thereby have duties towards you. Minimally, they have to let you do it, that is, they have a duty to refrain from preventing you from doing it: it would be wrong for them to stop you. One person's having a right, then, means that there is something about that person such that some other person or persons would be acting wrongly were they to do certain things to or concerning the first right—holder.

Rights are always "against" some other person or persons. "Special" rights are against specific other people, such as the person you bought the new vacuum cleaner from, who now has a duty to deliver it. "General" rights are against other people generally: your right to life, for instance, requires *all* others to refrain from killing you.

There is substantial moral controversy, of course, about which general rights we have and why we have them. The account of morality sketched here supplies a recipe for basic answers to this question: rights are those conditions that it is in everyone's interest that everyone should be protected in respect of. The essays themselves argue for some more specific answers.

But before we move to another subject, there is one distinction among types of rights that is too important to omit at this point; it will loom rather large in the essays to follow. This is the distinction between "negative" and "positive" rights (and duties).

Negative and Positive Rights

A right, as we have seen, is essentially a ground of duties or obligations on the part of others in relation to the right-holder. Those rights that entail only duties to *refrain*—duties *not* to do something—are "negative" rights. Jones's negative right to do x is Smith's duty not to prevent Jones from doing x. Of course there are many things Smith might do that fall short of outright prevention but would nevertheless make it more difficult for Jones to do x; a precise statement of that right will have to tell us which of these are to be proscribed and which not.

In still other cases, side-effects of what Smith does, rather than the directly intended point of his action, make it difficult or impossible for Jones to do it. So when we talk of rights of this type, there is ample room for consideration of just what we are thereby proscribed from doing. All, however, have this in common: you could completely fulfil the requirements of a purely negative right by doing nothing at all. As we sleep, we refrain from killing, lying to, cheating, or assaulting everybody in the entire world. Only if some antecedent duty is established, on some other grounds, can a non-action be held to "cause" anyone's injury: if we fall asleep at our post, of course, we are responsible for what we had previously undertaken to do or avoid.

But it is widely held that there are rights of another sort, called "positive" rights. These are rights that entail for others not just the duty to refrain from interfering or preventing, but also the duty to *help*, at least in the cases where the right-holder would not be able to do the thing without help. Positive duties call for action, not non-action; in the circumstances in which they apply, they cannot be fulfilled by doing nothing. If you will die unless I act, and you have a positive right to life that holds against me, then I must act; lying down and going off to sleep won't do. That is the defining difference between them. We shall say much more about this in relevant places, for issues about positive rights loom large in all the issues we will be considering. Moreover, it is all too easy for people to slip from one to the other.

Thus, for someone to have a right is for certain acts of other people to be wrong. The difference between negative and positive rights is due to the difference between the kind of duties these rights impose on those others: duties to refrain from interfering, in the one set of cases, or to do something to help, in the other.

Duties that ask us only to refrain leave us where we are. We may not like being where we are, and where we prefer to be might violate a negative duty; in that case, a duty to refrain is a cost to us. Duties asking us to do something, however, draw upon our resources, our repertoire of abilities, our time; thus, they impose costs in excess of whatever costs, if any, are imposed by being required to refrain. All costs require justification from the point of view of those on whom they are imposed. It is not always easy to produce that justification. But it is much easier in the case of negative ones than positive ones. It is very obvious that the benefit one gets from not being killed by anybody, or stolen from, or injured, outweighs whatever one might gain by doing any of those things to someone else.

Values: Moral and Non-Moral

We can, and very frequently do, make judgements of value that we don't think of as moral judgements at all. Whether Suzie should get a permanent is not a moral question; nor whether we should have a picnic this afternoon, or whether I should take up the sitar. But whether people are starving or not is something we suppose to be of moral importance. We talk as though moral value is involved in the latter case, but not in the former.

What is involved in saying that something is of *moral value*, then? Or are there any such things, once right and wrong are accounted for? I suggest this: moral values are things that there should be a *public* attitude about, namely an attitude of support (for what is good) or of disdain (for what is bad). Morality is always a matter of uniformities. A morally favourable public attitude towards x is one that there is reason from everyone's point of view that everyone should have, rather than leaving it entirely to individual taste. What makes you happy or unhappy is up to you; but to think that happiness as such is a moral value is to think that we should *all* be concerned about it. Everyone should have a positive attitude towards anyone's being happy, and a negative attitude towards their

being unhappy, whatever brings about the happiness or unhappiness in question—unless, of course, that person's happiness stems
from an immoral way of life, devoted to the doing of what makes
others miserable; murderers should *not* be happy.

Again, we will have much to say about such matters as we go
along. For the present, let's just note that whether we should have
a positive attitude towards goal G is one thing, but whether we
should *force* people to work towards G is quite another. The liberal attitude suggested earlier will in general object to using force for
such purposes. If you agree that G is a good thing, then you will be
thereby motivated to do something to achieve it; even so, we in
general may not compel others to do it. Your values, your ideals of
life, are yours, and it is for you to decide how much to do on behalf
of any given value that you accept. But recognition that there is
good reason for all to have favourable attitudes towards certain
things, such as other people's happiness, may evaporate when the
proposal is to *require* that all contribute to it. If you are required to
do x, then it does not matter that you don't want to do it; if you are
merely encouraged and advised to do x, the fact that you really
don't want to do it does matter, and morally decides the issue in
your case.

The Issues

Having made a number of distinctions and definitions that will be
important throughout this book—and are important in ordinary
life—we are ready to address the issues.

Broadly speaking, the first seven issues—suicide, euthanasia,
punishment, war, animal rights, hunger, and abortion—are life-and-
death issues. There is a certain logic to their arrangement. Suicide is
the special case where killer and victim are the same person. In
euthanasia, they aren't the same, yet the idea is that the victim benefits from the killing and may have requested it. Punishment and
war, on the other hand, have non-voluntary victims, and this raises
very different questions about their justification.

The issues of animal rights and abortion raise another fundamental issue. Both the animal and the fetus are involuntary participants: the farm animal is driven to the plough or the slaughter-
house, and the fetus is not consulted on whether an abortion should
be performed. Yet both of these actions are thought by many to be
wrong, while many others hold that they are not. Those issues raise

the question of just *which* organisms have the right to life. All? All animals? All humans? All post-fetal humans? Or what?

The hunger issue, on the other hand, poses acutely the question of the relation between killing and allowing to die. Is there only a negative right to life, entailing the duty that we not kill, or is there also a positive one, entailing that we must help feed the hungry and nurse the life-threateningly sick?

The issue of population control could involve discussions of killing, at a macabre extreme, but more normally it is about how many (and/or, perhaps, which sorts of) people are to be brought into being at all and about who is to produce them and why. It is at the "life" end of the life-and-death spectrum. Finally, the much-discussed issue of abortion is placed at the end of the series because, as will be seen, it touches on almost all of the issues raised in the preceding essays. To have considered them first will, I hope, make the task less formidable when we get there.

Issues about sexual ethics, marriage, and the family get a sizeable chapter of their own, though they could easily get many (and have rightly been the subjects of vast literatures). They are not life-and-death issues, as such, but clearly a major aspect of sexual ethics concerns acts that can and characteristically do affect the production of new people, while family matters have much to do with both the size and character of the generations produced by them. However, the focus in these issues is again on life, and especially its quality, rather than death.

Issues concerning discrimination, affirmative action, censorship, and pornography are important because they shape the kind of society we will live in, and not, mainly, because of their bearing on whether anyone will live or die as a result of the principles adopted. They also raise, in very acute form, issues about the liberalism that informs this whole study.

New to this edition is a short chapter on environmental ethics. In part, this chapter follows up on the chapters on animal rights and abortion, for some hold that the environment itself has rights, even though it is not an organism at all. And it does concern, very greatly, the question of what grounds we may reasonably base our insistence that others do or refrain from certain actions. Some environmental problems may be life-threatening, just as the global environment is life-sustaining for us humans. But in others, what is in question is what kind of environment we want: Clean? Beautiful? In whose view?

A concluding chapter about obedience to the law is added for a similar reason that Aristotle ended his *Ethics* as he did: to consider the interface between morals and politics. Of course, such interfacing will have been in evidence throughout, but the question of how and why political and legal institutions are authoritative looms very large in the life of any modern individual. At the heart of this is the question of obligation to do what is legally required of us. The difference between one attitude and another on this matter can be the difference between totalitarianism and a free society.

This does not pretend to be an exhaustive study; no book could be, for our subject, after all, ranges over most of human life itself. But the issues discussed are all prominent now and undeniably important in almost any society or state of society we can readily envisage. I hope that these essays will interest you, the reader, and help to sharpen your critical faculties. I hope also that the views I have tried to support are indeed the right views. Nevertheless, what matters is the truth, and not my or your opinions. These essays will be successful insofar as they take us closer to such truth as there may be in morals. Of that, each reader must judge for himself or herself.

The Literature

The reader will find few references in these essays to specific articles and books by the thousands of others who have contributed to discussion of these subjects. There is a definite reason for that. The point of this book is to set forth my views. Detailed discussion of others would take hundreds of further pages. Moreover, if this book is read in the context of a course on moral matters—which is how it was engendered in the first place—then it will surely be coupled with at least one among the many excellent anthologies that are widely available in this field. In any such anthology you will find a variety of essays on most or all of the topics discussed here. Getting acquainted with them is essential for a fully informed view. A few specific titles were mentioned in the Preface, a few others will be mentioned later on, and the reader will then be able to find much more. I hope that upon looking into these writings, the reader will be the more convinced of the wisdom of my own approach. But looking into them is essential in any case.

Summing Up

In all of the following chapters, I append a brief summary of my results. This opening chapter, however, with its many important distinctions, defies summary. The reader will, I hope, return to it now and then to re-read the accounts in which some important distinction is made, in the light of its later application to the real-life problems with which this book is mainly concerned.

Chapter Two

Suicide
and the Value of Life

Life-and-death issues head off our agenda. The first is challenging, though atypical: that in which individuals kill themselves or contemplate doing so. What are we to think of them? Is suicide morally wrong? Even if we decide that it is not, there is an interesting array of questions to raise. For instance, can it ever be rational? But we'll start with the question of its morality.

Morals and Murder

Those who think that suicide is morally wrong likely think that it is so because it's a kind of *murder*. No item of our common moral beliefs is more central, more "obvious." than that we ought not to kill people. But what do we believe when we believe this? As soon as we look at it with any care, this fundamental and apparently secure belief becomes less clear. For one thing, we see right away that it is misleading to say that our moral belief is about the wrongness of "killing" as such. Few think it wrong to kill someone who is trying to kill you, at least if there is no other way to prevent him. Self-defence is an accepted justification of killing, and by no means the only one.

Justification vs. Excuse

Self-defence isn't an "excuse" for killing. It is, rather, a *justification*. A justification is a consideration showing that the action was actually not wrong: if successful, it refutes the charge that the agent did the wrong thing. Those who kill in self-defence have not performed a regrettable action for which they may be excused; instead, they acted *rightly*. That they had to do this is regrettable, but what they did, given the circumstances, is not. An *excuse*, on the other hand, accepts the main charge, but aims to reduce its force, blunting or diverting the blame that might otherwise be forthcoming. "He slipped, accidentally pushing the trigger", or "He wasn't in his right mind" don't deny that he killed the victim, but do deny that he was fully responsible and thereby eligible for the standard allotment of punishment. If he wasn't in his right mind, then it isn't quite right to say that "he" did it. And so on.

The category of excuses is a fascinating and important one. Morality tells us what to do: it guides our deliberations, affecting our actions from within. But a lot can go wrong in the inner recesses of the soul, and some of what goes wrong is such as to render moral methods of control inapplicable or impossible.It is possible to suggest that every action is always excused: did not the agent always do his best? I believe the answer is in the negative, and will assume so in all that follows. Yet it is not an easy matter to say why that answer is justified, and unless we can, we should not be totally confident that it *is* justified. With regrets, we must leave the question dangling.

Killing and Murder

When we say that someone has been "murdered," we say more than that he has been killed. It seems, indeed, that we are already making a moral judgement: 'murder' perhaps means 'wrongful killing.' Of course, if this is what it means, then "murder is wrong" is a trivial proposition: killing is wrong when it is wrong! But when is that? We are no further ahead.

It is difficult to say whether that semantic claim is correct, but it does attest to the tenacity of the idea that murder is wrong. We won't try to settle that point and it probably does not matter. What does matter is why we think that some killings are indeed wrong and some not—why some killings are to be adjudged "murders" and some not. What is involved in this judgement? Here are at least three points.

First, that the victim was *eligible*: that is, possessed of the moral status that makes it at least prima facie questionable whether one is obligated to be concerned for its life. If we swat flies, we imply that their lives don't "count." We can kill but we cannot "murder" flies, or tomatoes. And if a hunter who shot a deer was described as a "murderer," we could infer that the speaker was a believer in life rights for deer. Most would not so label it.

Second, that the killing was *intentional* (perhaps even deliberate, though that isn't quite the same thing). We can accidentally kill someone, but we cannot accidentally murder him. Third, that the victim was *innocent*—had done nothing to merit being killed, had not somehow negated or abandoned his right to live.

All of these bring up profound and difficult questions, and we will be getting into some (but not all) of them in our further investigations. Meanwhile, the question is whether those three are enough. And the answer, I believe, is that they are not. The suicide is clearly "eligible," his act clearly intentional, and certainly he has (usually) done nothing to deserve being killed. But does he necessarily do something wrong in killing himself? I think not, and I suspect that most of us do not either. But many used to think so, and some still do. We must consider whether they have a point.

One way with this question would be to add a fourth condition such as this to our list: that the individual killed must be a *different* individual from the one doing the killing. But if we do that, we again would trivialize our investigation. We would be saying that we don't call suicide "murder." (Indeed, some say just that: suicide is wrong because it is self-murder.) But our question is, why not? What we want to know is, why should it matter whether the victim is a different person? Pursuing that question will lead us into the heart of the matter.

Suicide: Values vs. Rights

At the outset, let's distinguish two questions: (1) whether suicide is or could ever be a *good thing*, and (2) whether suicide is *wrong*. Those who think it is wrong may think that you ought not to commit suicide no matter how good a thing it may seem. But they may also, and do ordinarily, think that suicide is *bad*—indeed, "evil."

If we suppose, as we must, that morality is to be constructed out of the interests of those concerned, then whether suicide is wrong or not becomes a matter of whether you *have the right to do it*. Some people sometimes believe it to be in their own interests to terminate their lives; the question is whether we should let them do so. Nowadays many people do think that people have such a right: that in the end, it is *up to Jones* whether Jones should commit suicide. I believe they are basically right.

Of course it is "up to" Jones in the sense that if he decides to commit suicide, it is usually difficult to stop him. Suicide is typically possible. But being possible doesn't mean that it's right. We must consider the matter further.

Who's in Charge? On the "Ownership" of the Self

Some think that the question whether a given life should be taken or not is a matter of *value*: is that life a good one or a bad one? If it's valuable, important, worthwhile, then it should not be taken. Life is good, and that's why we shouldn't destroy it, whether it's ours or somebody else's.

But maybe that isn't the right question. If it is, then it should follow not only that if the life in question is a good one, then it should be preserved, but also that if it's a bad one, then it should not. We should then congratulate anyone who would remove this weed in the garden of humanity. That seems to be the way the Nazis felt about Jews. I trust that the reader would feel rather uncomfortable about saying any such thing.

Of course, one way to avoid that is to take the line that every human being *is* worthwhile, perhaps terribly so—"infinitely" so, some would even say. But how do we know that? And when you think of it, perhaps people who say that could be accused of not having any taste. If you claim never to have met up with a bad wine, or a bad game by the Canadiens, then perhaps you just haven't been around enough. And the same goes if you claim never to have met a worthless person.

The trouble with all this is that *we* are inquiring about the value of this *other* person's life. But what business do we have doing such a thing? There's a sense here, I suggest, of straying onto a domain that isn't ours. When we assess Jones's, we are doing it from *our* point of view. But what about *Jones'* point of view? Doesn't that count?

Indeed it does—it counts so much that in a way it counts *entirely*. Whether Jones should commit suicide is altogether up to Jones and not at all for us to decide. We might think that Jones would be better off dead, but unless *he* thinks so, then we simply aren't permitted to do anything about it. The converse of this, though, is that if he does think so, then that too is up to him. The onus is on those who would insist that people not take this option even if they want to. Should they be forbidden to do so, if it would be possible by forbidding it to prevent it?

We can perhaps help out the discussion here by considering some options. We can put it in terms of whether Jones is his (or her) own person or not, her own "boss." If Jones doesn't make the decisions about what Jones will do, then who, after all, does?

There would seem to be three possibilities of interest: God, society, and the state. Each deserves a word or two here—especially the first.

God

It is useful to address the issue of suicide in relation to religious ideas, both because they have been so widely invoked in discussions of suicide, and because this affords us a good opportunity to apply what we have seen in the introductory chapter concerning the general role of religion and religious beliefs in ethical matters. Down through the centuries, religion has played a tremendously important role in moral thinking in general; but it has perhaps played an especially prominent role regarding this issue. People who think that moral principles are literally the commands of God have thought, and taught, that God commands us not to take our own lives.

We have seen in Chapter One that theological ethics as a general account of morality is untenable, both in principle and in its social implications. As regards the principles of morality, religion simply does not explain or account for them. Rather, it presupposes them. The religion of a given community will confirm the morality of that community, whatever it may be. It is, as I put it, a fifth wheel, explanatorily speaking. Instead of God's commands being the basis of morality, it's the other way around: morality is the basis for one's conception of God.

Someone who is told that God commands x and that therefore x is right is, quite reasonably, assuming that if God is for it, it must be right. But that is because a "god" is, by definition, a morally good being. But then, how do we know what is right and wrong to begin with, so that we can know what sort of thing God commands? The person who is content to look this up in a book, such as the Bible, is in fact getting the benefit, such as it is, of someone *else's* home-work—that of the person or persons who decided that x is what God must be in favour of, since x is clearly right, rather than y or z. But somewhere down the line, someone has to be responsible for that thinking. Someone needs to tell us just *why* x is right, without trying to slough off the responsibility for that thinking onto the mind of "God." They need to level with us!

Theological ethics proceeds, of course, on the assumption that there *is* a God—obviously a crucial concern for believers. Yet, as all informed believers know, different people have different views. That is hardly surprising, since no view on such a subject can claim to be publicly provable. In addition, each proponent of a rival creed will, of course, have a rival morality to press. Prospects for moral relations between the holders of those rival creeds are not good, if morality were really founded on religion. Yet a reasonable moral theory is going to have to cope with the problem of formulating principles that can have the support of the non-religious as well as those of varying religions. Plainly no theory based entirely from *within* any one particular religion can do that. No non-religious person will accept that we must all do x because the god proclaimed by some particular sect told us to do it, any more than a Baptist will accept an obligation to do x laid down by the Pope. It doesn't take a great deal of study of the melancholy history of religious wars among humans to see the need for a completely non-sectarian basis for morals.

Is Life a "Gift" from God?

Now let us return to the question of suicide. Many people have sup-posed that suicide is wrong because life is a "gift" from God. This view has special problems, over and above those broached above. Gifts are supposed to end up in the hands of the recipient, who is in principle free to do what he wants with it—otherwise, how would it be a *gift*? It might not be very sensible of me to smash the new vase you've given me, but if it's really mine, I may do that. I might lose your friendship as a result, but you couldn't prosecute me for it, as you could if it was still yours. But the religious person who thinks that God forbids suicide plainly thinks that he *can* do just that. But you can't have it both ways.

And then, *to whom* is God supposed to have given this "gift"? Here there is a crucial problem. For if it's my very life that is the alleged gift, then before "I" got it, *there was no "me" to give it to*. My life is not an adventitious extra bit of baggage that I can either have or not have: it's me. But by the time I exist, it's too late: I can't refuse to be given life, for in order to refuse it I must already have it—only living people can accept or refuse anything. Clearly, a gift that I had no choice but to "receive" is not a gift at all. To claim that is a fraud. I could have no obligation to be grateful for something I couldn't possibly have refused, and therefore cannot be said to have "accepted."

We can "accept life," certainly. But in the sense that we can do that, we need not suppose it is literally a "gift" from anyone. Many people, including, I hope, the reader, are glad to be alive, even though they don't credit any person or god with their deliberate creation. If we are glad to be alive, it is because life is good, not because it originated in some particular way.

And so we return to the most fundamental problem in the application of theological ethics to this particular question: How does anyone presume to *know* that God doesn't want us to commit suicide? God must want the best for me, if he's to deserve the title god. Well, what if suicide *is* the best thing for me? In that case, surely, it would be impossible for God not to want me to do it. The problem, in short, is that we cannot know what God wants about matter x until we know what is right regarding x—the very thing we were supposed to be trying to find out by consulting the god in question.

Of course, the theorist might want to say that suicide *cannot* be good for me. But why not? Not, as we have seen, because God forbids it, for we can know that he does only if it is in fact a bad thing to do. But if it isn't, then he could have no business forbidding it. So we are back where we started: trying to find some good reason for thinking that suicide is or is not good for me, in the circumstances.

Whatever the status of the claim that we were "created" by a god, we are independent beings with minds and purposes of our own. That fact especially, taken together with facts about society, leads to the conclusion that we really "own" ourselves, set our own purposes and, so far as we can in view of our relation to others in society, make our own rules for the conduct of our own lives. And, of course, take responsibility for those rules.

Society and State

If it turns out to be untenable to think that God owns our lives, then it is surely even less plausible to think that society or the state does. After all, society is merely all the *other* people. If they didn't even own their own selves, why should they own anybody else's? (Imagine a slave society in which *everyone* is a slave—no masters!)

Likewise with the state, which is essentially just the bureaucratic aspect of society. Here are a bunch of people, perhaps elected, who, says this view of morals, are my absolute bosses. I have to do what they say. Well, why? Because they'll make me? But our question isn't whether they *do* make you do things, but whether they have any *right* to. So where did they get such a right if they do have it? The answer given by modern defenders of the state is that they get it from "the people". Yet insofar as this answer is right, it presupposes that the people in question are free to do what they want—including the right to vote for whomever they want—on the basis of their own reasons. The theory really assumes that individual people own themselves.

Recall, too, that we cannot identify justice with the laws of the state. Less obviously, we can't identify it with the merely received rules of society, either. For in both cases, they could conceivably be wrong. Laws can be unjust, mores can be irrational, cruel, arbitrary. Morality can't be identified with any of those things. And neither can the ultimate source of value for our lives. It seems that there is no coherent substitute for individual freedom as the fundamental condition in this area. When it comes to your life, the ball is basically in *your* court.

Back to Square One: Can Suicide Be Good?

Suicide is an intentional shortening of one's own life. We shall all die someday, no matter what we do. What we call suicide is a comparatively *sudden* shortening, as compared to the death that would otherwise have been brought about by the familiar causes of disease, accident, or the like. But it is instructive to compare the quick intentional deaths we call "suicides" with those in which people smoke or drink themselves to death, or expose themselves to fatal diseases such as AIDS. We don't usually think of these as suicides. But how do they really differ, except in the duration and the certainty of the dying process?

If suicide is bad, why is it? Evidently because death is bad. But why is death bad? This is an important question, and neither silly nor idle. It is, in fact, vastly intriguing and quite puzzling. Long ago, the Greek philosopher Epicurus pointed out that death is not a special kind of state or condition *of ourselves* that we get into, a state that might be unpleasant or painful or dreary. Instead, death is *non-existence*: "Where death is, we are not; and where we are, death is not. Therefore, death is nothing to us."[1] So this famous argument goes. It's a strong one.

Those who believe in immortality, of course, think of death not as a termination of life but as a *change* — what we may call the "change-of-address" view of dying, as opposed to the termination-of-existence view. We cannot, of course, claim to *know* that the latter view is the right one. But we certainly have no evidence in favour of the former, nor is it clear just what would constitute evidence for it. And it doesn't really make much sense, when you think about it. There is no good account of an after-life that doesn't collide pretty sharply with all that we know, from science and common-sense observation.

In any case, the non-existence view of death raises the more interesting problems. For if death is indeed non-existence, then clearly Epicurus's was right: it is, in itself, not something fearful, something horrible. It is not, in a sense, *anything at all*. Epicurus' conclusion was that death is not an evil, and in the sense in which evil is undesirable experience, he certainly had a point. But this brings up a question: why should we bother to get out of the way of the oncoming express train?

The Value of Life

If there is any reason to avoid dying, it cannot be that the state we then pass into is worse, for there is no such state. It must lie rather in the fact that death deprives us of our lives. If that life was a good one, then it deprives us of a good. If it wasn't, then it relieves us of an evil. Which is it? Clearly that varies. Some lives are terrific, some are awful. There is no a priori way to know these things; one needs experience.

Some deny that specific experience is needed to decide this. They suppose that life is *in itself* a good, an "intrinsic" good. But it is unclear what this important-sounding claim amounts to or just what it would prove if true.

What does it mean? That life is good whether or not it feels good, seems good, amounts to anything? Imagine that you are absolutely devoid of feeling: your eyes are open and you see, but you simply don't care about anything you see, you feel neither joy nor sorrow, love nor hate, hope nor despair. Your mind is just a living blank. Can *that* be good? Surely not. What makes it good must be things like joy, pleasure, the sense of accomplishment, and the other good things in life. But if so, a life pervaded with the opposite things, the evils of life, is not obviously one worth continuing.

Even if we supposed life was what philosophers call an "intrinsic good"—something good "in itself"—-that wouldn't prove anything about the value of suicide. It would show only that insofar as some choice would leave you alive rather than dead, then that would count in favour of it. But *how strongly* in favour? Other considerations might outweigh it. Life's being intrinsically good means that it gets some points just for being life; but the fact that it's going to be incredibly painful for the next ten years, say, could render its alleged value too small to make any real difference. Terrible pain may get more negative points than the positive points from being alive per se.

Once we appreciate this last point, we can also address an important question that has no doubt occurred to many readers already: why should there be just *one* answer to the question whether life has value? Couldn't life strike Jones as having value, while it strikes Smith as being quite worthless? Note, too, that it is misleading to talk as though we are all evaluating the same thing. For what John evaluates is John's life, and what Sue evaluates is Sue's life. As soon as we appreciate that point, then another becomes pretty obvious: surely John is in a better position than Sue to evaluate John's life, and vice versa. After all, John is the one who *lives* John's life. Each of us has just one individual life, and so the person whose life it is surely in a much better position to know what it's like, and therefore to evaluate it. Of course, outside information is often of use. But still, there is that ultimate difference of authority between A and B so far as A's life is concerned. A is the one who is in charge, who must and will make the decisions about A's life.

The Purposes of Nature

Some people suppose that nature has "purposes" that we are here to "serve." This curious view is not much subscribed to in the philosophical community any more, though it is occasionally encountered elsewhere. As so often, reflection shows that there are two distinguishable questions to ask about this. One is whether nature does indeed have purposes. And on this, the question soon moves to the meta-level: how on earth would one go about having *evidence* that nature has purposes? We understand talk about purposes in terms of individual minds. But nature doesn't have a mind. In what sense, then, could it have purposes? The other question is one that wasn't asked by the people who held this view, but is clearly important: even if nature did have "purposes", why should *we* pay any attention to them? If nature wants us to do one thing, but *we* want to do another, why should nature be thought to have the upper hand? Indeed, why isn't it the other way around?

Actually, that it is the other way around is something we could argue plausibly even if we accepted the premise of natural purpose. We might point out that we are, after all, rational, self-controlled organisms with minds of our own. Why would nature have made us that way if it didn't want us to *use* those minds? Indeed, seeing that we are natural, how could there possibly be a disparity between what nature wants for us and what *we* want? After all, the argument requires that we are natural. If we weren't, then there wouldn't even be a presumption that we should follow "nature's purposes" instead of our own: we wouldn't be citizens of the state that nature "rules."

This is not to say that we can get no help by observing and studying nature, including for example, the nature of our own bodies. Obviously we can learn a lot about health by studying our own biology. But, can we learn from biology that health *should be one of our predominant values*? That's quite another matter. "Nature" can't decide that for you, any more than can the New Democratic Party or the New Testament. *You* have to decide about that. Nature's decision simply is your decision.

Interlude: Do We Die?

There is one philosophically quite interesting argument for the view that people don't actually go out of existence when they do what we call "dying." The argument is that death is *inconceivable*.

There is a plausible-seeming argument for this. If you try to imagine what it is *like* to be dead, you draw (so to speak) a blank.

Nothing you come up with, such as the image of sheer blackness and silence, can be the right thing—for if death is literally nonexistence, then there is no "you" left to do any conceiving, of those experiences or any other. Death is the end of any and every experience whatever.

So far, so good. But from the fact that death is in this sense inconceivable nothing actually follows. For notice that our previous infinite period of non-existence, before we were born, is also inconceivable. What was it like being Me, 500 years ago? The trouble is that it wasn't "like" anything, for I simply wasn't there (nor anywhere else, either). Anything I *could* imagine on that subject would thereby be shown to be wrong.

Rationality and Suicide

Can life be so bad that suicide is rational? The subject of the *rationality* of an action is much in dispute (like everything else in philosophy!), but there is a familiar picture that seems pretty plausible and is pretty generally accepted. A person acts rationally when he arranges or selects actions in such a way as to attain as much as possible of what, on the whole, he prefers and, thus, as little frustration as possible. To act rationally is to act so as to maximize the overall value in one's life. Some would add that the individual must also have appraised his goals in the light of his best information, to be sure that those are what he really wants. My formulation in terms of what he "on the whole" wants is intended to imply some such condition. *Irrational* action, then, is action that involves some sort of mistake, some error, and especially some avoidable error, as when you act against what you yourself think to be your best interests. Has the suicide made some such mistake?

Here are some relevant scenarios: life seems to be meaningless; the future looks to be full of nothing but pain, or nothing but misery; if I continue to live, horrible things will happen to me (or to someone I'm extremely attached to or concerned about); I'm becoming increasingly incompetent, disabled, incapable of doing the things that matter; or I am nothing but a drain on other people's resources, a dead loss, not worth anything to anyone any more. All these and many others have figured as reasons for suicide. And all *are* reasonable grounds for suicide, it seems to me— if the descriptions in these various scenarios really do apply. But do they ever?

Is there any *general* reason for thinking they must be false? One obvious possibility is that they involve false predictions. Things will get better; you will get better; they'll find a cure for what you've got; the expectedly horrible things won't happen after all. But while it is possible to be wrong about such things, it is also possible to be right. We must go by the best evidence we can get, and it could go either way.

The other interesting possibility is that one's values are somehow *wrong*: true happiness is compatible with having cancer, or being confined to a machine all day long, or being a quadriplegic, or in constant pain. The question about this kind of suggestion is whether it's true in *your* case, even if it might be true for some few, extraordinary others. It might be thought that if Helen Keller or Beethoven can make it, then so can you. But that might not be true. You might be made of more ordinary stuff than they. And then what? Continued but unendurable life might just be stupid.

There is also the intriguing argument that false desires don't *matter*.[2] What the suicide wants to do is to die, and whether or not he acts on false information, he gets what he wants in that respect; nor will he be disappointed about that—or anything else! But there's some question about the logic of this. Suppose I want to achieve some great thing, and I commit suicide because I suppose I'm just not going to succeed. And suppose I am wrong—if I lived and persevered, I *would* have made it. Am I then "disappointed"? Perhaps the answer should be said to be yes rather than no, even though I will not, of course, experience that disappointment.

A very large question is raised by this: what constitutes a person (that is, an *individual* person)? What we know about people is that they occupy a stretch of time. Birth and death are (roughly) the boundaries of this period. Some believe that we in some way "survive death," and some that we somehow preceded our own births, but so far as the publicly available facts are concerned, the stretch from birth to death is all we have to go on. During the great part of this stretch, we have distinctive personalities and characters, and also distinctive sets of interests, aims, tastes, and so on. Our question is whether the *well-being* of a person is to be estimated, in part, by considering things that lie outside his temporal boundaries. Things that lie earlier certainly affect the circumstances of our lives, of course; but there is nothing we can do about any of them—there's no use stewing about it. But what happens after we are gone is another matter, for we frequently have desires, interests, and goals that transcend the boundaries of our own lives. We take out insurance to support our families after we die; we contribute to causes that won't be completed until after our deaths, if ever; some pursue posthumous fame. Is it *rational* to want any of these things? After all, we won't be aware of their success or failure. Once we die, nothing will matter to us since there will be no "us" to whom anything *can* matter.

True, but that doesn't settle the issue. Confronted with the realization that where my death is, I am not, will I cease having any interest in anything that goes on after it? Quite the contrary. We will keep on caring about our spouses and children, our friends, our associates, our businesses, our projects. We will do such things even though we look death, as it were, squarely in the eye, fully appreciating the force of the Epicurean view. One suspects a flaw in any argument that would tell us we are being irrational in doing such things.

"Why should I do anything for posterity? What has posterity done for me?" asked a wag. The answer might be: Nothing, but maybe it's worth doing something for them anyway. People have lived very satisfying lives working for people they'll never meet or know. If those lives are satisfying, who are we to say that they're silly? Maybe they're not so silly after all! But people like that may also be said to have lost something if their projects fail, and to have gained something if they succeed. In retrospect, their lives are better if things after they die go one way, and worse if they go another.

Courage

Is the suicide a coward? Is he throwing in the towel, deserting his post, or something of the sort? This is an interesting question, too. But some versions of it assume that we have "posts" to "desert," and what if we don't? Why should we think that we do? Some people have indeed taken up posts, built a network of relationships and dependencies with others. Having done so, they (and we) might be able to apply the notions of "courage" and "cowardice" with some plausibility. If Jones marries a woman with a handicap and five children to boot, then does himself in because he can't face the responsibilities he's taken on, he surely is liable for some criticism, and "cowardice" might be the right notion to apply.

But should we call Arthur Koestler a coward? Koestler, having written some famous and important books, found himself with a debilitating disease. He judged the expected suffering and especially the deterioration of his faculties to be the sort of thing that a good life can do without. He carefully arranged everything, including talking things over with his wife, who faced similar problems and felt the same way. They made out their wills, paid their bills, and so on, and the two of them then took a painless poison, ending their lives before these unsavory developments took place—and before anyone else was put to trouble and expense on their account. They believed that they were doing the wise thing. "Death with dignity" has since become something of a slogan.

We may think this quite rational, and yet not go along with that view of the matter. Some will "fight" to the end, refusing to let ill health, infirmity, and other troubles get them down to that extent. Can we say that some of these people are right, some wrong?

At a minimum, it seems to me that we have no business making it impossible for people to make such decisions. These are important, difficult, and *personal* problems. We can consider others' ways of dealing with them, learn something from them—and then must choose our own way. There seems to be no publicly supportable reason why people should not be left free in this respect.

Is Life "Infinitely Valuable"?

Some people do say, rather vaguely, that life has "infinite" value. Often those who say that mean only that you can't put a particular "price" on it. Even that is doubtful. My friends in engineering point out that if you are on a committee deciding how to spend a budget on roads, you must put a price on life, whether you like it or not. Suppose that by spending an extra $10 million you can make a particular intersection safer, to the extent that you can predict that there will be one less fatality at it over the next decade than there otherwise would be. But if you spend the $10 million on that, you won't be able to pave twenty miles of road over in another part of the county that urgently needs it, or any number of other worthwhile things. In fact, I am told, life in North America these days is worth somewhere around a half-million dollars. If you can save a life with less than that, you spend it; but otherwise it's better to spend it on some other project.

Is this merely a specialized context, of no direct relevance to you and me? Not at all! Focusing on some examples will help us to define the issues more carefully. Let's start with the trip to Toronto (a city about an hour's drive from the author's). Do we go by car, by train—or not at all? Going by car is, say, about ten times as dangerous as by train: the probability that you get back in one piece is about 10 times as great if you go by train as by car. However, neither is particularly dangerous. And the car is a lot handier, saving you many hours of waiting or riding in not very pleasant quarters, getting you just where and when you want, and so on. If you are like most people, you will choose the car, despite its greater risk. But you wouldn't do this if you really thought that life is *infinitely* valuable. Your expected life-duration is a few seconds or minutes greater if you take the train. (Your "expected loss of life" is the probability of getting killed times the number of years you'd otherwise live.) If life is infinitely valuable, then *any* saving of expected life would be worth buying at *any* cost, in convenience, productivity, etc. But since the danger of driving is exceedingly tiny anyway, the extra safety you get by taking the far less convenient mode of transportation isn't, in your view, worth it. The cost of the increased expected life is just too high.

Actually, if life were "infinitely" valuable, you wouldn't go at all, for certainly taking a train to Toronto isn't quite as safe as simply staying home, or even as safe as walking downtown (with due care). You might prefer being a 100-year-old stick-in-the-mud to being a 95-year-old who has really been around and done interesting things. But lots of us would prefer the latter life to the former. Are we irrational? Not at all. Indeed, we may look on the former as the irrational one. After all, he has purchased five extra-boring years at the cost of a reasonably long life of much more interesting living!

The Skier

People often engage in dangerous activities such as skiing, auto-racing, and mountain-climbing. And many of them smoke, too. All of these documentably shorten one's expected life by significant amounts. The average smoker lives about ten years less than the average non-smoker; the expected lifespan of a Grand Prix racing driver, until recently when high-tech racing car bodies came into use, was dramatically lower than yours or mine—about thirty-nine years, compared to our seventy-eight or so. Yet people do such things voluntarily. *They* obviously don't regard "life," just like that, as infinitely valuable. They insist that certain *kinds* of lives are better, even if they're expectedly shorter. Sydney Carton, the hero of Dickens's *A Tale of Two Cities*, voluntarily sacrificed himself so that Charles Evrémonde would live instead. Perhaps it will be said that in this case, he's prolonging someone *else's* life. True: but if he doesn't think his *own* life is infinitely valuable, why should he think anyone *else's* is?

The Problem in the Abstract

There are many different ways of viewing our futures even if we reject the view that life must be prolonged no matter what it's like. Suppose that we have some way of estimating the value of each moment (or day, etc.) of our lives. And suppose that we arrive at a time, t, *after* which things look bad. But how bad is bad enough to consider suicide? Consider these options:

(1) Suppose that although future life will have its ups and downs, the downs outweigh the ups: the *average* value of future life will be negative"—on the average, painful rather than pleasant, bad rather than good. Is that enough? Note that if this is the case, then you maximize the *net* value of your life, over time, by committing suicide at t(0).

(2) Still, some people might take the view that the good moments are worth living anyway, even if there are more bad ones. This is "maximize the positive": pain only counts against more life if that life would have (almost) no pleasure at all.

(3) But consider the hedonist Roman senator. In his view, he shouldn't have to put up with any nonsense at all. Even if the future holds mostly pleasure, the few moments of pain are not worth it. In fact, anything less than practically perfect isn't good enough: he commands his slave to run him through at the onset of the first substantial toothache.

What Do We think?

I think view (3) will strike most of us as silly; even view (1) seems a bit ungenerous, somehow. Yet view (2) seems rather too strong. Most of us, I suppose, will adopt a view somewhere between (1) and (2). We'll continue living even if life offers more pain than pleasure, so long as it offers a fair amount of pleasure. But hardly any pleasure isn't enough: we won't endure ten years of intense suffering for the sake of one nice afternoon.

Are any of these views *wrong*? Is there any *error* involved in any of them? Not that I can readily see at present. Some might think that all moments of time containing equal amounts of pleasure or pain (or whatever else is held to be ultimately valuable) should count equally. But even that isn't altogether obvious. Consider the man who does endure ten painful years, and on the last day of his life, there's a sudden remission of all pain. He spends a nice afternoon feeding the ducks, or talking with his friend, or just contemplating the sun setting magnificently over the distant hills. And he says, "It was worth it!" Who's to say he was "wrong" about that?

[At this point, go home and listen to Mahler's *Das Lied von der Erde*, or the opening movement of Beethoven's 14th String Quartet.]

Summing Up

Some bad arguments have been used against the legitimacy of suicide. But the basic issue is self-ownership: are our lives fundamentally our own, or aren't they? The view urged here is that they are indeed, and in consequence suicide is in principle legitimate. It might also be rational, and I argued against the idea that life is infinitely valuable, and thus worth prolonging at any cost. Nevertheless, it is not to be taken lightly. But there is much room for different views about the value of life, and we must each decide about this on our own.

Our lives are our own, in consequence
suicide is legitimate.
- might also be rational.
- life is not unfinitely valuable, worth
prolonging @ any cost.

Chapter Three

Euthanasia

The subject of suicide naturally borders on that of euthanasia, which might be regarded as a sort of other-assisted suicide. In general, euthanasia occurs when one person brings about the death of another in the belief that the latter's death is a good to that person. If we suppose suicide to be rational in some cases, then the main question about euthanasia will be how much difference it makes when the agent of the killing is not the same person as its patient (as we will call the one who is killed—"victim" would be prejudicial, and almost all subjects of euthanasia will literally be patients, under someone's care, so "patient" won't be too misleading). That is what we will explore below.

Some Vital Distinctions

Several different questions, to which people might well want to give very different answers, must be distinguished in this area. Great confusion can result from failing to attend to them. Philippa Foot observes that the term literally means "easy death": the intention of one performing an act of "euthanasia" is to "ease the death" of someone.[1]

On the verbal face of it, this can be done only if the person is dying, at least slowly, for otherwise there is no expected death to "ease." If the person would last another twenty years otherwise, then what should we say? Surely the term simply isn't precise enough to give a clear and definite answer to such a question.

All of us will die anyway, some time or other. But someone who shoots me this afternoon, claiming this to be "euthanasia" on the ground that otherwise I would have died painfully in hospital twenty years later, would be misusing the term (among other things!) even if, somehow, he could *know* that I would indeed otherwise die as he says. (The possibility of such a case sharpens our sense of the need to require the patient's consent.)

Here are some things that euthanasia is *not*: someone does not perform euthanasia on someone else if instead what he does is thereby meant to

1. *execute* him (that would be punishment, not euthanasia),
2. relieve him of his money (which would be murder, not euthanasia).
3. improve the human race's genetic profile (which would be eugenics, not euthanasia).
4. bring about the death of "human vegetables" (for which there is, so far as I know, no currently satisfactory word).

The first three are obvious enough, but the fourth needs a word of explanation. Modern medicine enables us to face cases of "brain death," where the organism over there on the bed, or in the machine, may be described as a living human body without a human mind in it. In such cases it must be questioned whether unhooking it from its machine is to be regarded as bringing about "death" at all. Such ex-persons, one might well say, are already dead, in any sense that counts. At any rate, the unhooking of "human vegetables" is certainly not a case of *easing* the death of anyone: no "easing" is possible for one who suffers nothing, and a human organism that is totally unconscious feels nothing and therefore suffers nothing.

A fifth category of exclusion includes the agonizing cases of young children with deformities, degenerative diseases, inoperable conditions, and similar horrors. These are important, and difficult; but we cannot easily extrapolate from these to any conclusions about the standard cases that define the main issues of euthanasia— the termination of a mature life soon to end in any case from fatal disease. Children are not adults, and the differences matter enough to put these cases in a very different category—and one we won't deal with here.

This last type shows us that it is not possible to separate neatly questions of definition from questions of moral substance in this area. That's one reason it is rather important to worry a bit about definition.

An Important Note about Semantics

Many of these issues of life and death require us to think clearly about some matters that can easily be confused. "Life" especially is one such. Since death is relative to life, what are we talking about when we talk of death and of "easy death," for instance? Trying to get clear about it affords a good opportunity to make some semantic distinctions that will prove important.

Definition

First, some words about the notion of *definition*. People talk of defining various things: "we need to define life," they will say. But *life* isn't what we define: what we *define* is the *word* 'life.' A definition is a *statement*: it purports to tell us the *meaning* (or meanings) of a word or term—a proposed explication or explanation of the word's contribution to sentences in which it is employed. Meanings are not, as such, definitions. Everyone who uses words does so meaningfully (we hope!), and thus when they use them there is a "meaning" to be got at. But the user need never have formulated an explicit statement *of* that meaning—why should she, after all? Definitions can be helpful in teaching words to new users, but among those familiar with them, we employ definitions only when there is a possibility of confusion or error, or when we might be able to learn something by attending explicitly to aspects of meaning that are usually, and quite properly, left implicit.

We can distinguish two general types of definition:

1. *Explicative*: this is where the word is already in use among people being addressed, and the purpose of the definition is to tell us what those people mean when they use it;
2. *Prescriptive* or *legislative*, where the definer is simply trying to explain how he is going to use the term in question, whether or not others use it that way.

The first type of definition can be right or wrong, correct or incorrect, for the point is to report a matter of fact - how people do use the word. The criterion here is the *usage of the reference group*; if they don't use it that way, then one's definition is wrong; if they do, then it's right. In the case of the second type, while one can follow through on one's claim that one will use it this way, there is no separate question of whether the intention of the user "conforms with reality": there isn't any extra reality for it to conform to. Definitions of this sort may be useful or useless, clear or fuzzy, and helpful or pointless, but they can't be "incorrect."

When definitions of the first type are correct, though, they are so just by correctly reporting other people's usage. Again, it is *not* a matter of the "true meaning of the word" conforming to "reality." Definitions of words "conform" to reality in the sense that they do indeed label, indicate, or describe the things that the people who use them intend to refer to. But they don't literally tell us, of themselves, facts about the world outside of those minds. For that, we need empirical investigation, not definition of terms. We use words to convey facts, but defining the words only helps to make it clearer which facts we intend to convey; it can never create those facts.

For example: In a familiar use of the word 'bachelor' it means 'unmarried man.' It's neat to be able to define a word in that fashion—few definitions are so simple—but sentences containing the word can mislead. Consider the statement "all bachelors are unmarried" This looks like the same sort of sentence as "all bachelors are neurotic," but it isn't. For if one is using the word in the sense just noted, then a thing *can't* be a married bachelor, for part of what is meant by calling someone a bachelor is precisely that he is not married. On the other hand, "All bachelors are neurotic" is indeed a genuine attempt to state a fact about the world—not about the *word* 'bachelor.' Bachelors, so far as the word is concerned, can be neurotic or not. To find out whether they are, one will have to observe the bachelors themselves, not just the term 'bachelor.'

Ambiguity and Vagueness

Many words are ambiguous and virtually all are to some degree vague. There's a difference between those two phenomena, though, which it is well to be aware of.

(1) *Ambiguity* is a matter of having more than one meaning. Each meaning might be quite clear in itself, but there are two distinctly different ones, creating a risk of confusion between them. 'Bank' can denote a riverside or a place to keep money, but there's not much danger of confusing the two. In the case of "life,", though, the danger is real, as we will see.

(2) *Vagueness* is a matter of the term's being to some degree unclear. We are uncertain what to say about some cases: where the term in question is T, are these cases examples of T, or aren't they? Is a suitcase a trunk? No, but if you make the suitcase large enough and square enough, it may be uncertain which to call it. There are hardly any words so crystal clear that there's never any uncertainty about whether it applies. In cases of great moral import, vagueness can be a major problem: we must be concerned about cases where it is not easy to draw lines.

Terms can be both ambiguous and vague. There might be two uses of a term such that the difference between them is a matter of degree, and it will be notoriously difficult to decide which of the two to use. Ideally, the world would just refuse to supply such examples, but the world is notoriously unco-operative in accommodating such wishes! Take tall, for instance: a six-footer is tall relative to an infant, but short relative to a giraffe. Whether we should say that 'tall' is ambiguous is moot, since height is a relational concept and thus we need to have a reference class in mind when we use it. Yet it can easily be uncertain which of two very different ones is relevant, as in my example, where a man at the zoo, holding a child by the hand and looking up at the giraffes, invites both, which would give opposite results. On top of that, even when the reference class is clear, tall is vague: a six-footer is still tall for a man in contemporary North America, but how about a man five feet ten and a half? The point is clear: vagueness and ambiguity can go hand in hand, or not, as may be.

"Life"

Is the word "life" ambiguous? Carrots and people are both kinds of living things, but in saying that both exemplify life, do we say the same thing about them? It seems clear that we do not, usually. Let's make at least a tentative distinction here:

1. *Biological* life: animals and vegetables exemplify life in this sense, while minerals do not. Nutrition, growth, and decay are processes common to all living things in a purely biological sense of the term.

2. Experiential or *conscious* life: in this sense of 'life,' only beings with *minds* have it. Awareness, thought, feeling, sensation, emotion occupy consciousness. Nutrition and growth, on the other

hand, require no consciousness at all. That's also true of many sorts of bodily motion: we may turn over in our sleep with no awareness that we do so.

It was noted above that the term 'euthanasia' is the wrong one to apply in the case where the question is whether to unplug a "human vegetable." We can terminate biological life without thereby terminating any experiential life. And vice versa: taking a sedative may put one out of consciousness for a time, though one's bodily processes hum right along.

The sort of life that most people have in mind when they regard life as *valuable* is life in our second sense. Spending thousands of dollars to keep a body functioning when no mind is attached to it would be regarded by most of us as pointless. But spending thousands to enable us to continue to have experience is something we do all the time, and that makes perfectly good sense to us.

If a sly devil were to come along and offer us what he bills as "eternal life," but it turns out on further investigation to be eternal *biological* life only, most of us wouldn't take him up on it and would question the sanity of anyone who would. He would (among other things!) be exploiting an ambiguity in the term 'life.'

Euthanasia and Suicide Compared

Some cases of euthanasia might be described as "second-party-assisted suicide." Suppose our subject wishes to die and would kill herself if she could, but her physical condition makes this impossible (she's paralysed from the neck down, say). Someone helpfully unplugs her life-support system or puts strychnine in her tea. Would this be "euthanasia"? No. Or, at any rate, not exactly, or not necessarily.

In the first place, many suicides are inspired by emotional or other considerations, not by physical suffering. In those cases, death is not impending, and so suicide does not "ease death."

Second, in some very important cases of euthanasia, the patient is incapable of addressing himself to the question whether he wants to live on. If someone else is to intervene and shorten that patient's life, it would have to be without benefit of the subject's compliance. But in suicide, which is necessarily intentional and normally even deliberate, this can't happen.

If we think that suicide is fundamentally morally allowable, and that people even have the *right* to engage in it, then it is very difficult to sustain a large objection *in principle* to euthanasia. After all, in these cases euthanasia differs only in respect of the *agent* of the death. Conversely, if one thinks that euthanasia, even in the case where it is urgently requested by the patient, is nevertheless *not* allowable, then it will be very difficult to defend suicide. Clearly the two are closely related in many cases. The ones of special concern to us are those where a principle covering suicide doesn't readily apply.

Consent: The "Living Will" Question

Does the consent of the patient always fully justify euthanasia? If not, why not? First we must distinguish two issues: necessity and sufficiency. To say that consent is *necessary* for justified euthanasia is to say that unless consent is given, the euthanasia in question would *not* be justified. To say that consent is *sufficient* is to say that if consent is given, then euthanasia *is* justified. The two are logically independent.

Some will deny that our lives *are* "our own," of course. They need to tell us where the discussion in the previous chapter has gone astray. But until a good alternative to that result is at hand, this consideration will surely be paramount. If we say that the subject's life really does, after all, *belong* to that person, then what else could matter?

Self-ownership strongly supports the *necessity* of consent. We may not take other people's lives into our hands: consent, at least when it is possible to obtain it, is surely *necessary* for justified euthanasia. But accepting its necessity, as we have just seen, does not automatically commit us to accepting its *sufficiency*. Still, the same idea, self-ownership, suggests that those other people, the patients themselves, surely may do so: it's their life, after all.

That view strikes me as very powerful. Is there anything to go against this conclusion? Sometimes it might be that someone electing to die in preference to what he sees as a miserable life had incurred strong and specific obligations to other parties and would be copping out by dying, thus violating those obligations. To assess that in particular cases would, of course, require a sensitive understanding of those cases bearing in mind that it cannot be easy to have obligations so strong as to force someone to continue to live against his own will. But they cannot be the normal cases; in those, our patient is assumed to be reasonably well aligned with the rest of his social world.

But things can still go wrong. First and foremost, what if we cannot obtain the explicit wishes of the person concerned? In some extreme conditions, consent of the patient is unobtainable. Yet she might be suffering greatly. Then what? An important contribution to resolving dilemmas of this kind has recently attained prominence: a "living will," a document in which the person concerned tells us in advance what she wants done in such eventualities. While in full possession of her faculties, she may have soberly elected death without strenuous efforts to prolong life as the preferable option when she becomes irreversibly and fatally afflicted.

This brings up the second thing: someone might not have made out any such will or she may have made out a living will and then, unbeknownst to us, changed her mind. Now what? And there is the question whether we might think her mistaken, and how, if at all, that matters.

Suffering and Consent

Some people prefer to live even though they suffer, and others do not. When suffering and willing diverge, which has priority? Do we put to death one who insists that he wants to live, despite what seems to us unbearable suffering? On the other hand, do we help out of life one who is not suffering but nevertheless insists that he *wants* out, though he cannot procure his own death?

Perhaps these are not altogether independent conditions. We might say that anyone who wants to die *must* be suffering and, conversely, that someone who prefers to live even though he seems to be suffering is thereby shown not to be suffering so greatly after all. But I don't think that those are reliable suppositions. Some people seem to be able to endure a lot more pain than others—but it isn't that they don't *feel* it. They do feel it, but it doesn't *bother* them as much as it would others.[2] To take an example at a much lower level of seriousness than the ones we are considering here, I almost never use painkiller when undergoing dental surgery. Many students find this astonishing. But my reason is not that it doesn't actually hurt in my peculiar case. It's just that I find the "cure" worse than the disease: being deprived of the power of intelligible speech for a few hours is a greater cost to a university professor than a few minutes' pain.

Something like that could also be true of death for some people. If one's mind is suffused with suffering and nothing else, then what indeed is the point of life? But if, though suffering physically, you are also inspired to noble visions, or find yourself still able to make a bit of progress in your work on seventeenth century Indian poetry, you may find that life is still, on the whole, worth living. It is not our business to second-guess other people in such important matters.

What Are Our Duties vis-à-vis Patients' Wishes?

I have argued for the dominant status of the consent of the individual whose life is in question. But we must be careful to see what this means, for it means only that we have the duty to refrain from acting *contrary* to the known preferences of the subject. It does *not* mean, however, that we have the duty to *follow* those wishes. In the useful terminology explained in Chapter One, patients have a *negative* right regarding their lives, but not a *positive* one. So if Jones says "Kill me!" you have the right to refuse, just as he has the right to kill himself, if he can, or to ask still others to do it for him. You might sign up, on request, to become the executor of a person's will, and similarly you might sign up to become the executor of his *living* will, obligating yourself to slip him the final potion upon request. But, equally, you may refuse any such request. To accede to it is to exemplify the virtue of charity, not of justice. Only if you have a prior commitment to this patient that you would not fail him in this last request does it become a duty of justice that goes beyond charity.

Thus the primary cases of euthanasia involve relations among consenting adults. As with all such cases, our business is only to refrain from interfering—not necessarily to join the club.

When Consent Isn't Conveyed

What do we do when the sufferer is unable to tell us what he wants? The first thing that comes to mind, certainly, is to try to find out what he would have said if he could have said anything. But how do we do that? We are looking for a very "iffy" piece of information, a "counterfactual," as philosophers call it; and they have been much concerned about the logic of such things.

It is established practice to let the decision be taken by the nearest available relatives of the patient. Two different considerations suggest that this is a reasonable idea. First, we think that near-kinship gives us more claim on a life than does the status of being a mere onlooker or stranger. Parents and their offspring have bonds that most do not, and close relations are more strongly concerned about each other than about outsiders. The very common acceptance of this attitude creates a presumption that it also holds in the case at hand. But it is only a presumption, and it could be overturned by contrary evidence. In *this* case, we may know that the patient was totally at odds with his relatives and would not want to accept their assessments as at all authoritative in his case.

The second point is that those with whom one has grown up and knows well are more likely to have enough evidence about one's personality, character, and interests than strangers. Long-time close associates, therefore, are reasonably thought to be able to say what the patient would have wanted, at least by comparison with those who knew her scarcely or not at all.

Rights vs. Values

But if this fails us, too, then where do we go? Some would counsel that, in that case, we must perforce sustain people in life. No consent, no euthanasia. That is a kind of fail-safe strategy, it is thought. But unconsidered acceptance of that strategy isn't wise, for that would be to neglect some important considerations.

The importance of a patient's consent or lack of it is asserted when we accept his *right* over himself. Of course, it comes first if we know what he wants. But where we don't, this right cannot be appealed to as a sufficient source of moral advice. We do not violate a patient's rights if what he has the right to is respect for his will, and yet there is no expressed will—thus leaving us in the dark about what constitutes respecting it. When a person writes up or otherwise conveys his will about a matter that is his by right to decide about, he invokes his own values, his considered preferences for how those things are to go. We then have guidance of the most authoritative kind. But when we have no way of getting at this will, there is no alternative but to approach the matter from the perspective of values. Now we have to think about the value of life versus death in this case, which, as we have seen, is really the value of a shorter as compared with a longer life, where the longer one, in the cases we are considering here, has much more pain and suffering in it than the shorter one would have.

In addressing such a case, whose values would we now be invoking? We can, and should, try to invoke the values of the subject, but these, we are assuming, are inconclusive in this case. This leaves us with no option but to decide as best we can by consulting our *own* values—our considered opinion about what's best to do in these cases, and thus about what sort of life is most worth living, or most worth living for this subject if we know enough to make any adjustments for it. Here the problem is to exercise a suitable objectivity. Suppose that our own preferences are, as we know, quite idiosyncratic. Unless we have special information about the case before us, we of course must be guided by what we know about normal cases, on the ground that a given case, absent further information, is by definition more likely to be normal than not. But this may not help very much. How many normal people actually have an opinion about whether they would prefer to die rather than suffer to such-and-such a degree? Very few, surely! To the degree that we lack information about typical cases, we are back to intuition and the affirmation of our own ideals of life. The point is that we would now be justified in this, for we have no other rational recourse.

Who Pays? Negative vs. Positive Rights to Life

When we realize that our own values do and must count, another question suddenly comes up. Suppose that our subject is being kept alive by very expensive, high-tech methods. Keeping him alive is costing somebody $20,000 per month. Does that matter? And does it matter *who* is paying for it? Contrary to what many citizens of modern welfare states may think, I believe that it does indeed.

To pinpoint the issue that faces us here, we need again to recall the distinction, defined in Chapter One, between negative and positive rights. This, in brief, is the distinction between rights requiring the rest of us not to interfere and those requiring us to help. We may resummarize them as follows:

Person A's *negative* right over person B to do x entails Person B's duty to *let* A do x (i.e., to refrain from interfering with A's performance of x). A's *positive* right over person B to do x entails B's duty to *help* A do x (i.e., to do something to enable A to do x), if A cannot do x unaided or with the aid only of persons who are will-ing to help.

In the cases where we want to say that the right in question is not a right to *do* something, but rather a right to *have* something, call it y, then the negative right of A to y is B's duty not to take y from A, or more generally to use y without A's permission, whereas A's positive right to y is B's duty to supply y to A if A doesn't already have it.

This distinction, we should note, is not the same as another that has become a familiar one in philosophical and political writ-ings, namely that between "welfare" rights, on the one hand, and "action" (sometimes called "liberty") rights, on the other. Let x be any liberty and one can make the same distinction. If x is some-thing A is currently free to do, for whatever reason, then his nega-tive right to that liberty is that we not deprive him of it; but even if he isn't currently at liberty to do it, then if he has only a negative right to it, we do not need to go out of our way to supply it to him; whereas if he has a positive right to it, then we do. The wrongly imprisoned prisoner has a right to be free; but does he have a right to be *freed* by *us*? That's an important question, and not one that is self-evidently answered by the sheer fact that he has the right to be free.

Or let y be some state of welfare or health. Then A's negative right to that state means that we mustn't deprive him of or worsen him in respect of that state of welfare or health; but his positive right to it would mean that if he doesn't have it, we may have to see to it that he gets it, if we can.

Now let us apply this to the crucial cases before us, involving our right to *life*. If that right is merely negative, then it only forbids us to *kill* people, that is, to deprive them of their lives. It says noth-ing about having to help keep them alive if they are dying from causes that we had nothing to do with. ("Thou may'st not kill, but needst not strive/officiously to keep alive.") But if their right is pos-itive, then we do indeed have to "strive" to keep people alive if we can. Thus the issue of who must pay is settled one way if the right to life is merely negative. In that case, others do not need to pay to keep someone alive, though it might be nice of them if they did. But if life is a positive right, then indeed we may all be obliged to pay (that is, to help pay, if we can) for such purposes.

The Issue of Active vs. Passive Euthanasia

These definitions assume, of course, that we can distinguish between refraining from intervening and harming, and between refraining from intervening and helping. To be of any application, they require that harming and helping are not the only two possibilities: that just sitting on the sidelines may be distinguished from both. Some writers claim to deny this. For example, James Rachels, in his now famous discussion of "active" and "passive" euthanasia, argues that there is no essential difference between killing someone and letting that person die. If that is really so, then we don't have to choose between positive and negative rights to life, for on what seems to be Rachels's view, we would have to say that whenever we fail to help someone, then it is as if we had *killed* him. If, on the other hand, people's right to life is to be regarded as essentially negative and *not* positive, then we do need to be able to make the killing/letting die distinction.

So who's right? I am, actually; or rather, *we* are, we being me and most of you, for we all do make such a distinction. We don't think that at every moment of the day we are or might as well be out there murdering all those poor innocent people who, after all, are dying by the thousands as we sip our tea and whom, quite possibly, we could be helping to live a bit longer. So we want the police to move heaven and earth to apprehend murderers, but we do nothing whatever about people who merely fail to save as many lives as possible.

Actually, the situation is worse than that—"worse," that is, if Rachels is right! Consider such latterly famous cases as that of Kitty Genovese, a woman who was attacked, raped, and murdered by a vicious criminal while no less than thirty-eight people watched from street corners and windows, yet none of whom even lifted a finger to phone the police. But they were guilty of no crime. Is the criminal law totally out to lunch? Or was there some basis for this distinction between the bystanders and the criminal?

In my view there is indeed a distinction, and a sound basis for it. The philosopher Philippa Foot, in her highly regarded article, "Euthanasia," isn't very clear about the basis, saying that killing and letting-die are contrary to "different virtues": it is *uncharitable* to allow to die when one could do something to prevent death, whereas it is *unjust* to kill. While I agree with her in that judgement, it is one thing to say so, but quite another to explain why the distinction matters. Most of us intuitively agree with her, I am sure, but could-n't we all be confused?

The first thing to do is to point out that, on the face of it, there are two different questions here: first, whether there is *any distinction at all*, and second, if there is indeed such a distinction, whether it matters.

Is there *any* difference between killing and allowing to die? Can we *tell* the difference? Sure we can! Rachels's example of the murderer who pushes the little boy beneath the surface of the water is one in which he clearly kills the boy; his other "killer," who merely stands by and watches while the boy drowns, *lets him die*. We have no trouble with those two. Notice that in the second case, the boy would have drowned even if the nasty uncle had been in Australia at the time. It would then be equally true that the uncle let the boy die, but implausible to hold him guilty of mur-der! In the first case, on the other hand, the man has to be right there; if he could establish that he was elsewhere at the time, that would prove that he didn't drown the boy. To kill is to bring about an alteration in the state of one's victim, from life to death, which the victim *would not have undergone had one not acted*. To let die, on the other hand, is to refrain from doing something which, if you had done it, would have prevented such an alteration of the patient's condition. The patient is not worse off for having been allowed to die than he would have been had the agent not even been around.

Of course a proponent of Rachels's thesis could say that allow-ing to die amounts to killing only when it would be quite *easy* for us to save the person and we nevertheless don't do it. He could say that the duty not to kill is the duty both to refrain from such overt acts as stabbing and also from such relatively inert "acts," or non-acts, as failing to rescue when we could do so very easily.

How easily? That's certainly one major problem. It's rare that you can save a life by merely lifting a finger. And it's a long way from there to spending $20,000 a month. Conversely, it is almost never difficult to refrain from acting. Consider this: all of us, at this very moment, are not-killing over five billion people! If inaction were equivalent to action, we'd have to be mighty busy people to rack up a record like that. Yet in fact, it's a snap—we don't even have to think about it!

So Rachels would be wrong if he really thought that there is *no* distinction. But he likely doesn't think that. Rather, he thinks that the abstract distinction that we've found it easy enough to make doesn't basically *matter*. Now, whether it does matter is, of course, a moral question, and one with potentially major implications, for if we hold that we have positive duties our lives are very much more complicated than if we only have negative ones. It is in almost all cases remarkably easy to observe negative duties. You can fulfil them completely by doing absolutely nothing. A positive duty, on the other hand, requires a definite commitment of your energy and time, or money, or other resources. Negative duties leave us much freer. (This has to be true, for it would be incoherent to hold that we did have positive rights but did *not* have negative rights to the same thing. Suppose that it was other people's duty to save us if they can, but they have no duty to refrain from shooting us if they happen to feel like it?)

A fair number of philosophers down through the ages, and a great many ordinary people, have thought that our right to life is essentially and primarily negative, not positive. We may indeed be criticized for not helping to save lives, if we could have done so, but we may not be jailed for it. On the other hand, we may indeed be jailed for killing someone, and we deserve no special praise if we do refrain from killing. It's what's to be expected. Those of us who don't kill people—luckily, that's almost all of us—are literally "only doing our duty." But those who jump into the icy water and save lives, at great risk to their own, deserve very special praise and commendation. They are heroes—they're not "just doing their duty." And even those who render small assistances deserve our thanks. If you save my life by merely walking ten feet out of your way and pressing a button, I still owe you thanks for it. But I don't owe special thanks to all those good people out there who refrain from killing me, as—happily for me—they do every day.

So let's go back to our question: what if it would cost a great deal of money to keep this person alive? If we had no fundamental duty to keep him alive anyway—it's a charitable and generous act on our part to keep him alive as long as we have—then is it not also our right to decide to stop rendering this assistance? Especially if he's in such bad shape that there's grave doubt about even calling it "assistance"? If we properly command our own lives, then we also should be thought to be properly in command of our own resources: it's up to us whether to help to keep a given person alive, whether that person is our self or someone else, or instead to spend our time and money on any number of other possible goods.

Special Obligations: The Health-Care Professional

At this point, we should recognize that there are people out there, health-care professionals such as doctors and nurses, whose relation to the sick and dying is quite different from that of the rest of us. The doctor has sworn to uphold life, to the best of her ability. The nurse's *duty* is to change the bedpan and inject the medicine in the right amount and at the right time. These are all positive acts for the care of others. If people only have negative rights to life and health, what about these people?

The short answer is that health-care professionals do indeed have those duties, but they are the duties of their jobs, their offices. And they assumed those offices or accepted those jobs voluntarily. Nobody has the duty to become a doctor, if they should prefer instead the life of the tennis player, or even the life of the vagabond, for that matter.

Taking the duty to keep others alive seriously raises the old question of liberty vs. slavery. Do other people own us, or do we own ourselves? If they don't own us, it means that they don't have authority or command over us, over how we shall spend our time and what we will make of our lives. We must respect each other's lives, not trample on them or just use them as we wish without bothering to ask; so we can't simply insist that they help us out when we are in a jam, perhaps not even if that jam is a matter of life and death.

On the other hand, most people would prefer to join an insurance pool, for instance, so that they could indeed count on the help of certain other people. And perhaps we can say that "society" in general "appoints" certain people, doctors and the like, to render major help. We can also say that it asks all of us to be helpful in general, to be ready to go out of our way a bit to assist our fellows when they are in trouble. But it's a long way from that to $20,000 per month. The idea that people simply have a *right* to our assistance, especially our substantial assistance, is anything but self-evident.

Canada, like many other places, has a public medicare system that in effect assumes that we have a positive right to life. Supporters might say that Canadians do have such a right—not, however, a right against everyone else in the world, but only against their own health officials, a right given to them by their fellow Canadians. But the trouble with the political version of an insurance pool is that this was an *involuntary* "gift" on the part of many of them—all those who would vote against the system if they had the opportunity and who resent paying the taxes by which it is supported. Obviously there are moral questions about this. Am I being "generous" and "helpful" to you if the way in which I demonstrate my generosity is to put a gun to my neighbour's back and tell him to pay your medical bills or I'll shoot?

killing our actions cause

The Patient on the Life-Sustaining System

The question of killing versus allowing to die *does* get problematic in one very important kind of case, that of patients who are already on life-sustaining systems. If Nurse B walks into Patient A's room and quietly disconnects the system or shuts off a valve that controls the life-sustaining medicine being continually dripped into A's system, is she then killing him or merely letting him die? Were it not for the system, he would be long-since dead; not installing such a system in the first place would be allowing to die. Nevertheless, the answer in this kind of case, on the face of it, is that Nurse B is indeed killing him. This is not like the case where we see the victim struggling in the water and are faced with the decision whether to jump in and try to save him. Rather, it's like the case where somebody else has already done that, and the victim is now in a boat waiting for further developments—but we gently tip the boat so that she falls in and drowns after all.

What we do when we shut down a system that someone else has put the patient on is to deny the patient a benefit (in this case, continued life) that someone else has a perfect right to give him, and did give him. We have intervened in a voluntarily formed relation between someone and someone else, and intervened in a quite devastating way. This is not a matter of merely "letting die." It may well be murder. Whether it is that or a morally excusable, or even commendable, act of assistance depends on what sort of shape the patient is actually in, on what his will would have been if he had been in a position to say, and other things.

On the other hand, where the question is whether to hook the patient up to a life-saving system in the first place, it's more straightforward. Here the issue really is whether we save or allow to die. Hooking him up saves him; not doing so lets him die. In the latter case, we have not killed him: we have, instead, chosen not to intervene in the course of nature. The disease, or whatever it is, is what kills him, and we (let us assume) had nothing to do with his getting that in the first place. So this is like the question whether to leap in and save the drowning man, except that it is normally a lot less risky to us.

Summary on Euthanasia

Let's try to say where we are. First, it is vitally important to distinguish euthanasia from several other issues. The question about euthanasia is whether it is permissible to "ease" the death of one who is dying anyway, or whose condition is at any rate so severe that it would likely engender thoughts of suicide in the patient. It is *not* the question of eugenics, nor of murder, nor of allowing human vegetables to die. Nor is it the question of what to do about defective newborns. (We will consider those, at least somewhat, when we discuss abortion.) There *is* a difficult set of questions about children with incurable degenerative conditions, etc. Those are important in their own right, but are on the margin of the euthanasia issue. Or just over the margin—since, after all, a major factor there is that we suppose that children aren't able to assess, effectively, the serious issues involved, and thus we don't have the option of acting in response to a request by another mature adult. I have not addressed that issue above, and am ruling it out of the present consideration.

Second, the standard case of euthanasia is one where we have the consent, or even the request, of the patient to "ease his passing." The patient is already dying, and suffering or otherwise in for an existence she prefers not to have to endure, and she is thus in the position of the rational suicide except that someone else has to act, for she cannot do so under her own power. If suicide is morally acceptable, then this type of euthanasia must be, too, in principle. And there are the same kind of questions: did she think it over sufficiently? Do we concur with her judgement, or should we resist?

Third, we have the cases where the patient has not left such a request in the past and is unable now to address the question. Here we must ask, first, what the patient would have wanted. We may be able to arrive at a plausible conclusion about this from past knowledge of the patient, likely to be had by her friends and relatives and not likely to be had by anyone else. Here the suggested conclusion is that we then do that, whatever it is, and assuming that we don't think her reasoning too much in error and that we are willing to bear the costs of the selected option.

Fourth, in some of these further cases, we will have no idea what the patient would have wanted, and then we must go on our own considered judgements of whether the person's life is indeed worth living. This requires us to have some sort of view, a philosophy of life. Most people will say: if her life is nothing but pain and suffering, and there's no hope, then let's pull the plug now. But some will not, and their view is certainly to be listened to with respect. What "most people" say is not necessarily the truth, after all.

Fifth, addressing the question of "active" versus "passive" euthanasia, we must distinguish two sorts of cases again: (1) those where the "passive" option is *genuinely* passive—that is, it's a question whether to do anything or not, and (2) those in which this is not the issue, for the patient is already hooked up and the question is whether to unhook, after which she dies. The difference between the second and outright killing is surely too small to bear much weight. In those cases, we may agree with Rachels. But not in the others.

Sixth, some crises in real life force a rapid decision. The patient is in utter torment, nothing can be done to save her, and the real question is whether to put her out of her misery now or let her suffer a few more hours and then die. Consider the case of the driver of the burning gasoline truck, pinned beneath the wreckage and screaming uncontrollably, who has a loaded revolver in the cab. Should we pull it out and shoot him when he implores us to do so? This would genuinely be *active euthanasia* in the full sense. And it is not obvious that the answer to this question is in the negative. Here again, we must agree with Rachels: sometimes the right thing to do is an act that would in other circumstances be terribly wrong. It will be very hard to do such an act, and it should be; but it may still be right. Still, I do not murder the driver if I fail to shoot him, nor am I the cause of his fearsome pains. On the other hand, I would wish that I could help him, and would be sorry if I thought that I could, yet didn't.

This should confirm that the question of euthanasia is not a simple one!

Slippery Slope Arguments

Euthanasia is one of many issues in which a familiar type of argument tends to be employed: the argument from the "slippery slope." The argument goes roughly like this: "If we allow euthanasia, then people will take advantage of it and start killing unwanted people." Euthanasia will edge over into eugenics or outright murder.

Arguments of this type are called "slippery slope" arguments because of two features:

1. The transition from the presumably permissible thing, F, over to the impermissible one, G, is *continuous*. Thus there is no place along the way that you can draw a precise and nonarbitrary line, separating definitely the Fs from the Gs. ("Up to just this point, it's merely euthanasia; beyond it, it's murder and you get sent to jail.")

2. Once you get started down the slope, you *can't stop*. So the only way to avoid the disastrous result is to draw the line right up at the top—disallow euthanasia, too, in the present instance.

Here we must make a very important distinction between two kinds of slippery slope arguments: "logical" and "psychological."

In the logical version, the proposed reason why we "can't stop" is simply the logical point made in (1): since we can't draw the line in a completely non-arbitrary fashion, we have no reason to stop at any particular place. Yet if we are to stop at all, we must do so in *some* particular place. Therefore, we can't stop at all. So the distinction between F and G has been steamrollered: F (say, euthanasia) is really no different from G (say, murder) after all.

The psychological version, on the other hand, says that what propels us down the slope is human psychology. People can't understand fine distinctions or they take advantage of any "loopholes" or "slack" in the rules. From the administrator's point of view, once you start allowing little exceptions at one point, for this group of people, you find yourself compelled to allow them at another, for that group. Before you know it, we're allowing outright murder.

There are rather different things to say about these two versions. Let's start with the logical versions, which are *very* frequent and *very* influential. Nothing can be more important than to appreciate that slippery-slope arguments of this type are *fallacious*. This can be illustrated easily with familiar examples. Consider, for instance, the case of the giant and the dwarf. The difference between them lies only in their height, which is a continuous variable. The difference between them can be divided indefinitely into tinier and tinier segments. Now consider a typical dwarf, say, three feet tall, and add a sixteenth of an inch. Is the person still a dwarf? Well, sure! Very well: then add another sixteenth to this last one. Still a dwarf? No doubt. But if we can repeat this argument indefinitely, then we shall have "proven" that dwarfs are actually giants!

The logical structure of the argument is this: If x is an F, then where n is some very small (but not literally "infinitesimal") amount, as you please, then an x which is F + n is also an F.

All we need is that one premise, and we're off and running, for new cases are always indistinguishable from the former ones, and their being indistinguishable is precisely what qualifies them for the same description.

Interestingly enough, you can also "prove" by this argument that giants are really dwarfs. Just start at the other end and instead of adding n to a dwarf, subtract n from a giant. This very fact shows us that the argument is no good. For, of course, dwarfs are *not* giants. If the argument were valid, it would "prove" two mutually incompatible conclusions: that dwarfs are actually very tall, and that giants are actually very short.

Lest giants and dwarfs be thought too far out as examples, consider the voting age. In Canada, if you turn eighteen on September 5 and the election is on September 6, you get to vote, while your friend whose birthday is on the seventh has to wait until the next election, which may not be until four or more years later. Obviously there is no correlation between political maturity and age close enough to tell us that your friend was not competent to vote on the sixth and you were. Considerations of administrative convenience, practicality, and a sort of fairness are what prompt us to decide on a definite legal age for drinking, driving, and other things. But on the other hand, children are not adults, and young people are not old people, despite the fact that children slowly grow into young adults, then into middle-aged people, old people, and so on, with no sharp breaks between.

The point, then, is that the absence of a logically sharp distinction between F and G does *not* in any way prove that there is no difference between Fs and Gs, and it especially doesn't prove that the concepts of F and G must be without moral importance.

But if we turn to the psychological versions of slippery slope arguments things are quite different. That the argument is fallacious certainly doesn't mean that people won't succumb to it: many university-educated people have indulged in them. Yet an administrator will appreciate the possible force of slippery slope arguments based on human psychology. On the other hand, though, suppose that there are really good reasons why we should allow F, and equally good reasons why we should disallow G. The fact that juries can deliberate for hours trying to decide whether Jones was guilty of murder or only manslaughter doesn't mean that there is no difference between them. Indeed, just the opposite: they deliberate because the issue is important. There is a difference—which is why we think it worthwhile to agonize over such decisions.

Empirical evidence is relevant to these matters, of course. We can look and see whether allowing F has in fact been accompanied by a significant increase in G. In some places, turning right on a red light is disallowed, in others it is allowed and has been for years. Clearly it would be possible to do a statistical analysis to see whether the accident rate is higher in the areas that do allow it. Similarly, it might be possible to do research to see whether places that allow euthanasia also suffer increases in murder. (This is not easy to do, however, since the very clever murderer who has disguised his deed as euthanasia would be very difficult to detect, since part of his cleverness is having a very good case for terminating the life in question. Only *he* knows that she didn't really want him to do it, say. But while we won't be able to discern undetectable murders, we *will* be able to notice whether there has been a marked increase in the incidence of "euthanasia" in suspicious circumstances.)

The logical version, on the other hand, requires no statistics or facts to refute; that is purely a conceptual matter. But it is a very important exercise, for a large part of whatever basis there is for supposing there is a problem on the psychological front is precisely that too many people don't realize that it is a fallacy. Nor is this surprising. One major part of the premise in the logical version is often undoubtedly true: you cannot, often, draw a non-arbitrarily sharp line between the two things. There is no precise height below which you are normal and above which you are tall. We just have to decide that for some practical purpose, such as when we are summarizing findings for a report or when we have to make an administrative decision. In short, lack of sharp, non-arbitrary dividing lines simply does not show that there is no such distinction as that of tall and short.

In practice, we may sometimes have to set up artificially precise criteria. Recalling our example of height, we might, for instance, set the minimum height for classifying contemporary North American males as tall at six feet. This is arbitrary in detail, but not at all arbitrary in principle. Males of 5' 9" really are medium, and those of 6' 2" really are tall, in Canadian or American society these days, even if ones of 5' 11-7/8" are so close to tall that for most purposes one wouldn't hesitate to group them with the tall; but males of 5' 10-3/4" are borderline medium, and it is a moot question whether to classify them as tall or medium. If anything turned on it, we could sharpen up such distinctions; but normally, nothing does. It is important to know both that any such problems can be resolved, if need arises, and also that often they simply do not need to be resolved.

But in important cases such as killing versus allowing to die, resolution is important—something *does* turn on it. If agent A doesn't push patient B into the water, he doesn't *murder* her; yet if he does nothing to save B, he is still culpable to some degree, though in the category of negligence rather than murder. And if he makes a middling, but failing effort? We won't have gone greatly wrong if he gets off with a substantial reprimand. These decisions illustrate both the need for and the possibility of arriving at workable solutions despite the presence of slippery slopes.

Psychology

The really difficult question is what to do when people step across lines, as they doubtless will, taking advantage of permissive rules. We must be very careful in making rules on the basis of irrational behaviour. We should never reward stupidity, even though we may have to guard against it. If in serious cases a great deal of good is done thereby, we should not disallow euthanasia. We risk playing into the hands of would-be killers by allowing it, but we condone a great deal of unnecessary suffering if we forbid it. The most reasonable solution is to allow it, but with considerable safeguards against possible abuse: committee decisions; more than one person including perhaps an expert, to be in on the deliberation; and so on.

But we couldn't even get that far if some fundamental matter of principle forbade euthanasia. So far as I can see, there is not. The subject is difficult, indeed; but, fortunately, it is not impossible.

Summing Up

Euthanasia differs from suicide in that someone else administers it to the patient. When the patient is able to make his wishes clearly known, we can assimilate euthanasia to suicide: there is no further objection in principle, though those selected to administer it have the right to refuse. But when we cannot know just what the patient wants at the time, because he is unable to communicate, we must ultimately decide, in the light either of what we know or can infer about what he would want or of our own considered views on the value of life. Once euthanasia is seen to be justified in principle, there is little support for confining euthanasia to its "passive" version, in which the patient is allowed to die rather than killed, despite the fact that a clear distinction between the two is possible and is often morally very important.

Chapter Four

Punishment, Capital and Otherwise

So far, we have looked at two closely related issues concerning possibly justified killing: of oneself, in suicide, and of others, in euthanasia. I have taken the general position that unless adequate reason to the contrary can be shown, we should let people follow their own judgement in matters that concern essentially themselves. In both cases, this "default option," as I termed it, seems often to be met. In most cases there is no good reason to prevent people from committing suicide from our own point of view; and out of regard for the subjects themselves, if they have considered the matter carefully and not made serious mistakes, there seems also no strong objection to either of these acts. But our next topic, punishment, is very different. Criminals, we suppose, normally do *not* regard it as in their interest to be punished. Consequently, the justification of punishment cannot be the same as for suicide and euthanasia. The subject raises many fascinating issues, of which I shall mention several, without trying to be comprehensive; and no one can doubt of its enormous importance, especially in legal contexts.

Definitions

Let's start, as usual, by trying to get a reasonably clear grasp of our subject. When A is described as "punishing" B, there are two essential features:

(1) What A does to B—call it x—must be *expectedly undesirable from B's point of view* (an "evil," as some would say).

(2) A does x *in response to* something B is believed by A to have done in the past. (That is at least claimed by A, whether A actually believes it or not.)

Some would also add a third, which I list for discussion:

(3?) A has appropriate authority to do x in this case.

I list this third one with a question mark, because clearly people often claim to be punishing others when they are in no such position of authority, there being no formal arrangement or institution bearing on the case. The philosopher John Locke held that in a "state of nature" all persons would have the right to punish any other persons who violated what he claimed was the "natural law."[1] In saying this, he did not misuse the term "punish"—we understand what he meant. It is better, I think, to regard condition (3) as a very important condition for *institutionalizing* punishment, as a highly desirable safeguard, rather than part of the fundamental concept. (We'll say a bit more about this later.)

Condition (1), however, is clearly essential. I can't punish you by giving you that long-desired trip to Hawaii, unless I suppose that it won't turn out to be so nice after all: perhaps you are deathly fearful of flying and it will be a long plane trip, or, more severely, your vacation is scheduled for just the time when a volcano will erupt under your seaside resort while you are there. In short, it is crucial that x be undesirable *from B's point of view*. What if the judge sentences B to be hanged, whereupon B's heart is gladdened? From B's point of view, the state has performed inadvertent euthanasia. We have to admit that something isn't quite right when that happens, even though the hanging would, to be sure, achieve what is almost universally regarded as an important purpose of punishment, that is, to protect people from the criminal from that time forth.

Another large question, especially in practice but also in the theory of punishment, is this: just which, if any, of the innumerable undesirable things we could do to people are appropriate for the legitimate purposes of punishment and which aren't? At one time, beating people and subjecting them to humiliation were typical punishments. We no longer think this right. Criminals in our society may be involuntarily confined behind bars, but while there, they are not to be tortured, beaten, humiliated, starved, or otherwise cruelly used. The American Constitution, for example, prohibits "cruel or unusual" punishments; and all First World countries today have similar views, whether constitutionally enshrined or not.

Condition (2) brings the question of justification to the fore. Condition (1) is enough to assure that the act we perform when we punish someone is of a type that is *normally wrong*: obviously, people may not routinely incarcerate, hang, or steal from each other. Acts of those types are prima facie wrong: they need justifying. Condition (2) locates the general sort of justification involved: B is thought to have done something to merit or *deserve* it.

These observations raise two questions, which together form the core of the philosophical subject of the justification of punishment:

1. *Which* things that B might have done *are* such as to make B eligible for this adverse treatment?
2. Most fundamentally of all, *why* does B's performance of such acts justify our treating him thus?

Once these fundamental matters are under control, we can then turn to the extremely important questions of specifics. Just which sorts of evils may we inflict on people for these purposes, and how do we correlate punishments with the malfeasant acts that earn them? Our answer to question (2), especially, is likely to say something helpful about that as well, but it is unlikely to give precise answers. In a discussion of this kind, we also must stop rather early on in such inquiries. But it is important to appreciate that they need to be made.[2]

Methodological Notes: Criteria for Punishment Theories

How are we to judge our progress in dealing with these difficult questions? Do we have anything to go by? As explained in Chapter One, there are, broadly, two approaches to moral issues: via a careful sifting of our "intuitions," or via a well-grounded theory that gives us strong reasons for supporting certain principles as morally correct. But we don't really need to choose between them; we can and should do both. If we have a general sense that certain things are central, we will not do well simply to ignore them. They may well offer guidance.

In the present case, there are indeed certain general desiderata, so important that we may well regard them as constraints on what could possibly be considered an acceptable theory of the subject. I am sure that every reader will agree with them. Here they are:

(1) The punishment must in some sense "fit" the crime: penalties can be too severe or not severe enough, or in other ways inappropriate.

(2) We may punish *only the guilty*. If we do x to someone in the name of punishing him for doing y, and he didn't in fact do y, then our punishment is prima facie unjust.

(3) The persons punished must have been *responsible* for the acts we are punishing them
for. Inflicting what are claimed to be punishments on those who were not relevantly responsible for their actions is also prima facie unjust.

(4) The procedures by which the persons to be punished are found to be punishable are also subject to certain requirements: they must exemplify "due process." Trials must be fair, the accused must have a chance to defend himself against the charge, and so on. This applies especially in formal institutions such as the criminal law system, but by no means exclusively. It is always a relevant consideration whether the punisher has sufficient reason for administering the punishment—whether he has ignored pertinent evidence, stacked or fabricated the case against the accused, and so on.

Institutional and Non-Institutional Justice

Before proceeding further, let me make two further observations, with associated distinctions. The first relates to our opening definition of punishment, in which I listed a possible third defining feature: that those doing the punishing must be "authorized" to do so. Clearly, there is no such requirement in our general use of the notion: anybody *can* punish anybody, and plenty of the cases in which people are punished without special authority are nevertheless justified. However, when society sets up formal institutions to administer punishment—the Ministry of Justice, the courts, the police—then scrupulous observance of "due process" comes to the fore. It now matters that everything be done in the light of public scrutiny; procedural safeguards become paramount, and claims such as that so-and-so had *no right* to punish someone, or to punish him for that particular action or in that way, become crucial.

We will, by and large, look at punishment in general here, rather than confining our considerations to institutionalized punishment. However, we have to keep an eye out for considerations bearing on punishment systems and will do so as we go along. My objection to capital punishment as an institution, for example, is based on just such considerations.

Anti-Punishment Theories

The second point to note now, just to avoid possible confusion, is that we are not assuming that the right theory will actually justify punishment at all. Some interesting theories in effect deny that punishment is ever, as such, justified. What we call punishment, according to these theories, is a sometimes successful but perhaps often unsuccessful attempt to do something else, and it is this *other* thing that is really the right thing. Those who think that crime is a sort of "disease," for instance, hold that we are never justified in punishing because one of its fundamental requirements, that people be responsible for their crimes, cannot ever be met: crime is really a psychiatric failing and the appropriate remedy is medical, not legal. To reject this theory simply on the ground that it denies what most of us think, namely that punishment is sometimes just, would be irresponsible. We shall look at both types of theories—two that do and one that does not view punishment as fundamentally justifiable—and we will try to cast an impartial eye on each.

With these points in mind, let us turn to the available theories. I will divide the field into three, offering some supportive and some critical comments on each. They have familiar names: *retribution*, *deterrence*, and *compensation*. (I shall modify the second, calling it the *deterrence/protection* theory, explaining why "deterrence" alone is misleading.) The first two propose to justify punishment, while the third is an anti-punishment theory in the sense just described. We'll consider them in order.

Retribution

The basic idea of this ancient view is that the *purpose* of punishment is to inflict evil on those who have done evil to others—no more and no less. It has long had, and continues to have, a certain appeal. It also elicits strong negative reactions from many people nowadays, and I am sure that most of us share both tendencies. There are good reasons for both reactions.

We've all heard the slogan, "An eye for an eye, a tooth for a tooth." The theory it seems to exemplify is called *retributivism*: that retribution is either the proper objective of punishment or, at least, the main objective. I shall first set forth what I take to be the principle of this theory:

The Retributive Principle: This principle holds that it is morally right to inflict evils upon those who cause evil, comparable to the evils they have caused others. Two points are of major importance here. First, the retributive theory holds that the retributive aim is legitimate *as it stands*—no *further* reasons are needed to justify inflicting pain on those who have caused pain.

Second, use of the vague term "comparable" is a deliberate attempt to leave open to consideration just what we are to take as constituting the acceptable sort of "comparability." The obvious dimension is quantitative: we should try to visit about "as much" evil on the evildoer as he has done. But what about the qualitative aspect? In Gilbert and Sullivan's *Mikado*, the Lord High Executioner has a delightful song that opens, "My object, Oh, sublime!/I shall achieve in time/to make the punishment fit the crime." He then proceeds to detail the specific horrors he would visit upon various colourful miscreants if he had his way: people who cheat at pool condemned to play with "elliptical billiard balls," and so on. It's a charming idea, and most people do see a certain ("sublime") justice in it. But, first, it isn't going to be so easy to work out in practice. And second, most of us also think that certain punishments are wrong in any case: torture, for example. Not even torturers, we think, are to be punished by being tortured in turn. Is that because we're just sissies, or is there some underlying reason for this reluctance?

The general idea here might be described as "moral accounting": the evildoer inflict such-and-such an amount of evil on us, and we "balance the books" by visiting a similar amount on him. Looking at it that way requires some sort of metric, some way of comparing one evil with another, enabling us to administer the appropriate punishments in return. But there is surely question whether there is any such metric. Won't we run into a problem with subjectivity? Won't one person's meat be another's poison? In principle the theory assumes that there is a *natural* metric, that in principle, there is such a thing as "*the* amount of evil" that B has done to C, so that we can coherently attempt to inflict a similar amount on B by way of punishing. And thus it would be possible for us to appraise objectively the justice of any particular sentence. This assumption is, to put it mildly, problematic.

Applying the Criteria to Retribution

The retributive theory seems to account nicely for approximately two and a half of our three desiderata. It says that a just punishment consists in the infliction of a *like amount* of evil on evildoers. If someone has inflicted no evil, therefore, the correct amount in return is zero: that person cannot be justly punished. So the theory meets requirement (2). And if we inflict more or less than the "like amount," then we have inflicted too much or too little, and we have a miscarriage along the lines of requirement (1): the punishment does not, in a now supposedly clear sense, "fit" the crime. It fits only if it is about *equal*. Both of these require, of course, that we are able to measure the crime, as discussed earlier, and if, as is all too likely, we cannot, then the theory isn't exactly shown to be false, but that fact would be very damaging to its claims to have satisfied these criteria.

What about the third one? That's where my "one-half" comes in: people can inflict harm unintentionally, accidentally, while insane, while asleep, and so on. The evils they thereby bring about are just as much evils as the ones people bring about intentionally. Why, then, are only the latter properly punishable, as our third criterion specifies? Why should we confine our punishment infliction to the *responsibly* guilty?

To answer this question, we need to look back at the most general conditions of morality. What are moral theories, moral rules, moral principles about? I have suggested answers to these questions: morality imposes (or tries to impose) restrictions on our repertoire of behavioural options. It attempts to get us to decide to act differently from how we might otherwise, by influencing our deliberations about what to do. But insane actions, accidents, and so on lie essentially outside the domain of deliberation. So the retributivist's answer to our challenge is that since he is advancing a moral theory, a theory about what it is right or wrong to do, punishing people who weren't responsible would be wrong because they didn't actually *do* the acts in question. Whatever caused those acts lay beyond the reach of rational deliberation and reflection.

Whether that is a sufficient answer is an important question, but it seems a plausible one, so far. What, then, are we to think of this theory?

The retributive theory apparently holds, explicitly or in effect, that it is *self-evident* that evildoers deserve to have evil done to them, for it says that the visiting of evils upon innocent people is *in itself* enough to justify the punishment response on our part. How would one test this claim? There is a major problem in all such appeals: when they encounter actual people who don't seem to *agree* with the allegedly self-evident principle, then there isn't anything the proponent can do about it except ask people to think again. And as a matter of fact, there are quite a lot of people who do not find it self-evident that we should do evil to evildoers. Some even find it self-evident that we should *not* do that. Socrates held that we should not harm others, whether those people are just or unjust. So, apparently, did Christ (Sermon on the Mount, in a famous passage: "when thine enemy smite thee on the cheek, turn your other cheek to him!"). And while retributivists might be inclined to reply to these people by sneering at them, that doesn't amount to an argument. The question, "*Why* aim at retribution?," awaits a satisfying answer.

Against the retribution theory, on the other hand, are considerations like this. Suppose the admittedly guilty party really does have a big change of heart afterwards and could live a useful life in the community? Why insist on keeping him behind bars (or under several feet of soil, if he's been executed)? Aren't we just losing something and gaining nothing?

The latter way of putting it brings up an idea that has been kicking around in social philosophy since early in this century when it was invented, or at least put in circulation, by the Italian sociologist/economist Vilfredo Pareto. Pareto proposed as a "criterion of efficiency" that we ask whether the new situation we are contemplating would (a) make anyone better off, while (b) leaving no one worse off? If it would meet those two conditions, then the new situation is said to be "Pareto-superior" (or "dominate") to the old. The trouble with retribution, in a nutshell, is that it looks as though it is sometimes Pareto-dominated by alternatives to punishing. Yet the retributionist seems to insist on forgoing this possible good for the sake of—well, what? That's the question.

But the anti-retributionists don't have it all to themselves. There are two things to bring into the picture, without which things would look very adverse indeed for the retributive theory. The first one brings up a fundamental question. In effect, who "makes" the moral rules? That is a question of moral theory, and as I have said in Chapter One, while we aren't supposed to be getting into moral theory in a big way, there is sometimes no alternative. This is one of those occasions.

I am persuaded, and I believe you, too, will be readily persuaded, that the only answer to this last question that makes any sense is that "we" make the moral rules. There isn't anybody else to do so, and if anybody else tried, we'd just have to formulate a new rule concerning whether we should pay any attention to that person's proposals. But now, let us remember that moral rules are rules about what *everybody* is to do, rules that they are to be *held* to and can't just "laugh off." Which rules can't you laugh off, then? One plausible answer is: the ones that *you* make. If you yourself say, "Okay, folks, everybody is to do x in circumstances C!,", then we'll certainly expect you, the author, to do so, and we'll feel authorized, by you, to treat you rather adversely if you don't. "After all," we say, "you didn't have to subscribe to that rule." Moreover, we say, you induced us to go along with it, on the understanding that you would, too. So if now we find you reneging, don't expect any sympathy from us!"[3]

But what rules should we suppose people are supporting when they act? Here we have two very different criteria to invoke. On the one hand, sometimes—not, perhaps, very often — we have verbal evidence of what people say they're for or against. That's very important in the cases where it applies, but it often doesn't. On the other hand, we have behavioural evidence. That is much trickier. But there are some helpful considerations we can invoke here. The most important of them is this: If a person does x in conditions C, then we attribute to that person support for the rule that it is allowable to do x in C — not, of course, just that it's O.K. for *that person* to do so, for after all, we are talking about rules for *everybody* (as I keep saying, with apologies if it seems like nagging!). If his proposed "rule" is that it's only okay, for him to do it, but not for anybody else, then we can respond with two points. First, we can ask, on what sort of general principle he will defend the exception? Sometimes we can, after all (well, he is the Prime Minister and we have to admit that he's got important things to do, so ...); but what won't do is the answer, "Why, just because I'm me, get it?" Well, we do get it, indeed, and have a very good response in turn: if that's what he's going to say, then we too will all feel free to make exceptions of ourselves—and there goes the rule! For the essence of these rules is that they are supposed to be authoritative over everyone's behaviour. But a rule to which everyone is an exception governs nobody. Worse yet, it leaves us in a situation in which all may do whatever they please.

Or, second, we can say this: "Uh, huh. But we see no reason to *accept* this stupid rule, and until you can come up with one that we do have reason to accept, the situation is that between the two of us, there *is* no rule on this matter." And that's important because it will have the same effect as the universal-exception option just noted: it leaves us free to do as we please.

That's all we need to make the point I now want to make on behalf of the retributivist. For the point is simply this: if we, for example, claim a right to deal with murderers by killing them, then *they*, at any rate, are in a poor position to object. After all, look how they treated their victims! Where, we may ask, were the rights to respect of one's person, and to a fair trial, and so forth, when they murdered poor so-and-so? If such rights mean nothing to the killer, then we shall feel free to treat him along the same lines as he treated his victim. We'll see how he likes *that*; and in any case, it'll rid us of him as a problem for the future.

I confess that I find this argument very persuasive. Many writers have from time to time talked about the duty not to kill people as though it just obviously applied in the case where the proposed victims are murderers. But why should it? If the point of the rule against murder is, roughly speaking, to protect us all from being killed, then that point is lost if it lets people get away with murder. Surely the point of distinguishing between those whose actions are acceptable and those whose actions are not is to single out the latter for different—and surely worse—treatment as compared with the former. The "everybody" whom the rules are to protect are all those who do not themselves break the very rules in question—the innocent, as we may reasonably call them. But as for the guilty, the point about considering them "guilty" is precisely that they are in some way and to some degree eligible for less protection, less good treatment, than the rest. And that's the retributivist's view.

This argument isn't intended to leave the retributive principle as self-evident. Rather, it provides an extremely compelling reason why we are at least morally permitted, on the face of it, to inflict evils on those who have felt free to inflict evils on us. The reason is understandable in terms of the moral relations in which we can most reasonably be thought to stand with our fellows.

On "Two Wrongs Don't Make a Right"

The foregoing reflections show that a familiar old saw about capital punishment, that "two wrongs don't make a right," involves a mistake, for what we do to murderers when we punish them is *not*, under the circumstances, another "wrong" at all. What *the murderers* did in the first place was wrong, of course, but what we are doing to them in response is not wrong but right. It is so because the criminal himself is evidently in favour of allowing this kind of treatment. We aren't doing something to him about which he has a reasonable complaint. And if not, then why can't we do it? And if we may do it, then of course it's not wrong, but instead right.

Punishment: A Right or a Duty?

Now we may restate the issue. Which of these two is the retributivist claiming: that it's *permissible* to punish (the guilty, in the appropriate degree)? Or—a much stronger claim—that we have a positive *duty* to punish them?

We can put this in terms of "weak" or "strong" versions of retribution. The weak version is that we have a *right* to punish, but that we aren't necessarily morally required to do it; the strong claim is that if someone has done an evil to someone, then we positively ought to punish the miscreant—we have a *duty* to punish.

Those who proclaim the strong principle should be asked, *To whom* do we owe this duty? They might think that we just simply do have it—it's not a duty "to" anyone. But we have rejected all such ideas where morality is in question: if it concerns no person, then it's none of our concern. On the other hand, one might argue that we owe this duty to the public, whom, after all, we are trying to protect. That's a fair argument, but it seems to move us away from retribution into the deterrence/protection view, which we'll discuss next. Another plausible idea is that we owe it to all those people who cared about the victim, or to the victim herself if she is still alive. Here again, however, we move towards another theory, the *compensation* theory; we will discuss that below, too.

Feelings

Meanwhile, there's another rather important factor to bring into this discussion—the way people, especially victims, *feel* about these matters. It is often argued against the retribution theory that retribution is merely a "primitive instinct," a "thirst for revenge", the implication being that such a thirst does not deserve to be slaked. Is this right?

Arguments about instincts do have the troubling feature that it is very difficult to know what to say about them. How are we supposed to establish that x is "instinctive" or not? And even if it is, what would that prove? What if it's an instinct that it would be possible, with a bit of work, to get rid of? Why worry about satisfying it in that case? The point is that we can hardly think that something is right just because it's instinctive.

On the other hand, we should admit that if there is a (virtually) universal behavioural tendency of a certain kind in people, then that creates a presumption that we should not ignore or suppress it without good reason. Eating, for example, is in some sense instinctive, and probably a good thing, too. Here arguments from sociobiology might be brought in. Perhaps the tendency to strike back at sources of hurt, out of a sense of danger or fear, has a high survival value. Imagine the cave man with a psychology like that of, say, a philosophy professor: "Hey, there's a sabre-toothed tiger over there, about to leap!" "Oh, yes? Sabre-toothed tiger, you say—how interesting! What variety? How long are his teeth? Yak, yak, yak ... "! Not surprisingly, professors are a fairly late development on the human scene....

It is not at all clear where an appeal to sociobiology will get us, to be sure. But perhaps we don't need to worry much about that, for we could just point out that people sometimes do get very great satisfaction out of revenge, and when you look at the unsavoury actions of those who inspired them with this desire, what's so bad about that? Why shouldn't they get such satisfaction, considering what has been done to them? Take, for example, the parents of little girls who have been raped and murdered, or of children snatched away from them in the middle of the night, dismembered and thrown into a dust bin—are we surprised that these people feel angry and vindictive? Why should we think we are superior to them if we don't?

Summary on Retribution Theory

My provisional conclusion on retribution is that, on the one hand, there is a pretty strong case for its being something we in principle have a right to, and the guilty are surely in no position to complain if we do seek retribution. On the other hand, retribution seems in many cases useless: there seems no longer any point in inflicting the penalty, which can also be costly and risky. But when there is point in it, retribution might well be compatible with protection/deterrence theory, though it is ordinarily thought to be its arch-rival. We turn to it next.

The Protection/Deterrence Theory

According to our next theory, which I call the "protection/deterrence" theory, punishment has a practical purpose: to prevent or at least minimize a certain kind of harm in the community, i.e., the kind intentionally inflicted on people by their fellows (as opposed to accidents, disease, floods, and other unintentionally imposed evils). Punishment is seen by the proponents of this theory as one device among many for making our lives better by reducing this major source of concern, the concern that other people—fellow rational beings—will bash us over the head, steal our goods, harm our children, hinder our pursuit of our daily bread, and so on. The aim is always the same, and we could simply call it the "protection" theory, since fundamentally the purpose of deterrence is also to protect; however, deterrence is a distinctive kind of protection. We will address the differences shortly. Meanwhile, we'll refer to it as 'PD theory.'

The PD theorist agrees with the retributionist that what we are basically concerned with is "crime," that is, harm-inflicting behavioural propensities. What *counts* as crime is the same on both theories. But PD at least appears to disagree with retribution as to *why* we should punish. As the seventeenth-century philosopher Thomas Hobbes put it in his classic statement of this point of view, the PD theorist bids us look "not at the evil that is past, but at the good that is to come." Hobbes would be impressed at the Paretian argument we broached above. If we would do better on the whole by not punishing B than by punishing him, then why punish? What's the point?

This fundamental feature of PD theory seems to raise a major problem. If we say that whether or not we should punish someone depends on what would happen *in the future* if we do, we seem to cut an essential link with the past, captured in our second criterion of punishment theories: that *only the guilty* may be punished. But mightn't we sometimes do more good by punishing the admittedly innocent? That is one of the classic challenges to this kind of theory. Closely related to it is that PD seems to collide with the first criterion, that punishments are to "fit" the crime: for if the degree of punishment is determined by how much good it would do to punish that much, rather than more or less, then why couldn't it be desirable to impose severe penalties for trivial crimes? Wouldn't that give us more deterrence?

There are, then, major problems to be solved for this theory. To deal with them, we shall have to begin by making some rather important distinctions. Especially, we must distinguish between the two aspects of protection: *prevention* and *deterrence*.

We *prevent* a certain harm when we bring it about that the harm doesn't occur, by making it impossible for the agent to commit the crime, no matter what he wants. We jam his gun, say, or kill him before he kills us. Slamming and locking a sturdy door may prevent the murder. Punishment, however, happens only *after* the fact. Necessarily, at the time of the punishment, we can no longer prevent the crime, for it has occurred in the past. Given a strong prison, incarceration will indeed prevent potential *future* crimes by that criminal. It might also reduce the incidence of crimes by others. That is where deterrence comes in.

We *deter* B from doing x when we provide him with effective inducement to *refrain* from doing x. Punishment cannot prevent the very crimes it punishes, but perhaps it can serve to prevent other crimes. The only significant way it could do this, however, would be by providing potential criminals with adequate motivation not to do the crime in question. Deterrence requires us to bring some further baggage along on our conceptual journey. Clearly potential criminal A cannot be deterred by our punishment of a different criminal, B, unless, at a minimum, A *believes* that B has been punished. Moreover, he has to believe that he was punished for doing the very thing that A is thinking of doing. The standard way of accomplishing this is to have a set of public rules, i.e., laws, saying what will and, by implication, what will not be punished. These rules must be public, for otherwise we must fail of our purpose: you can't deter people who don't know what they're supposed to avoid.

But mere publication of a rule isn't enough, for what deters isn't what's on a piece of paper somewhere but rather what happens when it is read, or heard about, by people who are considering whether to do what that piece of paper tells people not to do. And that, in turn, may depend on the efficiency of one's reinforcement procedures, such as the threat of police action. The plot, then, is thickening. We are into the rule of law and procedures for carrying out that rule. If deterrence is to be provided, that's how it will be provided.

We should pause here to point out that when we talk of deterrence, we don't have in mind cases where someone conscientiously concludes that he ought not to perform the harmful acts that our laws forbid. One can, certainly, be "deterred" by the thought that one will have done something wrong; and if we were all effectively subject to that kind of control, we would not need punishments at all. But we are interested here in what to do about those who have so little conscience that they are willing to commit crimes when it serves their purposes.

Deterrence and Punishing the Innocent

We can now attack the problems posed by our two criteria of punishment. First, what about punishing the innocent? The PD theorist can point to serious shortcomings with it. The point of punishment, according to this theory, is to protect innocent people. If the law goes around punishing them instead, then that's doubly bad: not only are we being harmed by others, contrary to what the system is all about, but we are further harmed by being forced, as taxpayers, to foot the bill for it. This is surely no way to "protect" people. Moreover, if we do punish the wrong man, then it means that the right man is still on the loose and likely still inflicting harms on people. Indeed, he's probably encouraged by the fact that the police seem to be perfectly happy to catch the wrong person, as long as they get *somebody*—so why should he worry? Punishing the innocent, then, ensures some basic failures of deterrence. And if it achieves any actual deterrence, it can only do so because of the *ignorance* of the public, who must be kept in the dark about what's really going on. This is not a safe way to run a public: hoodwinkery and deception, especially about such important matters, are among the very things governments are supposed to protect us from.

Our net result is that from the deterrence point of view, we must insist, as our ideal, that *all and only* the "bad guys" get punished (or if not punished, at least arraigned, recognized, detected—

which in some cases may be enough). For we want the potential criminal to suppose that the probability of his getting the punishment if he commits the crime is 100 per cent, and 0 per cent if he does not. That will provide the ideal inducement, if our penalties are rigged right and if they are effectively administered—large "ifs," unfortunately.

What about the next criterion—that a given punishment should "fit" the crime for which it is imposed? Here we need to emphasize that deterrence isn't a matter of "causation," as though punishment were a sort of neurological implant leading to reduced criminal activity. Rather than rewiring criminal brains, punishment deters because of its relation to the *reasoning* of potential criminals.

So what is the character of this reasoning? Roughly this: the criminal is out to gain by his crime, and we are out to try to persuade him not to commit it by showing him that he won't gain by it. Something or other must measure the "size" of the interest we are protecting, so that we can identify some crimes as more important than others. The PD theorist then suggests that by having a punishment "fit" a crime, what we should mean is that *worse crimes get more severe penalties*. Other things being equal, the crime with the greater penalty should be the one the criminal is more likely to avoid. If he's going to commit crime, we want to induce him to prefer lesser crimes to greater ones, just as what we really want is for him not to commit any crimes at all. So we attach more severe penalties to those crimes we consider more serious. That sends the right set of signals to the would-be criminal.

A third consideration, but one of immense importance, is this: since we are out to protect people, we should not myopically concentrate on protection from criminals only, for there is also a reasonable concern about protection from the criminal justice system itself. If we don't want to get killed by criminals, we don't want to get killed by trigger-happy policemen or "hanging judges" either. At some point the penalty for overtime parking becomes manifestly too high; any gain to the public from insufficiently regulated parking is outweighed by the enormous risks of that regulation. Thus we also have an interest in the procedural safeguards that are the concern of our fourth criterion, which applies to institutionalized punishment. Indeed, that institutions can provide these safeguards is one of the very reasons for creating them.

Now consider the justification of *actually imposing* a particular punishment, as opposed to the justification for having a system that merely threatens it. What does punishing accomplish, from this point of view? There are several good answers.

First, and most fundamentally, each fulfilled punishment serves the aim of deterrence by providing potential criminals with hard *evidence* that the public will in fact make good on its threats to visit these consequences upon miscreants. Conversely, each one who "gets away" adds evidence to the hypothesis that the law can be ignored. That is why we must make a determined effort to arrest every single guilty party.

Second, of course, if we punish by incarceration, then that will protect the public from repetition by that same miscreant while he's in jail.

Third, if our punishment is administered in the right way and is of the right kind, it might promote *reform*, inducing the miscreant to cease doing those things.

What if our criminal has already reformed? The PD theorist can cheerfully countenance forgiving and forgetting, where it is called for. He will, of course, have to make sure that the public is not misled, which is one reason why we should not easily be led to believe that real change of heart has occurred. But clearly it is in our interests to encourage such changes. So we must keep careful tabs on the allegedly reformed, publicize successes, and act swiftly to reincarcerate those whose change of heart turned out not to be genuine.

Moving to the responsibility criterion, it might at first sight seem, again, as though the PD theorist has no effective way to distinguish between the non-responsible and the responsible doer of harm. But it isn't so. We can distinguish between those whose behaviour is a function of their perception of costs and benefits, that is, of goods and evils as reckoned by them, and those whose behaviour is not. A system of penalties can *only* apply to the former, for that is the essence of the matter: morality is a certain kind of system of behaviour control, proceeding by verbal and non-verbal reinforcement to instil in each of us an internalized disposition to refrain from what is wrong and to do what is right. The punishment system, as a supplementary system for reinforcing the rules in the case of those who have insufficient understanding or mettle to achieve such internal self-control, turns to proffered penalties for those who can at least reason about the future well enough to appreciate the costs of crime. Those who are unable to respond even to that kind of behavioural influence are beyond the reach of the punishment system. We will have to deal with them in other ways. If they are a danger to us, for instance, then they may have to be contained, perhaps by detention in a psychiatric centre, but not by being *punished*. Rather, that is a type of "treatment."

The difference in practice can, of course, be unnoticeable. The psychiatric hospital may be every bit as loathsome as the prison. Moreover, there is a special danger in resorting to psychiatric incarceration, for it seems to offer a reason (or an excuse?) for simply setting aside any rights of the individual. The terms of "psychiatric imprisonment" have often been open-ended, and many people have lived out their lives in psychiatric institutions.[4] This looks, and often is, unfair—as wrong as unjust imprisonment. That this is a great danger is a reason why we have to think very deeply about how to balance our general interest in liberty against our specific interest in protection. How much increased risk of others' depredations are we willing to take in order to reduce our own risk of being ground under the wheels of The Justice Machine?

The Right to Defend Ourselves: The Least-Force Principle

Obviously, the acceptability of punishment as deterrence and therefore as a kind of protection is contingent on our having the moral right to defend ourselves. I imagine few will dissent from this, and in any case we will explore the issue more deeply in our next chapter, on war. Meanwhile, the point is that punishment becomes a kind of "defence" only when it is incorporated into a practice or system so that others may get the "message" that punishment is designed to transmit.

But how much may we do to defend ourselves? This is an important and interesting question, but without trying to get to the bottom of it, we may lay down one useful principle: that we should not use an "excessive" amount of force, that is, more than is needed for defence. It is an important safeguard to the citizen to know that if law enforcement officers are after him, they will expend as little force as necessary to get him. That's why the PD theorist is willing to let undoubtedly guilty persons go scot free so long as he is sure that no future harm will come from doing so—as it often does, no doubt; if we shouldn't be rigid about this, we must not be cavalier about it either.

We should use no more force than we need. But should we use less? Is there some upper limit on force, regardless of need? Is there, for instance, a principle that our preventive measures should impose no more damage than what is threatened by our potential criminal? That is a rather deep issue, but I shall suggest a correlative principle to the least-force principle. This might be called the "sufficient-force" principle. It says that we may use *as much* force as it takes to prevent an infliction of harm on the innocent.

Here's a test case. What if an aggressor is bent on only a medium-sized harm instead of murder, but he is so determined to inflict it that it would take severe violence, such as killing him, to prevent it? Consider the "stalker"—the man who becomes insanely attached to a woman so that he constantly imposes himself on her, despite persistent entreaties to stay away. This can impose serious psychological harm, even if a threat of physical harm doesn't accompany his behaviour (though it usually does). How much physical force may be used to keep him away? I think the answer is: whatever it takes, up to and including lethal force, though the latter would only be necessary if he resisted non-lethal force so strenuously as to impose a near-lethal risk on those trying to enforce the victim's right. My answer is viewed by some as too harsh. I leave the reader to think about that.

Capital Punishment and Deterrence

Now let's turn to the "supreme" punishment—capital punishment (CP). In the background lies whatever we decide about our right to defend ourselves; this must feed into the punishment system. Those considerations support the conclusion that we have the right even to kill if that is necessary to prevent ourselves being killed by an aggressor. What does this imply about capital punishment? The brief answer is that it would clearly justify it, *if* capital punishment could serve to protect us in the same way that shooting an aggressor might do, that is, by actually preventing him from killing or severely harming someone.

But is it ever "necessary"? Here we have again the problem that punishment looks "backward," and what we see is that the crime has already taken place. So we can no longer do anything about it. Clearly, capital punishment cannot be claimed to be necessary on that score. Any necessity here would have to stem from some other consideration. One such is that killing the murderer would prevent that particular person from repetition—ever. There is no doubt of its effectiveness for that limited purpose. But putting him behind bars for the rest of his life would also do that, so long as the criminal actually stays there.

For that matter, so would putting him there until such time as he ceased having his murderous tendencies. The snag there, of course, is *knowing* that he has ceased to have them. But while that is difficult, it is not always clearly impossible. And remember, we are not doing psychiatry here—just philosophy. We want to know what we should do *if* various things happened, such as the criminal's having a complete change of heart. Finding out whether this has actually happened is another problem.

For prevention purposes, as distinct from deterrence purposes, then, the argument is rather thin. Only if the cost of imprisonment were very great could a society justify execution in preference to imprisonment, so far as sheer protection is concerned. But what about deterrence? Can we argue that we "need" CP to provide sufficient deterrence for potential murderers? Clearly it would be absurd to maintain that the prospect of a lengthy or lifelong prison term has no deterrence value. It would have to be argued, not that deterrence can *only* be achieved by CP, but rather than it is *better* achieved.

To do that requires showing that CP reduces the murder rate more than imprisonment. That seems to be a question of fact rather than abstract argument. How, then, do we calculate the deterrent potential of a given type of penalty? There is a clear answer, in principle. We must first ascertain the following two magnitudes: (1) the gain to the criminal if he succeeds, times the probability that he will succeed; (2) the weight of the penalty in question from the point of view of the potential murderer we hope to deter, if he is apprehended and punished, times the probability that he will fail.

He then subtracts the second from the first (or, if we think of the second as a negative magnitude, then we add the two together). This gives us the *expected utility*, or *net* gain (or loss) of committing that crime. The "rational" criminal then compares the utility of committing his crime with the utility of doing anything else he can do instead. (What sort of benefit might this be in the case of murder? As we shall shortly see, this will turn out to be a crucial consideration.) If the comparison is between two different kinds of punishment, then our would-be criminal simply plugs in the weight he attaches to each and compares the overall result.

Suppose, then, that he gives greater weight to being executed than to being imprisoned for life (or some suitably long period)? Does it follow that CP will have significantly greater deterrence effect than long-term imprisonment? Not yet. For now everything depends on the other figure, the probability of apprehension. If our criminal knows that the chance of his getting caught is virtually zero, then it won't matter how much more weight he attaches to CP, for he can expect never to get that penalty.

Everyone has read murder mysteries in which fairly ingenious criminals out to speed their inheritances from rich uncles weave tangled webs, only to be defeated by an even more ingenious sleuth who managed to unravel the plot and bring him to justice. You might well have formed the impression that these are typical of murders. Alas, they are not, for it seems that very few murders are like that. Overwhelmingly, it seems, there are two sorts of murders: (1) crimes of passion: B gets extremely upset with C and becomes bent on doing him in; and (2) professional jobs in which B is completely cool. His victim is simply his target. No hard feelings, nothing personal: let's just do it, quick and clean, and collect our fee!

Now, as it happens, the type (1) murderer is, unfortunately, not particularly "rational." Not only does he characteristically leave clues all over the place, bungling the job, but in fact he very often confesses afterwards. And, most important for our present purposes, he doesn't *think* about the penalty. The prospect of either imprisonment or CP doesn't deter him, because he never even thinks about that. (In a set of interviews with Canadians convicted of murder before the death penalty was eliminated, who had since been pardoned or had their sentences commuted, not a single one said that he or she had thought at all about penalties. They just wanted to "get" the so-and-so who was, they supposed, causing their problem.) Type (1) murderers virtually always get caught. The probability of apprehension, in their case, is almost 100 per cent. But unfortunately, the severity of the penalty doesn't deter them because they aren't into thinking about penalties. They just let fly and face consequences later—when it's too late.

Type (2) murderers, on the other hand, are quite "rational"— terrifyingly so. They know how to do the job, they do it, and they walk calmly off without leaving a hint as to who did it or even why. So efficiently do these men pursue their trade that they virtually never get caught. (In the studies I have read about, it was noted that up to that time, still not long ago, *no* "professional" type killer had ever been convicted *of murder* in the United States.) This type of murderer's probability of apprehension, in other words, is effectively zero. So, no matter how much they dislike the thought of being hanged, the fact that they won't *be* hanged if they kill yields the result that there is no deterrence to be had from CP or from anything else.

That leaves scarcely anyone left to be the type of "medium-rational" murderer who might be deterred by the thought of CP but not by imprisonment. And this is borne out by such statistical studies as have been done. To my knowledge, not a single one of the many studies that have been done on this matter confirms a definite superior deterrence value for CP. (It's a very, very tricky project, to be sure. People have compared states or provinces before and after the time at which the laws changed, either from or to use of CP; they have compared places with similar ethnic, economic, and other sociologically significant compositions but different penalties for murder. All to no avail. The situation is that essentially nobody in the field thinks the evidence shows that CP shows a clear superiority in this regard.)[5]

Clearly, what you and I had better believe on this matter is that if we are going to favour CP, it should not be on grounds of superior deterrence value. In deciding whether to be in favour of CP, then, we must look elsewhere, at least in the present state of things and in our part of the world. Which is not to deny that in some special situations the death penalty could be effective: in Nigeria many years ago, a situation of near civil breakdown, with numerous murders and armed robberies, was brought rather quickly under control by instituting summary executions via firing-squad, plain for all to see. But that kind of situation is *very* different from the normal ones that an on going institution of CP is framed against. On that matter, we do well to recall that in early nineteenth-century England one could be hanged for all sorts of crimes, including pickpocketing, yet pickpockets were known to operate in the crowds watching the hangings!

So where else do we look? In two directions, I suggest. First, of course, one may feel that retribution is a sufficiently weighty aim of the law to justify CP even when it is not justified on deterrence grounds. Coupled with this, and often, I think, actually identified with it, is the sense that we owe the relatives of victims of murderers a certain satisfaction. That's an important consideration, actually; but it is not clear that it is part of retribution, properly speaking.

We will say more about it below when we discuss compensation. In any case, for every person ready to support the right of victims to satisfaction or to promote retribution as an abstract moral ideal, there are a dozen who are appalled at the whole idea and consider capital punishment uncivilized, unworthy of decent people in these enlightened times. Any policy is going to prove politically difficult.

The Problem of Executing the Innocent

However, there is another factor to consider, one so important that it can hardly be overlooked. Indeed, as I will now argue, it can hardly be thought not to be decisive in current circumstances. This is that, life being the sort of thing it is, you can only execute someone once. If you make a mistake, it's game over: there is no way you can undo the deed or make any sort of compensation to the unfortunate victim of the justice system. Execution of the innocent is an irremediable injustice.

Now, one might respond to this by suggesting that if we put in place sufficiently extensive safeguards, then, hopefully, no innocent persons will ever be executed. But this idea, so plausible at first sight, runs quickly into problems that lead to a dilemma. Legal safeguards are administered by people—by our fellow, fallible human beings. Our legal system places very great weight on jury trials, for instance, and juries of necessity consist of ordinary folk like us, not gods or supermen. The fact must be faced: it is humanly *impossible* to achieve that ideal situation in which all and only all those murderers who *deserve* to be executed *are* executed by the familiar workings of the criminal justice system.

Thinking about this some more, the dilemma begins to loom. Juries must work to a certain standard of evidence. In the U.S., it's "beyond a reasonable doubt." All right: how much doubt is that? When does reasonable doubt cease and neurotic doubt begin? Suppose we set our standards *very* high, verging on the neurotic. This will make it more likely that the people who do get executed, if any, are actually guilty. But by that very same token, it assures that a good many cases where the accused is actually guilty will not yield convictions.

If, on the other hand, you relax the standards materially, then you will indeed convict more. But as a result, it is virtually certain that some among those convicted are actually innocent. A modest perusal of the sort of convictions we've had in Canada over the years surely is enough to satisfy any reasonable person of what I have just said: there is *no* realistic option of getting the standards *just right*, so that nobody gets innocently executed and yet all the really evil people do get executed.[6]

Now think back to what we have noted about deterrence. The criminal forms his estimate of the probability that he will get convicted and executed by seeing *what happens to the others*. If he notes that very few people get hanged, then he himself will reasonably conclude that his chances of hanging, even if apprehended, are pretty small. This moves the likelihood of deterrence towards the value of a lesser penalty, such as long-term imprisonment.

If the evidence just doesn't support capital punishment as having serious differential deterrent force, as seems to be the case, then where does this leave us? I suggest it leaves us with the conclusion that imprisonment is the preferable option. On any view, after all, the prospect of being executed by the very people who are supposed to be protecting us is an evil we ought to avoid unless there is a truly enormous advantage in the system that entails a significant risk of it. And given the evident weakness of the appeal to retribution, what is there to say? A system in which a very few get executed, so that it is very likely (though not certain, remember) that those few really do deserve it, while the great majority of murderers perforce end up with incarceration as their only type of penalty, is not obviously superior in any interesting way to one in which none get executed. But if anyone continues to think it is, then let's at least appreciate that the reason is not that we, the public, are thus made "safer." The evidence points to the conclusion that CP accomplishes literally nothing in that respect.

Might CP at least be preferable on grounds of economy? Some would no doubt reject any such considerations as too crass even to be considered here, but I do not agree with them. Again, however, there is some relevant evidence available. Hauling a man out and shooting him is cheap, indeed. But that cannot be the way a modern state takes care of such matters. The costly process of elaborate court procedures and appeals, plus the expensive equipment needed for a modern, public execution that is not also offensive and distasteful, make CP anything but cheap. Back when resources were limited, jails weak and expensive, and justice rough, capital punishment was no doubt very much cheaper than incarceration. But here and now, both methods are simply inordinately expensive. We are told that it costs the equivalent of a full professor's salary to keep a prisoner in a modern penitentiary; but capital punishment is now so expensive that the interest on the money you spend on it will pay the lion's share of the bill for the incarceration. So there doesn't seem to be much in it, one way or the other.

Restitution (Compensation)

This brings us to our third view about punishment: that in fact the proper response to intentional damage and harm inflicted by one person on another is neither to get back at him by visiting him with like evils nor to use him as a cog in the deterrence-machine, but instead to require the aggressor to *make up for* the damage inflicted. This view, then, rejects punishment, strictly speaking, for what matters, says the restitutionist, is victims, and what matters about them is their rights. To set things right again is surely the thing to do, if it can be done.

It is a fascinating idea, but fraught with extreme difficulties. First, of course, we must have a clear idea of just who is due the compensation in question. And second, we must arrive at some tolerably clear idea how to assess the appropriate levels of compensation. A few observations are in order on both points.

It may seem obvious who matters: the victim. That, in fact, is the point of this theory. But if a thief prowls a neighbourhood, it is not only the particular house he eventually burgles that sustains a harm. What about the others, who only *might have* been robbed? Does the robber owe them something for frightening them?

Regarding the second, we do, fortunately have an abstract idea about how to proceed. In principle, it's all up to the victim. Only she knows how valuable the things that have been taken from her are to her. So it seems we should let her decide.

But how is this to work? Well, the criminal takes something away from her—in the easier cases, a material thing, such as her car. But what if it's the full use of her left arm for the rest of her life? Indeed, what if it is her life itself? In the last case, of course, we have the problem that there is nothing we can do any more for the victim, since she is now dead. But tabling this last case for the moment, the indicated procedure would be that the victim has to find a level of compensation, C, such that she is as happy with C, given that the crime took place, as she would have been if the crime had not taken place at all. That's a tall order in many cases, though in others it's not. We can imagine having our ancient VW stolen and replaced by a spanking new Toyota that we think more than makes up for all the nuisance occasioned by the theft. But that is less likely in the case where what was taken was the use of both of one's legs.

Clearly, the levels will often be very high. What if they are higher than our criminal could possibly pay? Do we then resort to imprisonment or even execution as punishment for non-payment? If so, punishment has returned to the theory after all. But if not, then it is not clear where we go next. A criminal's knowledge that he will be required to pay, literally, for his crime could serve as a deterrent, just as the prospect of jail is likely to. But if there is simply no possibility that he could pay up, the prospect of deterrence from this source diminishes.

What are we to do about these people who commit crimes they can't possibly make restitution for—kill them? Many would think that is going too far. But on the restitution view, it's not a matter of going either too far or not far enough, but of going in the wrong *direction*. For it may do nothing at all for the victim, one way or the other. Killing the miscreants doesn't promise much in the way of compensation! If A stole a million from B, then executing A isn't going to get B that million back.

Execution might satisfy some. In Muslim law, a murderer's life is turned over to the nearest relative of his victim. That relative can choose among execution, outright forgiveness, or something in between, as desired. One has to be rather bloodthirsty, one would think, to prefer another man's death to, say, a substantial payment of money or something of the sort. But it does happen. In fact, we are told, the relatives characteristically opt for capital punishment. Interesting. But one doubts that they really regard it as adequate compensation. More likely they are just catering to their own retributive instincts.

This leaves us with the thought that while compensation may with some plausibility be regarded as the ideally right way to respond to depredations, it is a way that leaves us with a lot of work to do to translate the theory into practice. We can imagine taking out crime insurance, for instance. The insurance company would do its best to apprehend the criminal and make him pay. How far this will get us is not entirely clear at present writing. Meanwhile, though, the difficult demands of this theory make it very doubtful that we can solve the problems of criminality by turning crime over to the *civil* courts—any time soon, anyway.[7]

A Sober Afterthought on Punishment

Before concluding this discussion of punishment, one thing needs to be emphasized much more strongly than I have yet done: the distinctly second-best nature of punishment as society's response to the problem of criminality. People who commit crimes try to make themselves better off at other people's expense. This requires the potential victims—all of us, including criminals themselves - to take measures to protect themselves, including the punishment system. All of this makes life worse for everyone. The basic problem lies in the fact that potential criminals do see crime as "paying." Yet if they are brought up with a strong aversion to getting their way by making life worse for others, they would not think that way. Most of us refrain from crime not because we might get caught and punished, but because we have an attitude of abhorrence for such activities: we think them wrong. That is surely the best reason. Punishment has to be a stopgap, a second-best—perhaps a necessary evil, but certainly an evil. To reduce that evil, we must do two things. In the first place, we must confine the scope of what is punishable to a narrow range of interpersonally inflicted harms. (Much of this book is devoted to arguments for that conclusion.) And second, we must use such moral influence as we have in our power on whomever we can to adopt the moral outlook in the first place. At the top of this list will be our own children. Bringing them up with the right attitudes is far more effective in reducing these evils than any punishment system for adults that anyone can devise.

Summing Up

Punishment involves treating people in ways we normally have no right to treat them. What justifies it, if anything? We considered three main theories: retribution, protection/deterrence, and restitution. Each has something to be said for it: that those who do evil simply *deserve* it, that we must punish in order to protect ourselves, and that what is really just is the exacting of suitable compensation rather than punishment. This last, I believe, is the best, in principle, but it seems so difficult as to be scarcely possible to substitute it for punishment, which is best viewed as a complex system of social protection. So in practice, the protection/deterrence view is what we must settle for. It gives a reasonable account of the main requirements of justice, calling only for useful punish-ments (in contrast to retribution) that are proportionate to the crime, for punishing only the guilty, and for punishing only the responsible. And in light of familiar and well-established facts, that theory gives very little support to capital punishment, at least in our time and circumstances.

Chapter Five

War

Individuals may not pursue their ends by violence. But what about states? Are they any different in this respect? It is widely thought so. In any case, are there reasonable moral restrictions on how war may be pursued when (and if) it is justified? Those are our questions in this chapter.

War may seem to be a strictly political issue rather than a moral one. But there is no such thing as a "strictly political issue that is not a moral one," if by this is meant that morality just isn't even relevant to the matter. There are, to be sure, questions about political tactics and strategy that are not moral issues: whether to run this candidate in that district, and so on. But political *issues*, as we have seen, are certainly moral issues. Political questions are about what to do, and things that are of moral concern are at stake.

So how is war a moral issue? If you are in a position of command and must decide whether to commit money and troops to a war, then you must satisfy yourself that you would be doing the right thing. If, like most of us, you are not in such a position, there are other decisions for us to make concerning the war: whether to resist a military draft, whether and how to voice opposition or support for a given war, whether to vote for candidates who oppose it, and so on. To discuss these issues efficiently, we will proceed rather as though one could decide the whole of same major issue concerning war by oneself, and of course this is almost never true. But our view on the lesser matters that we do have influence on must depend on our view about the larger one: if the war is immoral, then our business is to oppose it to whatever extent is possible and at least not to support it in ways that we can avoid. So we shall simply go ahead and discuss war as such: first, whether and how it can be morally justified; and second, whether there are right and wrong ways of fighting a war, right and wrong weapons one can choose to employ, and so on.

Three Options: Militarism, Pacifism, and Defence

I suppose the most widely held view about war, nowadays, is that it can be justified, when clearly necessary, for defence against aggression, but that aggression itself—the making of war for purposes of national gain rather than defence—is wrong. This fairly standard view is subject to attack (so to speak) on two fronts: from the pacifist, who insists that war isn't justified even for defence; and from the militarist, who holds that war is simply an instrument of state policy, to be used whenever it would promote the ends of the state.

Militarism has become something of a whipping-boy for moralists in our time. But it shouldn't be. We must try to consider the view rationally and not settle for what may be a merely emotional aversion to it. Then we will take up pacifism, in a similar vein, where the danger is a merely emotional adherence. We conclude with a longer discussion of defence, the view that most of us, very likely, consider to be the right one. The analysis in this chapter will, I hope, clarify and solidify this conviction.

Militarism

Should we make war whenever it suits national purposes? For that matter, should we do so whenever it looks as though we would win? One can imagine individuals with that kind of temperament. They exult in their physical strength and skill, and they simply enjoy beating up on people. Someone who does that would quickly get a reputation as a bully, and in a community such as you and I live in, he would soon find himself in prison. Our preceding discussion of punishment applies to his behaviour. But if the "bully" is the government itself, then nobody is in a position to "punish" it in our usual sense. Still, we may think that's what the bully deserves, whether or not anybody can actually do anything about it. But other states might threaten wars with punitive intent, and that possibility poses a further interesting case for discussion: is it all right to do *that*?

However, the more interesting question is not whether states may make wars just because they "like to fight," but for such familiar purposes as enslaving the conquered people, taking their natural resources, expanding their own empires, and the like. In all these cases, actually, the state in question is attempting to expand its domain of political and economic control. Thus, one might broadly refer to militarists as "imperialists" without serious distortion, even though on most of these occasions they are not after empire in the narrow sense. Continuing our analogy with individual cases, their behaviour is more like that of the professional thief than the bully.

Well, what's wrong with imperialism if we can get away with it? An important question, to be sure. Individuals who engage in violence for such reasons are denounced as thieves, assassins, mobsters, and ruffians. Is there any reason why we shouldn't think the same thing of states that behave analogously? Hitler claimed that Germany needed *lebensraum* ("living space"); so when his neighbours refused to surrender their countries without a fight (though many did just that), he sent his armies in to invade them. But we think you can't just steal somebody else's land or house because you claim to need it, and people who do that are behaving wrongly. Why not think the same of Hitler? We can imagine two (related) kinds of answer to this. One proposes that property is essentially the province of government; the other that might really does make right, in the end.

The first is the idea that states actually *define* the whole notion of property, and thus have the right to decide what should belong to whom. If they invade their neighbours, therefore, they aren't "taking other people's property," for those other people's "property" is only "theirs" because *their* government enacted laws protecting their use of it. So if our government comes along and bashes the first government out of the way, then the way is clear for us to rewrite all the rules—isn't it? The victorious king will give Northumbria to Sir Guy, and Wessex to Sir Geramond, and so on, after which those areas will actually *belong* to those gentlemen—won't they?

That takes us to a large and very fundamental subject: property rights and their foundation. We can hardly pursue that very far here, but I want to offer this suggestion about it: if the State isn't the source of our rights to personal security and liberty, then it isn't the foundation of our property rights, either. Our property is the result of our work, our involvement in the world, and these in turn lead to our making arrangements with our neighbours. To suppose that people have the right to life, and yet no right to property, is to take with one hand what you give with the other. Our lives are our activity, our chosen patterns of creation, work, fun, and the rest of it; and all those things require property rights. "Life" doesn't matter to us independently of our *lives*. Should we say that the people enslaved by conquering armies had their right to life respected, since they (or at least a lot of them) were, after all, still alive afterwards?

I suggest, in short, that this statist view of property makes no more sense than the statist view on human rights, and that the state can no more define property than it can define life itself. If we have a right against the state to be alive at all, we also have the right to live our *own* lives, in accordance with our own values and interests. And if we have that right, then we have the right to use and occupy bits of the world and incorporate those things into our lives on our own terms—not the state's. If we accept that, then our claims to property do not depend on the lawgivers, but rather on what we and others have done and the agreements we have made. I propose that it is the duty of the state to uphold these interests, not to flush them down the drain by "redefining" them or to act as though everything belongs to itself, which in its high and mighty wisdom dispenses all good things. Governments may not commit theft against people outside their boundaries any more than they may do so against people inside them.

Does Might Make Right?

The other suggestion to consider is that states can do whatever they want because might makes right, at least at the level of world politics. I have a little more sympathy with this idea, which has an appealing sense of getting down to the nitty-gritty. Rational people pursue their own interests, using their powers as best they can. So if A can simply get what he wants from B by sheer force, then why shouldn't he?

But there is a good and sufficient answer to that at the individual level: nobody is the Big Boss, and anyone who thinks he is simply makes himself into a target for the rest of us. The idea that we should *approve* of what bullies do, just because they do it, is too absurd to bear serious discussion. If bullies bent on destroying us for their personal gain won't listen to reason, then there's only one thing to do: kill 'em! That's what they're asking for by such behaviour; they leave us with no other reasonable option. Those who insist on war will, of course, get it. All we can do is hope that those of us on the side of peace and decency will be able to muster enough force to defeat them. But this is, one hopes, a case of right making might, rather than vice versa. The soundness of the idea that nobody should be able to get his way by force is such as to move most of us to rally to the cause of dealing, by force, with those who give us no other alternative.

We may, then, accept the premise that morality would indeed be unable to condemn effectively the actions of super-individuals. But we should still reject the conclusion that we should let Joe Biceps do what he wants, for Joe Biceps is not a super-individual but just another flesh-and-blood mortal who happens also to be a bully.

What about states, though? Some of them can make more plausible claims than Joe Biceps, can't they? Here there is a difficult and painful lesson to be learned, one that is taking humankind much longer to learn than it usually does for individuals. Big states might try to push around little ones. But does that give them the right to do so? Not at all!

Why not? First, because little states, seeing that big ones might have an interest in invading them, will be induced to make coalitions with other states so as to equalize the fight. What promised to be quick and clean little wars will turn into protracted and messy ones. And there are other considerations. Most notable among them is this: if the cause of the war is an interest of the big state in acquiring wealth from the small one, then war just isn't a good way to do that, for in a war, *everyone loses*. The victors lose a lot of soldiers and spend a great deal of money on equipment, especially in modern warfare. (This is to admit that things might once have been different: investments were relatively lower, prospective gains much higher, in the third millennium B.C.). By the time a modern state has "won," the war has cost far more than it would have cost simply to *buy* the things it wanted. Even if the enemy wouldn't sell, one could likely make do without it much more profitably than by making war. In modern times, wars for such reasons are utterly absurd. Defence, however, is another matter entirely. When one's very life is at stake, then any cost is justified to preserve it.

Nor should we ignore the very large "if" in the question as to why big nations shouldn't feel free to beat up on small ones *if* they can get away with it. First, of course, there is the fact that national states pursue their interests *at the expense* of many (often most) of its own people: those who lose their lives, their dear ones, and a sizeable fraction of most incomes in the process of subjugating the enemy. If we agreed that one person may not kill another merely to advance his own fortunes, then we must surely also agree that he cannot do so merely to advance someone else's. If the sacrificed soldier died defending his own loved ones or at least his own countrymen who were under threat, that's one thing. But if he dies merely to increase their access to other people's goods—goods to which they had no right in the first place—then his nation has wronged him, as well as its victims.

What if a soldier dies in an effort to liberate some other country? Here is another potent source of evil. Liberal countries, most notably the United States, have in recent times been willing to send armies to the "defence" of other countries that haven't asked for their help or manifestly did not want it. The most notable case is that of the American involvement in Vietnam, contrary to the wishes and, on any reasonable view of the matter, the interests of its people. That conflict affords a wealth of insight into the ways of power. Partly despite and partly because of the democratic nature of its political system, America's leaders involved their country in a war both hopeless and evil, leading to the expenditure of hundreds of billions of dollars and fifty thousand American lives, plus some hundreds of thousands of Vietnamese lives, and all for literally nothing.[1]

Of course a nation can fight for other reasons: glory, pride, a "place in the sun." Are those things that are worth having at such a price? A plausible answer is no. If one party can fight for glory, so can another; and there is no way for such fights to end satisfactorily for all concerned. If the only reason for fighting was to come out ahead, then whoever does it simply invites everyone to go home, lick their wounds, and come back another day. There are less costly and even, arguably, more interesting ways of achieving glory: sports, for example. Nation A's team can compete with Nation B's on the hockey rink, the baseball diamond, or in any number of other safe and exciting competitions. Given many and frequent games, all can win at something as time goes by. Best of all, the victorious hockey players merely walk off with the trophy—not with the bodies of their opponents. Millions of citizens of both countries enjoy the spectacle on TV, whether their side won or lost, and it all looks to be a vastly better alternative than war.

On the other hand, the very reasons that compel us to accept a general right of defence apply equally forcefully to nations. The basic principle here is the right of association. We value *this* group of people that we belong to and reasonably refuse to allow some outsider to come with guns and tanks to kill our friends, neighbours, and other fellow partakers of our accustomed lifestyle. Giving up such things is tantamount, often, to giving up our lives.

My tentative conclusion is that militarism is not plausible. No matter how strong any given state is, its power isn't sufficient reason for the rest of us to concede it the right to do whatever it pleases. And if perhaps it was prudent at some times in the past to make wars in order to pursue national objectives other than defence, it isn't so at the end of the twentieth century. War is too expensive and can achieve nothing worth having that honest toil and trade won't get us far more of, far more efficiently.

Perhaps this discussion doesn't do full justice to militarism. Down through the ages men have displayed courage, indeed heroism, and many other moral virtues in the conduct of war. That must not be lost sight of. But is the opportunity to display those virtues enough to make war *right*? Surely not. That would be like arguing that a doctor who went around spreading disease in order to demonstrate his prowess at curing the resulting patients was acting morally. He isn't; and neither is the ultra-courageous mobster, bully—or state.

Pacifism

We move next to the extreme opposite challenge to war, which is known as *pacifism*. The pacifist opposes war because he opposes violence. So far, so good: all of us, I hope, are opposed to violence. But the term "pacifism" should be confined to a distinctive doctrine, rather than just used to rename familiar views. The sort of view we will discuss here doesn't just oppose the use of violence for the sort of purposes we all agree are unjustified. Instead, the pacifist insists that violence may not be used for *any purposes at all*, including the purpose of defending ourselves against the violence of others. This idea has fascinated many people, including the founder of Christianity—whose professed adherents, however, have often been fully as bellicose as the "heathen" they have so often fought against, as for example in the Crusades and the Thirty Years' War.

Pacifism, as we discuss it here, is the refusal to use violence even to defend people against the aggressive violence of others. But what is violence? It has at least two importantly differing connotations. On the one hand, it can refer simply to rapid and sizeable transfers of energy, as in volcanic explosions and tropical storms.

On the other, it can refer much more narrowly to damage intentionally inflicted by some people upon others.

That the two definitions diverge greatly is illustrated on the one hand by such things as auto accidents, where there is violence in the first sense, but none in the second—the damage done is not intentionally inflicted by anyone; and by boxing matches, where there is intentional infliction of damage, but it is fully voluntary on the part of all concerned. And on the other, it is illustrated by non-violent murders such as putting poison in the victim's tea, which requires only minuscule and moderately paced energy transfers. The pacifist, of course, opposes the use of violence in the second sense distinguished: he's as opposed to poisoning as to blowing people up with high explosives, and he usually agrees that driving cars is permissible despite the probability that accidents will sometimes happen and even, if perhaps reluctantly, that people may, if they are fool enough, engage in voluntary pugilism.

These and other cases suggest, in fact, the need to be more precise about the pacifist's intentions, for we can distinguish several different levels of non-resistance to aggression. Just what does the pacifist want to allow people to do about would-be aggressors? May we do (1) nothing at all—just allow the intruder to walk all over us, pushing us out of our houses, raping our wives, tossing the children into incinerators? Or (2) are we to confine ourselves to *verbal* opposition: try to reason with the intruder, talk him into being a nice guy? Or (3) may we go further yet and use "non-violent resistance"? May we lock the doors, make them of steel, and "non-violently restrain" the enemy when he arrives?

One can imagine going even further than any of these in the direction of "turning the other cheek." One could be downright helpful to the enemy, opening doors for him so that he can molest your family or yourself still more efficiently. But in fact, no professing pacifist advocates that, and scarcely any go so far as the purely passive response depicted in (1). Pacifists, they say, are not to be "passive-ists." Almost all pacifists not only allow but insist on both the second and third of the listed options. I will not further discuss those who would reject them, if there are any. But there are hard questions to address to those who would draw a fine line between, on the one hand, threatening a potential intruder with violence or death and, on the other, doing one's best to frustrate him in ways short of violence. There are three questions to ask those who want to make much of that distinction.

In the first place, does it really *make sense* to condemn all violent means, while allowing supposedly non-violent ones? Second, what if "non-violent defence" ends up costing more innocent lives than defence by violent means? Finally, what if such methods cost more in *other* terms than those involving the possibility of violence?

The first question raises the fundamental theoretical problem of pacifism. The view has it that we may and should resist violence as much as possible, so long as we use *non-violent* resistance. But such resistance does, after all, frustrate the aggressor, preventing him from achieving his intended goals. This raises the question, what is the fundamental objection to violence? Is it not the frustration of the victim's desires? Reflection strongly suggests this. Why, then, should one way of doing this be allowed when another, equally or more frustrating, is forbidden?

The reply that pain and death are evils is inadequate, for it assumes a special status for those evils that most people don't actually give them. Ordinary people will put up with a lot of pain to achieve important objectives. We painfully toil up mountains simply to get to the top, cheerfully contract colds from kissing our loved ones, risk injuries skiing down icy slopes. And every mother bears her children in pain, which is readily and greatly outweighed by her love for the resulting infants. Given all this, how can it be sensible to draw an absolute line between those ways of frustrating an aggressor that inflict pain or injury on him and those that do not? Why may we not go further and take measures that threaten or risk the infliction of injuries? The pacifist, one begins to realize, is appealing to us on the basis of what turns out to be a quite idiosyncratic schedule of values.

The second question is more immediately embarrassing to the pacifist. Suppose that we want to confine ourselves to non-violent defensive methods, but the best available ones won't be as *effective* as some that do involve the threat or actual use of violence. You build stout walls, but the enemy forces occasionally get through and murder some innocent people. But suppose that they would have desisted if instead you had marched up to the enemy's camp and made it clear that the next time they engaged in certain aggressive activities, you and your stout-hearted fellows would proceed to beat them to a pulp? This enemy, let us suppose, won't listen to gentle words, but is extremely averse to the prospect of violence being done against himself. What we are envisaging here is that, as a result of your speaking to him in his own language—the language of sticks and stones rather than words—less violence is actually done. What is the pacifist to say if there are such cases? He can't easily ignore evidence that willingness to use violence sometimes works better towards effecting the very goal the pacifist would seem to be primarily attached to—peace.[2]

Here's an interesting case in point. In a sizeable American city some years ago there was a rash of rapes. The police decided to respond to this problem with an experiment. They offered to equip any interested woman with a handgun, provided she took lessons in using it for self-defence. Several hundred women—but still, less than 1 per cent of the female adult populace—took the program and were accordingly armed. The experiment was well publicized, and lo! The incidence of rape in that community went from epidemic proportions to virtually zero in an amazingly short time. Yet no rapists were actually shot! The sheer knowledge that their victims were quite possibly going to be armed and ready to kill if necessary was sufficient to make them desist. There is little question of any practicable training in "non-violent defence" being more effective than that and a great deal of reason to believe it would have been far less effective. And we can point to such historic examples as the Nazi occupation of the Rhine lands in 1937, where a very modest amount of French resistance would almost certainly have averted the slaughter of World War II.[3]

Given this, we must ask, how can the pacifist rationally suppose that the women-arming program was immoral? If we are serious about women having the right not to be sexually molested and we find a method that very effectively protects them without harming any innocent persons—or even, quite possibly, the potentially guilty ones themselves, though it *threatens* plenty of harm to them—then how could we take the view that the latter method must nevertheless be forgone in favour of much less effective ones, those using non-violent resistance? Such methods will, on the evidence, surely leave a trail of molested victims, perhaps shorter than the trail left if nothing at all is done, but still, much longer than if violent resistance is threatened in an effective and controlled way.

The serious pacifist might profess that non-violence is of so high an order of obligation that one must adhere to it no matter how high the bodies stack up around one (and, of course, one's own will likely end up on the pile soon enough). But the pacifist who takes this route pays a very high price indeed, a price in terms of a value that he must surely prize. For how could his program make any sense if he did not think peace a *good*? To take this route is to go even further in the direction of assuming idiosyncratic values. Normally people have no such categorical aversion to violence. In fact, what they have is a conditional rejection of it: they will refrain *if* others refrain, reserving the right to defend themselves by any means necessary against those who do not.

This brings us to our third question, concerning pacifism's further costs. So far we have questioned whether pacifism really makes sense in terms of its own goals. Now we must ask whether those goals—peace, in particular—should have the weight pacifism assigns to them? Suppose that we do find a method of non-violent resistance that is highly effective, but also very, very costly in terms of our other values. For example, imagine that we all move underground and keep the entrance heavily barred, admitting persons only when we are certain that they will not use violence against any of the inhabitants. Obviously, our freedom of movement would be extremely restricted, while the cost in hours spent building those stout walls or digging out that cave is also immense, since we may be sure that the protected people would have much preferred to spend their time doing other things. Well, if such methods are available only at such costs, then why *must* they be employed in preference to cruder, more violent, but equally effective methods that would leave people a lot freer to live the kind of lives they would much prefer to live? How much must I give up merely so that some violent person does not commit violence?

Depending on how it is formulated, these arguments show that pacifism is either radically incoherent or highly idiosyncratic. It is the former if the pacifist's argument is based on results. If the pacifist objects to violence because of its cost in terms of certain values, such as preserving lives, then the objection is irrational if it can be shown that the result of using or threatening violence, in a given case, would be to save more lives. To preserve their position, pacifists would then have to argue that violence and the threat of violence are never actually necessary to preserve lives. That is an implausible claim, and one that seems to be empirically refuted by many cases, such as the one about rape, or for that matter the apparent efficacy of police forces, in the better cases anyway, in keeping the level of violence down in large cities.[4]

If, on the other hand, pacifists appeal, say, to the "sacredness" of life, then the trouble is that most people simply do not regard life as sacred in the relevant sense. We are quite prepared to risk our lives, if need be, to live the sort of lives we much prefer; why, then, can't we threaten the lives of others when they propose to deprive us of ours? Of course, the pacifist might reply that we have the "wrong" values. But to this we have a further reply: morality is not for the few who share the pacifist's peculiar set of values. Our question, when we are in the realm of morals, is whether there is a directive that can reasonably be addressed to all persons, calling upon them to refrain from certain activities. To support such directives, there has to be a basis in the values of the persons addressed that would make acceptance of those directives reasonable for them. If the only sort of values that would do this, in the case of a given proposal, are those that virtually nobody has, then our prospect of success in proposing it as a moral principle is nil: it's a non-starter. Morals are for people, not just for angels, eccentrics, or saints. Until such time as the pacifist can persuade us to embrace his strange preferences, his program is hopeless as a proposal for general morality.

The Pacifist Argument

Why did the pacifist think his principle right in the first place? He apparently advances an argument like this:

1. Violence is wrong in and of itself.
2. Violence in self-defence is violence.
3. Therefore, violence in self-defence is wrong.

But the argument is fatally flawed.

(1) What is meant by "wrong in and of itself"—that violence is *always evil*? If the word "violence" is used in the first of the two familiar senses distinguished at the outset, then this claim does not seem to be true. We don't think boxing immoral, though we may think it silly. And if violence were always wrong, there would be no identifiable distinction between the sadist who inflicts pain just for the fun of it and the dentist who inflicts pain now in order to save pain in the long run.

(2) Regarding the second premise, we again encounter the ambiguity of the word "violence." It might be objected that when innocent people defend themselves against assailants by using weapons or fists, what they do shouldn't be called violence, so that the claim, "violence in self-defence is violence" should be rejected. However, we won't use this argument here, since the issue does not turn on words but on ideas.

(3) The most important objection to the argument is that it deduces the wrong conclusion from its premises. From the premise that violence is wrong, what follows is not only that we should normally *refrain* from it, but also that we should *resist* it rather than let people get away with it. Violence is wrong when used against the innocent; its use against the violent, on the other hand, may be the only way to deal with them and is surely justified. Of course, just to *say* this would be question-begging against the pacifist. But on the other hand, for him to assert the third claim just on the basis of the first two premises would also be question-begging.

Non-violent resistance might be practised in hopes of having a positive, peaceful effect on others. Buddha, Jesus, Gandhi, and Mother Teresa are examples: they have probably inspired many people to peaceful ways. But this argument will not suffice. Their practice requires an extraordinary willingness to sacrifice oneself to one's ideals—Jesus was executed and Gandhi was assassinated. And not just oneself, but one's friends and family, may be exposed to great risk by adhering to this principle in certain circumstances. Most of us aren't prepared to pay that kind of price for "peace," if pacifism even succeeds in bringing it—which, as we have seen, it often won't. We do not find such a life attractive. In fact, we don't even find such pacifists morally admirable. If they want to sacrifice themselves, that's one thing. But what about their families and others who look to them for protection? What's so morally admirable about letting them get shot, tortured, and raped?

Perhaps the most important of the pacifist's arguments goes like this: if everyone were to practise pacifism, then all people would be safe, since there would then be universal peace—a pure ideal that we all, I trust, agree to be morally laudable. But the argument is quickly undone. True, the world would be a more peaceful place if everyone practised pacifism. But the very same is true if everyone stuck to the doctrine of refraining only from *aggressive* violence, reserving violence for the defence of innocents. For if no one aggresses, then there is nothing to defend against, no occasion for violence, and so the world consisting of people who adhere to the principle of using violence only in defence against aggressors would be precisely as peaceful as if all were pacifists. So pacifism is no improvement on the ordinary view in that respect. But as soon as we get back to the real world, in which there are lots of nice people but, unfortunately, a fair number of rotters as well, the picture changes completely. Here the pacifist's practice seems to have the effect of letting the rotters get away with murder in all those cases where the murderer doesn't happen to be the type who is charmed by displays of non-violence. And that's outrageous.

In short, pacifism is full of severe problems: of coherence, of appeal to ordinary people, of demands on our psychic resources, and probably of information about the real world. This brings us to our third view, the familiar one that distinguishes between aggression and defence, and allows us a right to violence when and only when that is necessary for defence.

The Right to Defend Ourselves

Is there a good reason for thinking that there is a right to self-defence? Indeed there is. To start with, let us remember what a right is: to say that one has a right to do something is to say that others have the duty to let you do it. But why should one be entitled to *enforce* that right?

The answer I would propose is that if we aren't allowed to protect a right, then the very claim that it is a right is meaningless. The claim that others may not interfere or in any way prevent you from doing what you have a right to do is not meant as a mere verbal gesture or an expression of wishful thinking. It has teeth. What it says is that if it comes down to a contest between you, the right-holder, and some would-be violator of that right, then you are the person who should be defended, not the violator. If the only way to ensure that you "win" is to knock out the aggressor, then so be it.

The right to self-defence in this sense is very basic, and the argument for it quite simple. For most of us, there is no point in morality if it allows people to walk all over us because of our adherence to it. Patsy morality isn't for us. What *we* want is our lives. We can't have them if others may just invade us at will. Violence is the number-one enemy; therefore, people charging in and bashing about, getting what they want without having to work for it or by voluntary exchange with willing suppliers, are not to be permitted to get away with those activities. If they cannot be persuaded by peaceable means to desist, so that we are reduced to choosing between using force or being murdered, robbed, and otherwise assaulted, choosing force is greatly and obviously preferable. To deny this is to throw over the prospect of morality having much effect in the real world.

It's of utmost importance to realize that if we weren't such nice guys, the nasty ones wouldn't be able to do this to us. Instead, there would be general warfare. And in that case, neither of us would "win": we would both lose, and lose big. What makes it alone reasonable for us to become nice people is that other people do so as well. If they claim to have done so but then resort to violence anyway—to the very thing morality is supposed to free us from—then we must be entitled to return to it ourselves. That's what makes morality a fair and reasonable arrangement. That, and nothing else, in the end.

Our topic is war, and wars, of course, are fought between states and not between particular individuals. We must ask how much difference that makes, and especially whether, perhaps, it makes *all* the difference? But how could it? If our concern against other individuals is that they not attack us, the same is true regarding individuals who happen to be from other states. We have the same reason not to allow violence by people in strange uniforms as by our neighbours. If we do not resist, we are just as dead in the one case as in the other.

The "Just" War

Is war ever just? The pacifist says no. But pacifism, as we have seen, won't do. It would be irrational to give up the right to defend ourselves: the pacifist's cure is worse than the disease. Still, there are the questions of when war *is* justified, and of what we may and may not do in fighting wars, even when they are.

Here we turn to the hoary doctrine known as Just War theory. Philosophers generally take this theory seriously, for it is powerfully plausible. We will take a brief but sympathetic look at this doctrine, without claiming interpretive fidelity to its original exponents.[5]

Two Branches

We may think of a Just War theory as a completion of the following sentence-form: "Party A justly participates in a war with Party B if and only if...." Our job is to fill in the blank. There are two branches of Just War theory. In the first branch of our inquiry, we will have to show that the *reason* (or "cause") for which A fights the proposed war is a just one. The other branch concerns one's *conduct* of such wars as satisfy the first branch. Once you have a just cause, can you then do just *anything* in your efforts to win it? Just War theory says no: there are still restrictions that moral beings ought to observe, even though what they are justly doing is, in a sense, trying to kill each other. Let's say a bit about each branch.

Just Cause: Who Is To Be Defended?

What, then, justifies A in waging war against B? We have accepted the answer that war is justified only if it is necessary for defence. But whom may we defend? And just what about those people may we defend? Finally, what constitutes "necessity" here?

Let's start with the first one. I have argued that we are surely allowed to defend ourselves. But may we defend *only* ourselves, or do we get to come to the aid of another beleaguered friendly nation? If no one may help others, then that is very bad news for the weak. Little states cannot stand up long against big ones, after all. Prohibiting help is simply throwing the game into the laps of the big guys. But then, the *other* big guys are hardly going to stand for that!

Thus we arrive at the same conclusion as for individuals: states may engage in war *only* to defend either themselves *or* other *innocent* states (that is, other non-aggressive states). Despite what William Earle seems to want to say, we must rule out of court those who make war for any other reason.[6]

Notice, of course, that if everyone lived up to this specification, then there wouldn't be any wars, for on this view, the only way one party can be justified in fighting a war is if another party who is not meeting the specification fights first. Wars between decent states are just not going to happen.

Defend What?

If we may defend ourselves, just what about ourselves may we defend? Our lives, of course. But what else? Or rather, just what are we to include in a "life" for this purpose? How about our property, for example? Suppose that the enemy is "only" after our industrial wealth or certain non-food resources such as oil. May we "trade lives for oil," as some critics of the Gulf War put it?

There's an easy right answer to this: you bet! Remember, the enemy is, we are supposing, *attacking* us. He isn't merely offering to *buy* those resources—we'd be happy to arrange a suitable sale, quite possibly. But no: he wants to take them by force, whatever we may think of it. Of course, it matters whether we acquired the things in question legitimately in the first place. But suppose we *did*?[7]

Reflection leads rapidly to the conclusion that we may defend *whatever* is legitimately ours against attacks by others. If we kill them, that's their fault: all they had to do was be peaceable and there would have been no problem. The example may be extended. Not just oil wells, but your CD collection, your new pair of running shoes, or whatever may be defended from anyone who proposes to acquire it from you by force or fraud.

Most wars have been fought for possession of land. This is "possession" by *states*, of course, and that brings up important and fundamental questions. Rarely have wars been fought over *individuals'* possession of land. Often, we may suppose, it would have been possible for everyone concerned to make mutually advantageous trades with particular members of the "enemy," eliminating any need for resort to violence. Jewish settlers in Palestine, for example, sometimes did buy their land from former Arab owners. But when collective, wholesale expropriation set in, that led to war. People will fight to retain their land, as well as their families and their ways of life. They are perfectly right to do so. Those things are worth fighting for.

Necessity

When we claim that defence is "necessary," what do we mean? The general idea is that other methods of achieving agreement have failed. Clearly that implies a duty to seek out those other ways. We must try to negotiate if we can, to look for reasonable terms on which the problem with the expected aggressor can be settled. Nowadays, we might take our case to the United Nations, for instance. Negotiation is our first resort. If that fails, we should build up our defences and warn the enemy of the consequences if he should attack. And if he actually does, then defence is indeed necessary.

But may we attack only if he actually attacks us first? There is a problem about confining defensive effort in this way. What if the enemy is rapidly building up his forces and we can see that if we do not attack now, we will certainly lose the war he will soon start? The forces of Nazi Germany could easily have been defeated in the years before World War II actually began; when it did begin, it did so on Hitler's terms, not the Allies'. Wouldn't the European countries he picked on have been justified in pre-emptive attacks?

We cannot just rule out pre-emption. But we must be fully justified in thinking that we are in a situation justifying it: we must have objectively monitored the enemy's troop build-up and movements. In fact, nations have usually been very reluctant to engage in such warfare, even when it would surely have been reasonable to do so. There is, alas, no easy way to settle the question of when a war is genuinely defensive.

Just War-Making: The Least-Force Principle

Suppose that we have the general principle for just cause fairly well in hand, then, what about the other branch of the theory? Here, too, we have a nice general principle: the *least-force principle*. What this says is that even if one's cause is just, one may use only the amount of force required to eliminate the threat, not to go further, inflicting damage for its own sake or for purely punitive purposes.

As we saw above, it is a sign of peaceful intentions that one be willing to discuss one's case, to negotiate rather than just assuming it and proceeding without regard for the others. And in this connection, there is another common-sense principle to observe: not to attack the enemy's negotiators. That requires that we be able to recognize them, of course, and so we come up with a common convention such as the white flag, whose bearers are to be respected. Thus is bloodshed spared and peace made possible.

The least-force principle has two major areas of application, in its turn: protection of non-combatants and minimization of injury to the combatants. Each has a clear rationale.

Let's start with the combatant—non-combatant distinction. There is a presumption that non-combatants are no threat to us, so there is no need to defend ourselves against them; if we shoot them, we act as aggressors rather than defenders, warmongers rather than peacemakers. We make this distinction on the presumption, as I put it, that *they* aren't the problem for us—they aren't the ones we have a quarrel with.

But alas! The presumption may not clearly be true. If non-combatants don't pull the triggers, they may nevertheless *make* the triggers—work in munitions factories, for instance. And aren't those factories eligible targets? Reflection on this raises a serious question of where we are to draw the line. Suppose that our non-combatant merely grows food, but some of it is fed to the troops? Couldn't starving those troops be an effective method of combat? And mightn't we promote that end by burning the enemy's wheat fields, say? One common strategy of attackers in earlier times was to starve the enemy into submission by siege warfare: surrounding the city, preventing all exit until they ran out of food. Can we declare that wrongful, so long as the war is fought for just cause?

There is another way that the combatant/non-combatant distinction tends to come unstuck. What if your weapons are such that it becomes very difficult to hit only the enemy's military personnel? Bombing from airplanes, for example, was and mostly still is very inaccurate. If it's a large bomb, then even if you hit precisely what you aim at, you are still likely to destroy the neighbours while you're at it. This is an especially acute problem with nuclear weapons, of course.

As to the enemy soldiers, one must remember that they are only fighting for their country—they are not personally "out to get us." Revenge, therefore, is out of order. So is using more force against them than you need to. If method A attains the appropriate military objective just as well as method B, but A kills fewer of the enemy, then we ought to use method A. We would certainly want our enemies to do the same, and we are assuming that there is no *military* justification for doing anything else.

Similar considerations apply to the treatment of prisoners. Once they are non-combatants there is no excuse for mistreating them, e.g., by feeding them inadequately. Besides, if the enemy's troops are aware that they will be well treated by our side, then they have maximum inducement to surrender readily. What could make more sense than that? A recent book recounts extensive inhuman treatment of German soldiers after the end of World War II by the American government. The war was over and all of those soldiers were only too interested in returning to peaceful life; yet, according to this well-documented account, they were deliberately kept in POW camps on subminimal diets and without shelter; as many as a million may have died as a result.[8] If this study is right, it is a shocking example. Few wars have been more popular in America than World War II, where the foe seemed to represent as pure a case of evil as one could readily imagine. But nobody is purely evil or purely good. And however evil the policies of his government, the individual enemy soldier may not be regarded as merely the incarnation of that evil. As they are likely to be more or less normal and probably hapless fellow humans, we should do nothing to embitter or enrage them.

The principle of least force has thus far been neutral on another matter of fundamental moral interest: should we not only minimize unnecessary force against the enemy, though attaining our objective in the most efficient way, but *also* do so at some *cost* to efficiency, specifically by incurring some avoidable danger to our side? The Persian Gulf War of 1991 provides an interesting case for reflection. The allied armies, immeasurably superior in weaponry, equipment, and training, slaughtered Iraqi soldiers at will during the few days of ground combat, at trifling cost in casualties to their own troops. The "kill ratio" is said to have been about 500 Iraqis killed to one allied soldier killed. Now, let us suppose that the allied generals could have won the war one day later and saved half of those Iraqi troops—at the cost of twice as many casualties to themselves. The "kill ratio" would, let us suppose, have been a "mere" 125:1. We would have saved 50,000 Iraqi lives at the cost of 200 allied lives. It is extremely difficult to know such things in the heat of battle, of course, but if Allied commanders could have known this, what should they have done?

It may be noted that this policy of sparing many enemy lives at the cost of a few of our own would not have gone over well with the parents of those few extra dead soldiers on the allied side. We may be very sure of that. (One didn't hear of *any* American mourning expressed at the size of Iraqi losses.) Yet we should pause to ask whether exclusive concern with the minimization of one's own casualties, regardless of how many of the enemy are sacrificed, is really an acceptable one. Again, this is not an easy question to answer. But if the Americans ever get into a war in which the ratio was more nearly the other way around, it would be interesting to see whether they would then be more sympathetic to a principle of avoiding massive enemy casualties when not strictly necessary for achieving legitimate objectives, even at the cost of a very few extra casualties to one's own side in the process.

The relevant Just War principle for these matters, as advanced by medieval thinkers, was called "proportionality": the amount of damage one does should be proportionate to the good to be attained. But putting it that way raises a problem. Must I use less force to protect my CD collection than my house? If an armed robber arrives in the dead of night bent on removing my CD collection from the premises, do I have to let him go if my only way of stopping him is to shoot him? If he instead is after my Ferrari, which is worth as much as a house, do I then get to shoot him?

It is plausible to say that the *enemy* is the one who should bear this in mind. It is for him to ponder the question whether to risk his life for a mere CD collection. But does justice require that our efforts to resist him be limited by the value of the object being defended? No doubt it is imprudent to risk our lives to defend objects of minor value, just as it is for the thief. But while it may be imprudent, do we actually have *no right* to do it? On reflection, I think, that can't be correct. As in Just War theory, first we should *warn* the thief, if we can, and then *threaten* him ("hands up or I shoot!"), if there is time; only when all this has failed may we actually shoot. But by that time, we may well be defending our lives and not merely our property. Which, I suggest, is no surprise when one thinks more deeply about it: for our property, the things we have been working and striving for, *is* a very considerable part of our life. It is not really surprising that practically all the wars ever fought have been fought to acquire or defend pieces of real estate.

Nuclear Deterrence

The development of nuclear weapons has intensified reflection on Just War theory in recent years. Large nuclear weapons can destroy sizeable cities with one explosion. Missiles can deliver those weapons accurately and so swiftly that shooting them down en route is virtually impossible. Any nation possessing such weapons is in a position to inflict catastrophic damage on anyone it wants to, with no possible defence by the intended victim—*except* the kind of "defence" that consists in a suitable counter-threat, that is, *deterrence*. A's threat to annihilate B is countered by B's threat to reciprocate. B may not be able to shoot down the enemy's missiles in flight, but he can discover that they are on the way and have time to retaliate if he is well prepared. Nations seeing this to be so, and able to do something about it, were very well prepared indeed.

Is the threat of nuclear retaliation morally permissible? Many have thought not. They reason that by the time the enemy's missiles are on the way, one's own nuclear response would do no good: the damage to oneself will be done anyway, and one will only inflict useless casualties on the enemy. Those who talk this way, of course, presume that retribution is not a just aim of war, and surely that is one question one would want to consider carefully. However, one would have to point out that even if it were, the trouble is that the victims of our megatonnage will consist almost entirely of innocent civilians instead of those responsible for the attack. All those factual points are true, and important. But on the other hand, if you refuse even to consider using nuclear retaliation, do you not lay yourself open to attacks and the threat of same ("nuclear blackmail")?

Such was the hard question of the forty years following World War II. Each side told the world that it was only arming itself against possible attack by the other. If that was really true, then the situation made no sense at all. The correct thing to do is what was eventually done, more or less: start a policy of tentative unilateral cuts to see what one's opponent does; if he follows suit, then cut some more. This policy makes sense because trying to be "superior" in nuclear weapons is obviously futile, while trying to be "equal." always in practice amounts to looking as though you are trying to be superior, since each side separately decides what counts as "equal". Yet actually having *less* weapons than the other side, it is agreed, makes no discernible difference to deterrent capability—a state that won't risk the obliteration of 75 per cent of its populace won't risk 50 per cent either. But it makes an enormous difference to the reading of intentions. A state clearly equipping itself to do *less* harm to the enemy than its enemy aims to do to it is obviously not a state bent on conquest.[9]

As in the case of punishment, there is no "solution" to such problems at the strategic level. The only real solution to the problem of private crime is to bring people up with strongly internalized, deeply negative attitudes towards damaging others and their property. An analogous point may be made of nations: they must come to respect each other and, to a modest degree, trust each other. Above all, they must renounce *paranoia*: nothing destroys prospects for peace more effectively than the belief that everybody is out to murder you the moment you let your guard down. Our problem is solved only when we realize that there is nothing to be gained by a nuclear war (or any war) *and* we take this as a good reason for dismantling nuclear (and other) weapons, reducing threats to everyone. Happily, it appears for the present as though the world is on its way to just such an outcome. Let's hope the appearance is not an illusion.

War in the Post-Nuclear Era

Since the eclipse of the Soviet Union as a "superpower," and especially as a power whose political ideology is belligerently opposed to that of the mixed-capitalist states that form the "front-line" states in today's world, the threat of nuclear war has subsided—but the incidence of smaller kinds of war is at least as great as ever. Notably, there are wars ostensibly caused by ethnic rivalries, as in the former Yugoslavia and the Middle East. Do these smaller but very fierce conflicts call for any serious revision of our principles? I think not; but perhaps they do call for some further elaboration. Primarily, of course, we may rehearse the same reasoning as we used on behalf of property rights and more generally the right of each and every person to life and to the liberty to pursue, peaceably, the kind of life that person chooses to pursue. This applies to groups as well as to individuals. It is very easy for ethnic and religious groups to suppose that their way of life is *the* way of life for all, and, likewise, it is inevitable that such an attitude will result in wars with the many others who do not accept their choice. It would be easy to say that the main moral of these recently prominent causes of unrest in the world is the front-rank importance of religious toleration.

Too easy, actually. For there is another lesson, less easily learned and much less easily acted upon. Supposedly rival groups of Serbs, Croats, Bosnians, and others had been living for the most part peaceably, and side by side for many years before the recent troubles in Yugoslavia. Likewise, the supposed enemies in Rwanda, the Tutsi and Hutu tribes, had been living mostly peaceably, with extensive intermarriage, for a considerable time before the massacres of the late 1990s. Why do such people become bitter enemies all of a sudden? It is always clear that the immediate occasion is political: the power-seeking of strongmen prompts them to exploit these rivalries by associating them with material benefits or supposed material injustices, thus fanning what are in fact tiny embers into serious flames that can result in near-genocidal levels of violence. It is not difficult to say what sorts of actions are in the wrong and for what reasons; it is not easy to say just how they can be dealt with.

The United Nations has been near-powerless in these disputes, and it has been so especially because of its reluctance to breach the principle of non-intervention into the affairs of independent states. The UN Charter explicitly holds that "No state has the right to intervene, directly or indirectly, for any reason whatever, in the internal or external affairs of any other state."[10]

It is not difficult to see why a political body consisting of the representatives of sovereign states should want to adopt such a principle, nor is it difficult to muster some sympathy for it as such. Yet we should be very concerned about its long-term effects on the lives of ordinary people. The control of political power has always been a major concern, but its importance has surely increased enormously in contemporary times. How to control it, however, is a major problem indeed.

Two hundred years ago, the philosopher Immanuel Kant (1722-1804) wrote a famous treatise, *Perpetual Peace*, in which he proposed as the "First Definitive Article for perpetual Peace" that "The Civil Constitution of Every State Should be Republican."[11] The efficacy of Kant's proposal was tested recently by an author who made an empirical survey of wars since there had begun to be, in the modern sense of the term, liberal states of the sort meant by "republican." He found, strikingly, that there had never been a war between two liberal states as such, though sometimes liberal states had been aligned with non-liberal states on opposite sides in a war.[12] This certainly suggests that the impetus towards democracy in the modern world is not misguided in this respect—although achieving democracy in backward areas or areas riven by politically fanned ethnic hostilities is quite another matter.

But those matters have to do with means, not with basic principles. That our basic principle should be broadly of the kind embraced here is not, I think, in doubt.

Summing Up

No principle of morals is more fundamental and far-reaching than that violence is wrong. It is wrong because as a way of settling differences it is *inefficient*, leaving both victors and vanquished worse off than the methods of peace. Even so, we clearly have the right to defend ourselves. Pacifism, the view that we do not, is broken-backed in principle, holding up non-violence as a supreme value and thereby depriving us of our only means of preventing great harm when aggressors descend upon us. But wars can be justly or unjustly carried on as well, and we have argued that we should indeed be ready to employ violence to the minimal extent necessary, sparing the innocent if possible—which may not be the case when nuclear war is threatened. Even in that melancholy instance, the right to defend oneself comes first: nuclear blackmail is no more to be tolerated than any other kind. Fortunately, the problems of nuclear war seem soluble, since it is so clear that nobody can hope to win one.

Chapter Six

Morals and Animals

Do animals have rights? Or, for that matter, any moral standing at all? This is another very interesting and theoretically tricky issue, and another that we can't hope to resolve without recourse to moral theory. The main question is whether there is any inherent reason to put animals in a different moral category than people—say, outside it altogether. If we do have any moral relations to animals, then of what sort are they to be? Will they be in the category of duties of benevolence, or are they in the category of *rights* or duties of justice enforceable by law? In fact, many countries have rather extensive legislative protection of experimental animals, though none, as yet, extending the right to life to cows and chickens.

First Question: The Moral Status of Animals

I have argued that morals, if they are to be rational, must amount to agreements among people—people of all kinds, all pursuing their own personal interests, which are various and do not necessarily include much concern for others and their interests. But people have minds and apply information gleaned from observing the world around them to the task of promoting their interests, and they have a broad repertoire of powers including some that can make them exceedingly dangerous as well as others that can make them very helpful. This gives us reason to agree with each other that we will refrain from harming others in the pursuit of our interests, to respect each other's property and grant extensive civil rights, but not necessarily to go very far out of our way to be very helpful to those we don't know and may not particularly care for.

But now let us consider the case where those "others" are animals, incapable of articulate speech, possessed of reasoning faculties that are very hard to compare with our own but obviously not oriented, as ours are, to absorbing and formulating vast amounts of information about the world and using it as effectively as possible to a vast variety of ends. Now add to this that the creatures in question can be quite useful to us in ways that typical humans are not: good to eat, equipped with insulating furs and hides, and so on. It is also true that these creatures apparently feel pain and some sorts of pleasure, that they have some kinds of interests, certainly including eating and certainly not including higher mathematics, literary production, masked balls, or any other of the activities we regard as "civilized." It is also true, by and large, that these creatures are not much of a threat to us, except in a few special and easily avoided cases. To primitive man, wild animals may have been a serious and constant threat, but no longer. Indeed, it is more nearly the other way around. The normal activities of the vast numbers of people on our planet tend to be incompatible with the flourishing of wild animals in the vicinity, and because of our vastly superior resources, those are conflicts that humans overwhelmingly tend to win. On the other hand, domestic animals flourish as never before under the watchful eye of their owners, though often at the price of a fairly early demise as they are turned into hamburger, leather upholstery, fur coats, and other desirable consumer items. The contemporary scene may present something of a paradox, then: as never before, animals flourish, and yet they are killed in great numbers. By and large, no contemporary legislature grants animals the right to *life* as it is normally understood; yet they do grant them some protection against wanton cruelty. Is this as it should be? The argument of this chapter is that, for the most part, it is.

What do we do about threats from other organisms? In the case of people, we can make a deal with them, inducing them to adopt an internalized attitude of disdain for murder and the like, and erecting appropriate institutions to penalize those who fail to acquire such aversions in sufficient degree. But what about animals? It is not wise to try to make a deal with your normal polar bear, wolverine, or crocodile. You either build a fence or shoot the critter, but so far as inducing *moral restraint* is concerned, forget it! Animals, in short, are essentially incapable of moral activity. If we adopt moral restraints in relation to them, it looks as though it will necessarily be a one-sided affair: the animals gain everything and we gain nothing. This is not an ironclad generalization. Particular people have sometimes established very good relations with particular animals—horse and rider, man and dog, opera singer and cat. But this is not a social contract extending to all animals or even to all members of any one species. Each is a specialized case, dependent on the attitudes and interests of certain individual people.

And just as there isn't much capacity for general reciprocity in animals, so, too, there is no motive on our part to seek it. Most of us don't really *want* to establish "good relations" with the typical steer, being rather more interested in the steak or hamburger to which it may contribute in the not-too-distant future. And we don't *need* a social contract with the cow, for we have by far the upper hand. Given their dim intellects and bovine ways, cows can supply us with what we want from them without our having to make any general concessions of the type that animal moralists plump for. So why bother? Perhaps you have a "thing" about morality, a *special* interest? But special interests are no good for moral purposes. One person will befriend a cow, and that's fine; but the next will milk the beast, and eat her later on. People differ. The question, then, is this: why should those of us who want to eat cows have to submit to the self-ascribed "moral" ministrations of those who want to make them charter members of the moral republic?

Different Foundations?

Most philosophers these days reject the contractarian viewpoint, though not, in my judgement, for good reasons. They instead go along with contemporary philosophers such as Tom Regan in thinking that we should approach moral issues "intuitively."[1] Whether we must go along with them in this is a disputed question;[2] but let us see where it takes us.

Why would we think that animals actually have "rights"? And which rights would they have? Most people don't like the idea of causing random suffering for no reason. That supports a principle against being cruel to animals. However, there is also a question of just what constitutes cruelty and what the limits of this principle are. Many people, I'm sure, think that if we could find a cure for cancer by performing experiments on thousands of monkeys in ways that are extremely painful and later fatal to the monkeys, we should still go right ahead. People, they will say, count far more than monkeys. Most people think animal experimentation permissible, so long as it could lead to something important for us.

When philosophers like Regan deny this, then, they go *against* normal intuition. Regan's own arguments, indeed, are much subtler, appealing to supposedly deeper levels of our moral consciousness-es. He claims that we are being *inconsistent* if we think it's all right to torture animals in order to discover facts, no matter how important they are to us. Why? Because we are against torturing humans to find out those same things, even if it would work. We may not just take people and torture them to death, with the justification that the results will be very important for humanity. So how can we say this about animals?

To this, the normal person will respond that it's because they're *only* animals, implying that they don't count for much. So at this point Regan must appeal to his intuition about the moral equality of all organisms—down to molluscs or thereabouts. He will say that we can't treat animals that way because of their "inherent moral value," which is allegedly equal to ours. But most of us don't think it is. Regan needs an argument to go against this normal intuition, and what he supplies is another intuition that is, so far anyway, definitely *not* normal.

He does supply an argument, though: what about the insane, the feeble-minded, and infants? Aren't our duties to them the same as to ordinary people? If they are, then where would we draw a line that would rationally divide animals from us? This is, in short, a slippery slope argument, and as such is subject to familiar objections. Moreover, ordinary people would be puzzled by the comparison. They agree that the blind, the demented, or even perhaps the feeble-minded do indeed deserve good treatment from us. But in their view, even a demented person is way "above" an animal—even a very intelligent animal, such as a German shepherd.

It's not entirely clear, to be sure, why they should think that. But then, one trouble with appealing to intuition is that intuitions aren't supposed to come with nice clean arguments attached to them. In fact, the point of an appeal to intuition is precisely that argument is not needed, indeed, not possible: it's just what you *do* think, upon consideration, and that's supposed to be enough.

As we have seen before, however, it is *not* "enough." What if many other people have an intuition—as they do—that people are *superior* to animals? If so, what is Regan doing trying to show us that this intuition is *baseless*?

On the other side of the comparison, people might well deny that "human vegetables," human bodies that are alive but whose brains have ceased to generate any consciousness whatever, are any better than animals. But then, they also think that those human bodies no longer have normal human rights. They may quite properly be disconnected from life support systems, for instance. In short, once we get humans that are clearly no "better" than animals, in the respects that are so familiarly regarded as relevant in these matters, then they are also no longer entitled to the usual human rights.

There's a further large point that the Regan view doesn't adequately recognize. Almost every human has a special relation to some others: parents, friends, neighbours, children, and so on. Those special relations generate special moral concern. We cannot simply refuse to extend any concern to subnormal or weak humans without contravening the interests of their normal loved ones and inviting similar treatment of our own loved ones. This is untrue of animals, who do, of course, have families, too, but those families are just more animals. The point is that they have no special relations to humans. All those that do get rights in a derivative way: to assault such humans is to violate the rights of their kin and those who care for them.

There is one important exception to this last point. But this exception also serves to support my view, not Regan's. I have in mind those cases where the animal is owned by some human. Many animals belong to particular people, as pets, work animals, zoo animals, or whatever. Those animals are, of course, protected by virtue of their *owners'* rights. You may not harm my dog even if you may kill strays without compunction. You can't kill my horse, even if horses as such don't have rights, for it's mine, and I do have rights, including the right to the use of this horse. That, indeed, is what it is to be "mine": it's for me, and not you, to say what may be done to what is so called. Of course, Regan might say that animals cannot be "owned" for the same reason that people can't be. We rightly outlaw slavery. However, the analogy is question-begging. Since we don't think animals *are* people, we don't think of our use of them as "enslavement," a category only applicable to beings like ourselves, possessed of articulate reason and the rest of our distinctive features. So until he can show otherwise, he can't object to ownership either. That very same owner, however, is free to kill the animal for his purposes, if that is his interest. All things considered, then, the slippery slope argument, appealing to marginal cases, doesn't prove what it is supposed to.

What about killing animals for food? The case of animals is different from ours in a fundamental respect here, too. Cruelty is indeed wrong; but even if we think it wrong in the case of animals, killing an animal needn't be cruel—it needn't inflict a lot of pain, the pain is very brief, and it isn't wanton, since we then use the animal for good purposes, such as culinary ones. Killing *people* that way, of course, would not be right: you and I aren't willing to be killed for any such reasons; we draw the line quite narrowly at self-defence. But then, we humans are able to complain, whereas animals cannot; and their inability to do so is connected with another important feature. So far as we can see, animals don't have the sort of articulated vision of the future that you and I have. Why don't *we* want to die? Because we can look ahead to the future, have values and plans about it, puzzle about it, worry about it, and so on. Animals apparently can't do that. Perhaps we don't *know* that they don't, but the "apparently" is really pretty strong. The inability of animals to articulate or spell out any such vision—which is a pretty complex thing to do—strongly supports this judgement, for how could one entertain complex visions of one's own future in the complete absence of articulate speech? And on the other hand, why wouldn't an organism capable of that kind of cognitive complexity also be capable of learning to communicate in an articulate way with us?

If animals can't really represent their own lives to themselves in the sophisticated way we can, one could argue that it really can't plausibly be claimed to *matter* to the animal whether it lives or dies. It will, indeed, take action to ward off danger—but then, so do ants and flies, which even Regan doesn't think have any rights. If having genuine, rich emotional and cognitive *lives* is morally important, then animals just don't qualify. So why, even if we sympathize with animals, should we be overly concerned about killing them?

So far as I can see, then, common-sense views about animals don't accord with Regan's on the major points. There remain questions about cruel treatment, and Regan is on solider ground here, for most people, I believe, do think that outright cruelty to animals is morally objectionable—though they don't think that even such treatment is wrong provided it is necessary for a good purpose, as is claimed, at least, in the case of laboratory research into certain diseases. The basis for the objection to cruel treatment is surely sympathy, just as it is for our dealings with infant humans. But that interest, which in any case is surely not universal, doesn't take us far. For there is no obvious general public interest that supports the extension of general rights to animals.

As always, there is the question of how we are to support claims in this field. Regan thinks he can draw on our "moral intuition," and I have suggested that if we try doing that, we won't clearly get his results. But I also hold that we should not do this by way of seeking solid support for our views, for intuitions are unreliable. Rather, we should think of our intuitions as themselves just more or less indicative hunches or guesses at principles that can and must, in the end, be supported independently. Regan thinks that we can come up with only one reasonable conclusion if we try to be consistent with our main intuitions. I don't think so, and in any case it wouldn't be his principle. It would instead be our familiar view, allowing people to use animals for any normal human purpose and only objecting to very cruel ways of so using them.

The basic point is that we have principles for dealing *with each other* that have implications about the cases of animals. Given that we both can't and also don't need to make a general "contract" with the animals, the right conclusions about people's relations to animals must be subordinate to our firmly grounded conclusions about how to treat *each other*: we should let each *person* do pretty much as he or she wants. If some wish to hunt, they may; if others don't like hunting, they needn't, and can also protest—but they can't intervene to prevent others of different mind from hunting. They also have the option of buying the animals the hunters wish to hunt, or the land on which they would hunt them, declaring those lands off limits to hunters. The same with furs: if some people like to wear furs and others are willing to grow or kill animals to provide them with furs, then the people who don't like this can protest. But they have no business ganging up on them with legislation and the like: that's not fair, any more than it's fair for Catholics to gang up on everyone else and declare a state church. It begs the question to assume that animals are in the same moral class as you and I, and wrong to assume that people who like hamburgers are morally inferior to people who don't. Manifestly, animals are *not* in the same moral class as we, in the obvious respects that count for the generation of publicly compelling moral principles.

Utilitarianism

Another note might be helpful to readers of articles on this matter.[3] Some philosophers profess (as I once did[4]) to accept the utilitarian view of morals. According to this view, every organism that has interests, and especially that is capable of pleasure and pain, automatically counts morally. We are supposed to aim to "maximize" the overall positive utility of all creatures, great and small. If animals can benefit from certain of my actions and be harmed by others, then I should, other things being equal, perform the first sort and avoid the second.

Even if we were to accept utilitarianism, as I no longer do, what about this "other things being equal" clause? Suppose that I like to *eat* certain animals. Do I then get to count my pleasure in eating the animal against its pain in being killed? Utilitarianism seems to have to say that I do. We may not kill and eat people, says the utilitarian, because what they lose from doing so greatly exceeds what we gain. But with animals it may well be the other way around: what the animal loses is relatively modest, what we gain considerable.

And there's another point. Does the utilitarian say that we can produce more utility by producing more creatures to experience it? Do twice as many people, other things equal, constitute twice as good a thing, morally speaking? On one understanding of utilitarianism, at any rate, this is exactly what we should say.[5] But if so, another interesting consideration arises regarding animals. Consider domesticated animals, such as cows and chickens. We like to eat them, so we grow them intentionally—and take good care of them before they're killed. In consequence, there are far more of these creatures, due directly to our habit of eating them, than there would be if we didn't like to eat them. Left in the wilds the cow would not thrive, but in our farmyards they prosper and multiply. Does this justify our killing of them? The utilitarian of this type can say yes.

I don't accept utilitarianism any more, but it's important to appreciate that even if we grant some moral standing to animals, it needn't follow that we should all be vegetarians, avoid wearing furs, and refrain from using animals for research or experimentation. The more radical point of view of this book, however, proposes that there is no case for basic moral standing for animals and that our dealings with them should be guided entirely by considerations of our own interests. Among those interests, to be sure, are sympathy and an interest in pets, which we like to treat well. We may also admire the aesthetic variety and remarkable powers of so many animal species. These certainly constitute real sources of support for generally treating many kinds of animals with much more concern than inanimate objects—but not for giving them full-fledged rights.

Nutritional Considerations

Vegetarianism is increasingly popular these days, at least among University-educated and literarily informed people. Some of its support comes from what is claimed to be a moral aversion to eating, and thus killing, animals. That is the kind of case considered and rejected above. However, an independent source of support comes from nutrition. It is claimed that a diet reliant on meat from animals is worse for us than a carefully assembled vegetarian diet. Some may even claim that the latter is aesthetically superior.

Both of those kinds of evaluation, however, need to be carefully distinguished from moral evaluation. Even if the nutritional or aesthetic arguments were correct, would this show that we have the right to prevent the heretical who continue to relish and flourish on a diet of animal flesh from doing so? Certainly not, in the view here defended. And we should always be very careful about foisting our tastes in ways of life on others. Precisely that, so far as I can see, is what would be done by a vegetarian who agitates for legislation to deprive others of the right to pursue their favoured ways of life.

A different argument appeals to a claim that raising animals for human diets is inefficient, in that it takes much more land to grow food for animals who are then eaten by people than to grow grains for people straight off. But this influential argument is heavily involved in matters of fact, and its involvements are largely wrong, as it turns out. First, there isn't any problem about feeding the world's population with the diet it wants, as we will be detailing further in the chapter on the environment. And second, the alleged inefficiency involves a mistake. The kind of grains you can feed to animals can be grown on soils that won't support rice, wheat, or vegetables. So the choice isn't between supporting ten people per acre on beef and supporting fifty people on wheat: it's between supporting ten people per acre on beef or supporting no people per acre on anything that can be grown there. (This is reflected in the relative prices of the various grains in question. No farmer who could grow people-crops would grow animal-crops on the same soil; he maximizes his profits by raising whatever will grow best there, given prevailing prices.)[6]

Summing Up

I have argued that animals have no basic rights. We do not need to extend that status to them, both because we could not make a mutually beneficial "agreement" with them even if we wanted to, and because we have no reason to do so. The ancient and common-sense view that we may make such use of animals as suits *us* is the right one. But what does suit us? Perhaps they have more to offer than we may have thought, and on that account we should not be wanton with them. Typical animals do nothing to harm us, and are often interesting, not only to the scientist but to the normally curious. This gives almost all of us sufficient reason not to treat animals with wanton cruelty. But that is all.

Chapter Seven

Feeding the Hungry

Throughout history it has been the lot of most people to know that there are others worse off than they, and often enough of others who face starvation. In the contemporary world, television and other mass media enable all of us in the better-off areas to hear about starvation in even the most remote places. What, if any, are our obligations toward the victims of such a terrible situation?

This can be a rather complex subject, for different cases differ significantly. We must begin, then, by distinguishing the main ones. First, we should note that the word 'starve' functions both as a passive verb, indicating something that happens to one, and as an active verb, designating something inflicted by one person on another. In the latter case, starvation is a form of killing and comes under the same strictures that any other method of killing is liable to. But when the problem is plague, crop failure due to drought, or sheer lack of know-how, there is no obviously guilty party. Then the question is whether *we*, the amply fed, are guilty parties if we *fail to come to the rescue* of those unfortunate people.

Starvation and Murder

If I lock you in a room with no food and don't let you out, I have murdered you. If group A burns the crops of group B, it has slaughtered the Bs. There is no genuine issue about such cases. It is wrong to kill innocent people, and one way of killing them is as eligible for condemnation as any other. Such cases are happily unusual, and we need say no more about them here other than to note, as I will, that the most substantial recent cases could readily be regarded as cases of something amounting to murder, rather than the other kind.

Our interest, then, is in the cases where murder is not the relevant category, or at least not obviously so. But some writers, such as James Rachels,[1] hold that letting someone die is *morally equivalent* to killing them or, at least, "basically" equivalent. Is this so? Most people do not think so; it takes a subtle philosophical argument to persuade them of this. The difference between a bad thing that I intentionally or at least forseeably brought about and one that just happened, through no fault of my own, matters to most of us in practice. Is our view sustainable in principle, too? Suppose the case is one I could do something about, as when you are starving and my granary is burgeoning. Does that make a difference?

Duties of Justice and Duties of Charity

Another important question, which has cropped up in some of our discussions but is nowhere more clearly relevant than here, is the distinction between *justice* and *charity*. By justice I here intend those things that we may, if need be, be forced to do—where our actions can be constrained by others to ensure our performance. Charity, on the other hand, "comes from the heart": 'charity' means, roughly, caring, an emotionally tinged desire to benefit other people just because they need it.

We should note a special point about this. It is often said that charity "cannot be compelled." Is this true? In one clear sense, it is, for in this sense charity consists *only* of benefits motivated by love or concern. If instead you regard an act as one that we may forcibly compel people to do, then you are taking that act to be a case of *justice*. Can it at the same time be charity? It can if we detach the motive from the act and define charity simply as doing good for others. But the claim that charity in this second sense cannot be compelled is definitely *not* true by definition—and is in fact false. People are frequently compelled to do good for others, especially by our governments, which tax us in order to benefit the poor, educate the uneducated, and so on. Whether they *should* be thus compelled is a genuine moral question, however, and must not be evaded by recourse to semantics. (Whether those programs produce benefits that outweigh their costs is a very complex question; but that they do often produce *some* benefits, at whatever cost, is scarcely deniable.)

On which side of the moral divide, then, shall we place feeding the hungry? Is it to be regarded as unenforceable charity, to be left to individual consciences, or enforceable justice, perhaps to be handled by governments? Here, we are asking whether feeding the hungry is not only something we ought to do but also something we *must* do, as a matter of justice. It is especially this latter that concerns us in the present chapter. A great deal turns on it.

We should note, also, the logical possibility that someone might differ so strongly with most of us on this matter as to think it positively *wrong* to feed the hungry. That is an extreme view, but it looks rather like the view that some writers, such as Garrett Hardin,[2] defend. However, it is misleading to characterize their view in this way. Hardin, for example, thinks that feeding the hungry is an exercise in *misguided* charity, not real charity. In feeding the hungry today, he argues, we merely create a much greater problem tomorrow, for feeding the relatively few now will create an unmanageably large number next time their crops fail, a number we won't be able to feed and who will consequently starve. Thus we actually cause more starvation by feeding people now than we do by not feeding them, hard though that may sound. Hardin, then, is not favouring cruelty towards the weak. The truly charitable, he believes, should be *against* feeding the hungry, at least in some cases.

Hardin's argument brings up the need for another distinction of urgent importance: between *principles* and *policies*. Being in favour of feeding the hungry *in principle* may or may not imply that we should feed the particular persons involved in this or that particular case, for that may depend on further facts about those cases. For example, perhaps trying to feed *these* hungry people runs into the problem that the government of those hungry people doesn't want *you* feeding them. If the price of feeding them is that you must go to war, then it may not be the best thing to do. If enormous starvation faces a group in the further future if the starving among them are fed now, then a policy of feeding them now may not be recommended by a principle of humanity. And so on. Principles are relatively abstract and may be considered just by considering possibilities; but when it comes to policy pursued in the real world, facts cannot be ignored.

Our general question is what sort of moral concerns we have with the starving. The question breaks down into two. First, is there a *basic duty of justice* to feed the starving? And second, if there isn't, then is there a basic requirement of *charity* that we be disposed to do so, and if so, how strong is that requirement?

Justice and Starvation

Let's begin with the first. Is it *unjust* to let others starve to death? We must distinguish two very different ways in which someone might try to argue for this. First, there are those who, like Rachels, argue that there is no fundamental distinction between killing and letting die. If that is right, then the duty not to kill is all we need to support the conclusion that there is a duty of justice not to let people starve, and the duty not to kill (innocent) people is uncontroversial. Second, however, some insist that feeding the hungry is a duty of justice even if we don't accept the equivalence of killing and letting-die. They therefore need a different argument, in support of a positive right to be fed. The two different views call for very different discussions.

Starving and Allowing to Starve

Starving and allowing to starve are special cases of killing and letting die. Are they the same, as some insist? In our discussion of euthanasia, we saw the need for a crucial distinction here: between the view that they are literally indistinguishable and the view that even though they are logically distinguishable, they are nevertheless *morally* equivalent.

As to the first, the argument for non-identity of the two is straightforward. When you kill someone, you do an act, x, which brings it about that the person is dead *when he would otherwise still be alive.* You induce a *change* (for the worse) in his condition. But when you let someone die, this is not so, for she would have died even if you had, say, been in Australia at the time. How can *you* be said to be the "cause" of something that would have happened if you didn't exist?

To be sure, we do often attribute causality to human inaction. But the clear cases of such attribution are those where the agent in question had an antecedent *responsibility* to do the thing in question. The geraniums may die because you fail to water them, but to say that you thus *caused* them to die is to imply that you were *supposed* to water them. Of course, we may agree that if we have a duty to feed the poor and we don't feed them, then we are at fault. But the question before us is *whether* we have this duty, and the argument we are examining purports to prove this by showing that even when we do nothing, we still "cause" their deaths. If the argument presupposes that very responsibility, it plainly begs the question rather than giving us a good answer to it.

What about the claim that killing and letting die are morally equivalent? Here again, there is a danger of begging the question. *If* we have a duty to feed the hungry and we don't, then not doing so might be morally equivalent to killing them, perhaps—though I doubt that any proponents would seriously propose life imprisonment for failing to contribute to the cause of feeding the hungry! But again, the consequence clearly doesn't follow if we don't have that duty, which is in question. Those who think we do not have fundamental duties to take care of each other, but only duties to refrain from killing and the like, will deny that they are morally equivalent.

The liberty proponent will thus insist that when Beethoven wrote symphonies instead of using his talents to grow food for the starving, like the peasants he depicted in his Pastorale symphony, he was doing what he had a perfect right to do. A connoisseur of music might go further and hold that he was also doing *the right thing*: that someone with the talents of a Beethoven does more for people by composing great music than by trying to save lives, even if he would have been *successful* in saving those lives—which is not very likely anyway.

How do we settle this issue? If we were all connoisseurs, it would be easy: if you know and love great music, you will find it easy to believe that a symphony by Beethoven or Mahler is worth more than prolonging the lives of a few hundred starvelings for another few miserable years. If you are one of those starving persons, your view might well be different. (But it might not. Consider the starving artist in his garret, famed in romantic novels and operas: they lived voluntarily in squalor, believing that what they were doing was worth the sacrifice.)

We are not all connoisseurs, nor are most of us starving. Advocates of welfare duties talk glibly as though there were a single point of view ("welfare") that dominates everything else. But it's not true. There are all kinds of points of view, diverse and to a large extent incommensurable. Uniting them is not as simple as the welfarist or utilitarian may think. It is *not* certain, not obvious, that we "add more to the sum of human happiness" by supporting the opera than by supporting OXFAM.[3] How are we to unite diverse people on these evaluative matters? The most plausible answer, I think, is the point of view that allows different people to live their various lives by forbidding interference with the lives of others. Rather than insisting, with threats to back it up, that I *help* someone for whose projects and purposes I have no sympathy whatever, let us all agree to *respect* each other's pursuits. We'll agree to let each person live as that person sees fit, with only our bumpings into each other being subject to public control. To do this, we need to draw a sort of line around each person and insist that others not cross that line without the permission of the occupant. The rule will be not to intervene forcibly in the lives of others, thus requiring that our relations be mutually agreeable. Enforced feeding of the starving, however, does cross the line, invading the farmer or the merchant, forcing him to part with some of his hard-earned produce and give it without compensation to others. That, says the advocate of liberty, is theft, not charity.

So if someone is starving, we may pity him or we may be indifferent, but the question so far as our *obligations* are concerned is this: how did he *get* that way? If it was not the result of my previous activities, then I have no obligation to him and may help him out or not, as I choose. If it was a result of my own doing, then of course I must do something. If you live and have long lived downstream from me, and I decide to dam up the river and divert the water elsewhere, then I have deprived you of your water and must compensate you, by supplying you with the equivalent, or else desist. But if you live in the middle of a parched desert and it does not rain, so that you are faced with death from thirst, that is not my doing and I have no compensating to do.

This liberty-respecting idea avoids, by and large, the need to make the sort of utility comparisons essential to the utility or welfare view. If we have no general obligation to manufacture as much utility for others as possible, then we don't have to concern ourselves about measuring that utility. Being free to pursue our own projects, we will evaluate our results as best we may, each in our own way. There is no need to keep a constant check on others to see whether we ought to be doing more for them and less for ourselves.

The Ethics of the Hair Shirt

In stark contrast to the liberty-respecting view stands the idea that we are to count the satisfactions of others as equal in value to our own. If I can create a little more pleasure for some stranger by spending my dollar on him than I would create for myself by spending it on an ice cream cone, I then have a putative *obligation* to spend it on him. Thus I am to defer continually to others in the organization of my activities and shall be assailed by guilt whenever I am not bending my energies to the relief of those allegedly less fortunate than I. "Benefit others, at the expense of yourself—and keep doing it until you are as poor and miserable as those whose poverty and misery you are supposed to be relieving!"[4] That is the ethics of the hair shirt.

How should we react to this idea? Negatively, I suggest. Doesn't that view really make us the slaves of the (supposedly) less well off? Surely a rule of conduct that permits people to be themselves and to try to live the best and most interesting lives they can is better than one that makes us all, in effect, functionaries in a welfare state? The rule that *neither* the rich *nor* the poor ought to be enslaved by the others is surely the better rule.

Some, of course, think that the poor *are*, inherently, the "slaves" of the rich, and the rich inherently the masters of the poor. Such is the Marxist view, for instance. It's an important argument, and very influential. It is also wrong. In the first place, its account of "masterhood" is not what we usually have in mind by that notion: the wealthy do *not* have the right to hold a gun to the heads of the non-wealthy and tell them what to do. Legally and morally, both are held to the same strict requirement, to refrain from inflicting evils on anyone, rich or poor. And second, the idea that the rich and the poor are somehow at loggerheads with each other is, so far as "capitalist" economies are concerned, precisely the opposite of the truth, for insofar as wealth is made in free economies, there is only one way to make it: by selling things to other people that those others *voluntarily* purchase. This means that the purchaser, in his view, is made better off *as well as* the seller by the transaction. Of course, the employees of the owners of businesses also become better off, via their wages. The results of this activity are that there are *more* goods in the world than there would otherwise be and that all concerned are better off.

This is precisely the opposite of the way the thief makes his money. The thief expends time and energy depriving others, involuntarily, of what they worked to produce, rather than devoting his energies to new productive activities. The thief, therefore, leaves the world poorer than it was before he set out on his exploitative ways.

Marxists assimilate the honest accumulator to the thief. Rather than being, as so many seem to think, a profound contribution to social theory, that is a ground-floor conceptual error, a failure to appreciate that wealth comes about precisely because of the prohibition of theft, rather than by its wholesale exercise.

Of course this Marxist, view also encourages the "poor" to rise up and revolt and "socialize the means of production," with consequences familiar to the world. In socialist countries, almost everyone is worse off than almost everyone in "capitalist" ones: Russian, Chinese, and Cuban poor are poorer than their North American counterparts, and middle-class Russians *far* poorer. If we are impressed by that result—as it seems to me we should be—then we will consider the Marxist program an effort at wholesale theft, with the expected results that theft always has: making people poorer, not richer.

Poverty and War

It is hardly surprising if people who feel they are up against the wall—and who might well be right in assessing their situation in just that way—should be tempted to resort to violence in their efforts to stay alive. If they have been persuaded of a claim that they have a *right* against the more fortunate that the latter share the wealth with them, that will give the violence in question an ideological support that is likely to make the results more intransigent and more disruptive. And one natural reaction on the part of middle-class and, perhaps especially, wealthier people is to adopt the attitude that we do indeed have a fundamental duty to help feed the starving, undercutting the reasons for "class war" or theft. It is difficult to say whether this reaction does more harm than good. In one way, surely, it's the former: for this reasoning really does involve an assumption that might makes right after all, and that is a view that undoes the good we can all hope for from morals.

Mutual Aid

The anti-welfarist idea, however, can be taken too far. Should people be disposed to assist each other in time of need? Certainly they should. But the appropriate rule for this is not that each person is duty-bound to minister to the poor until he himself is a pauper or near-pauper as well. Rather, the appropriate rule is what the characterization "in time of need" more nearly suggests. There are indeed emergencies in life when a modest effort by someone will do a great deal for someone else. People who aren't ready to help others when it is comparatively easy to do so are people who deserve to be avoided when they themselves turn to others in time of need.

But this all assumes that these occasions are, in the first place, relatively unusual, and in the second, that the help offered is genuinely of modest cost to the provider. If a stranger on the street asks for directions, a trifling expenditure of time and effort saves him great frustration and perhaps also makes for a pleasant encounter with another human (which that other human should try to make so, for example, by being polite and saying "thanks!"). But if as I walk down the street I am accosted on all sides by similar requests, then I shall never get my day's work done if I can't just say, "Sorry, I've got to be going!" or merely ignore them and walk right on. If instead I must minister to each, then soon there will be nothing to give, since its existence depends entirely on the activities of people who produce it. If the stranger asks me to drive him around town all day looking for a long-lost friend, then that's going too far, though of course, I should be free to help him out even to that extent if I am so inclined.

What about parting with the means for making your sweet little daughter's birthday party a memorable one in order to keep a dozen strangers alive on the other side of the world? Is this something you are morally required to do? It is not. She may well *matter* to you more than they— and well she should. This illustrates again the point that people do *not* "count equally" for most of us. Normal people care more about some people than others, and build their very lives around those carings. It is both absurd and arrogant for theorists, talking airily about the equality of all people, to insist on cramming it down our throats—which is how ordinary people do see it.

It is reasonable, then, to arrive at a general understanding that we shall be ready to help when help is urgent and when giving it is not very onerous to us. But a general understanding that we shall help everyone as if they were our spouses or dearest friends is quite another matter. Only a thinker whose heart has been replaced by a calculating machine could suppose that to be reasonable.

Note, too, that the duty to help is a "moral" one in a closely related but not identical sense of the word 'duty' to the one I have mainly been employing in this book. This is the sense in which morals have to do with what's in our souls rather than what others may enforce by threats of punishment and the like. To feel sympathy for the unfortunate is, we may well think, to be human—even though we realize that apparently some humans manage not to feel so. We have ideals of humanity, and this sense of commiseration and fellow-feeling is prominent on most of our depictions of this ideal. I share this ideal, while realizing that it is far from the only ideal that people might reasonably espouse. And it is precisely that realization that forces us to the conclusion that the duty to relieve others in distress cannot reasonably be classed as one to be enforced with threats of jail terms and the like, that is, by taxation. It is, instead, enforced by the expressed support of one's fellow sympathizers and by our spiritual mettle.

Charity

One of the good things we can do in life is to make an effort to care about people whom we don't ordinarily care or think about. This can benefit not only the intended beneficiaries in distant places, but it can also benefit you, by broadening your perspective. There is a place for the enlargement of human sympathies. But then, these are *sympathies*, matters of the heart; and for such matters, family, friends, colleagues, and co-workers are rightly first on your agenda. Why so? First, just because you are you and not somebody else— not, for example, a godlike "impartial observer." But there is another reason of interest, even if you think there is something right about the utilitarian view. This is what amounts to a consideration of *efficiency*. We know ourselves and our loved ones; we do not, by definition, know strangers. We can choose a gift for people we know and love, but are we wise to try to benefit someone of alien culture and diet? If we do a good thing for someone we know well, we make an investment that will be returned as the years go by; but we have little idea of the pay-off from charity for the unknown. Of course, that can be overcome, once in awhile—you might end up pen pals with a peasant in Guatemala. But it would not be wise to count on it.

The tendency and desire to do good for others is a virtue. Moreover, it is a *moral* virtue, for we all have an interest in the general acquisition of this quality. Just as anyone can kill anyone else, so anyone can benefit anyone else; and so long as the cost to oneself of participating in the general scheme of helpfulness is low—

namely, decidedly less than the return—then it is likely to be worth it. But it is not reasonable to take the matter beyond that. In particular, it is not reasonable to become a busybody, or a fanatic like Dickens's character Mrs. Jellyby, who is so busy with her charitable work for the natives in darkest Africa that her own children run around in rags and become the terror of the neighbourhood. Nor is it reasonable to be so concerned for the welfare of distant persons that you resort to armed robbery in your efforts to help them out ("Stick 'em up! I'm collecting for OXFAM!").

Notes on the Real World

If we are persuaded by the above, then as decent human beings we will be concerned about starvation and inclined to do something to help out if we can. But taking this seriously, as a realistic program for action in the world we actually live in, raises two questions. First, what *is* the situation? Are there lots of people in danger of imminent demise from lack of food? And second, just what should *we* do about it if there are?

Regarding the first question, one notes that contemporary philosophers and many others talk as though the answer is obviously and overwhelmingly in the affirmative. They write as though people by the millions are starving daily. It is of interest to realize that they are, generally speaking, wrong, and in the special cases where there really is hunger at that level, its causes are such as to make a very great difference to our answer to the second question.

In fact, starvation in the contemporary world is *not at all* due to the world's population having "outrun its resources," as Garrett Hardin and so many others seem to think; nor is the world even remotely a "lifeboat," as implied by the title of a famous article on the subject.[5] On the contrary, we now know that the world can support an indefinite number of people, certainly vastly more than there are now. If people have more children, they can be fed, or at least there is no reason why they couldn't be, so far as the actual availability of resources is concerned; nor does anyone in the affluent part of the world need to give up eating meat or driving Porsches to enable them to do so. In 1970, harbingers of gloom and doom on these matters were reporting that by the 1990s there would be massive starvation in the world unless we got to work right away, clamping birth-control measures on the recalcitrant natives and enforcing vegetarianism on us affluent North Americans. But events have shown them to be totally wrong about all this. Now at the end of the twentieth century there are perhaps a half-billion more people than there were then, and rather than starving, they are not only eating, but eating better than ever before. All, that is, *except* for those being starved at gunpoint by their governments or by warring political factions. Meanwhile, Western nations piled up food surpluses and wondered what to do to keep their farmers from going broke for lack of demand for their burgeoning products.

In fact, *all* of the substantial starvation (as opposed to the occasional flood) in the middle to later parts of the twentieth century has been due to politics, not agriculture. In several African countries, in Nicaragua for awhile, in China until not long ago, in the Soviet Union for most of its unhappy career, the regimes in power, propelled by ideology or a desire for cheap votes, imposed artificially low food prices or artificially inefficient agricultural systems on their people, thus providing remarkably effective disincentives to their farmers to grow food. Not surprisingly, they responded by not growing it. The cure is to let the farmers farm in peace, and charge whatever they like for their produce; it is astonishing how rapidly they will then proceed to grow food to meet the demand. But the cure isn't to have Western countries send over boatloads of wheat. Even if the local government will let people have this bounty (they often don't—corrupt officials have been known to go out and privately resell the grain elsewhere instead of distributing it to their starving subjects), providing it indiscriminately hooks them on Western charity instead of enabling them to regain the self-sufficiency they enjoyed in earlier times, before modern Western benefits such as "democracy" enabled incompetent local governments to disrupt the food supply.[6]

We must also mention countries with governments that drive people forcibly off their land, burn their crops, or outrightly steal it from the peasantry, as in Ethiopia and Somalia in the early 1990s. Those countries combined such barbarities with the familiar tendency to prevent Western aid from getting to its intended recipients. Nature has nothing to do with starvation in such cases, and improvements in agriculture are not the cure. Improvements in politics are.

This means that the would-be charitable person faces a pretty difficult problem when he turns to the second question: What to do? In cases of natural disaster, as when a huge flood inundates the coast of Bangladesh, there will be short-term problems, and charitable agencies are excellent at responding quickly with needed food and medical supplies. Supporting some of those for dealing with such emergencies is likely a good idea. But in many other cases, there is very little that an outside agency can do. Tinpot dictators equipped with modern assault weapons and armoured cars are not exactly examples of sweet reason at work, and only governments normally have the kind of clout that can open doors, even a crack, to the sort of aid we might like to give their beleaguered peoples.

There are many organizations whose enthusiastic volunteers go to Third World communities to try to help them in various ways. Their efforts meet with variable success, especially because the fundamental question of what constitutes "help" is so hard to answer. Do we help a native tribe in Africa that has maintained its way of life for thousands of years when we get their children learning arithmetic and wearing jeans? Or do we only destroy what they have and replace it with something very difficult for them to cope with? As a case in point, a travel writer[7] describes how one community in Madagascar was given an efficient modern pump for its communal water supply, which provided plenty of clean water and relieved people of long trips to polluted wells. It stopped some years later, by which time the people who installed it had long since gone, and nobody knew how to repair it. Interestingly, they didn't seem terribly concerned about this turn of events and made no effort whatever to get someone to fix the pump, but simply went back to the old ways, uncomplainingly and inefficiently. Apparently *they* didn't realize how terribly "essential" this pump was. Do we really know better than they? Why are we so sure that we do?

Helping people who are *very* different from us is not an easy matter. Did all those missionaries who descended on the hapless Africans in the past centuries do them a lot of good by teaching them Christianity, or by bringing the infant mortality rate way down so that families accustomed to having a manageable number of children surviving to maturity suddenly found themselves with six or seven mouths to feed instead of two? Or by building a road to enable tourists to drive up to the village and give the natives all sorts of Western diseases their immune systems were totally unprepared for? There is surely a real question here for thoughtful people, however well-intentioned. Our efforts could well create disasters for the people we are trying to help, as well as impose pointless costs on ourselves.

The sober conclusion from all this is that, with the best will in the world, it might still be better to spend our money on the opera after all. We are unlikely to act well when we act in ignorance, and when we deal with people vastly differently from ourselves, ignorance is almost certain to afflict our efforts.

Summing Up

The basic question of this chapter is whether the hungry have a positive right to be fed. Of course, we have a right to feed them if we wish, and they have a negative right to be fed. But may we forcibly impose a duty on others to feed them? We may not. If the fact that others are starving is not our fault, then we do not need to provide for them as a duty of justice. To think otherwise is to suppose that we are, in effect, slaves to the badly off. And so we can in good conscience spend our money on the opera instead of on the poor. Even so, feeding the hungry and taking care of the miserable is a nice thing to do and is morally recommended. Charity is a virtue. Moreover, starvation turns out to be almost entirely a function of bad governments rather than of nature's inability to accommodate the burgeoning masses. Our charitable instincts can handle easily the problems that are due to natural disaster. We can feed the starving *and* go to the opera!

Chapter Eight

Abortion

The social problem of abortion is easily the most divisive issue of all those we discuss in this book—at least here in North America. It's interesting to speculate on why this might be so, but it is not our task to do that here in any detail. We should note, though, that this issue is perhaps more likely than any other to evoke intense feelings. This is understandable, for most of us who have children love those children and very much wanted the prenatal organisms from which they emerged to come to term and grow up into lovable children and good people. But it is a mistake to transfer our strong feelings about that into an area—*other* people's fetuses—that isn't ours. And, of course, it is wrong to base morals on emotions. What you or I may feel about this or that does not, in and of itself, stand as the basis of a rule for others, and that goes for this emotion-charged aspect of life as much as for any other. We must do better than that.

We can hope that some of the divisiveness will turn out to be due to misunderstanding of a kind that can be cleared up. Undoubtedly, for example, many people have religious views about abortion. Those people must take seriously the points made about religious ethics earlier on. If only an irrational or vindictive or sadistic "god" would favour a given view, that is surely a reason for abandoning the supposed god in question rather than taking that view to be the truth. Instead of speculating further about motives for disagreement, let us look at the arguments and construct the best position we can. Perhaps we can hope for agreement by all who look at the matter carefully.

The Issue: Is Abortion Permissible?

As usual, it will be well to begin by reminding ourselves, as precisely as possible, of the issue. It is, in brief, whether people who want abortions are to be *allowed* to have them—whether, in short, abortion is *morally permissible*. There are two logically possible alternatives to saying that it should be. One would be that abortion is morally *required*. That option, of course, may be dismissed out of hand: no one thinks abortion is generally obligatory—only a fanatical misanthrope could hold that. The other is that abortion is morally *impermissible*, that is, forbidden or wrong. That quite definitely is an option that many people favour. We must choose between abortion's being generally allowable and its being generally not allowable. We will be examining arguments supporting one or the other of those two possibilities.

We will not be discussing personal issues: whether any particular person should have an abortion in one or another set of circumstances. Of course if the restrictive view is right, then all such people would have to be given the same advice: no. But if the liberal side is chosen, then each pregnant woman who considers abortion will have to decide what she shall do. The answer will depend on her knowing what she wants and what her capabilities and circumstances allow— things that writers of philosophy books certainly cannot know.

When the question is whether people are to be allowed to do something that they very much want to do, then the onus is on those who propose to forbid them: they must justify the forbidding. On the other hand, one does not need, in general, to make a positive case for allowing people to do what they want. Consequently, we need only to examine proposed cases *against* and see whether they establish some solid reason why people should not be allowed to do this.

Whose issue is this? Like all moral issues, it is *everyone's*. The people whose specific actions would be forbidden by a restrictive abortion principle are mostly doctors who are able to perform abortions, of course. However, it is pregnant women who will be forbidden to seek their services and punished if they avail themselves of those services; in that sense, abortion is uniquely a woman's issue. But it is an issue for all of us whether we will try to prevent or interfere with women who seek and doctors who provide abortions, or vote for politicians who in turn would propose to impose such restrictions (or lift them if they exist). As with all moral issues, we address everyone here.

Two Perspectives

We may distinguish between arguments against abortion by the criterion of whose interests the argument centrally turns on.

1. Most turn on claimed rights *of the fetus* itself.
2. Other arguments look to the interests or rights of some or all *other* people. For example, considerations of population control, which have induced some countries to switch from permissive to restrictive abortion laws, are sometimes appealed to.

Few writers have put much weight on arguments of type (2), and for good reason. For if we try to consider what interests others have in the matter, the answer is of the general sort that they are interested in the *existence* of the persons whom the fetuses in question would become if abortion is not chosen. But that interest can be furthered by *any* procedure or policy that has the potential to increase or decrease the number of humans. The objection along these lines, if it worked at all, would apply to other things, such as contraception, as much as or even more than to abortion. In fact, abortion would then be objectionable only *as* a contraceptive: the objection to it would be that it reduces the number of people. But both contraception and simple abstinence have that effect and account for far more cases of unproduced children than abortion. Such arguments, then, are extremely weak as they bear on abortion.

Abortion and Murder: The Argument

The argument for the wrongness of abortion on grounds of what happens to the fetus—that its life is terminated—in general goes like this:

1. Murder is wrong.
2. Abortion is murder.
3. Therefore, abortion is wrong.

This argument is clearly valid—its conclusion follows logically from its premises. The question is whether it is *sound*—are its premises true?

Regarding premise (1), one must note that it is sententious as it stands. Indeed, it can be viewed as trivially true without semantic violence: *murder* could reasonably be defined as *wrongful killing*. But the statement that *wrongful killing is wrong* is not very helpful! What we want to know is, which killings *are* wrong, and why.

What we need, then, is some such premise as

1(a) *Killing* is wrong.

But this premise is regarded by most people as obviously false, in view of our lack of scruple about eating animals. At the least, it's too sweeping. Killing *what* is wrong, and when? Needing an answer to this, we might at first propose this as our principle:

1(b): Killing *people* is wrong.

That would be closer, at least—though, as we have seen, there are those who think that killing animals is wrong as well, and possibly for the same reason that killing people is. But few who oppose abortion would want to accept that. We will assume, for the sake of argument, that the usual view about animals is justified: people may kill them for many purposes that would not justify them in killing people, such as to eat them or use their hides to make shoes. However, there are still problems, for most people would agree that 1(b) is also inadequate, since they would accept the rightness, in some cases at least, of some acts of killing people: killing in self-defence, perhaps capital punishment, suicide, and euthanasia. It would be better still to say some such thing as

1(c): Killing *innocent* people is wrong.

Even this, however, will not quite do. Euthanasia requesters are innocent, but they want only to die. I have argued that euthanasia can be and sometimes is right. So the principle must be modified once more:

1(d): Killing innocent people *who do not want to die* is wrong.

Plainly this is getting a lot closer. Even so, it would be difficult to refine 1(d) to the point where we would have arrived at a generalization with no important exceptions; indeed, most moral philosophers are inclined to think that such an "absolute" generalization is impossible. Luckily, however, it doesn't matter for the abortion issue, for we can now easily enough see why many people would deny that our original argument is sound. They would claim that the *second* premise, namely that abortion is murder, is false. Here are three ways in which they might deny this. First, it might be denied that fetuses are, in the relevant sense, *innocent*. Second, it might be denied that abortion is, in the relevant sense, *killing*. Third, we could deny that fetuses are, in the relevant sense, *people*. Each deserves some discussion.

Are Fetuses Innocent Victims?

Those who make the first criticism, concerning the "innocence" of the fetus, argue as follows. A pregnant woman supplies essentials to the fetus for nine months. People cannot be obliged to do this for just anybody—only for special, invited guests. But suppose that a starving person comes to your door and insists on your feeding him for nine months: do you have the duty to let him in and start feeding him? No. Even if he will die of exposure and want if you don't take him in, you still don't have to. It would be nice of you, to be sure, but it is, after all, your house (and your life). So if you show him the door, then it's not really a matter of killing an innocent victim, according to this argument, but of denying services, however essential, to an unwanted stranger.

In reply to this, it could be pointed out that in most cases, the fetus does not simply come to its mother's door from out of the blue, as it were, for the mother was normally responsible for its being there. If the act of sexual intercourse that led to conception was involuntary, as when it is caused by rape, then there would be a clear case of this type. But in cases where conception was voluntary the argument is surely weaker. After all, pregnant women normally knew what they were getting into when they engaged in acts likely to result in pregnancy.

In some cases, conception is due to technical problems in the preventive devices used. Such cases present special problems. A defective contraceptive device producing unwanted pregnancies would be analogous to the case of a neighbourhood that is positively teeming with beggars who will show up at table the moment you leave one door unlocked even for a moment. Would it be right to hold the house owner responsible for their care for the next many months? Or may the owner summarily eject them? The latter certainly sounds plausible.

Of course, it may be questioned whether the comparison is fair. Sperm and eggs are not exactly beggars, for they are entirely devoid of responsibility for their actions. Only the adults whose act brings them together can be held responsible for anything here, and the trouble is that in these cases, they took precautions but the precautions failed.

Whatever we say about that, it would surely be much more difficult to make a strong argument for abortion along these lines if it is agreed that fetuses do indeed have the same right to life that is generally attributed to normal adults. I don't normally have the right to kick you out in the cold, to starve or freeze, just because my invitation to come and visit got into the mail by accident. On the other hand, neither do I have the duty to put you up for nine months, no questions asked.

Pressing this kind of analogy very hard shows us that it is problematic at crucial points. The analogy implies that fetuses get their rights exclusively by virtue of the invitation of their parents. Almost all opponents of abortion will deny that, and thus little progress in the debate is made by invoking the analogy.

A closer look, then, suggests that the basic issue remains this: do prenatal human organisms have rights independent from what parents may, of their own free wills, extend to them? Specifically, do they have strong negative rights to life, as such? That can't be settled by invoking the analogy between fetuses and rational adults, for we can only invoke that if we already know the answer. Accordingly, discussion of this fundamental issue will occupy the main part of this chapter.

Killing, Letting Die, or Separation?

But first we must turn to the second criticism of the argument. Do we, in having an abortion, strictly speaking *kill* the fetus? Or should abortions be regarded, instead, as cases of allowing to die?

The argument that they are not outright killings appeals to the fact that the immediate point of an abortion is to *detach* the embryo from its life-support system. This usually results in death, to be sure, because an embryo cannot care for itself; still, that is a further fact, lying beyond the bounds of the abortion itself. The point is that it need not be the purpose of the abortion operation to kill the embryo. In fact, it is now technically possible, with very early abortions, to transfer the organism in question to a test-tube environment and/or to another womb. Clearly, if the supposed victim can survive the operation, it is not murder. And the new technical possibility creates a third category besides killing and letting die: separating and letting live, by transferring the fetus from one environment (its mother's womb) to another (a test-tube or even, perhaps, a different woman's womb).

Thus there are two distinct issues, in principle:

1. Do we have the right to *terminate pregnancies* before birth?
2. Do we have the right to *kill fetuses*?[1]

These could have different answers. If the objection to abortion is that it's killing, then, at least in principle, a procedure by which

fetuses are detached without being directly killed might be regarded as morally no more objectionable than allowing distant victims
of starvation to die. And a procedure in which the embryo is safely
transplanted elsewhere should be entirely acceptable, since in that
case the fetus doesn't die at all.

We should appreciate that making this distinction does not
automatically preclude affirmative answers to *both* questions. In fact,
any combination is logically available—someone could conceivably
object to transplantation without objecting to killing or, though this
is most unlikely, to transplantation but not to killing; and in any
case, issues about that would lie outside the abortion issue. However, we should also appreciate the force of an argument that can apply
in certain cases, notably of pregnancies due to rape or deception. It
can be argued[2] that in such cases, a right merely to transfer the fetus
elsewhere isn't enough, for a woman might insist that there *not be* a
child who originates in the way that this particular fetus would have.
A woman who has been raped may insist that she has the right not
to be forced to become the mother to any child resulting from the
violent or deceptive act of the man who raped her and who would
be its father if no abortion fatal to that fetus takes place. For she
hates him—as well she might—and is utterly aghast at the prospect
of spending her life with the constant reminder that someone out
there exists only because of what that man did. Does she have this
right? Of course, it isn't the fault of the fetus or the child in question
that its father was who he was and became its father in the way he
did. But that's no consolation to the prospective mother.

Again we can see that discussions of this kind presuppose that
fetuses have some kind of rights, some special moral status that
must be respected, so that abortion would at least have to be justified by making fine distinctions or appealing to special considerations. If fetuses have no such rights, however, then such discussions
may be sidetracked. The woman in our preceding example, for
instance, need have no qualms whatever about seeking an abortion
if the fetus she is carrying has no moral status in its own right.

Letting Die and the Principle of Double Effect

In the preceding section, we pointed out that abortion is not necessarily killing and then mainly addressed the cases where the fetus
doesn't in fact die, owing to special medical technology. But we also
need to consider the much more frequent cases in which the fetus does

die. Even in those cases, it is not normally true that the physician performing the operation was intending to kill the fetus or that the pregnant mother was literally directing her physician to do so. Their intention is only to *terminate the pregnancy*; the death of the fetus is a
side-effect, not literally part of the aim in aborting. The question is: in
view of the fact that the death of the fetus is virtually certain and clearly foreseen, does that distinction *matter*? Or is it a distinction without
a difference, as one of my old professors used to say?

According to one tradition of moral philosophy, it does. That
tradition invokes a principle known as the "principle of double
effect." According to it, we are strictly forbidden ever to *intend* evil,
either as part of our aim or as part of the means by which we intend
to try to achieve that aim. Thus, killing someone out of sheer cruelty is forbidden, and so is killing someone in order to get someone
else out of a jam; but killing someone as the foreseeable but unwanted result of some other process, such as saving an innocent life, is
quite another matter. So long as that other process is legitimate in
itself, the principle of double effect says that the unintended "second
effect" may nevertheless render the act morally permissible, provided that two conditions are met: first, that the evil is unavoidable if
the good end is to be achieved, and second, that the evil is not so
great as to outweigh the good accomplished by the act. For example,
if a physician performs an operation to save the mother's life, and
this operation unfortunately results in the death of a fetus she is carrying, then it may still be allowable to perform the operation. This is
on the assumption that saving the mother's life is more important
than saving the fetus's life and that there is no way to save both.

I mention this principle here because it has been very widely
invoked, and has historically been very influential. Nevertheless, I
think it is too shaky to hang very much on. The main problem is
that the identification of agents' intentions can be very tricky. May
we go into depth psychology and say that whatever the agent *said*
he was trying to do, what he *really* meant to do was, say, to "strike
a blow at motherhood" or some such thing? And just how are we to
distinguish means from side-effects? Can that distinction really bear
much weight? Surely if I can foresee that my act is going to kill
some innocent people, then I am just as responsible for it as if I were
actually intending to do so, am I not? And finally: don't we always
prefer that our means not lead to any other effects than the intended ends? Can't we always claim that unfortunate effects are "secondary" ones rather than intended? Couldn't the robber who kills

his victim claim that he really just wanted the money, and its owner just happened—alas!—to be in the way? Mightn't *all* evil be unintended, at bottom?

We will not try to resolve that one here. Clearly, if the death of the fetus were not thought to be a great moral evil in the first place, then the whole doctrine would be unnecessary anyway so far as the abortion issue is concerned. That is the claim we will now explore.

Fetal Rights

Are fetuses among the things that have the right to life in the first place? That is, are they among the things that we are morally required to refrain from killing? Should the intentionally inflicted death of a fetus count as murder or not?

To appreciate the question, recall our working principle, that killing innocent people who do not want to die is wrong. Now we must ask what the basis of this principle is. Just what is it about those whom it is wrong to kill that *makes* it wrong to kill them? It's useless to reply, "They have the right to life," for that is what we are asking here—which entities *do* have such a right, and why? And that is a question which, I believe, cannot be answered convincingly without a good answer to the question, Why? *Why* think that things of that kind do have rights, in particular the right to life?

There are, I think, two basic possibilities to consider. I shall call them the "biological" and the "psychological" views. The first holds that what fundamentally has the right to life are biologically (genetically) human *organisms*, and they have this right just because they are such organisms. The psychological view, on the other hand, holds that what has this right are only organisms that have "souls", or "minds," and that they have that right only because of their having those souls or minds.

This second option is both obscure and perhaps ambiguous; but here are what we may think of as two more definite versions of it. One variant identifies mind with rationality: we have this right because, as Aristotle's classic definition of man has it, we are "rational animals." The other variant holds that rationality isn't exactly what does it. Rather, the basis of rights is due, somehow, to the fact that we are *psychologically* human: that we have what I will describe as articulable, complex, and value-permeated consciousness. Normal adults are my model for this. We'll consider each of these three (the biological and the two versions of the psychological) in turn.

Bodily Humanity

Is it by virtue of being merely biological humans that people have the right to life? It is worth pointing out that most people do not think so. Consider the famous case of Karen Ann Quinlan, whose body lived on years after her "soul" (in either of the senses distinguished) had, so far as we know, completely ceased to be: she became brain-dead as the result of an accident. Thereafter she was, as nearly literally as can be, a human vegetable: though definitely alive, she had no consciousness at all. Her body continued to function, though only because it was hooked to a life-support system. The question then arose whether to unhook her. Even many Catholics, including her own parents, thought it would be permissible to do so. Eventually this was done, and Karen's body did finally die. Most people seem to have approved.

Even those who didn't agree may have disagreed only because they thought that there was some chance that Karen Ann's psyche would, by some miracle, resume functioning after all. However, that possibility is beside the present point, for it does not support the biological answer to our question. Instead, it depends on the outside possibility that the psychological criterion would apply after all, despite all evidence. To keep the two distinct, therefore, we must suppose that there was absolutely no chance of this happening. Would those who disagreed *then* think there was any reason not to allow Karen's body to die? (It is not clear whether death is quite the appropriate concept to apply to a completely mindless but functioning body. When we eat vegetables, we don't think of them as "dying"! However, on the purely biological view we are considering, that is what we would have to say.)

On the Concept of the Soul

To say that because people have something called "souls" it is wrong to kill them may well be quite right, as we shall see. But since the idea of soul is hardly a clear one, everything depends on what we are to mean by it. In its most usual sense, I think, the word designates our *consciousness*, our experienced life. That is the sense I will employ, and it will be discussed shortly. But first we should dwell a little longer on the possibility that something else is meant. Considering this will help to fix our minds on the crucial issues here.

Imagine a view of soul according to which just *anything* might conceivably have one: your dinner fork, the tree in your front yard, even the rocks in the hills. But what could people who imagine such things be imagining, anyway? My guess is that they're really thinking that the fork, or the tree, or at least the rabbit, actually does have *experience*, somewhat as we do, if perhaps more inchoate. Comic-strip artists amuse us by their personifying of cats, dogs, and the occasional cactus. But it works by turning them into a very unusual sort of *human*, really—that is, by endowing them with personality and conscious experience, rather than just leaving them to be animals or plants.

What if we carefully detach any implication of consciousness from our use of the term "soul," so that it simply designates a metaphysical somewhat having *no* necessary connection with our actual, conscious life? Then, surely, possession of soul would become utterly irrelevant. If it is impossible to tell by any kind of observations whether a cactus has a soul or not, then the thought that a cactus might have one isn't going to make any difference to your behaviour. It won't keep you from carving up that cactus, if for some reason you want to do so. Someone who insisted that you not do so on the ground that you would be severing that cactus from its "soul" would have to be putting you on—or perhaps putting himself on. For this supposed idea of soul would be completely useless, and therefore meaningless. Needless to say, we cannot erect an important ethical principle on any such basis.

Rationality

Is what gives us rights, then, our rationality, our "faculty of reason"? This seems to go in the right general direction. Yet there is a question as to what that right direction is. To see this, we must make another distinction, between two aspects of rationality as we normally understand that idea. These are (1) information-processing, and (2) thought. At first glance, these may seem the same. But by thinking more closely about it, we can pry them apart.

Regarding the first, if rationality is only the ability to do calculations, make strictly deductive inferences, store bodies of data and search them effectively, etc., then these are all things computers can do. Yet the idea that computers have *personal lives* is surely silly. They are valuable objects, of course, and their *owners* have rights over them that the rest of us must respect. But to grant computers rights on their *own* account, because they too are "rational," is to suppose that computers *have* an "own"; and most of us find it impossible to believe that they do.

This brings us to the second option. People are plainly not just information-processors: they also *think*—a quite different matter. Thought, after all, involves consciousness, awareness: to think is to have thoughts occurring in one's mind, subjective representations of what's going on around us and of the relations among them. Thinking, to be sure, *involves* information-processing. But it goes beyond it in this vital respect: the thinker is a conscious, experiencing being, one who not only calculates but *knows that* he or she is doing so.

It is certainly plausible to suppose that thought is an "essential attribute" of people, to put it in philosophical jargon. What we mean is that part of what we are saying when we attribute personhood to people is that they can think. But is it *the whole* of it? Neither I nor you really think so. For thought is, one might say, intrinsically *bloodless*. We distinguish thought, strictly speaking, from feeling, having emotions, acting, intending and so on. Now, imagine a computer that could not only process information but genuinely think while it's at it—it would be aware of its various rational processes. But it wouldn't, let us suppose, *care* about what it was doing. Suppose it was completely indifferent to everything, didn't care what it thought about or why, or whether it continued to think tomorrow or simply expired. Such a computer would indeed be a remarkable thing—if, of course, one could really have any reason to think that it did actually think and not just undergo complicated electronic alterations. But would it have *rights*—personal rights against the rest of us, rights not to be mistreated or killed? I suggest that it would not, that on anything like our usual views about these matters, rationality in the restricted senses we have been considering really isn't sufficient for having rights—though I think, and I take it we all think, that rationality is clearly necessary. If we are right about this, then the Aristotelian view isn't adequate.

Personhood

We now come to the third view: that what matters is possession of "soul" in the familiar sense of having what I shall vaguely call a *developed phenomenal psychology*. I add the word 'phenomenal' for the important reason that plenty of organisms have a psychology in the contemporary sense of the word: they have behaviour patterns, and some of those patterns are pretty complex. But we humans have much more than just an "edge" on animals in the respects I'm here concerned with. People have highly articulated life experiences.

They remember their personal pasts right back to childhood; they have plans that they know about, think and worry about; they have elaborate, articulate, verbally mediated interactions with other people. It would be impossible and it is certainly not necessary to try to pin down precisely what is common to all of us that makes us people, except perhaps to note that among the most important common features of people is that they are so *different* from each other—we have individual personalities, a sense of ourselves as individuals, as distinctive lives. "Self-consciousness" is the appropriate term here. We are conscious of ourselves as distinct persons with lives of our own to live and impending deaths to face as best we can.

Of course, we are not conscious when we are asleep or stunned, and we suppose that we continue to have rights when in those conditions. Yet if we were *always* asleep, would we have any rights? Surely not: we would then be in Karen Quinlan's condition. However, the sleeping body you see before you is *mine*. Before going to sleep, I had extensive plans about what to do when I awake, and I'm not about to allow others to make incursions on my body while asleep. The owners of sleeping bodies are the active nonsleeping persons that precede and follow the sleeper, and in whose service the sleeping body sleeps. It is those owners who have rights—among them the right not to be killed or damaged while asleep.

Taking all this into account, I suggest that if we reflect on what sort of beings we think have rights, then there is our answer: individuals with complex personal consciousness. Most people do not think that animals, for instance, have rights, or at least not the crucial one here, the right to life—not seriously, and not on their own account (imagine that we had the right to life, *except* in case someone felt like eating us!). We distinguish strongly between animals and people, even though the former no doubt experience pleasure and pain. Why? Surely the distinction is of this type: human consciousness is complex, articulate, and spans a considerable reach of time from infancy to the present and, by imagination, well into the future, even into fantasy-land. Capturing the scope of human experience is a never-ending job, richly preoccupying the work of novelists, poets, biographers, historians, and many others. A very large gap separates the normal human from any other animal as well as from robots and computers, and it is this fact of complex experience that especially marks the difference. Attributions of "soul" specifically to people are really attributions of that feature.

Let us use the term 'person' here to designate entities that have personality in the aforementioned senses. They think in the subjective sense and do not just engage in information-processing; they can and often do articulate their experience, they identify other persons, converse with them, think back and forth along the tracks of their own histories, and have values—things they care about, plans, projects, and the rest of it. All of this is perfectly familiar to any adult, or any child beyond infancy. And it is what we especially think of as qualifying an individual for rights.

Are Fetuses Persons?

If this is the right story, then the question is whether fetuses are persons. And the answer is pretty easy and straightforward: it is obviously extremely implausible to suppose that they are—that prenatal human organisms literally have *personal* lives. Fetuses simply aren't the phenomenally self-conscious beings we are talking about. Not until they become infants will they have genuine experiences, become aware of themselves as individuals, develop an articulate grasp of their surroundings, or have anything quite as fancy as thoughts, plans, hopes, and interests. The "mental life" of a fetus is utterly on the biological level. In this respect, indeed, fetuses would seem to be well below the level of, say, cattle—whose meat most of us are quite ready to eat without a twinge of conscience.

Of course, it may be claimed that we are mistaken in our view of animals and that we should all become vegetarians. (Readers who started late should consult Chapter Six, on animal rights.) Here I have only tried to identify which sorts of features we think qualify an entity for rights, and not to develop a theory of *why* those are good reasons for attributing rights to the entities that happen to have them (namely, us). But the basic theory developed in previous chapters has a clear and significant implication for the question of abortion. The suggestion is that we extend rights to various organisms on the basis of our *interests*, mutually considered. We want rights for ourselves because rights are protections: rights, if recognized, get us or secure for us things that we decidedly want. For you to grant me a right is for you to agree to refrain from doing whatever this right is a right that you not do; your acceptance is sincere only if you do so refrain. And vice versa. In short: I grant you this right provided you grant it to me. Morality, according to this view, is a sort of "deal," a "social contract," an informal agreement among everybody that they will treat each other in various ways and not others. If there is no point in making such an agreement, then there would be no reason to accept the commitment it involves. In the case of animals, there is no point, because no need, to make such a deal. With people, there decidedly is. But where do fetuses fit in this scheme?

It is clear that the same is true of fetuses as of animals in one crucial respect: we cannot make deals with them since they lack the level of articulate consciousness necessary for doing anything that complicated.

The other crucial respect in the case of animals is that we do not need to make deals with them, because we have nothing to fear from them nothing to gain by attempting to make such arrangements that we can't get without them. In this respect, the situation between us and human fetuses is rather different. For given the biological facts, fetuses are essential if there are going to be future people at all, and we do have a great and general interest in the existence of people. Moreover, human parents-to-be usually have strong emotional interests in the particular fetus that the female of the pair is carrying. This is all perfectly natural and normal, and results in a remarkably reliable supply of future people.

However, we must take account of the fact that there are occasional cases in which the mother-to-be does *not* have that positive emotional interest in her fetus's becoming a child. Her interest in those cases is apparently quite the reverse—actually negative. Such women lack the typically positive emotional interest that normally provides one excellent reason for carrying a fetus to term. The question we must ask about the unusual cases, then, is whether there is any decent reason for *requiring* them to carry those fetuses to term against their desire and their perceived interest. And the reflections above suggest that the answer to this is normally in the negative. We do not have interests of a type sufficient to override the right to live our lives as we see fit, and in particular to use our personal selves for our own rather than other people's purposes. That is the general right that all of us do have very good reason to attribute to all of us. And that right calls upon us to allow people who are different from ourselves to *be* different, so long as they do not thereby endanger our own pursuits of our various lives.

Our Right to Our Bodies

A major part of this right focuses centrally on our relation to our own bodies. The general right to run our own lives implies, in this respect, specifically that other people may not use our bodies in ways contrary to what we want. And that right, on the face of it, conflicts with any proposed restriction on abortion, for the person who proposes to forbid abortion is in effect forcibly requiring women who do not want to continue their pregnancies to continue them nevertheless. Sometimes these women are pretty desperate. Back in the days when abortion was illegal, a great many women had "back-street" abortions, often with dire consequences for their health. There has to be a very strong reason to put people involuntarily into a situation where they would be driven to do things like that. A reason to the effect that fetuses had the right to life just like you and me would certainly be such a reason— if its premise were true. But it is not. Fetuses do not have intrinsically personal selves, as you and I do, and so, on the face of it, there is no such reason for granting them rights of the usual kind. Unless that conclusion is faulty, it becomes very difficult to see what else might justify us in so restricting this familiar, general, and extremely important right.

Is there, then, some reason to overturn that finding?

The Slippery Slope, Again

If fetuses do not qualify for rights on intrinsic grounds, there might still be other reasons to grant them rights. We will discuss some of those reasons later. However, there are two important arguments on the basis of which many people claim to believe that fetuses must nevertheless be granted the same status as adults anyway, despite the foregoing considerations: the argument from slippery slope and the argument from potentiality.

According to the slippery slope argument, we cannot draw the line between things that clearly do have rights (us) and things that, on the face of it, would not qualify (fetuses). It is important to understand that the slippery slope argument applies *only* against this background. If it is argued that fetuses have rights for some other reason, having nothing to do with personhood, then slippery slope is irrelevant. Here, however, we are interested in examining the argument itself, which has been extraordinarily influential. That makes it the more important to appreciate that it is frankly worthless. (Slippery slope arguments have been discussed already in Chapter Three, but some of the main points will be reviewed here, with specific attention to the context of the abortion issue.)

What is meant by the argument's premise that we "cannot draw the line" between non-right-holding fetuses and right-holding adults?

Here we should distinguish several importantly different claims:

1. It is impossible to demarcate the "above-the-lines" from the "below-the-lines" *at all*— there just isn't any such distinction.
2. It is impossible to draw a *precise* line between them.
3. It is impossible to draw a *non-arbitrary* line between them.

Which applies here? Plainly (1) does not, for a presupposition of this argument is that fetuses, *as they stand* (that is, given only the properties they have *while they are fetuses*), do not qualify for these rights. That was the point of the preceding analysis. Thus, we do have the demarcation that (1) denies: between a set of entities (including fetuses) that do not have inherent rights and another set of entities (including normal adults) that do have them. (The "properties" of fetuses considered here include, of course, only those exemplified or manifested during the fetal period. The capacity of fetuses to grow up and become non-fetuses is another matter, and will be considered next, when we discuss the potentiality argument.)

Nor does (2) hold. For we *could* draw as precise a line as you like: for example, on the child's 1st birthday, to the hour—before it, no rights; after it, full rights—Bingo! Just like that! The claim that we "can't" draw such a line, therefore, taken literally, is false.

What claim (2) is really getting at, then, is better stated in (3), for it no doubt is true that it is extremely difficult, and likely impossible, to draw a line that is *both* precise *and non-arbitrary* between fetuses and infants, infants and toddlers, toddlers and tots, and so on.

To put the problem in perspective, we should notice that it doesn't just apply to stages of the growth of humans but to virtually all of the distinctions we make in normal life. Dining tables shade off by tiny degrees into end tables and coffee tables, full-size sedans into compacts, mansions into bungalows...and plenty of those matters of degree are of considerable importance. The right to vote, for example, is something you suddenly get on your eighteenth birthday in Canada. Obviously this is arbitrary: nobody supposes that at midnight of your eighteenth birthday, you are suddenly transformed from a snivelling political incompetent into a very fountain of wisdom, able to be entrusted with Your Country's Destiny! (It's a nice idea, but we don't have the budget for it—fairy godmothers are getting pricier all the time!)

One possibility, therefore, would indeed be to draw a line that, while arbitrary in its *precise* location, is still in *roughly* the right place. If we are to have a voting age at all, for example, then some-where in the late teens or early twenties is reasonable, whereas set-ting it at seventy-three or -six, for example, would clearly be way off the mark. Where would it be in the case of abortion, though? (I will, in fact suggest below that setting it at birth is an excellent choice, though for a rather different reason.) The point is that one can solve problems of this general type satisfactorily enough. Slippery slope considerations locate a difficulty, which can be annoying, but it is very far from being insuperable because it is a logically soluble problem. Yet that is what the argument claims is insoluble.

Meanwhile, let us remember the general logic of the slippery slope argument. Any distinction that is fundamentally a matter of *continuous degree*, you will recall, will eventually lead to absurdity. Our "tallest dwarf" becomes not a dwarf at all, but a giant. So there is no sense at all to the claim that the argument actually proves something subtle and important that we had not noticed before about giants and dwarves. And there's worse: for the argument is reversible. Just as the slippery slope argument would "prove" that dwarves are giants, so it would "prove" that in fact giants are dwarves. All you have to do is start at the other end and, instead of adding subtract a tiny bit each time. Clearly such arguments, if they were sound, would eradicate a great many obvious and important distinctions: the large and the small, the tall and the short, the important and the trivial, saints and sinners.... An argument that has such implications is, of course, silly.

In short, we simply have to realize that when we deal with inherently imprecise distinctions, we will have to make somewhat arbitrary categories in practice, as required for our purposes. Between "tall" and "short" we can insert "medium"; or, if needed, we could add "medium-tall", "medium-short," and "medium-medi-um." Every distinction will generate its own small slippery slope problem, and every such problem can be solved as you like by fix-ing an arbitrarily precise line, if there's any reason to do so—which there usually isn't. But in the case of abortion, there are some very good reasons, indeed. It will matter that we set it here, or there. So it is worth thinking about it and getting it in a plausible place.

We may note that there are rather good reasons, based on con-siderations partly of the slippery slope variety, for extending the rights of normal adults to any non-standard cases: the lame, the incompetent, the feeble, the subnormal, the poor, and so on. All of these constitute special problems, but there are good and obvious reasons for not regarding them as organisms simply available for eating or otherwise maltreating them. One is that any of us could become disabled or otherwise subnormal, and we do not like to think that we would be subjected to bad treatment just on that account. Another is in the slippery slope category: where *would* we draw the line between those competent enough and those insufficiently competent for being awarded the right to life? Moreover, every human is someone's daughter or son, parent, sibling, friend, and so on. Our affective attitudes have little regard for competence. Until people get to the Karen Quinlan state, they matter to someone. This is enough to support a general proscription against bad treatment of such cases.

However, there is no similar argument against abortion. Fetuses are not yet anyone's friends or loved ones, and in any case, their special relation to their mothers—being literally inside their bodies—is enough to overwhelm any other affective considerations.

Taking No Chances?

It might also be argued that we ought to draw the line between adults and fetuses as conservatively as possible. After all, we don't want to take even the slightest chance that a genuine right-holding person might be accidentally killed owing to an overly liberal abortion policy, do we?

But that argument makes sense only if it is *possible* that we are wrong about what fetuses are like, so that a tighter policy would guard against really possible errors. But it isn't "possible": there is simply no reason to think that lurking inside the soul of the fetus is a real person such as you and I, only it's in hiding, so to speak. We are being amply conservative in this respect if we draw our line at birth or even several weeks beyond. (See below for a discussion of infanticide.)

And meanwhile, the supposedly "conservative" policy, in its efforts to guard against the remote chance of error about fetuses, will sacrifice the very real interests of millions of women (and, very often, of families—for it is often a couple who sees that it can't afford the financial or the emotional or some other sort of costs of another child). It is characteristic of tyrants that they seize on trivial or remotely likely wrongs in order to impose major costs on their subjects by way of "prevention." Such would the case with be restrictions on abortion, so far as the argument is concerned.

Potentiality

The other argument intended to support rights for fetuses despite their lack of inherent eligibility for them is the potentiality argument. This argument appeals to the fact that fetuses are, after all, *potentially* persons who, of course, will have rights when they realize that potentiality. Therefore, the argument concludes, they have those rights right *now*. Skeletally, the argument is this:

1. Fs are potentially Gs
2. Gs have rights
3. Therefore, Fs have rights.

The first question to ask about any argument is whether it is valid: does its conclusion, at least, *follow* from its premises? Let's ask this of the potentiality argument. Does it pass this test? It does not. Joel Feinberg gives an excellent counter-example: the President-elect of the United States, during the three or so months between election and inauguration, is as "potentially" President as you can get without actually being President. Nevertheless, he has none of the powers and rights of office until he is actually inaugurated.[3] Here's another: If you are a young Canadian, then you are a potentially retired Canadian; all retired Canadians are entitled to Canada Pension Plan incomes; therefore, you are *now* entitled to a Canada Pension Plan income.

Obviously something is wrong here. What's wrong is that the conclusion of the argument is not the one stated. What it actually implies is that the persons in these examples *potentially* have the rights of the positions or situations they will eventually attain. But that is far from actually *having* them—and having them is what is in question. If fetuses only potentially have the rights of persons, then they do not *actually* have them. And if the right they only potentially have is the right to life, then that means they do not have it now.

It also means that if an abortion is had now, then there is no possibility of ever violating the rights of the individual that this fetus would have become if an abortion were not had, for having an abortion precludes this from happening. The "potential person" in that fetus never becomes an actual person—i.e., it never becomes *a person*. And if there is no person, then there are no rights of that person to violate.

Why might people have thought that the potentiality argument is a good one? Here is one possibility. Some things we can do to a fetus would make life much worse for the individual it later becomes. Smoking and drinking while pregnant, we are told, can leave a child with serious health problems in later life. But fifteen-year-olds have a right not to be damaged. So if you can damage them well in advance, e.g., when they are fetuses, then that is a very good reason for not inflicting that damage and for thinking that it is wrong to do so.

Abortions, however, are different. If you abort fetus x, then there will *not* be, later on, some person who is worse off than she would have been had there been no abortion, for if there is an abortion there is later *no person at all* who grew from that fetus. Thus there is no person who is now harmed, by comparison with how she would have been had an abortion not taken place. There is no person whose right to life was violated very early on. If that right can only be had by a person, and fetuses are not persons, then abortion does not violate any person's right to life. Potential people are not people and do not have rights, any more than possible people do. Neither of those expressions refer to people, and only people have rights.

Abortion and Population Issues

Could there be other reasons for thinking abortion generally wrong, even if we grant all of the preceding points? One line of thought goes like this: people are *valuable*, and we should promote the existence of valuable things. Therefore, we should not prevent children from coming into existence.

The first problem with this argument is its premise. To assert, as if it were a simple fact, that people are "valuable" will not do, for reasons we have considered. To whom, we must ask, are they so valuable? *Who* values them? Obviously, most children are highly valued by their parents, and one would hope that all are. However, the pregnant woman seeking an abortion obviously does not value the existence of the person her fetus would become if she had it, or at any rate not sufficiently to persuade her to bring it into existence. What right do *we* have to insist that she have it on the basis of a premise she regards as false?

Besides this fundamental consideration, there is another aspect of the argument crucial to deriving its conclusion. It requires a major premise telling us *how many* people there should be. Only if the new person whom this fetus would become is required to reach the proposed level would it follow that the woman should be made to have it, even against her will. But very few premises of that kind could possibly support a particular conclusion like that.

One that would is this: there should be *as many people as possible*. But aside from the obviously disputable nature of that idea, it has to be pointed out that from it would follow not only prohibitions on abortion, but also on contraception and abstinence, for whenever it is possible for two persons to produce a baby, and they don't do it, then those two people will not be producing as many people as possible. On this remarkable view, it seems, most people should be constantly copulating!

In short, the view that people are valuable must be spelled out in terms of a general population policy. And such a policy, as we have already seen, need have nothing especially to do with abortions. For example, there could be monetary incentives to have children, as is now being done in Quebec. What *won't* follow is a plausible case for general moral prohibition of abortion. For that matter, just the opposite might follow. Considerations of overpopulation might create a plausible argument for an extremely liberal abortion policy, as in Japan. Countries already overburdened with people hardly need a rule *against* abortion on such grounds. Some would be tempted to require them rather than prohibit them. All in all, then, appeals to the public value of new people make an extremely dubious source of support for restrictions on abortion.

Infanticide

The general view I have been supporting raises a question that many people regard as decisive. It concerns the bearing of liberal abortion on infanticide. The problem is this. Wherever we tried to draw a line between fetuses and persons, it could hardly coincide with the moment of birth. Newborns are still far from having the sort of personal properties we argued to be essential for inherent rights, however rapidly they acquire them. Thus if we allow abortion, would we not be forced, on such premises, to allow infanticide as well?

But we do not need to rest the case exclusively on the possession of inherent personality, for there is a different kind of difference between the abortion situation and the infanticide situation, which I am inclined to think makes all the difference, at least in societies like ours. This difference is that fetuses are inside their mother's bodies, attached by *natural* means, whereas born infants are detached. Requiring that the pregnant woman retain and deliver the fetus is enforcing pregnancy. It's a case of forcing someone to do something *with her body* that she does not want to do with it. After birth, however, we have a separate organism that can be transported without any further imposition on the body of the mother. If the mother doesn't want her newborn, then, she can give it to others without any invasion of her rights over her body. Once the baby is born, she can give it away without any physical costs. Perhaps there are emotional costs, but if those impel her not to have the child, they would surely also lead her to have an abortion, if available—as it would be, in the liberal view I have been arguing for.

Infanticide was widely practised in more primitive societies. That is surely because the medical technology of those societies simply wasn't advanced enough to enable them to have abortions. In societies that do have such capabilities, then, parental interest in infanticide would have to be very rare and very special. And public interests begin to exert themselves. How strong should the rights of parents over their children be—so strong as to include the right to destroy them? It seems to me that we can make a good case for stopping short of that, provided that abortion is allowed and available as an option. Thus, parents anxious not to have their impending children could have an abortion. Arguably, if a mother can put up with pregnancy for that rather longish period, then she can certainly put up with someone else's having the still-unwanted resulting child. And given the overwhelming social interest in good treatment of children, including infants, I would take it that we could be justified in forbidding infanticide, so long as we allow abortion.

Fathers

I have thus far said nothing directly concerning a rather important secondary issue: should fathers, along with the mothers, have rights concerning their unborn offspring? There are vexed questions nowadays about surrogate mothers hired to bring children to term by would-be parents incapable of producing them on their own. A father who participated voluntarily in the conception of an infant he would like to have, and who is willing to help with its care, surely has a claim to consideration against a mother who changed her mind in the course of pregnancy. But does he have an actual *right* against her that she bring it to term? A contract could have been signed, though it usually isn't, and surely nothing short of that would give him that kind of right. Our argument for the rights of mothers to abortions depends mainly on their physical, gestative relation to the fetus, not their genetic relation to it. So it is difficult to see that there is anything about male parenthood to get us beyond the point that affection and personal commitment reach to. Those, of course, can certainly create moral obligations on both wives and husbands. And those are characteristically, and happily, enough. Appeal to the rights of fathers is insufficient to alter our conclusion on abortion.

Summing Up

The question of abortion is primarily whether a woman wanting one may be denied it by her society. Our indicated conclusion is that no argument that is both consistent and liberal could support restrictive policies on abortion in circumstances generally like ours. Fetuses clearly don't have what it takes to claim the benefits of morality; and so far as extrinsic considerations are concerned, clearly the rights of people to their bodies are enough to assure mothers of the right to abortion, except in extremely special cases. A social need for more children is so unlikely and so weak as to offer no real support for a restrictive abortion policy. Special agreements with someone, such as her husband, that she will have the child could make it wrong for a woman to abort, but even such an agreement wouldn't easily support a legal prohibition on her having one. We are left, therefore, with the fully liberal view, giving women a general right to abortion on demand. Society, we must conclude, may not chain mothers to the delivery bed any more than to the marriage bed.

Chapter Nine

Population: How Many People Should There Be?

Our discussion in the previous chapters bring up a fascinating subject: How do we decide how large a population to have? Is there a "right" number of people for the world? Of course, there can be a population problem in a particular locality, or in a particular school building or home, for that matter; and consideration of such cases may afford us some insight into the global issue as well. But the global question about population is interestingly special.

What makes it special is the following problem. In any undertaking, we must, of course, take into account the interests of people who would be affected by what we might do. But when we contemplate bringing new people into existence, how and why are we to take into account the interests of the new people in question—that is, of possible future generations? Do they count equally with the people already here? Or do the latter have priority? Or, as some seem to suppose, do the newcomers actually have priority?

Why is this a problem? Because in the special case of producing new people, we, the people already here, the people who would be the parents of these new people, have it within our power to determine whether the further people will *exist* or not. In normal situations, we are dealing with other people who are here independently of what we do: we deal with them as separate agents. Thus we can deal with those others on the basis, to a very large extent, of *agreement*. But when we look to the future, the people who are "there" aren't in that position. We can't make a deal with them on the subject of whether they are to exist or not. Until people exist, you can't deal with them, yet once they do exist, it's no longer an eligible subject for discussion whether they shall come into existence—for here they are! (Readers will recall a similar point about regarding life as a gift from God in the discussion of suicide. Regarding future generations, it is we who are, as it were, in the role of God.)

Of course, other people's children aren't brought into existence at our will. As far as we are concerned, they are independent. We can, however, deal with their parents, and one of the matters for negotiation with them is the terms on which they are to have children. There are two questions of interest in these negotiations. One is the central question of this chapter: What considerations are relevant as regards the *number* of children to be had? Is there, especially, any good reason for saying that some people may and others may not have any children at all? The other is: What are the rights of the newcomers? How are they to count in the "negotiations"? Does the fact that they do not yet exist make any difference to their standing, and especially to their rights?

Population Policy

One idea about the first question is that we should assign a certain value to each life and then adopt the population policy that would maximize this value. The question about this seemingly plausible idea is whether it makes any sense.

What is this value to be? Some would assign value to life itself. Presumably that would suggest that the right policy is the one that maximizes the number of people there are. It doesn't follow that the policy would result in there being an utterly enormous population, for that depends on resources, which we will discuss below. If they are limited, then it would be possible that the population over-reaches its resources, resulting in less people, or even no people, in the longer run. (If you put ten people in a chamber that has only enough air for nine, does one die or do all ten die? It could be the latter if you aren't careful.)

Few of us would think it valuable to have people around no matter what their lives were like. What if you could have a vast number of perfectly miserable people, or a much smaller number of people who were happy? It seems obvious to most of us that the smaller number should be preferred.

Why is that? Perhaps because we think that happiness itself is a good thing: if so, then the more the better! Maybe—but a couple of points should give us pause. Does it matter, in particular, how this happiness is *distributed*? Happiness seems fairly clearly to be a matter of degree. Suppose we could somehow measure it. Then we could imagine having to choose not only between, say, a happy population and a miserable one, but between two happy populations, one of which was happier than the other—or, more interestingly yet, two equally happy populations overall, but one of which was larger than the other. In the latter case, there are more people, but each person is on the average *less* happy than in the other. Now what? Which should we prefer, and why?

It might again seem obvious that in that case we should prefer the smaller population to the larger, since each person is happier in the smaller one. Perhaps. But some people might reason differently. They might say, "It's not as though anybody in the larger population is actually *suffering*—it's just that they aren't *as* well off. But just think: more people enjoy this happiness. Isn't that better? The smaller population denies the happiness of human life to some people!"

The latter reasoning leads to acceptance of what Derek Parfit[1] calls "the Repugnant Conclusion": that we should prefer an enormous population of just barely happy people to a much smaller population of extremely happy people, so long as the *total* happiness, the sum of all the individual barley happy people, was the same or slightly greater in the larger population. Must we prefer that? Or is there, in fact, any "must" about it?

Does anything push us in one direction or the other? There is one interesting argument in favour of the smaller but individually happier population: happiness is, after all, an individual kind of thing. *We* would rather be happier than less happy, after all. Indeed, each of us wants to be as happy as possible. Now, think of these two possible populations as if they were, say, places we could move to. If I "move" to P1, I know that *I* will be happier than if I move to P2, the larger but individually less happy one. That makes sense, doesn't it?

But in so thinking, we have fallen into a subtle logical trap. For it's not a matter of "moving," after all. It is, instead, a matter of being *born* into one or the other. And of course we might say, "Well, I'd rather be born into one than the other, too!" But who is this "I" who is asking what sort of life "he" would prefer to have? For after all, by hypothesis "he' doesn't *exist* yet! A non-existent "person," after all, can't make choices; and as for existing people, it is too late for them to cease to exist, for here they are!

Logical Traps

Here we have to alert ourselves to the possibility of tripping up on the peculiar semantics of these questions. We talk as though "non-existent people" refers to some *kind* of people. But obviously this isn't so. A "non-existent person" isn't a *kind* of person, for the point of the phrase "non-existent person" is precisely that there *is no such person*.

To help see the oddity here, think of a room empty of people, such as your closet, and ask how many non-existent people there are in that closet right now. If non-existent people were a kind of people, they would have to be individual people—that being the only people there are. But then you should also be able to count them. Yet it makes no sense whatever to talk of the number of non-existent people in your closet. The whole idea is just a muddle, a semantic illusion.

On the other hand, there's nothing logically peculiar about *future* people: they, indeed, are just people, like you and me—it's just that they happen to live later than we do. So there's nothing logically problematic with the concept of future people. Nevertheless, there is, as we observed at the beginning of this discussion, the fact that *whether* they exist depends on what *we* do—on what people living right now do. About this, we have our choice. And when we think about this, the potential for misleadingness comes into view. For instance, it might be said that we "have the power of life or death over these people," as if we were some sort of Oriental potentate juggling our subjects' lives like so many pieces on a game board. But it's nothing of the sort. Once your child is born, you will have the sort of "power" over him that a parent does—which, for awhile, is considerable. But the fact that he was born as a result of your decision, and that you might have decided otherwise, won't result in your having any particular power over him. And "those" who are not born as a result of your negative decision will not suffer from the fact, nor even notice it at all.

Instead of talking about "future people," there is a temptation to talk about "potential people." But to do so is, again, to invite misleading talk. The obvious way to use the notion of a potential person is in the context of reproductive biology: a two-celled human organism (zygote) might reasonably be called a "potential person," for if you do the right things it will end up being a person, like you and me—it will grow up to become one. But then if you go back further, to the stage before even that two-celled organism existed, what then would there be to call a "potential person"? The separate cells that, if united, would make up the zygote? Or their component molecules? Or perhaps the idea in the mind of a possible parent? It becomes very clear that so-called "potential people," in contrast to future people, are *not* people.

There's also the expression 'possible person.' This is a particularly treacherous expression. The idea of a "possible person" is that there might *or might not* exist anything for that description to apply to. Thus, we can't quite say that a possible person is a non-existent person, for *some* possible persons do exist—for instance, you do. It must be possible for you to exist, since you actually do: actuality entails possibility, as logicians put it. But other possible persons do not exist. For instance, my fourth child does not exist, since I have but three. Now, consider one of these "possible people" who ends up not becoming actual. Suppose that I contemplate having another child, but my wife and I decide not to have it. One might imagine that we've even got so far as to choose a name for it, say, Lynn. So shall we now say that "Poor Lynn doesn't even exist!"? Should we say that we have "denied" Lynn "existence"? Of course not. For you can't "deny" anything to a merely possible, that is non-actual, person. It will suffer no pangs from such a "denial." Existence isn't a good that goes to some but not others. Existence is a precondition for having *any* human goods at all; in the absence of existence, there is no subject for any such goods, or the lack of them, to go to.

It need do no harm, then, to talk loosely of "possible" and "non-existent" and "actual" people, so long as we just remember that only the latter are people, whereas the former are only ideas in our minds or else assorted pre-personal entities. Thinking about possible and potential and non-existent people might give us a headache, but there is no need to worry about those "non-existent people" *themselves*. As far as "they" are concerned, there is no problem, for there is nothing referred to by 'they' that can have, or lack, any problems.

Population Values

Let's return, then, to our main question: how many people should there be? There is a fallacy, as we have seen, in the suggestion that the smaller population "denies life" to all of the "people" who don't exist in it but who would have existed in the larger one. "They," we now see, weren't denied anything at all. Nonexistence isn't something that makes the non-existent person unhappy: instead, the whole subject of the happiness *or* unhappiness of that "person" doesn't arise. There is no such subject, no person whose happiness or lack of it is in question. So having a smaller population is not something done at the "expense" of the people who might otherwise have existed.

Does it follow, then, that we *must* prefer the smaller population? It does not. For consider one of the less happy people in the larger population. What is he less happy *than*? "Less happy" is a comparative: in order for person A to be "less happy," there must be some case for comparison. But in the present case, what is it? We can compare the happiness level of the hypothetical less happy person in P2 with the level of some hypothetical person in P1, but what is the point of doing so? From the point of view of the hypothetically less happy individual in P2, what matters is whether *she* is less happy than *she* would have been if, say, *she* had been born into P1. The trouble with that, though, is that she might very well not have *existed* in P1, since it is, by hypothesis, *smaller* than P2.

To flesh out such abstract possibilities, let's consider what kind of scenarios in the real world we might pick to exemplify P1-P2 choices. Suppose the dictator of Xanada announces to his people the following good news: he will greatly increase the happiness of Xanada by forcing all the adult women in the population to have a minimum of three children. This, let us suppose, is something that none of those women actually wants - the one or two children each woman already has is just fine with them. But once the decree goes into effect and they've had their third—at great cost in personal happiness to themselves—there are all these new Xanadians, and they, on the average, are well above the zero-happiness level, so their extra happiness more than outweighs the loss to the people who have been forced to have the extra children. So, reasons the dictator, the Xanadians are happier!

What this does is to treat Xanada as if *it* were the moral unit, an entity whose interests are what really matters. That's a natural line for a dictator to take, since it helps him to justify imposing all sorts of things on his unwitting people. But it's a fraud. In *this* situation, should all those women be overjoyed at the dictator's result? Or should they be good and angry, as they most likely will be?

Clearly the latter is the correct answer, unless they change their minds, which is beside the present point. Only the interests of individuals matter, and the "interests" of possible individuals, as such, do not. The people who didn't want more children are not selfishly preferring their own happiness to that of the possible people they might otherwise bring into existence. Having decided not to have any, there *are no* further people whose happiness or lack of it is to be compared to their own.

Here's another scenario. This time the dictator announces that he's found a way to make a dramatic improvement in happiness: just kill off all the unhappy people! That will make the *average* happiness of the populace much higher, you see. Well, should anyone regard this as an improvement? Hardly. For making the "average" person "better off" is, in this case, nothing but arithmetical sleight-of-hand. In point of fact, nobody's happiness has been altered at all, except for the unfortunates who are killed off.

Even in their case, some theorist might urge, their *happiness* hasn't really been affected. Dead people are not less happy than they used to be; for they are, really, just newly non-existent people who feel nothing! Right?

But this is another subtle mistake. As pointed out back in Chapters Two and Three, what makes death a disvalue to us is that it greatly shortens our lives, and what constitutes value for us is the prospect of satisfying our desires. And we *want* to live. So we should credit all the killed people with a net *reduction* in happiness, since they would, in their own view, live lives with much less valuable experience in them than if they had been allowed to live. This is so even if, as we are supposing, their experience isn't very valuable.

What these examples illustrate is how easy it is to bamboozle ourselves in this area by mistaking collectivities for people, possible people for people, and arithmetical hocus-pocus for real estimations of the well-being of real people.

Individual Values

The views we have just been considering raise a major question: can we really compare one life to another in the way they require? Indeed, *may* we do so? Who is this "we" who get to do this, and why do they get to do it? We manipulate notions of happiness as if the aspirations and ideas of the people whose happiness we are supposed to be talking about didn't count. But surely they *do* count—

isn't that why we're talking about making such calculations in the first place?

In fact, what people think and want is so important as to raise the question whether the *general* happiness is even the right thing to talk about because particular people will have ideas about the quality of life. They may not take to the view that one person's happiness is as good as another's, given an equal "amount" of it. They might think that some people's *way* of being happy is stupid or contemptible. In any case, it is easy enough to imagine them not being especially interested in most other people. They have their own lives to live.

Nor is the concept of happiness particularly clear. Is the mystic who spends his life in a monastery or a cave happy? How about Beethoven, who gave up any hope of domestic happiness because he thought his music was more important? (And aren't the rest of us lucky he did?) Should we say that he not only gave up domestic happiness, but gave up on happiness itself—accounting his life as a creative artist more important, greater? Or should we say that he found his highest happiness in his art? The extreme difficulty of deciding what to say here illustrates how difficult it is for *us* to come up with firm judgements about *other* people's lives.
Limited Resources?

Much has been said in recent times about "overpopulation." raising the spectre that humanity might "run out of" resources to keep it going. Therefore, it is reasoned, we must cut down on the world's "out-of-control" population. This remarkably popular set of views calls for reflection—and for more than a bit of empirical knowledge.

The reflection it calls for is this. *If* there were "only so much to go around," how would this imply that the world should go in for general population control? If it is proposed that we should have less people now so that there can be more people in the future, then the question arises why we should prefer future people to present people? If there are only going to be N people on the earth in the whole of time, why should it matter whether most of them live now, or are instead strung out over the next 10,000 years?

If it is supposed that happiness is happiness is happiness, and it doesn't matter who has it, then it seems, offhand, as though the total value of humanity—those N people—will be the same no matter how they are distributed in time. So it simply would not follow that we should have "population control." That would only follow if, for instance, you felt that without such control we will have the *wrong* N people! Cut down on the number of black people so we can have more white ones, perhaps? Or on the not-so-bright so that we can have more of the super-bright? How about having more people who play Parcheesi?

People: Lottery versus Market

If there really is a finite resource base to support people, then we are in for a sort of competition to see which future population we will have—more like the one *we* want or more like the one *they* want—for any number of different "theys." Such a competition could get pretty nasty. One imagines race wars, border wars, "ethnic cleansing," and worse.

If the situation were like that, what would be a fair way to have the competition? We have seen that fairness in this matter cannot consist in giving each possible person an equal chance to become an actual person: that is unintelligible, both because the number of possible people is infinite, and because there's no reason to be concerned about the interests of possible people, since there is no such thing as an interest of a possible person. There are *possible* interests of such "persons," if you like; but only *real* interests count. What we would need to be fair *to* are the potential parents, that is to say, the actual people on the earth now who want to have children.

In principle, we could run the competition as a lottery, giving each couple one ticket. Then we draw, awarding as many places as there is room for new people. The winners, who have won fair and square, then get to have the children.

A different way to do it would be to give each person the number of child spaces we think there is room for, and then let each person use that right as they wish, either by having the child *or* by selling it to somebody else who wanted children. Some would rather have the money, some the children. Each could make use of her opportunity as she saw fit. This, surely, would be the preferable way. No one would be able simply to impose a cost on others by having more children than she or he was entitled to, and all those who wanted to have a full quota of people of a certain kind in the world would give their children-producing rights to the right selection of potential parents from their own point of view.

Resources Unlimited

Fortunately, however, neither scheme, nor any other, turns out to be necessary. Further reflection and a modest amount of factual information show us that the population situation is not like that at all. It is a mistake, indeed a fallacy, to think that our world is necessarily in a situation of limited resources, permitting room for just so many and no more. There is no competition, no zero-sum game, as the decision theorists call it. (In a zero-sum game, A's gain is B's loss: whatever one player gains, the other player loses.)

Many people nowadays will find what I have just said heretical or wildly optimistic. The antidote is to check out the facts. To begin with, the food supply in the world has kept right on expanding along with the population. Those who, in the 1970s, ominously projected massive starvation within a decade or two have been proven dead wrong. There was, and is, no problem about the *resources* necessary to feed or clothe people. Nor is there a problem about the resources necessary for us "rich" people in the "advanced" countries.

But it isn't really just a matter of how the facts happen to be, for the whole idea that resources must be fixed, and thus limited, is based on a fundamental error, which we might call the materialist fallacy. In fact, resources do not consist in pieces of stuff. We do use pieces of stuff, to be sure: but how much we can do with a given piece of stuff depends on how ingenious we are, not just on how much of that kind of stuff there happens to be. The more ingenious we are, the less natural stuff we need, and so the less it matters what the particular amount of stuff we have to start out with. Technical know-how enables us to make silk purses out of sows' ears, a Honda out of a very modest amount of iron, silicon, and a few other natural substances. Moreover, our consumption is a broad recycling process. We raise food, eat it, and then make more food out of the garbage from the first lot. That's just the way nature works. Fertile soil consists largely of the decayed remains of earlier plants. So long as the sun shines and the rains fall, there is literally no limit, in principle, to how much food people can raise. Even if the rain were to stop—which it can't—we can run a pipe to the sea, remove the life-killing salts from it, and raise food again. What's needed isn't more of any particular kind of matter, but greater knowledge. And knowledge is *not* finite. It is growing, indeed burgeoning, all the time, and there is and can be no end in sight.

In today's world, what is its single most important resource? A plausible answer is sand! This lowly stuff contains the silicon from which are made the microchips that are the "brains" of computers. And the calculational and memory-enhancing capacities of computers underlie almost all technical advances nowadays, both in human systems management and in the development of material goods. Yet all this computing power comes from trivial quantities of one of the most abundant natural resources there is. The crucial factor is sheer human ingenuity, which is what designs and operates the computers.

In short, there is no theoretical limit to the number of people there can be, nor on how much "happiness" they can attain so far as resources have anything to do with it. (How much they do have to do with it is, of course, the subject of unlimited discussion, contemplation, and experiment. It is a fact of life that a poor peasant can be as happy as a multimillionaire playboy. On the other hand, the rich, in general, live longer and have far more varied lives than the poor, and almost everyone prefers being rich to being poor.)[2]

People are our primary resource. The reason any one of us is as well off as he or she happens to be today, in any respect involving the use of goods or services, is that there are all those other people out there, creating the light-bulb, the computer, the airliner, the works of Shakespeare, Bertrand Russell, Beethoven, and so on. The more people there are, the more nice things they can and will make and do for each other. Other people are of literally incalculable value to us. To choke off the supply of people and be as niggardly as possible about how many we will allow is to decree that human progress slow to a crawl or even a halt. The pessimism about people that is so popular currently is as absurd and self-defeating as it is unnecessary and ill-considered.

Who Pays?

It costs money to raise children, as any parent is well aware. There is a lengthy time lag between the infant we start out with and the productive, interesting human being we hope to end up with after a couple of decades of care, concern, and expenditure. Children are an investment. When it is successful, the output from our new human will eventually more than make up for his or her input costs. Who should pay those "capital costs" and who should get the returns?

What complicates this question is that, normally, returns to investment go to the investor. Yet the parents who expend so much of their income and energy to support their children are not the main beneficiaries of the latter's production—at least, not at the monetary level and not in the short term. Of course, parents do benefit emotionally and spiritually—with any luck. The parent who has done a good job will reap pleasure and satisfaction from the family life that children make possible, both before and after they grow up. Still, pleasure and satisfaction don't pay the bills.

What about the poor, though? If one can't afford to feed the children, then what? Are they to starve? We are back to the problem of feeding the hungry, except that now the subjects are our very own children.

In fact, developed countries all provide extensive support services for children, whose cost is born by everybody, not just the parents of the particular children benefitted. The most substantial of these is education. All children in the developed Western world (or the North) can look forward to many years of education without their parents having to bear much if any of the tuition expense. And many other services are provided to the poor.

In this book, we cannot go too extensively into strictly political philosophy. But the institutions of the modern welfare state have many problems, and it is reasonable to regard at least some of these as moral problems. The main one is this: why should other people bear the expense of your children? There is also a rather plausible general answer: it's because other people get the lion's share of the benefit from your children.[3]

But the answer is distressingly undiscriminating as it stands, because the specific way in which they benefit from your children, after all, is by purchasing the goods and services that those grown-up children eventually produce. That's how your children will (you hope) make their living: by doing useful things for others in exchange for the money with which, in turn, they buy the necessities and luxuries of life. And the reason those grown-up children are able to do this is that their parents did such things before, and did them so well that they could afford to raise those children.

This system has an extremely desirable spin-off: it means that the world is populated by the people we most want to have in it—those who will do the most good. Contrast this with the cases in which we, the public, support young people who are unemployable, enabling them to have children, all at our expense, after which we support the jails into and out of which they will yo-yo away their mid-lives in their efforts to support the drug habits that will also no doubt greatly increase their maintenance cost, and finally the pensions on which they will live in their old age and the hospitals and nursing homes in which they will spend an increasing proportion of that old age. In such cases, we, the public, are the losers throughout. We will have spent sizeable portions of our incomes with no return whatever to ourselves—not to mention all the victims of their crimes—and for that matter, precious little to the alleged beneficiaries. And that does not sound like such a good idea.

Of course, if you think that people are "intrinsically valuable"—teen gangs, druggies, murderers, suffering cancer patients, and all—then maybe you won't think it's a bad investment. But surely some discernment is in order? Wouldn't it have been better still if your investment had also paid off for *you* and for all the other people who also helped, involuntarily, to pay the bills?

Our Responsibility for Future Generations

The alternative idea is to take the view that basically each of us should take responsibility for our own children, just as we should for our own lives. Those who do nothing for others deserve nothing from those others; and those who have children without the resources to support them may end up with a lot of poverty-stricken children on their hands. People who do that can and should be regarded with shame, and if we take their children off their hands and bring them up ourselves, their parents should not regard that as "social justice" at work, but rather as an enormously lucky thing for them and an act of great generosity from us. For just as the world does not owe you a living, neither does it owe you support of your children. That is *your* job.

It is also basically up to us what kind of children we will have, insofar as we can influence that. We can marry the sort of people we think will be more likely to produce the sort of people we want to have around and who will do well in training and educating them in the best way, according to our judgement of how we want them to mature. So long as we do not do so at net cost to others, as when our children become serial murderers or gangsters, we shall each, in our small way, be able to play god—that's one of the opportunities life affords. It is not, on the other hand, an opportunity that other people have the duty to extend to us. If and insofar as they help us out, it should be, in principle, because they benefit in the long run from the help they've given us, by virtue of our making it worth their while by helping them or others in turn.

Of course, if we leave the question of future generations in this way to individuals to deal with on their own, then nobody will need or be able to decide how many people the world will have. The question is, why should anybody be able to decide a thing like that? That's reasoning for dictators, not for free men and women. My conclusion is that there simply is no duty to reproduce to any particular extent. How many children you should have depends on how many you want and can afford. There is no inherent limit from the outside world on how many people we can have in this world, although if the population of the world were to approach the trillion level, for instance, most of *us*, at least, would find that very uncomfortable. But then, we may be sure that in that case the cost of housing and living-space would become inordinate. (It already has in Tokyo and in most of the great cities of the West, where average family sizes do not, to put it mildly, make a "population explosion" at all likely! In fact, most of the current industrialized countries would have *declining* populations were it not for immigration. Expanding wealth, it seems, reduces people's interest in having children and, curiously, their perceived ability to afford them.) At the other limit, we could all stop reproducing. If we did that, the human race would, of course, eventually die out. If we don't like that, as most of us don't, then the cure is simple: reproduce! But this also doesn't look to be a problem any time soon. People wouldn't be around if they didn't have a substantial reproductive drive.

Nor, as we have seen, is world overpopulation a problem. In various particular places there might be felt to be too many people from one point of view or another. Some find Hong Kong, for instance, uncomfortably densely populated. To each his own on that matter of taste; but Hong Kong, despite its trivial natural resources, is quite wealthy by world standards, due in part to its very density. More people in close proximity means that transportation and communication are extremely efficient per capita. On foot, you can reach 50,000 people within a fifteen-minute radius in Hong Kong. Even if you have a Land Rover, you can't do that in Saskatchewan. That means that you can avail yourself of the services of an enormous number of people in Hong Kong and can look for a market for your services from them far more easily than in uncrowded places.

And then there are places like Canada, with its vast prairies, forests, mountain ranges, and tundra, for the most part scarcely populated at all. Indeed, this country can very reasonably be regarded as a spectacular case of underpopulation. Yet Canadians do pretty well, too, Canada being among the "rich" countries; and many of us enjoy the wilderness and the great open spaces. In today's world, and for a very long time to come, we can take our pick. That's surely not a bad thing.

There is an idea that we ought to see to it that we leave future generations a world that is in at least as good condition as when we found it. There are two points to make about the suggestion. The first is that it is not a clear one, for different people have different interests, and they conflict. If you leave the world in a certain condition, for the benefit of those who like it that way, then there are sure to be others who would want you to leave it in quite a different way. The second is that in any case, so long as people are tolerably rational and given a reasonable interpretation of the requirement, it is surely utterly easy to meet, almost no matter what the material world we leave them is like. In fact, leaving them a world reasonably well stocked with people who are morally decent is the best thing we can possibly do for them. Given that, the rest is easy, people being what they are. What they will all do with the world they inherit is *up to them*, a point that it is not always easy for us parents to appreciate. The possibility that other people might turn out to be competent human beings in their own right is one we should start considering fairly early on!

Summing Up

The idea that there is a population problem is intriguing. And it seems pretty clear that if there is such a thing, it would scarcely admit of any clear solution in the abstract. Do people have a right to be born? That makes no sense. Is there an allocation problem? If the world could only hold just so many people, then there could be, if people wanted to have more children than there was room for. A solution might be at hand as well: give each current adult a reproduction-quota right, which could be bought and sold.

Yet it turns out, on careful examination, that there is no such problem in the real world. There is no basis for saying that people in general are morally required either to have more children or to have less. There is some basis for saying that more is generally better, to be sure. But that does not entail a duty to reproduce, any more than the supposed problem of global scarcity turned out to be a basis for a duty to refrain from reproduction. Resources are not limited in such a way that the world can only "hold" so many people. We need not worry about whether the rich are somehow using up scarce resources at the expense of the poor, for the answer to this is also in the negative—resources expand with population, contrary to what many think. In principle, we may each have as many children as we personally want and can afford to have. There is, in the end, no "problem" to "solve."

Chapter Ten

Morals and the Environment

The Subject

The environment of an organism, in the broadest sense of the term, is everything outside it; the environment of the human species as a whole is everything non-human. But more narrowly and relevantly, the environment is that part of the rest of the universe that we relate to and that affects us significantly. Distant galaxies may explode with unimaginable violence, but it makes no difference to us whether they do or not. A snowstorm in our town, on the other hand, though cosmically insignificant, matters a great deal to us. The snowstorm is a part of our environment in a sense that matters; the galaxies are not.

Few topics have received so much attention in recent decades as the environment; and, in a way, it deserves the attention. After all, we exist because of our environment, and it's the only one we have. So far as we currently know, only this one planet in the entire universe is suitable for human habitation—it is certainly the only one within practicable distance from us. In turn, each individual one of us thrives, or the reverse, in a home, and then a village, farm, forest, or city; what is outside but near to us obviously matters a great deal. People spend lives altering their near environments in ways hoped to make them more suitable to their interests—cleaning out the garage, planting flowers, and so on.

All of this matters a great deal, in detail. Indeed, it matters far too much for present purposes. Each of us will have some small part of the world under our particular influence—our property. We will generally be concerned that that property be in what we regard as good condition. Other parts of the world belong to other people, and we assume that they are taking care of those parts. We may occasionally have advice for some of them, but only very rarely would we actually have a right to step in and alter the arrangements they make.

All this detailed caring for little bits of the world, however, is not the focus of recent attention to "the environment." That subject is the larger environment that is more or less common to us all, and in which changes can make a lot of difference to many or all people: if the earth were to dry up or its mean temperature to increase by 100° Fahrenheit, life would become impossible. There is current concern about the melting of the polar ice-caps, the depletion of ozone in the upper atmosphere, the exhaustion of oxygen should the earth be much further deforested and the "carrying capacity" of the earth, whose burgeoning population might lead to exhaustion of resources necessary for life. Such scenarios form the principal impetus to environmental writings over the past few decades.

It is not clear where we should stop. After all, germ-carried diseases and accidents might reasonably be regarded as environmental matters; and if we include our relations to our fellows as well—the social environment—then the topic of environmental ethics includes engineering and medicine as well as ethics. And even that doesn't quite exhaust the subject, for in another direction we get into aesthetics—our interest in natural beauty, especially—and in still another, attitudes of a religious kind, or nearly so.

We may distinguish three concerns about the environment:

1. The health and survival concerns of people.
2. The more strictly aesthetic interests, as in preserving beautiful wilderness areas.
3. Finally, the view called "Deep Environmentalism"—that the environment, in whole or in part, has some kind of intrinsic value, and even that it has *rights*, moral standing on *its own* account, rather than just because of its relation to our own interests.

These three points of view differ radically. On the first view, the reason we ought not to damage trees or canyons is that we ought not to damage other *people*—the ones who own them, or who depend on their being one way rather than another. On the second view, the damage consists in ugliness or reduced beauty. On the third, to damage such things is to violate their own moral status—the trees or canyons themselves: we owe good treatment *to the tree*, for the *sake* of the tree, not because of the greater good we might derive from a tree intact as compared with a tree fallen. (Or we owe it for the sake of "the world" or "the ecosystem.")

Most of the issues that make it into the newspapers are of the first type. I will conclude that that is as it should be; but the other two are philosophically interesting, and their implications very important. So we will consider them, in reverse order.

1. "Depth" and the Environment

Most people will probably find the third view odd or bizarre on the face of it. Why should we be concerned about the survival of a tree or canyon *for the sake of* that tree or canyon? The reason for this reaction, I think, testifies to the inevitability of the general approach to morals set forth in Chapter One. We all want to do our best. We would like our environments to cater to *our* interests, in whatever ways are possible, and at the least not to hamper or threaten us. In the case of the human environment, our methods of attempting to bring it about that we do the best we can is, generally speaking, by reasoning—that is, by appealing to the reason of other people. We can see that we humans—all of us—have much to gain by co-operation and much to lose by its opposite, such as warfare. What makes it possible for others to achieve that co-operation with us is that they, like we, have minds of their own. Like ourselves, other people also take in information, redirect their actions in the light of it, and in consequence can make arrangements—agreements, contracts, and the like, with us or others. We can readily understand the point of a rule to keep those agreements. Above all, a survey of our general interests assures us that we need rules against *violence*. With persistent training and any luck at all, those rules will have considerable effect. It is that training, the habituation of our fellows to nonviolence and to being helpful to others, that has enabled humans to achieve the remarkable progress, material and otherwise, that we have experienced and benefited from through the centuries.

In contrast, trees, stones, grasslands, icebergs, headlands, and so forth do not have that capacity. There is no use trying to discuss with a canyon how best to enable us and it to get along to mutual benefit. The canyon cannot address this matter, nor does it, in any intelligible sense of the word, "care" about itself. It has no mind, and therefore no concept of itself or anything else to inform that caring. Because this is so, the sense in which canyons, rivers, trees, and the like might be "damaged" or the reverse, well or badly treated, is one that has nothing directly to do with morals. A canyon cannot be immoral to us, even if its walls collapse and it buries us; lightning does no moral wrong when it strikes us dead or destroys our house. On the other hand, if we destroy that house or that canyon, that matters not a whit to it: canyons and buildings simply don't care what we do to them or to anything.

The flourishing or non-flourishing of non-human things has no *direct* relation to morals, I have said; but 'directly' is the operative word here, for even the good or ill of our fellows has nothing *directly* to do with our practical deliberation. My respect for you is called for because of what I have to lose at your hands if I do not, or to gain if I do. You *react* to my behaviour: what I do to you affects what you do to me. So even if we have no native sympathy with each other, we will, nevertheless, if we are sensible, arrive at a mutual understanding of how we are to behave towards each other.

Now, what happens to natural things can certainly affect us too. But how are we to deal with that fact? Not by making *arrangements* with them; the methods by which we humans deal with each other are simply not available when it comes to dealing with canyons or trees. They have no desires, interests, or intentions, no reasoning powers to steer their responses to us in one way rather than another, and no emotions to affect the quality of those responses. The idea of a tree or a canyon coming to "agree" that it ought to do this rather than that is simply not available. We saw that this was true even with animals, which are at least sentient beings; it is still more obviously true of trees or mountains.

I have classified environmental concerns into three, according to whether they affect our health or prosperity, our aesthetic sensibilities, ourselves at some deeper spiritual level. This last one, which we will consider now, is very different from the others, and especially from the first. Effects on health obviously matter and will motivate the affected people to do something about it. But spiritual concerns are in another boat altogether. It is certainly possible for humans to develop attitudes of affection and respect for non-human entities. But is there any *reason* to do so, if we don't already happen to feel that way? That is, is there a reason that can be articulated and which, when articulated, must be accepted and found persuasive by everyone? On the basis of all we know at present, the answer is in the negative. There is often reason to do one or another thing about our environments, but the reason recognizably stems from our practical interests. And for most of us, most of the time, those interests are not of the type that we might have in, say, our sweethearts. But the "deep environmentalist," as he is called, seems to think that is just about what they should be: we are to love the environment, somehow, for *its own sake*.

Philosophers who urge the claims of non-human bits of the environment as if they had moral standing in their own right talk as though they were the friends of the oppressed and downtrodden, or at least the hitherto ignored. But that is misleading. Protecting rivers and hills, rocks and trees is, in fact, very expensive. Those natural things do not care what we do to them, or anything else— but the *people* who would involuntarily have to bear the costs of "spiritual respect for nature" will indeed feel it, and do care about that. The net effect is that deep ecologists are engaging in extravagant pseudo-moralizing. They are putting one over on the rest of us. Who, they in effect say, are we mere people—the five or so billions of us who have houses to build and gardens to plant—against the fifty trillion trees that a handful of eco-sympathizers claim to represent?

To this there is a simple answer: we are *people*, and the rest of the world is *stuff*: it has no vote; it cannot in any literal sense of the word have one, and it should have none.

"The Environment" Isn't The Environment

It is perhaps useful to add that the idea of there being some one thing called "the environment" that "needs protecting" (as it is, preservation in its current state, or returned to some past state) is a muddle. The environment consists of a whole lot of things, and a whole lot of animal species, plants, and the rest of it. And it is ever-changing, as the forces of evolution, wind and weather, viruses and gene-frequencies go on. Species have no interest in preserving species, nor in general the individuals comprised in them;

and the world as a whole isn't even a species. In the course of hundreds of millions of years, the roster of species flourishing on our planet has changed incredibly. It is a peculiar conceit of a few members of *homo sapiens* that "all life is valuable" and that *we* have a duty to preserve biodiversity for its own sake. Believing that there is such a duty will result in officials forcing a man who has invested millions of dollars developing an upscale resort complex to cease his activities on the ground that they endanger one particular rare species of bird, thus threatening biodiversity. Thousands of people's pleasant vacations, and this man's income, will thus be sacrificed to a value that neither he nor very many others hold.

Is that right? Many environmental philosophers think so, but without reason. The actions they advocate amount to eco-gangsterism, and the value on which it is based is fraudulent. That is not how people should relate to each other. In real terms, what cases like this appear to amount to is that people with certain tastes are enabled by the law to force other people who do not share those tastes to act in accordance with them anyway.

If that description of the matter is to be rationally rebutted, it must be by showing that the disappearance of this one species of bird, or whatever, really is important to humanity in general, despite appearances. But important in what way? A few people might have enjoyed spotting those birds; a few others might have wanted to study their habits for scientific purposes. But people's needs are not to be sacrificed to the whims of others with supposedly "superior" tastes. From the moral point of view, none of us is better than any others: we must refrain from imposing our tastes on others, no matter how high of brow we may think ourselves to be. The bird-spotters and the scientists, then, must demonstrate that people's lives would be seriously worsened, and even endangered, by activities such as those of the investor in question— which means, of course, taking into consideration the thousands of potential customers of that investor, who would enjoy the altered environment he proposes to create very much more than the continued existence of a half-dozen X-crested warblers. What must be shown is that *we* are generally endangered in respect of our lives or healths, and not merely in respect of the non-fulfilment of some other people's personal world-views. Absent such a demonstration, there is no case for forcing such people to desist from the humanly useful activities they proposed to engage in.

The "deep environmentalist" view of these matters, in short, is found, on closer examination, to be thoroughly *immoral*. ("Better to kill a man than a snake!"—as one enthusiast for that view, we are told, has said.)

Who Owns Nature?

One way to put this question is: to whom does nature *belong*? Who is to determine what nature is to be used for? Whose purposes should it serve? These familiar and frequently-asked questions are misleading, for they imply that "nature," as such, does belong to someone—to "all of us," usually—and that "it" is a sort of unified "thing" that must be maintained as is, forever. But that presupposition is very far off base. Nature is a whole lot of stuff, of all sorts. It is not, insofar as it is nature, "owned" by anyone, but is instead simply *there*. Ownership doesn't happen until someone undertakes to use parts of the natural world and in relation to someone else in such a way that difficulties arise that are best resolved by recognizing rights over things. There are many ways to use these many natural things, and in detail they will vary enormously from one person to another (and from one organism to another). Even so, these different ways of using nature are mostly quite capable of being pursued by diverse people in diverse places, without seriously, and especially without adversely, affecting each other. You can build one sort of house in place X, while I build a very different house over in place Y—no problem. We both can live happily in our different dwellings. You can enjoy walks in natural forests over there, while I walk along the sidewalks of a large city over here—and we can trade places, too, if we want. Diverse activities can be coordinated to mutual benefit, and the process of co-ordinating them takes place all the time, all over the world, largely without fuss.

The ideas we are presently considering, however, are not so readily resolvable. If you have a view about how the *whole world* should look, your view must clash fundamentally and unavoidably with that of any who would like it to look some other way. And when we bring a "spiritual" dimension into the matter, these rival views will have the force of rival religions, dividing humanity into warring camps. Just as the proper solution in the case of religion is freedom of religion, with the state and the community taking no sides on the matter, so, too, the proper solution here is freedom of metaphysical orientation. No one of such views may be made the official one, to be used as a basis for pushing rivals around, any more than with religion, where giving one of them official status is precisely what has occasioned the discomfit, or even torture and death, of innumerable "heretics" down through the centuries.

2. The Aesthetic Dimension

People often have aesthetic tastes and pursue aesthetic purposes. One may simply want to contemplate certain portions of nature in its unaltered form—gaze admiringly at a broad valley, or the starry heavens above, or breathe it in, or immerse oneself in it, as when walking through a forest or take a swimming in the ocean. Some claim to derive intense pleasure from contemplating nature as a whole. Such experiences easily inspire people to do something to preserve—or to bend—nature for those purposes.

There are other people involved in these matters. The world does not belong to aesthetes or to believers in animism, and certainly not to one particular set of aesthetes. Their claims are no better (or worse) than anyone else's, so far as the public is concerned. The special qualities of their tastes or beliefs does not give them moral authority over other people. Beauty may or may not be "in the eye of the beholder," as the saying has it, but certainly it is something about which tastes vary enormously. Just as with religion or Deep Environmentalism, the problem of reconciling these divisions is not properly solved by declaring one of them to be in the right.

Sometimes there is a good deal of agreement about some such matter. For example, few of us enjoy litter in public parks or on highways. On the other hand, some like desert landscapes, others lush green valleys, and so on. Happily, the world is large enough to afford a great variety of scenery, and the productive work of humans, in many people's estimations, often enhances the landscape rather than destroying its beauty. Again, it is clear that there is no one way that the whole world ought to be, so far as visual beauty is concerned—and no one way that it can be, for that matter. A coherent moral principle about such matters must enable the diversity of tastes to co-exist on co-operative terms, and such terms do not consist in declaring one party's aesthetic outlook to be the right one, and all others to be wrong. Nor should they simply allow the majority to rule. There is a better way. But it can be best appreciated by moving to our third category, that of the specifically human values of human health, human survival, and the flourishing of human individuals.

3. Human-Centred Problems

Environmental problems of the latter kind are twofold. One concerns overpopulation via resource exhaustion: might there be so many people that we will use up all the resources necessary for sustaining human life? The second concerns health and risks to it that arise as by-products ("externalities") to human uses of bits of the environment.

Both of these are really forms of one fundamental problem: What is the right way to allocate or allot natural resources among potential users and how do we decide who gets to do what and with what? The "better way" hinted at in the preceding section will emerge especially from reflection on this last question. So we'll start with this more fundamental question, then return to the first two.

First, the Solution

How are we to reconcile the immense variety of conflicting interests in nature? The bad way is to decide whose tastes or interests are the "right" ones. That question, if asked, will be decided one way by aesthetes, or by the politically ambitious—and another way by others, and still another by yet others. It is, in fact, a non-answer—indeed, a fraudulent or pseudo-answer—one that fundamentally re-raises the original question while diverting the attention of the discussants.

But there is also a good answer to the question, and so far as I can see, the only good answer. It says, first, that people are to be free to use bits of nature as they please, and thus must each respect every other person's right to do so as well. This leads to the familiar idea of private property. Those using bits of nature that have not been previously used by others are to be regarded as *entitled* to continue to do so as they please: others may not invade and despoil just as they please, but must instead obtain the consent of the owner. As more and more things come under human use, property acquisition will proceed not by setting forth into unowned nature but by trading, buying, and selling what various people already have and have worked on. People will often be motivated to relinquish their right to what they currently own by being offered something they regard as better. Usually these offers will take financial form, and generally (but not always) the owners will sell to those who offer the highest price.

This suggests the solution to the kind of problems we have been considering, as well as the further ones we are about to discuss: how much are the different parties willing to pay to have their interests realized? If Group A will pay more, then its interests regarding the use of that particular item will get realized; if B offers to pay more, then B's will be realized. That is a good measure of the net benefit to be had, and it measures it in a way that is beneficial for all concerned. For note that B is not simply left out in the cold—as he would be if instead the matter is decided by a group of legislators with the power to force one or another "solution" upon him. Market solutions mean that those whose interests in that particular item do not, as a result of their closer transactions, get pursued, will now, with their newly acquired cash, be able to pursue some other interests. Moreover, these other interests will be regarded by B as *more important* than the original ones: it was worth more to B to relinquish his claim on the original item, given its cost under the circumstances, than to exchange for possession of something else. You get this acre of land in a valuable urban location, I get a condo in Florida. You acquire my bit of land with a small vein of gold running under it, and I set up a pizza shop in Edmonton.

How Everybody Can Win

What's important about this "market" system, in short, is that it is "win-win": that is to say, all parties emerge from the transactions better off, in their own view, than before. This is so when the original parties had enormous disparities of relative wealth as well as when they did not. When Microsoft sells you a piece of software that you value, you judge your several hundred dollars to be well spent: you are better off with the software than with whatever else you might have bought with the same money; and Bill Gates is now, say, several hundred dollars wealthier than he already was—which (at present writing) is very wealthy indeed.

What will surprise some readers, and very likely anger some others, and be rejected out of hand by still others, is that this "market" solution continues to be the right one in the special case of scarce resources that could possibly be exhausted, just as it is for any other cases. The key to the matter is that as desired things become scarcer, then—provided they are owned by persons interested in making money—the price goes up. This increase in price has two very useful effects, socially speaking. First, it means that those resources will go to the people who really want them, as evidenced by how much they are prepared to give up in order to have them; and for the same reason, they will be people who are likely to put them to good use, since otherwise their expensive purchase may lie idle. Second, it will motivate the other people who did not get the items in question to find alternatives, so that they can get along without the scarcer item. In both cases, the result is that people get more value out of the scarce resource: a given unit of it goes farther—does more things for more people.

But mightn't we run out of certain things altogether? And wouldn't that create a case for government or other forcible intervention or something of the sort? That is the standard view on this matter. But it is the wrong view, as I shall now try to show.

Scarcity and Natural Resources: Exhaustion?

Many human purposes in using parts of nature require the transformation of those parts into something else. An apple is transformed into energy for nourishing and propelling a human; a tree might get turned into firewood, a log cabin, or thousands of sheets of writing paper; coal or oil might be converted into mechanical motion as when powering cars, or making asphalt for paving, or warmth for buildings. All of these uses require more or less know-how, or as we now call it, "technology," low and high. And all of these uses are regarded by most people as much preferable to leaving nature as it was—leaving the oil in the ground, or the trees unaltered in the earth.

Uses of natural items that require their transformation into something else raise, of course, the question of supply. In some cases, the transformation is (so far as we presently know, anyway) irreversible: the original natural substances are used up. Of course, nothing is used up in the sense that its material particles and contained energy literally disappear; the supply of matter in the region of the earth is nearly constant, and of matter/energy in the universe likewise. But specific materials, such as tungsten, say, more or less slowly disappear from our particular planet. In many other cases, natural items are moved around a lot and considerably transformed, as when water is boiled or frozen—but then they change back, as when ice melts or steam condenses. These cases bring up the subject of resource conservation or exhaustion, and thus of "sustainable development," in a now-modish phrase. Let's discuss this important subject.

Is there a realistic possibility that we humans will run out of resources necessary to sustain life? Or at least to sustain the kind of life-style that we in the "rich" countries have achieved? Many people, and perhaps the ordinary person on the street, apparently think so. But there are very good reasons for thinking that the answer to that, so far as we can see, is actually in the negative. The main reason is that the essentials of life for people are all renewable, rather than being exhausted upon use.

Food

Let's take the most obvious of them—food. The food on my plate disappears when I eat it, yes—but everything returns to the earth by and by, and new plants and animals appear. As a matter of fact, the nutrients out of which living tissues are made come mainly from the air, so that the mass of living matter on earth, rather than decreasing, *increases* over time.

We know how air renews. We are part of a cycle, in which we breathe oxygen in and carbon dioxide out, while plants do just the reverse. Equally obviously, water renews, and without even changing very much in the process. Food is part of the cycle and the chain. When humans increase their food production efforts, the results increase the base for the next round. And so on.

Without going into details about all these mechanisms, we need only point to the gross facts about food production to realize that claims about global "overpopulation" and "carrying capacity" are groundless. During the twentieth century, the world saw an amazing increase in population, due mainly to the fact that by the later part of the century people all lived so much longer even as the global birth rate showed a marked decline. Yet, contrary to what the reader may suppose, food production has more than kept up with all the new mouths to feed. In the 30 years from 1961-1990, world population rather more than doubled, but the average number of calories per person increased markedly, especially in the poor countries—as one might have hoped—by about one third, according to standard estimates. Starvation, about which people hear so much when it happens, has been limited in this century almost entirely to politically caused food shortages such as forced evictions and migrations of people, or simply imposed starvation, as in Stalin's treatment of the Ukrainian kulaks. It wasn't nature's fault, nor was it the fault of ordinary people trying to get by in the world.

What we now know is that once an area has a reasonably free agricultural system, where producers are able to set their prices by negotiation with willing buyers, it soon becomes self-sufficient or better. When China, which had been using collective agriculture and state-controlled prices, freed up its agriculture, output increased so dramatically that by the end of one decade it was actually exporting food, even while its inhabitants were enjoying much better diets than before. Its policy of forced population control, which it had used for decades, had done no good for the food situation, but free agriculture solved those problems; its population control measures were probably completely pointless.[1] In general, the story about food production shows that Malthusian fears about "overpopulation" are far off the mark. So far as food is concerned, there is *no* population problem, no problem of "carrying capacity" for the globe, and there need never be one.

This subject has provided the occasion for one of the most spectacular mistakes in the history of social science—the "Malthusian" hypothesis (soon repudiated by its author), according to which humankind's tendency to reproduce makes for an exponential growth in population, while its agricultural efforts can meet only with arithmetical increases in production. It is puzzling that Malthus should have arrived at so arbitrary a hypothesis about how agricultural resources increase—except that humans are wonderful at spinning elegant explanations of things they know nothing about. To see how arbitrary his "explanation" was, just suppose that available land is fixed, that agricultural technology is also fixed, and that all cultivable land is actually under cultivation by the available methods. In that case, the potential for increased production per acre is not an arithmetical increase - it is *zero*, regardless of how much additional labour is expended. On the other hand, a single farmer armed with a radical improvement in agricultural methods can double or triple his crop in a single season. To generalize as Malthus did is to ignore reality.

Happily, the combination of conditions in which additional effort is fruitless virtually never obtains, save for very tiny particular areas for brief periods of time. In the first place, the whole world's supply of agricultural land is not fixed, but is itself a function of agricultural technology: forests are cleared, swamps are drained, even areas covered by the sea are made cultivable, as illustrated by hard-working Netherlanders with their pumps and dikes, resulting in areas of land not available to earlier residents of northwestern Europe. Second, and of far greater importance, people can increase the number of calories and other nutritional desiderata got from a given amount of land by improvement both in methods of cultivation and in the very plants that we cultivate. The result is that we grow more and better food from less and less land. And there is no predictable rate for increases from this source. A farmer with a new species of wheat, or a new method of planting it, could double his output in a year. The new hydroponic farming technology enables incredible amounts of food to be grown without using any agricultural land at all. The upper floors of tall buildings, for example, will do. Malthus's idea captivated the imaginations of academics for a century and more, but it is, to be blunt, technical poppycock. Those who accept his arguments do not know what they are talking about.

Agricultural production is a subject that few city-folk and few academics appreciate—starting with Marx, who scoffed at the "idiocy of the countryside." The picture of agricultural production entertained by these literate and otherwise intelligent people seems to be that *nature* does all the supplying, and all *we* do is pick things up: a fixed number of apples, and (oh, dear!) at this rate, eventually they'll all be picked! But everything possible is wrong with that picture. Nature is the base from which we work, indeed: but *everything* is done by people—ingenious and hard-working orchard-keepers learning ways to grow more and more apples per tree; agricultural scientists developing new and better varieties of apple; other clever people designing better tractors and trucks, and much, much more. No work, no food: in the sweat of our brow, says the Lord, shall we eat bread. But the sweat is not just from muscular exertion: it is, far more, from cognitive exertion, from learning what works and what doesn't—how to get more from less. Nowadays, in fact, the amount of literal sweat is much reduced. Farmers in North America have increased their yields per acre of wheat, corn, soybeans, and so on, to an extent that few can appreciate who don't live on farms, and meanwhile they sow, plough, and reap in air-conditioned comfort. The net result of all this activity every-where is that the contemporary world grows more food per person than ever before, despite there being many more people to feed than ever before. And meanwhile, it also enjoys an *increase*—not a decrease, as writers on this matter who haven't looked up the facts tend to claim—of forested land and recreational land of all types. It is fascinating that people can write solemn apocalyptic books, such as Paul Ehrlich's popular *The Population Bomb*,[2] at the very time when their ideas are being refuted all around them. The contem-porary reading public has been exposed to more misinformation about the physical aspects of the world around them, I think, than about any other subject today.

Other Resources

That is the story with food, you may be thinking, but what about all the other resources on which we now depend? Is there not a con-cern about sustaining the contemporary lifestyles of the well-off people in the world? And what about extending this lifestyle to oth-ers? Is not the North exploiting the South? Surely aboriginal peo-ples can never end up with one car per family, if we in the northern hemisphere insist on hogging all the resources necessary for them to achieve that level? Again, despite the virtual ubiquitousness of an affirmative answer to this question— inculcated into all heads in grade schools and even in universities—the answer is in fact nega-tive. But here the reason, though rather like the case with food and population, has nuances worth appreciating.

As noted, some natural resources tend to get "used up." If the uses to which we put those things are such as to make resupply of the same item impossible, and we kept on using them in the same way and at a steady rate, then it would no doubt be possible to run out of those things altogether. Despite that, however, there turns out to be no reason to think that we will ever "run out" of *any* of them, and absolutely no reason to think that even if we did we would be depriving ourselves of any of the good things they cur-rently enable us to have. The picture that people are being sold when those disaster-scenario claims are made is, like the Malthusian picture, totally wrong.

In the first place, none of those things *is* literally necessary for life, nor for living in the high style to which we have become accustomed. In fact, none of them is specifically necessary for *any* of our amenities. The reason for this is that our wealth consists of human-made goods and services, and those goods use up very little in the way of natural resources; above all, they don't require any *particular* resources. Buildings are massive, but are made mainly of concrete, brick, and the like—materials that present no scarcity problem and are in any case indefinitely reusable. Buildings nowadays still use a fair amount of wood, to be sure; but wood is biological, it is easy to grow more when needed, and that is exactly what we do. In fact, we grow new forests more rapidly than we use up old ones.[3] The world's forests, except in the Amazon,[4] are increasing, not decreasing—a point that seems to have been overlooked by many advocates of paper recycling and the like. "Save the Trees!" is a completely pointless slogan. Many buildings still require steel, of course; but it is not in short supply, either. The world's supply of iron ore is currently estimated to be sufficient to last thousands of years, even at current rates of use.

Now consider a product built of some natural material that is so scarce that we possibly might run out of it—*if* current rates of use are sustained for more than, say, a few decades. Then what? The answer is easy. If those resources are, as they should be, in the hands of profit-seeking individuals and companies, then their scarcity means that their price will go up. By the time the item gets really scarce, few former users will still be using it—they will, as most of us always have, be happily using other things that are cheaper. And, too, in the meantime ingenious people will have set to work not only making it possible to use the cheaper resources, but in almost all cases, to make the resultant products better as well. To take a small but wholly typical example: collectors of recordings of music, such as this author, were gladdened by the move in the late 1940s from heavy 78 rpm records to much lighter long-playing records made entirely of polyvinyl. These slim discs held about five times as much music, weighed much less, and sounded a lot better than their predecessors. Their production also made far less demand on expendable resources, vinyl being made of stuff for which there is no supply problem. Then to complete the picture, in the 1980s compact discs supplanted LPs, an even tinier quantity of cheap plastic replaced a much larger one, again the resulting quality of sound was much higher, and yet huge production makes basically no draw at all on expendable natural resources.

A colleague remarked one morning that he'd acquired a neat device for his new car that was intended to be magnetically attached to a handy metal surface—but there were no metal surfaces! Durable and safer plastics had replaced steel in all those areas. Yet only collectors and antiquarians would value a 1927 or 1947 car above its 1997 successor—so much more comfortable, durable, safer, faster, and in every way better. This story is repeated everywhere in modern life. The greatly superior range of options enjoyed by contemporary citizens of wealthy countries depends not on the use of irreplaceable resources, but on the more and more ingenious use of less and less rare materials. In short, our well-being depends on technology. And there is no limit to technological development—no limit to the amount of useful information we humans might eventually acquire, and by means of which we can turn cheap and plentiful materials into exotic and useful devices, playthings, tools, and so on indefinitely. The question in all cases is whether we can do better by continuing to use the increasingly scarce item, or by shifting to something else. Which we do depends on one thing above all others: human ingenuity, the growth of technical knowledge.

When we think about the matter carefully, we will realize that there is no strictly natural item that is valuable in and of itself irrespective of human knowledge or interests. And human interests, apart from a very few very basic ones, change. We will always need food, water, air, and a local environment falling within a certain temperature range. But none of those involve resource exhaustion of a relevantly interesting kind. We depend on the sun for energy, and it, some billions of years hence, will no doubt exhaust itself and turn cold, or blow up spectacularly, in both cases destroying all support for life on earth, and/or the earth itself. But while that is charming to contemplate for purposes of writing science fiction, its practical relevance for anybody's life in the foreseeable future is nil. For all practical purposes, we can expect a continuing flow of energy from the sun, indefinitely. Water and air are naturally recycled. We breathe out CO_2 and breathe in oxygen; luckily, plants do just the reverse. Both we and the plants can tolerate considerable variations in the proportions of the two gases, and within those wide limits, we can co-exist happily forever. We drink water in at one end, and out it comes later on at the other, to be recycled through the earth and air until once again it goes through us. Here humans can and do help matters along, cleaning the water more quickly than would the natural environment, or moving it from one place to another. There is no question of exhaustion, except at very local, idiosyncratic, and temporary levels. Given technology and plenty of energy—which we have - water can even, if necessary, be desalinated and piped in from the ocean, as is increasingly done in Arabia. In almost all other places in the world, much cheaper solutions are available.

The same story is repeated everywhere. Are we running out of oil? One would think that we *must* be—yet every year the estimates of remaining resources increase rather than decrease, and to the consternation of Arab sheiks its price goes down rather than up. And at the same time as people find more and more natural oil, others also find ways to use less of it. A modern well-insulated house with high-efficiency gas furnace will keep families in northerly climates such as Canada's more comfortable at a tiny fraction of the cost in resources required to feed the wood or coal stoves used by their great-grandparents, whose frame houses had leaky walls and windows, or by their parents with their inefficient furnaces and mediocre insulation. In fact, houses have been built that require no furnaces at all, even in cold Ontario. There is currently no reason to go to that expense except to show that it can be done; but the fact illustrates the point that there is no such thing as unavoidable human dependence on particular, expendable natural resources to maintain life in comfort.

As the late Julian Simon observed, a good way to go broke nowadays is to invest your money in natural resources such as gold or copper. The reason for this is that we learn to use less of these things for old purposes and to use other and better materials for many of those and a great range of new purposes. Diamonds may be a girl's best friend, but the major action with diamonds is in industrial applications, and most diamonds so used are now synthetic. Plastics of a great variety of types have replaced metals. Carbon fibre racing cars protect their drivers far better than the steel or aluminum ones formerly standard—and there is no shortage of carbon. The story goes on and on. When we get to the further reaches of current technology, it soon becomes clear that the idea that mankind may collectively be facing resource shortages, threatening the lives of us all, is completely without foundation. It is a bugaboo, made from misinformation, misinterpretation, and bad reasoning—period.

The word 'period' will offend many readers of the above, but it is meant seriously: there is, in the end, *nothing at all*—except muddle, misunderstanding, and arbitrary speculation—to the case for the idea that mankind is going to run out of x or y or z and that we therefore must start to conserve. If the reader looks carefully into the mandated conservation efforts of our time, he will find that the same story holds for all of them. Governments require us to recycle paper. Why? Because we will run out of trees? But trees are growing so fast around the world that new growth vastly outstrips harvests for commercial and industrial purposes; and recycling takes much more energy than manufacturing new paper. Again, governments require elaborate sortings of garbage so that various components of it can be recycled. But the recycling takes more energy and on the whole more resources than the original cans and bottles and cardboard in question. Is it feared that we will run out of land to dump garbage in? This idea is popular, but a modest amount of arithmetic shows it to be baseless. All of the garbage expected to be produced in the United States for the next 100 years, if simply dumped on the ground, would make a pile 300 feet deep about the size of Abilene, Texas; covering the whole country to that depth would take 41,000 years.[5] But even now only a fraction is dumped, and the more expensive the land gets on which we dump the garbage, the greater the inducement to do something else with it, such as burning it by a clean method, promoting decomposition, and so on. As with all stories about scarcity, this story assumes that no other ways of dealing with wastes are available or ever will be. Since many other ways already exist, that assumption is already known to be false. Like the others, this story of resource scarcity is essentially fraudulent.

No better example of modern life improvement can be pointed to nowadays than the computer and its associated Internet. And what material resources are required for computers? The heart of the computer is the microchip, which uses a decreasing amount of a material so plentiful that even the most dedicated environmentalist must blush to talk of "scarcity." Yet one microchip can do more useful work than a hundred nineteenth-century steam engines. A human being spending a day at his computer, and going out for a jog beforehand or at lunchtime, will have worked more interestingly and more fruitfully than any coal miner, without using up any resources of value other than his own time. But he will have used that time better. Another human may spend his day practising the violin, or rehearsing for the dramatic production to be mounted the following week. Millions of people spend their time in institutions of learning or research, all with the most trivial use of natural resources. Writers depicting a world of steadily and inevitably diminishing resources as a result of the ravages of modern life, could not readily be more in error about the character of the world around them.

The lesson in all this is that the material needs of humans are not met by more or less rapidly depleting a large heap of natural stuff. That picture is entirely misguided. Instead, our wants are predominantly and increasingly met by intelligently transforming diminishing amounts of scarce natural stuff into artificial but much more useful goods of immense variety. The primary ingredient is not *stuff*, but *ingenuity*; and with this, our species is remarkably well endowed. A good idea is rapidly spread around, and other bright people improve on it or apply it to different areas. Meanwhile, the people who are served by all this are free to buy or not as they choose, and their choices in that regard exert powerful pressures toward the production of what is most wanted, and the non-production of what is not wanted. This rather simple mechanism is amazingly effective, especially because it requires no direction or control from above. Quite the contrary: almost anything a government is likely to try to do in this area is sure to be counter-productive. If it was truly beneficial to do the things governments supposedly require people to do for their own good, after all, they would most likely do those things; that it instead requires force to get them to do them is virtually a certain indication that those things are not beneficial after all.

A further, sober reflection on all this is in order. If we look around for the *major* waste of resources in our time, we shall look not to humanly pleasurable or useful activities, but above all to war, where huge machines are blown to bits, huge ships sunk, billions of small bits of steel expended, and all for the purpose of destruction rather than constructive improvement of human life. Such activities are genuinely wasteful in every sense of the word, looked at in the large. If anyone benefits from war, it is at most the politically ambitious and perhaps the industrialists they employ at such high cost, not the long-suffering populace who bear its costs in such depressing degree. Yet wars are by-products of government, not of rational economic activity by individuals trying to improve their lives. People engaging in commerce for mutual benefit do not shoot each other—that is hardly a mutually beneficial activity. When money can be made in the weapons business, we won't have to dig much to see that it is the force of government that lies behind it. Governments extract taxes from their citizens, and use the revenues thus gleaned to create a market for bombs, tanks, and fighter planes. If you want resource ill-use, look always to the use of coercion and force by possessors of political power, not to the typical voluntary activities of ordinary people.

Most readers at this point will be thinking of environmental problems that they have read about in newspapers and magazines. Fires and floods are routine occurrences; but our subject here is global problems—large-scale looming disasters that are supposed to affect mankind as a whole. Here we need evidence of a large-scale type—and such evidence tells entirely against those who prophesy doom for mankind. The actual evidence is that the human race has more and better food to eat, better houses, more cars, much more and more interesting entertainment, more opportunities to witness the glories of nature or to walk in the forests, and in general, more of everything good—at the same time that we live longer, on average, than humans have ever done before, despite cancer, cigarettes, auto accidents, and the rest of it.[6] Moreover, there is no inherent reason why we cannot continue to improve, nor why the whole of the human race cannot enjoy that abundance.

Epilogue on Resource Exhaustion: The Vanishing Species

Let us return now to the sample case mentioned many pages ago, involving the resort developer versus the bird fanciers and ornithologists. Note, first, that agreement on the matter as it is usually conceived is out of the question. On this current view, either we require everybody to make sacrifices to save the birds, or we require bird-lovers to stand and weep as the last members of the X-crested warbler go under. Of course, enthusiasts might manage to preach to our resort developer and convert him to their ecocentric views. Freedom of speech permits them to try to do just that, after all—if the developer will listen. But in the extremely likely event that the bird-lovers fail in this endeavour, then what? The familiar answer is that the parties purporting to be on the side of the environment will fax their members of Parliament or other persons in a position to coerce the newcomers. And if, as is likely, they are successful, then our entrepreneur is out several million dollars, and the many thousands of people who might have enjoyed a vacation at his facility are deprived of that opportunity. Total loss to the public: $20 million or so. Total gain to the public: a few bird fanciers enjoy the knowledge that there may be a dozen more spotted white-crested thrushes than there otherwise would have been. Some few people will have extracted minor benefits from others, at enormous expense to the latter and without compensation. How much of that sum would these people have been prepared to pay for this benefit, if they had had to do so in order to get it? Probably very little. Net cost to society: a whole lot.

It will be replied, correctly, that *future* bird watchers are also deprived of their satisfaction by the building of the resort. That's true. But then, why do they have any more right to have their interests satisfied than future vacationers? And how would one calculate such things? There are thousands of bird species in the world for bird-watchers to enjoy. The marginal cost of one less species is something, no doubt—but *how much*? That is something for present bird-watchers to consider, and insofar as they feel themselves to be representing these people, they should stand ready to invest in the future of bird-watchers by subsidizing the spotted white-crested thrush—by buying up the property and preserving it for the birds. If they are unwilling to do so, then we will have to infer that the interest in question is not as great as they supposed.

Many writers talk as though the disappearance of some species is a cosmic disaster, and that it is the sacred duty of humans to impoverish themselves (or rather, their neighbours) to prevent this from occurring. Yet Mother Nature, over the past several hundred million years, has managed to exterminate species by the million. If we want to adopt the values of Nature, there is a much better case for abetting wholesale destruction than for preserving species.

Meanwhile our developer, of course, is also looking to the future. In investing millions of dollars in the area, building hotels, swimming pools, paths through the woods where guests may commune in peace with the birds, and so on, he is betting on the future. He is estimating that people will find their enjoyment enhanced so much by these facilities that they are willing to pay a great deal for it, thus justifying his investment.

So, who is right? The market provides the correct solution. Those who value birds, snails, and so forth, should be buying up the sort of habitat they will thrive in, thus helping to ensure what they see to be the future of ornithologically interested humanity. Those who value pleasant swims, the ocean air, and so forth, more than they value the sight and sound of one particular species of rare bird will buy vacations at our hypothetical resort. And in fact, as is already being done in more rational areas in our world, still others, noting the increasing market for eco-vacations, will buy up that land, preserve the species, and make a handsome profit by arranging tours for ecological enthusiasts to view the last members of a rare species in their native habitat. Again, the market provides the correct, win-win solution.

The point here is not that species will, necessarily, be preserved after all. It is that those species will be preserved in which there is enough genuine interest to make it reasonable for humans to get together, voluntarily, and preserve them—and not otherwise. The values of an élite coterie of ecological enthusiasts have no special status as compared with those of people with more ordinary and mundane interests. But they can meet, to mutual benefit, in the marketplace. That is the way to respect the rights of all concerned.

Pollution and Health

The final set of questions to be concerned with has to do with health and safety. Some human activities generate by-products that are harmful to human health. Here, at last, we will surely need government or the equivalent, will we not? That is what most people think, and they may possibly be right about some things. But which?

The general category of most concern here is pollution. What gets polluted is the air, water, and sometimes earth. But these present very different problems. Air is ubiquitous: smoke ejected into the air at point X very soon makes its way to point Y, and thence into the lungs of people far removed from the original source. Moreover, it is often very difficult and likely impossible to know just who is to blame and who are the victims of particular pollutants. That is what makes pollution an example of what economists call "externalities": costs involved in the production of certain goods that are borne by people who did not get the goods in question.

The same can be true, though in less degree, of water. Common dwellers on the shore of a lake will experience the impurities dumped into it by others on that lake. Other lakes around, however, may be quite unaffected. Rivers have a direction; those upstream pollute the waters of those downstream and not the other way around. Contaminants in water spread more or less in ways that are trackable and containable at greater or less cost. And while earth may be polluted, the pollutants do not distribute very widely, in general. If owner A's land is infected, it is usually going to be his immediate neighbour who is to blame, not someone miles away.

Pollution, on the face of it, is morally problematic, because it involves the worsening of others' condition. Your lungs, your stomach, and other parts of your biological system can be poisoned by the activities of others, and since those bodily parts are indeed yours, those activities are, on the face of it, wrongful. But here we come upon three very important points that complicate matters greatly.

The first is that all of these things are very much matters of *degree*. There is no substance of any kind of which the human body cannot tolerate even one molecule, and all known poisons are such that a great deal more than that is necessary before their effects on people become toxic. Moreover, substances that are poisonous in high degree may be essential to life in lesser quantities. The human body normally contains a bit of arsenic, and any number of other toxic chemicals. On the other hand, every ingestible substance, no matter how nutritious, is a case in point: if you are force-fed enormous quantities of anything, however necessary for life if taken in the right amounts, you will die. Yet if you are deprived altogether of those same things, you will also die. This is the principle laid down by Paraselsis many centuries ago. When asked what is poisonous, he replied that everything is a poison, and yet that nothing is—it all depends on the amount.

Second, there is considerable variability: poisons are rather variable from one person to another. Some people have allergies to nuts. If A invites B to a party, at which the dessert includes a hint of pecan flavour, B could easily die as a result of what was intended to be a benefit. Some people can tolerate amounts of substance x that would be fatal to others. North American tourists visiting Central America or Africa usually cannot drink the water that is the normal fare for the local inhabitants. Those who didn't succumb to its con-

taminants in infancy now thrive on it. People can be slowly habitu-
ated to diets that will sicken or kill others if suddenly exposed to
them.

Knowledge of both of these variables is essential if we are to
exert reasonable controls on our actions in relation to each other.
But we now come to the third and probably most important of
them. Few things we can do cause no alien substances of any kind,
in any degree, to be inflicted upon anyone, but the levels may be
low enough so that they are quite prepared to have us perform
those activities anyway—especially when the levels are vanishing-
ly low, as they characteristically are. But even when they are not,
they may constitute part of a price that on the whole is worth paying. The noise of a great city is endured by all, especially when
they walk the city's central streets; but most people are quite willing to endure those sounds in exchange for the other benefits of
city life, often travelling hundreds of miles at considerable
expense to do so. Automobiles emit pollutants in their exhausts;
yet the benefits of automobiles, both to their drivers and to those
who benefit from the improved services and levels of production
that automobiles provide, far outweigh the costs of their pollution, and that was so even when automobiles were far more pollu-
tive than they are now.

In fact, if there were no motor vehicles, we would not only be
far poorer than we are, but less healthy as well. Longevity has
increased greatly in the industrialized countries, despite the levels
of pollution that are the by-products of their industries. This is
undoubtedly due in considerable part to the better diets and
improved health care that reliable and efficient transportation
makes possible. If the ambulance that carries a heart attack victim
to hospital had to be horse-drawn, many patients would be dead by
the time or arrival—not to mention that horses pollute far more
than cars anyway.

Environmental Fallacies

Perfect Purity

The first lesson of all this reflection is that any policy that tells us
that the right level of pollution is *no* pollution is, to put it bluntly,
absurd. Zero pollution is unachievable, and close approximations to
it are almost always far worse than modest pollution, when their full

costs are appreciated. If it is proposed to spend huge sums cleaning up the external atmosphere, the unwary taxpayer should know that the average home has an atmosphere far more polluted than the external air, even in busy cities with considerable industry. Despite the fact that he spends half of his hours in that comparatively very polluted air, that same average taxpayer is going to live to be eighty to ninety years old at current rates. The extra money he would be required to spend on reductions of air pollution may well be a waste of money: a vacation in Hawaii or an improved stereo system could easily be a far better investment.

The situation is this. Most people live in environments that are clean enough to support a good and long life. When they become fatally ill, it will rarely be due to any of the usually cited causes: environmentally induced cancers, for example, from chemicals in one's after-shave lotion, are very rare. And when there are such, it is usually self-imposed, as when the cancer patient spent the last twenty years smoking a pack of cigarettes a day, or the heart attack victim has avoided the foods that would have prevented his condition, or has eaten too many of those that promote it. For all these people, extra expenditures to clean up the environment are not worth making. The smoker who lives in Los Angeles is poisoning himself at a rate that makes the effects of its frequent smogs trivial by comparison. For other people, such expenditures, up to some point, may be worth making. But what point?

To know this, we must have an estimate of the health-promoting effects of the proposed cleanups. We must then compare those benefits with the proposed costs. If the probability of getting cancer is improved by one thousandth of one percent, at a cost of $500 per capita, that expenditure will not be worth making. But if the same benefit can be obtained for, say, $25 per person, it is likely worth it for almost anyone. In a political environment in which we are continually told that all pollution is evil and that anything spent on pollution is a good investment, the likelihood that environmental proposals are soundly based from the point of view of the ordinary citizen is very low.

Back to Nature

In today's political atmosphere, the average citizen probably thinks that pollution is a uniquely contemporary problem brought on by industrialization. Such citizens will be interested to hear how far from the truth this actually is. Primitive peoples have a life expectancy roughly half that of contemporary industrial countries. What brings this about? The brief answer is: polluted water, infested food, and wood smoke. Modern water purification methods avoid the first; refrigeration, cooking, and care in the initial preparation of food deal with the second; and the use of efficient furnaces burning natural gas— a fuel, by the way, not available in "nature"— and of electric ranges, greatly reduce the net dangers associated with the third.

An acquaintance used to drive a car with a bumper sticker that read, "Split Wood, not Atoms!" This charming slogan was, we now know, about as badly informed as one can imagine. Wood smoke is among the worst sources of air pollution known to man, whereas the generation of electricity by nuclear means is a method as near as we know to absolute purity so far as air pollutions are concerned. Nuclear generation is also safer than any other method, when all costs are taken into account, even compared to hydroelectricity— hydro dams have a way of bursting, drowning many people, whereas the dangers of nuclear generation are well known to engineers and readily containable. One top scientist puts things in perspective by pointing out that the use of coal and other fuels instead of nuclear energy costs several hundred lives per year in the United States.[7]

Probably the chief benefit of modern science to mankind was the discovery of the germ theory of disease. This led to our ability to test water for microorganisms likely to cause diseases, and also to the use of routinely sterile methods of supervising the birthing process. Clean water and clean births lower the infant and child mortality rates by quite spectacular amounts, by comparison with which, probably, all the other benefits of modern medicine pale. Primitive peoples are victims of these micro-organisms at a rate that amounts to devastation by contemporary standards. The discovery of this one source of pollution, with comparatively cheap and simple methods of cleanup, has gained more useful life for more people than all of the higher-tech resources of modern medicine put together.

The plausibility of "Back to Nature" as a formula for healthy living is, in short, zero. Those who say this probably mean that if you could go back to just the right parts of nature, under just the right conditions, and armed with an arsenal of modern scientific knowledge about the environment you would then be living in, you could probably do very well. Moving us all back to seventeenth-century rural technology, on the other hand, would certainly get us seventeenth-century levels of health and life expectancy along with it.

Health Above All!

The most fundamental, perhaps, of the fallacies that infect current thinking about the environment is the idea that physical health in particular is so important to us all that nothing else counts by comparison. This is a view that does not correspond to the practice of very many people. Almost everyone we know, including ourselves, has a lifestyle that could be healthier. To achieve that greater degree of health would involve abandoning that lifestyle, or modifying it so much that its main benefits would be much diminished. When this is the case, we must consider which is more important. And it may be either one. The writer who must spend an hour a day exercising if he is to avoid a heart condition may conclude that it is well spent; but if he does so at the cost of what would be his best work, it will not be so obvious.

Some lives are very risky indeed. The mountain climber and the racing car driver engage in activities with a quite significant probability of early death. They make efforts to decrease those risks, but reducing them to negligibility is probably out of the question. Nevertheless, people knowing the risks prefer to engage in those activities. The expected shorter but more interesting life seems to them better than the less interesting but less risky alternatives.

This brings us back to the ideas explored in early chapters on life and death. We choose what we shall do on the basis of our values, and those are highly variable from one person to the next. We are not in a very good position to tell our neighbour what he ought to do with that life, and that includes nagging him about his health. All of us value our health to at least some degree, and almost all of us value it quite highly. But making it the dominant interest of our lives is another matter. And imposing it on people at the cost of what they hold dear is not something we have any business doing— so long as what they do hold dear is not, in its turn, significantly dangerous to the next person.

The Exotics: Global Warming, Ozone Depletion, the Weather

Some of the issues about the environment involve quite technical matters; opinions of experts will vary more, and it will be hard for the ordinary person to know what to make of them. The claims made about "global warming" are among the foremost of these. One sees the phrase occurring in the news, and in any number of papers in the journals, as if this were simply a phenomenon, an established fact like the change of the seasons. It is nothing of the sort, however. With a modest amount of research we can unearth the following points. First, the earlier claims made about global warming were based on models, and especially on computer programs, known to be faulty even at the time. Their predictions have been refuted quite resoundingly by ensuing facts. Consensus among the climatologists whose special subject this is has it that in the later part of the twentieth century there has been no global warming at all in the Northern hemisphere, and very little in the Southern hemisphere. Second, the whole subject is extremely sensitive to data selection. Since the weather is both constantly changing and very variable from one place to another, one needs merely to find the appropriate regions and periods to provide evidence for just about any trend you like. Whatever else, readers need to be wary about the sources of global claims. The best source is undoubtedly that of infrared satellites, which are the only technical devices at present that can accurately measure average wide-area temperatures. These have been used for some decades, and during this period they show no warming whatever in the northerly regions where theory suggests that warming should be most serious. Third, there is a good deal of talk about the "greenhouse effect," primarily because here at last is an area where legislators can get into the act. There has definitely been considerable human contribution to a build-up of gases of that kind in the middle and later parts of this century. But it is simply assumed that these contribute to global warming and, as just mentioned, that actually is not happening. Moreover, greenhouse effects can be benign, not just malignant. (In fact, the tenability of human life on the earth is due to it: without greenhouse gases, daytime temperatures would be well above the boiling point, night-time temperatures intolerably cold.) It is now thought that the main effect of the twentieth century's greenhouse gas build-up is to reduce extremes of temperature, and this in turn may have contributed to the increase in agricultural productivity experienced in our hemisphere.[8]

The ozone layer's comings and goings have been in the news primarily because the high-tech tools needed to observe it did not exist until recently; but its instability is legendary, and there is no cause for alarm from that quarter either. The most notable point about the current controversy and its legislative impacts is that the only significant effect on human health from even quite substantial ozone thinnings is increased exposure to ultra-violet rays, which in turn increase the likelihood of skin cancer. The effect of ozone thinning on this important variable is comparatively trivial, equivalent to moving at most a hundred miles south if you live in the northern hemisphere. But the risks of over-exposure to the sun are well known and easily avoided, by wearing a shirt. Legislation requiring people to forego the benefits of Styrofoam or to pay a great deal more for their refrigerators because their manufacturers are legislatively prohibited from using the cheap and very effective gases hitherto normal for such things is hardly justified for the purpose of enabling people to keep their shirts off a few minutes longer.[9]

All of which is enough to illustrate that the reader should not take much in this area at face value. What one should do is to use common sense. The world is doing quite well by us humans: the sea levels are not rising though claims about global warming imply that we should already be experiencing seriously adverse effects. We aren't.

There is little doubt that hypotheses about these matters can be made precise and can be confirmed or disconfirmed over long runs of time. But there is no reason to think at present that anything urgently important is happening. By comparison, enormous floods requiring concerted action by hundreds of thousands of people are real and a familiar feature of the human scene. There is no difficulty seeing that flood waters about to engulf one's neighbourhood are a serious problem, and in such cases affected people will do very well to work together to contain the damage, and should be ready to assist people in need of help. And people have been ready in that way, down through the centuries. If any of the currently touted "crises" and "ecological disasters" were of anything like that degree of seriousness, we would again be ready to respond. But they are not.

The best advice to the person on the street is to remember the story of Chicken Little. The claim that the sky is falling was exciting, indeed, but vague and completely unsubstantiated, and the frantic activity in the neighbourhood inspired by the shrill circulation of that story was completely unjustified. We seem to be in the same situation today: vague stories, but this time backed by scientifically sophisticated findings, are used to arouse the citizenry to what are actually irrational responses—required recycling, heavy-handed environmental regulations entailing costly hearings and surveys, prohibition of very useful substances, and other expensive measures have been the order of the day. But that things are pretty much the way they have been for a long time, are certainly well within the limits that we can live with, and in general are improving rather than the reverse, is the unexciting but heartening report of science more carefully looked at, and of informed common sense.

Summing Up

The subject of the environment has been treated to an extraordinary level of public misinformation, probably unequaled by any other subject in modern times—one would probably have to go back to medieval "science" and theology to equal it. We are told that the human population is out of control and headed for self-extermination because of its excesses, that people are using up vital resources at a rate promising disaster, that ordinary and apparently useful human activities are endangering our lives, and in general that mankind is in the midst of a vast "ecological crisis." The truth on all these matters turns out to be quite unexciting, if one's taste is for grade B thrillers. It is, on the other hand, very exciting indeed if one is interested in the well-being of the human race.

The basic problem with the popular picture is its assumption that the good life consists in "using up" scarce and essential natural resources, so that the better we all live now, the worse life will be for future generations or the folks in the poor countries. That turns out to be a complete mistake. The world faces no population problem, so far as prospects for human nutrition and life are concerned: high population densities have brought greater output of food per person, not less, and greatly enhanced options for interesting and useful activity. Our increasingly better lives in the wealthy countries use up less and less irreplaceable natural resources, and in a great number of cases already use effectively none at all. Nor is there any reason why the benefits we enjoy can't also be enjoyed, as time goes on, by everyone in the whole world. To achieve this, all we need is normal voluntary human activity, with very few externally imposed controls. Refraining from killing and enslaving each other will do far more for the human race than any amount of "environmental regulation," and if we can manage that, the future for mankind looks very bright. So our environmental duty, as ordinary citizens, is simply to refrain, as usual, from activities that obviously injure our neighbours, to continue to earn and spend our money in the best ways we can think of, and to be grateful for the innumerable opportunities for good living that we have inherited from the generations of clever and hard-working people that have preceded us, and that are daily being created by so many among the present generation.

Chapter Eleven

Sexual Ethics: Sex, Love, Marriage, and Family

The topic of sexual ethics is very broad, and many of its issues are very personal. Thus it is specially important to distinguish at the outset between two issues:

1. Which arrangements regarding sexual matters should we be considered to have the *right* to? What are we required to do in this area, and what are we required to avoid?
2. Which arrangements would be *best* for you?

Neither question is an easy one in any of these areas, but (1) is, I think, generally a lot easier than (2). Moreover, (2) is only somewhat a question for general philosophy, though it is very much a question for your personal philosophy of life; but that is something that mostly lies beyond the confines of this book. What we can do about it is mainly to sketch some interesting possibilities; but you must choose, and only you are likely to have most of the relevant information—much of it emotional in nature. For philosophers to try to discuss such things would be like asking whether playing hockey is more fulfilling than sailing. A *philosophical* theory that tries to answer such questions would be eligible for rejection on that count alone. We theorists need to understand our limitations.

Issues

There are four subjects, variously related, that we will look at here: sex, love, marriage, and family. We should start by explaining why I list these as four different subjects, for some would object even to that, insisting that they are inseparable. But there is a clear reason. They are not only logically but actually independent. People can and sometimes do have sexual relations whether or not they love each other, whether or not they are married, and regardless of any actual or contemplated family involvements. People can and do love each other independently of sex, marriage, or family—not only because there are more kinds of love than the kind you "fall in," but also because even with that kind it is quite possible for two people to love each other, yet refrain from sex, marriage or family. Notoriously, people can and sometimes do have sexless, loveless, and childless marriages. We may think that this is too bad, of course, but that's not the point here. The point, rather, is to think about them and see whether we still think it's "too bad" after we have done so. Finally, people can have families without being or getting married, without loving each other, and even without sex (for example, by adoption; or nowadays, by recourse to new medical technologies).

There are four subjects, then, and so the question is, how should they be related? Answers vary widely. But in almost all human societies, it is pretty safe to say, a set of practices on all of these matters, in general, tries to align them with each other more or less closely. In basically "European" countries (such as all those of the Americas), the cultural paradigm is that all four are supposed to go together: person A is to have sex with person B if and only if A also loves B, is married to B, and has or wants to have a family with B. Some non-European societies, including some North American indigenous peoples, deviate interestingly from the European paradigm. Perhaps we can learn something from them.[1]

This paradigm is very imperfectly mirrored in our actual practice. One sees polls indicating that perhaps 60 per cent of all married women and 80 per cent or more of all married men report having had at least one extramarital affair; people getting married with no prior sexual experience with persons other than their marital partners are now quite rare. Divorce and subsequent family breakup are very common, to the point of being nearly typical. And so on. Yet, despite these facts, there is still a general attitude that the paradigm represents the way things really *ought* to be. Adulterers often agree that adultery is immoral; when families break up, the warring spouses may agree that it is too bad that it had to come to that; when people get married and conclude that they are sexually incompatible, they regard that as a great misfortune.

When these attitudes are used to appraise people's behaviour quite generally, then they are moral attitudes in the sense we are concerned with in this book. When, on the other hand, one adopts a certain ideal of behaviour for oneself, at the same time agreeing that other answers might be better for other people, then the values you hold are personal ones. We must, as usual, remind ourselves that while this book is primarily concerned about social morality, personal values are what life is all about. Your values are *you*—the stuff of your life. Obviously, they are important. In our discussion of the present issues, we can perhaps make many useful points to consider or take into account in trying to shape your personal values as well as the public, social norms that are our primary concern. So I won't avoid observations on that level; but it will be important to understand in what spirit they are to be taken. Namely, they are suggestions or depictions of possibilities, but definitely not moral requirements.

So, for example, if we ask whether the Western paradigm is a good one, then that question can be understood to mean: would *you* be happier adopting and at least trying to conform to this paradigm? And the answer might be affirmative. But if we then ask, "But what about everybody else?"—meaning, are we going to insist that they adopt it as well?—then a very different answer might well be indicated. With these prefatory remarks in place, let's try at least to scratch the surface of these inexhaustibly interesting subjects.

Sex: The Biological Background

The background of our subject is biological. Humans are equipped by nature with a sexual system of reproduction. Not all living things are: amoeba reproduce by fission, the organism's genotype simply splitting down the middle, the resulting clones going their separate ways.

In view of the pace of developments in genetics and biotechnology, nobody can speak with confidence about what is possible or impossible. In the past, and mostly still in the present, humans wanting children had to find sexual partners, perform a sex act on an occasion when the woman's eggs were available (a short period each 28 days), and then wait for nine months, during which any number of things could go wrong. At birth itself, still more things could go wrong, and quite often did. Today this picture must be appreciably modified as a picture of what *must* be. Humans have been conceived as well as nurtured outside of wombs, and we can hardly be sure what will come next. Nature, then, does not constrain our options in this area nearly so severely as it did not long ago. For most people, however, the standard procedures remain the norm, and we can expect them to be so for a long time to come. Fortunately, the rates of infant mortality or maternal mortality upon delivery are extremely low; few women need fear for their lives or those of their offspring if they should choose to have children. So we deal in terms that are true for by far the most part—but still, not in terms of certainties and inevitabilities.

From Biology to Sexual Ethics

It was never true that the Western paradigm itself is "natural" in the sense of being the only possible way to do these things. Consider, for example, the idea that the *purpose* of sex is reproduction. The term "purpose," unfortunately, is seriously ambiguous in this context. We must distinguish between at least two understandings of the claim:

1. The *biological function* of human sex organs is reproduction.
2. People *ought to want* children when they perform sex acts.

That these aren't the same thing is easy to show by example: the function of a dum-dum bullet is to make a quite enormous, ragged hole in the victim—but let us hope that people do not generally have as a *purpose* the making of such holes in their fellow humans. Or again: the fact that the biological function of our kidneys is to strain out various poisons from our system doesn't mean that it is immoral to use a kidney dialysis machine.

Concerning the present subject, then, our question is how the undoubted biological function of the sex organs relates to their purposes from the point of view of those whose organs they are. In particular, we should ask where sexual pleasure fits into the picture. Sexual intercourse is, typically, highly enjoyable to those who engage in it (setting aside for the moment the very important cases in which it is involuntary for one party). It is obviously true to say that in many cases, and probably in most cases, the purpose of copulation is pleasure rather than reproduction. In saying this, I am of course talking about the actual conscious motivation of those concerned: what they look forward to is a pleasurable experience. Not only do they not look forward to the production of children, but they characteristically go to some lengths to prevent their production.

Again, remember that we must distinguish the question, Why *do* people engage in sexual activity? from the question, Why *should* they? This last question has to be understood against the background of the answer to the first one. Given that most people are motivated to engage in sexual activity by an interest in pleasure rather than reproduction, is there any reason to insist that they shouldn't be, that they should instead confine themselves to the reproductive purpose?

"Natural" Purpose

A widely employed response to the above is that the reason is that reproduction is the "natural purpose" of sexual activity. But to say this seems to be to attribute "purposes" to "nature," and this is a very problematic attribution, for nature, after all, does not have a mind, and so it can hardly have purposes in the sense in which you and I do. There are, as suggested, "natural functions," but these are understandable as claims about the structures in question, showing what they are capable of doing, how they typically work, and also about their role in the ongoing biological world. Were people to cease using these organs for reproducing, they would cease reproducing; and if they did that, then ere long, the human race would die out. If we think (plausibly) that that is a bad thing, then we have a good answer to "So, why engage in it?": in order to reproduce. But we have no answer at all to the question, "Why not sometimes engage in it for other reasons, too?" (or even, for those reasons *instead* of procreation).

Actually, that is too weak, for indeed we have an excellent reason to do so: it's nice. The answer, "because I want there to be future children of mine" is a good one, too: it points to another interest to be achieved. But then, pleasure is also an interest, as are various other things that possibly could be promoted, on occasion, by sexual activity.

Hedonism and Sex

Sexual pleasure is widely viewed as the very archetype of pleasure, the clearest, simplest, and most straightforward example. But anyone with a modest amount of personal experience will be quick to qualify this picture. A typical sex act between two contemporary adult humans is an extremely *personal* experience: personal in the sense that those involved are not just getting their sexual organs massaged; rather, they take themselves to be relating in an important way to the *particular* person who is their partner on that occasion. They often desire that partner in a highly specific and very intense way. It matters to them that they are doing this, and they suppose, and at least hope, that their partner is responding not only with enjoyment but with love and appreciation. Many specific values are involved in sex, and to treat it as if it were like chocolate ice cream is simply naive. Indeed, the simpler gustatory pleasures, by and large, are actually purer examples of pleasure than sex.

But that is only to say that life is complicated. It is also true that in many cases sex is a source of great pleasure to those involved. We should not demean or underestimate that. Whether narrowly hedonistic or intensely personal, the point is that the range of emotions and feelings involved in sex is often not directly concerned with family, and only incidentally with marriage. Of course, sex has something to do with reproduction, but those who engage in it need not consciously intend or desire reproduction. Any connection with biology is a good deal less direct.

It is presumably true that sexual activity is induced by very basic motives inherent in our biological constitution. Unfortunately, though, it is not at all obvious just how that factor bears on the situation. A rapist, for example, will not and should not be let off from the charge of rape by claiming that he was "driven" to do it. Whatever the sex drive is, it is present in all of us, yet most of us manage to desist from rape. Indeed, quite a few people abstain from sexual activity altogether. Whatever the deep-lying nature of the sex drive may be, it is compatible with a huge range of sexual behaviour, including a virtually total lack of it.

Sex and Beauty

Many people spend a lot of time and energy trying to look attractive, and making observations on the attractiveness or lack of it, of other people. When we fall in love, a major factor in our psychological involvement is often our appreciation of the *look* of the beloved. Countless poems and works of music and art are devoted to beauty of person, especially that of women. This is often described as "sexual attractiveness," and so indeed it is—in some way. But it isn't so easy to say just what this "way" is. If we ask what qualities we have an eye for in the way of sexual attractiveness, one might think that the first answer that comes to mind should be suitability to reproductive functioning. But it doesn't take much reflection to see that that answer is quite strikingly wrong. Many women who don't look anything like the typical erotic superstars of the day are just as sexually capable in every way as are those celebrities. A squat and "ugly" woman will have children just as efficiently, nurture them just as well, and likely provide her mate with as much sheer sexual pleasure as Helen of Troy herself. When men have sexual preferences for beautiful women, the basis of these preferences in purely biological terms, if any, is mostly incomprehensible, and the same goes for women's preferences for men. While physical beauty's capacity to motivate sexual interest and desire is beyond doubt, yet it must be admitted that "sexual" beauty seems to be a unique category of pure aesthetic attraction bearing little relation to reproductive functioning. I find this astonishing and rather wonderful, frankly. But it certainly adds to the mysteries here rather than explaining them.

We should add that it is perfectly possible and not at all unusual for a man to agree that a certain woman is very beautiful, yet have no particular sexual interest in her; and he might agree that a woman he is keenly sexually interested in is not as beautiful as some other. The correlation between the particular kind of beauty of person that we tend to associate with sexual attractiveness and actual sexual attraction would seem to be very imperfect. And again—a good thing, too!

Sex and Love

While reproduction is, for the most part, not the immediate object of sexual activities, those activities are, on the other hand, quite typically concerned with *love*. Typically, yes—but not always. Sexual desire for another person is decidedly not the same thing as love. We can say that sexual desire is a *type* of love, but this is only helpful if one could then show how it is related to the other types—for example, that to be animated by that kind of love is also to be animated by other kinds. But is it? Three kinds of cases provide important evidence on this matter.

First, there is *commercial* sex—the prostitute, who is quite willing to perform sexual acts with anyone willing to pay the price. The prostitute doesn't love her clients, doesn't claim to, and doesn't even want to. She does want her customers to have a good time, for they will then return, increasing her income and saving on advertising costs.

Second, there is the rapist, who appears, if anything, to *hate* his victims; his sex act is an expression of anger rather than love, of the desire to dominate and even destroy his involuntary "partner" rather than to give her good experiences and advance her general well-being.

Third, and most important, we have the participant in "casual" sex. A sees B in a bar, likes the way he looks, strikes up a conversation, and soon they find themselves in bed. Very soon after that, A has forgotten all about B, including his name (which perhaps she never learned), and probably vice versa. Is this to be called "love"? Is their sexual activity to be described as "making love"? The answer is not obvious, but a negative answer seems quite plausible.

We can set aside the example of the prostitute as one in which no real feeling is involved — it's just business. As for passion, she is an expert actress; she fakes it all. For our purposes, then, the feelings of her customers are more important as evidence about the relation between sex and love. Clearly *they* don't do it for the "money," since they pay the price rather than receiving it. Their motives seem to be more like those of casual sex.

We can't set aside the rapist, however, for his activities vividly show us that sex can be combined with horrifyingly negative feelings about others. They certainly show us that sex isn't identical with love. Only some kind of depth psychology could support such a claim: perhaps the rapist is a failure, one who can't attract women to normal, voluntary sex, and so, in fulfilling his desires in this repugnant way, he expresses a longing for something he never had and perhaps cannot have, as well as his envy and hatred of those who do. This is an interesting possibility, but it requires going far beneath the surface of the motivations involved.

The category of "casual" sex seems the most important in this context. Here there is no negative motivation such as the rapist has, and no commercial motive like that of the prostitute. There is mutual erotic attraction, to be sure. But can the motivation of those engaged in casual sex be properly described as "love"?

Three Sorts of Love

The preceding point inevitably brings us to the question of just what love is. We can sympathize with the view that it is ridiculous to try to define such a thing, and agree with P.J. O'Rourke who observes, "No aspect of love is so ridiculous that it hasn't been exhaustively reviewed by the great thinkers, the great artists, and the great hosts of daytime talk shows."[2] But fortunately, we are not really trying to do all that. Rather, we are trying to identify the senses of the word "love," which should be a much more doable task. Here we may avail ourselves of a classification of long standing among theorists on these matters, which distinguishes three sorts of love: (1) *eros*, or erotic love, which we may almost identify with sexual love (not just sexual *desire*, which is not regarded as necessarily involving love at all); (2) *philios*, or friendship; and (3) *agape*, or generalized benevolence towards all people.

The classical trio strangely omits a fourth kind of love, for which I'll coin the term *familias*.

This is the love that parents feel for their children, children for parents, and siblings for each other—"family" love. It can't easily be identified with any of the classic three types: perhaps it is a species of "eros," though that will be quite misleading to contemporary ears. But it is surely at least as pervasive as any of them. However, our main concern for the present is love between (previously) unrelated adults, so we will leave this important kind of love to one side for the moment.

Which of these best describes our subject? Of course all are important, but not equally so for present purposes. Clearly agape for instance, is not the sort of love we are talking about here, for what we are concerned with is personal, unlike the generalized feeling for all humankind. But what about philios? Isn't love at least partly friendship? That does seem reasonable: one who had no friendly feelings at all towards another could scarcely be thought to *love* that other. But again, it certainly isn't sufficient: you can like someone very much, find his or her company altogether pleasant and interesting, and yet have no sexual desire for him or her at all. It is a familiar phenomenon, and often enough the source of dilemmas. People have wished that they did have the sexual kind of love for people they loved only as friends, but have realized that they do not and sometimes must take care to avoid giving an impression that they do. And the reverse is frequently true, too: we might wish that we were not sexually attracted to someone we very much want to be friends with—a friend's spouse, for example.

Nor are we done with complications, for the relation between love and sex, even when it is sexual love, isn't simple either. "I love him/her more, but he's certainly not as good in bed as so-and-so" is an attitude often encountered. A might *desire* that B maximally satisfy A sexually, and yet it might be that another person would actually do that better. This might lead to a dilemma, of course. And it might well be a pretty good reason for avoiding multiple relationships: if you confine yourself to one partner, then the fact that you would get more pleasure from someone else could be a good reason *not* to become involved with that someone, for doing so might complicate both your life and that of others. This and indefinitely many other examples again illustrate the complexities of this subject.

Nevertheless, I believe we can arrive at a fairly unified concept of the sort of love we are talking about: I suggest that love is (1) erotically sexual, but with (2) a friendship component, and (3) some desire for commitment.

It is erotic in the sense of being a case of *personal desire*: desire for the other person as such and not just for that person as a general type. In matters of love—of the "heart," as we say—"chemistry" is of the essence. This doesn't mean that love is *irrational*. But it does mean that it is not essentially rational—not a matter of calculation but of feeling. Yet it is perfectly reasonable to respond to one's feelings.

Here we should quickly add a note about biology. Sociobiologists may tell us that even though *we* do no "calculating," yet our *genes* do. It is not very clear what sense it makes to talk of things such as genes making "calculations," but presumably the biologist's idea is not a silly one. The kind of calculation excluded above is, simply, not explicit, "up-front" calculation. And we must also add quickly that lovers do plenty of calculating once they are in love. How do I contrive to see her more often? Can we afford the gift we'd love to make as an expression of love? And so on.

That's eros. Next, we note that these feelings of love are indeed friendly. This is to say, first, that they are not malevolent or domineering, but also that they are not, for instance, ideological or merely principled. The person who proposes marriage out of one of those motives may be cruelly misleading the other, who wanted love, not duty or membership in the party.

And finally, there is the element of commitment: an ongoing, open-ended tendency to act for the well-being of the beloved in a way that doesn't depend exclusively on how one happens to feel at the moment. There is passion at a moment, to be sure. But when is it love? At least in part, it's when it looks into the future and sees, and wants, the beloved to be there: you want to be near him or her the day after tomorrow, to promote the other's well-being into the indefinite future. (Why indefinite? Because if one says, "I will love you for two weeks!" that seems puzzling. To feel for two weeks the impulse to indefinite commitment, however, is quite possible and, perhaps lamentably, frequent enough.)

Love at first sight is indeed not only possible but fairly frequent. But what happens at that first sight is not just a desire, say, to have sexual relations with that person as soon as possible; rather, it is the desire, which arose all of a sudden, to be near and with the other for the indefinite future.

Obviously love is a matter of degree. But the lover, *qua* lover, aspires to a high degree of it and thinks that higher is better. But it seems reasonable to insist that all three of these components are necessary to love of the kind that concerns us here. And that is the kind that, as the songs have it, makes the world go around.

Sexual Philosophies

What principle should we use to govern our sex lives?

(1) We might—starting, some would say, at the bottom—try suggesting that one should aim at maximizing one's overall sexual satisfaction. But surely this would have to be qualified severely to be at all plausible, at least to most of us. Is one to maximize this, *regardless of all else*? It isn't clear what that means, but let's suppose we have some way of deciding which of two alternatives would produce more sexual satisfaction; and suppose, further, that this alternative has all sorts of costs on other fronts. To take a trivial example: while you are making out, the eggs burn. You might be prepared to forgo a little bit of sexual satisfaction in order to have a good breakfast. That doesn't seem irrational. Or, to take examples closer to home in moral theory, suppose that the cost of more sex is that the neighbours burn to death in a fire, which you can prevent by

phoning the fire department instead of finishing the latest sex act: shouldn't we pick up the phone in that case?

(2) If we weaken the proposed principle by suggesting that one ought to maximize one's sexual satisfaction "other things being equal," it will be a lot more plausible—but then, we should realize how *very* weak this is. For example, St. Thomas Aquinas, though a monk, might accept it. It's just that nothing that really mattered to him would ever have been merely "equal"; for him, those other values would always outweigh any attraction of sexual pleasures. And so, I presume, he never did engage in sex.

(3) Perhaps we should try another tack and say that our purpose is to maximize our *emotional* satisfaction, construing sexual satisfaction as merely a major component of that. There again, the effect on one's sexual activity, narrowly considered, might be quite drastic. All sorts of emotional considerations might weigh against seizing various opportunities for sexual activity.

(4) Surely it would be most plausible of all, if we go in this direction, to suggest that one aims to maximize one's overall *happiness*. That puts the sexual question into the right perspective, at any rate: whether to pursue more sexual satisfaction or instead to go for more of some other sort of value would depend on which would promote one's total happiness more. But how does one find this out? Nobody can say precisely, and moreover, we surely would expect the answers to vary immensely. We would also expect that in almost all cases sheer sexual pleasure is far from the only component in the happiest life.

The Liberal View of Sexual Activities

This diversity again supports the general liberal position in morals: an interest in others' good would recommend not trying to prescribe for them in areas where we have to admit that we don't know the answers. To some limited extent, one can say what has and what hasn't worked for oneself; this might be useful, both to oneself and to others. But we shouldn't be very confident in such matters. And anyone who has been in love will be aware of the difficulty, amounting to futility, of setting aside such feelings.

As in every other context, the liberal view says that people are to be allowed to do what they want unless their preferred activity adversely affects others—where the adversity is *not* assessed in terms of the moral attitudes of those others, but rather of their own interests as seen by them. We may do what we please provided it does not involuntarily worsen the personal situations of others. In the case of sexual activities, these are, so far as they go, not such as to affect parties beyond the interacting persons in question, unless there are special arrangements between one or both and outside parties—as there often are, to be sure. But apart from that special case, then, the principle would seem to imply that we should, *prima facie*, allow any sexual activities taking place between fully consenting adults. (Not all are: sometimes consent is qualified by deception or relevant ignorance.) If engaging in those activities has long-run adverse effects on those people themselves, then they will do well to change their ways. But it is for them to judge that matter and up to them to act accordingly.

On the face of it, the liberal view would allow homosexuality, prostitution, and "non-normal" sex. Whether it would allow extra-marital or premarital sex depends on other considerations, especially whether such activities might be inconsistent with marital or family duties. In the case of very young people, of course, the liberal principle becomes inapplicable or at least considerably qualified: the parents of child C, especially, are to have a major voice in the matter, even against C's desires. How far that authority extends, and how long it lasts, are difficult questions, which will be only somewhat addressed below, when we consider family issues.

This book began by defending the liberal view in general. If we accept that outlook, then the main question about any activity under scrutiny is whether it has, either obviously or on closer examination, potential for significant negative effects on others. That will be my procedure in this inquiry, though of course we must always be on the lookout for cracks in the liberal edifice. It is probably in sexual matters more than any other area of life that people tend to draw back from the implications of liberalism, which calls for acceptance as legitimate of practices that some view with great discomfort or dismay. Still, the question always is: why should *my* discomfort or dismay entitle me to debar those who differ from pursuing their chosen ways of life?

Non-Standard Sex

People pursuing sexual pleasure don't confine themselves to the standard male-female act of sexual intercourse. There are all sorts of deviations from that paradigm: homosexual, autoerotic, and non-standard heterosexual stimulation is frequent. Of this there is certainly no doubt. Now, many moralists will insist that people seeking such pleasures cannot be healthy or happy. But that at least seems not to be true. Not all homosexuals are unhappy, for instance, and those who are may be so not because they are homosexual, as such, but because of the social pressures they must bear because of their sexual orientation.

The question is much discussed whether homosexuality is natural or acquired. Very likely the question is too obscure to admit of any answer, and certainly we won't try to decide it here. But does it matter? However they got that way, typical homosexuals have no desire to revert to the heterosexual syndrome, and most would say that there is no possibility of their doing so. A moral principle based on the assumption that the way they are is wrong isn't going to get very far with such people—and, for this purpose, they are the ones who count. Unless some very solid reasons can be found to object to homosexual behaviour, then, the result of social objection to it will be that a lot of people's lives will be made miserable merely to accommodate the moral views of others. Speculation about the intentions of homosexuals hardly constitutes such reason.

There is an obvious point to make about homosexuality, however. A society consisting entirely of homosexuals would, obviously, have no future, so long as its members confined themselves to strictly homosexual activity. That's hardly a trivial point. On the other hand, however, their attitude can easily be that there are plenty of others to take care of that, and that attitude is apparently justified: the world's population continues to increase, despite a considerable incidence of homosexuality. At the risk of offending some well-meaning people, it must be pointed out that in many religions the adoption of a non-sexual way of life is looked on with great favour, and a considerable number of adherents do just that — monks, for example, in the Roman Catholic and Buddhist religions. If the objection to homosexuality is founded on non-reproduction, that is equally an objection to monkhood and nunhood. But the reply is the same. Were there a serious danger of major depletion of population, then such people would have to consider modifying their ways in some respects. But there is not, as things stand. And there seems also no danger of homosexuality increasing greatly in future, nor for that matter of religious seclusion.

Perversion

It is widely believed that some sexual activities are "perversions." What is that supposed to mean? Why is it thought to matter?

(1) Policies are sometimes called "perverse" with a clear meaning; such policies are so poorly framed that they are likely to frustrate the very ends they are designed to achieve and to bring about other evils worse than the ones they are supposed to prevent. For example, someone might take a "perverse pleasure" in needling his friends. But in the case of what are called sexual perversions, that understanding of the term does not apply, for the participants aim at certain kinds of pleasure and presumably often do really succeed in achieving it. How, then, are they "perverse"?

If the claim is that these activities don't actually please, then that would indeed be perverse in this clear sense: but it evidently reflects ignorance. People often get a great deal of pleasure from these activities. If the claim is that they are "disgusting," then the trouble is that they apparently don't disgust the people who enthusiastically engage in them; so we are left with an argument that says "x disgusts *me*; therefore *you* ought not to be allowed to do x." Not a very satisfactory argument!

(2) Another possible meaning is not so clear: it is that such people are *misusing* various parts of their own bodies and/or other people's—they use them for the "wrong purposes." To those who speak this way, it is obvious what the purpose of sex organs is—reproduction—and to use them for anything else is clearly wrong. But that is very far from obvious. If you use your knee to support a table instead of to walk with, that isn't perverse; if you use the dictionary for a doorstop or a paperweight, no one takes issue. More generally, things can be used in all sorts of ways besides the standard or the defining way such things are used. Yet when someone stimulates a sexual organ with a tongue rather than with the matching natural organ, that is claimed to be "perverse." Why? The idea that things ought not to be used for any but their "natural purposes" seems either unintelligible or absurdly implausible. It certainly won't bear the weight of a general prohibition on unusual sexual practices.

Sexually Transmitted Diseases

Sexual activities have an essential biological side to them, bringing different people into intimate, bodily contact with each other. As a result, there is a potential public health aspect to sexual relations: assorted diseases await the unwary, transmitted with varying degrees of efficiency by sexual contact. AIDS is the most virulent of recently important ones, the others having been largely, though not completely, gotten under control by modern treatments. Where AIDS is little understood and sexual looseness is typical, the chances of infection are extremely high. If there are multiple relationships among a sizeable populace, the chance of some communicable disease spreading is greatly increased, as compared with a populace in which people are generally and reliably monogamous. One reads that many African countries are faced with a potential population reduction at the hands of the AIDS virus comparable to that brought about by the Black Death in Europe in the fourteenth century (one out of three or four).

There are several strategies to consider against the threat of sexually transmitted disease. One can cease having sex at all (or not start); one can stick to one reliable partner who is not infected; or one can take measures to try to ensure either that one's partner is not infected or that even if he or she is, one won't end up with the disease oneself. The latter method is, of course, the chanciest, whereas the first is perfectly secure, so far as we know, and the second is as secure as one's partner, which often means just about perfectly secure. One of the important features of monogamy is that it amounts to a virtually complete guarantee against the general spread of sexually transmitted diseases, since it confines any such diseases to those two people. And unless one of them has it congenitally or by some unlikely chance, their relations will not pose a risk to each other either.

Yet we cannot assume that the least risky method is necessarily the best. Life is risky and a more rewarding life can be a riskier one too. What does matter is that we not impose unknown and unexpected risks on others. That is a responsibility that we must all insist on, whatever form it may take in a particular case.

Love

According to the Christian New Testament, the fundamental commandment is "love ye one another." But Christ surely couldn't have meant by *love* here what the poets and writers of popular songs mean by it. He presumably meant that one ought to have an attitude of general beneficence and goodwill towards all. Or if he really meant the sort of thing that lovers feel towards each other, then his dictum would have to be regarded as downright perverse. Not only do people not love everyone, and not only are they incapable of doing so, but they should not try to do so. The central reason is that if you love someone, then you want to pay that person a level of attention that is incompatible with extending the same to everyone, or even to more than a very few people.

Some advocates of monogamy hold that you can't extend it to *anyone* else. Perhaps they attach a specifically sexual connotation to the love they insist should be restricted to one other person. After all, there is plenty of non-sexual love: the love of parents for children, for instance, is a familiar phenomenon, and can be quite as intense, and motivate people to do equally extraordinary things, as the love of a sexual partner. And charity, which is one sort of love, is encouraged by most religions and all normal people, and extends very widely.

Most people place a very high value on love of all types, and perhaps the highest value on love between spouses. Such love is not easy to analyse, but it seems at least to be a sort of mix of friendship and erotic attraction. Lovers want to spend a lot of time in each other's company, preferably without other people around; and they want to engage in sexual activities with each other. They find much enjoyment and satisfaction in these things. Is that what the high value attached to it consists in? Is what's valuable about love what it does for the lover—and if so, is *that* what it does?

Here there is an interesting problem. It is claimed that love, at last, is the most perfectly unselfish emotion. People in love may think that they are totally devoted to their beloveds—totally and selflessly. But is this true? And if it were true, would it be rational? One might think that it is out of place to talk about rationality here, on the ground that love is a sort of madness while reason is cold and abstract, But that is a misunderstanding. For consider what sort of madness it is: not simple insanity, which no one could desire. Rather, it's claimed to be a "divine" madness, a very good kind of madness—in short, a highly desirable state to be in. Clearly it is rational to want to be in desirable states. Still, perhaps the implication of the idea that love is a madness is that there are some downsides to love that the lover too readily overlooks. The vaunted selflessness of love may be a good example. Who would want to be a slave, for instance? If to love is to be nothing more than a slave to the beloved, then that surely looks like a downside—though it's hard to see how it could be overlooked.

But, fortunately, it is a sheer mistake to think that love is totally selfless in this way. Suppose that you find everything you do for her completely unpleasant. Is that love? Indeed not. If you are allegedly loved by someone with that kind of attitude, you are well advised to steer clear. Surely the right way to look at this is that *love is both other-interested and self-interested*, and moreover, it is the first because it's the second. Or as poets and mystics might put it, it is the union of self and other, lover and beloved. That is what's so interesting about it. *You* feel good, elated, inflamed, inspired, enthused, delighted *by* the person you love, and you do nice things for her because you enjoy doing them. If doing such things becomes a drag instead, then the flame of love has flickered down, the relationship has become unsatisfying to you, and you've got problems—as does your supposedly beloved. Such a relationship has gone sour and has ceased to be love. For love desires, demands mutuality, and when it doesn't get it, the lover is miserable, as may well be the beloved who has no interest in returning that lover's affection.

Here, then, is a conjecture about the value of love: it is the highest human good because it is the most conspicuous example of a disposition that exhibits what economists call "positive externality." Cases so called are those in which the actions of one person benefit another without that other person's having contributed to the cost of producing the benefit. If the producer is happy to supply the benefit in question, then the whole transaction, so far as it goes, is positive for all concerned. That's what happens in a successful love relationship: the other's good is your good, and vice versa—A's pleasure generates pleasure in B, and vice versa; thus their actions have positive pay-offs for both parties. Thus love, as common sense has long known, is the exact opposite of hatred: there, A benefits only from B's harm—the more satisfied A is, the *less* satisfied B is. Hatred is maximally divisive in relation to its object, while love maximally unites lover and beloved. A further recommendation of love is that it is open to all parties. It requires no particular resources: lovers need only each other's company, basically, and the rest is secondary, window-dressing. Rich and poor alike can share in the joys of love—and the sorrows and snares as well, of course.

But we properly become concerned about others' loves when they start generating negative externalities to those outside the charmed circle (usually a dyad, actually). Suppose that Jason, out of love for Hephaestia, slays someone who has offended her or goes forth and robs the First National Bank of Athens so as to be able to provide her with the world's largest natural pearl, which she greatly desires. We may call that a perverse love, but that isn't a very helpful thing to say. What matters is that it is *immoral* love, love motivating actions that inflict evils on others. One of the main things that lovers have to bear in mind is that they are not the only two people in the world, that they still have duties towards the rest of us and that we cannot be expected to support them when their love impels them to do evil to others.

Jealousy and "Free Love"

The passion of love varies in duration, from momentary to lifelong. The momentary versions are of only modest interest to us, except insofar as they might incidentally lead to or disrupt larger involvements, such as family or the agent's relationship to another lover or to some cause. But the real thing, as it is quite reasonably known, notoriously tends to generate complexities. Among these, problems of *jealousy* stand high on the list. A loves B, B loves A, and B hears, and is inclined to believe, rumours to the effect that A also views C with favour, and in consequence B takes a dim view both of A's imagined or real proclivities in that respect and of C. This can lead to dire consequences indeed, as so much literature and the popular press amply attest.

What should we think of jealousy? People seem to be genuinely ambivalent about it. On the one hand, it is regarded as a vice, to avoid if we can. On the other hand, we tend to view with suspicion anyone who professes an unjealous love. And jealousy certainly isn't surprising; perhaps it is "natural," though whether that means anything more than that it is typical is not clear. What makes jealousy unsurprising is that lovers *want* their beloveds: they want their time and attention, and they don't want these eroded or deflected by other romantic interests.

Traditionally, jealousy has been regarded as more nearly a woman's passion than a man's; there has been some perceived asymmetry between the sexes. Buttressed by the recent science (if that's the right word) of sociobiology, a theory to the effect that men and women differ in their basic sexual motivations has gained currency: basically, it is said, men want to have sex, whereas women want to have children. The role of Man in the reproductive process is momentary, but not that of Woman: she's in it for nine months minimum, and then after that she tends to be the primary caretaker of her offspring for many years. Sociobiologists hypothesize that every organism wants to maximize the incidence of its own genes in the population. Given their different roles in reproduction, men do this by mating with many partners, but women, once pregnant, have no further need for sex during the ensuing many months and more—but they do have need of support, someone to help supply sustenance and shelter for the longish period of domesticity needed to get offspring to the point where they can survive by themselves. So while Man's impulse is to go a-roaming, Woman's is to keep Man chained to the domestic establishment. Jealousy acts to increase the cost of outside involvement for the male.

This account—rather elegant in its way—may well explain something, though it surely oversimplifies the picture. (For one thing, male jealousy and female roaming are both frequent enough to require an epicycle or two in the theory.) But what matters to us as individuals, whatever our sex or role may be, is whether one partner is jealous when the other is not. That gives rise to special conflicts, whereas mutual jealousy supports mutual fidelity as the obvious compromise, while mutual unjealousness, if genuine, supports mutual tolerance.

These should not be seen in moralistic terms. The jealous one isn't "in the right" and the other "in the wrong," or vice versa; rather, there is a problem, and if the parties to it are to relate well to each other some accommodation must be made. The jealous one's behaviour may have the effect of depriving the other one of some desirable experiences, ones that might not have had any significant effect on the other one—jealousy itself being the only thing that stands in the way. Jealousy in that sense would seem to be an inefficient emotion, a vice, and needs to be conquered. Yet it can't be ignored and won't just go away because we tell it to.

On the other side, there is some question what a "completely unjealous love" would mean. There are people who don't get particularly upset when their mates go off with others occasionally. If they were to do so very frequently, of course, the question would arise what the point was; but within limits, some people seem to manage it. (We'll return to that when we get to marriage.) The net conclusion is that "jealousy problems" are probable and require a solution tailored to the needs of the particular couple involved. The main line of solution is to try to identify a real interest underlying the jealousy, and then see whether the jealousy can be isolated and perhaps wither upon being so. But perhaps not; and if not, an adjustment must somehow be made or real trouble may ensue. Things are rarely easy in these matters.

Can Love Be Required?

Familiar marriage ceremonies have laid it down that the persons becoming espoused are to "love, honour, and obey" each other, or words to that effect. The specific implication, sometimes explicitly put, is that these people have a *duty* to have these attitudes towards each other. Now, it is clear enough that obedience and perhaps even honouring can be commanded, but love seems to be another matter: surely it cannot be directly commanded, and it is unclear that it can be literally commanded in any ordinary sense of that term. It is, after all, a feeling; and feelings, notoriously, are not the sort of things you can just turn on and off at will. Perhaps one could have a duty to *act as if* one loved someone, champing at the bit the whole time; but that wouldn't be the same thing as genuine love.

Yet people have often enough accepted it as their duty to love certain people. Take one's children, for instance: it is quite familiar to insist that a parent love his or her children, perhaps love them equally, and a lot. Still, are such things really possible? It is our duty to treat our children well, and a parent who attacks, violates, unfairly accuses or reproaches, or unnecessarily chastises his children is certainly eligible for plenty of criticism. His children are to be pitied, and indeed, *he* is to be pitied. For if you don't enjoy and have affection for your children, what is the point? We can say all this, and still a doubt remains that love can be, properly speaking, commanded or required. Can the parent who feels no love be condemned for not feeling it?

There is no very easy answer to this. If people can't just have those feelings on demand, they can still do things to increase the probability that they will have the warm feelings we identify with love. And if there is someone whose affections you are anxious to be the object of, then you can do much to deserve them—and much to turn them off. If you are successful, the other person's affections will in turn, very likely, stimulate those warm feelings. One can regard a loving relationship as a sort of psychological investment, and for normal humans its potential returns are great. One might even end up being happy, for it is common wisdom that none of the other avenues to happiness is as likely as this to produce results. Folk wisdom to the effect that a solid and reliable love is worth more than wealth and power, for example, strikes me as being just that: wisdom. But people do vary, especially in regard to the *capacity* as well as the opportunity for manifesting that kind of love. It is not reasonable to insist that people do what they cannot.

Marriage

Talk of "marriage" here is in danger of confusion, stemming from the fact that in all societies there are marital *institutions*. There are often recognized ceremonies and legal forms; when people talk about "getting married," they usually mean becoming united as pre-scribed and sanctioned by those forms. But just what do those forms have to do with the subject we are interested in? The Neanderthals presumably lacked legal marriage, but they certainly had mates. And in our own society, there are informal relationships having much the same effect as legal marriage. So I will specify our subject in this way: marriage is a relationship with long-term, open-ended mutual commitment. (Such relationships can also obtain in same-sexed couples. How much of the following applies equally to such cases is a moot point, to which only slight attention will be given.) A "spouse" or "mate" for our purpose is, to put it in academic terms, a lover with tenure.

There are important questions about how and even whether a legal institution regarding such relationships should be framed. But our more immediate question is what we should think of this, that or the other relationship of the general type. Is there a specific type of marriage arrangement that society should support, perhaps to the exclusion of others? In Canada at present, for instance, bigamy and polygamy are illegal, and homosexual marriages are not recognized. Yet typical Canadians would merely be surprised, probably not shocked, and very likely not outraged if they were to encounter people with three wives, two husbands, or same-sexed couples who regarded themselves as married. Would they *disapprove* of such arrangements? Some very likely would, to be sure; but a good many would not. In moral as distinct from legal terms, the institution of marriage in our society is by no means uniformly defined.

Should we disapprove of some or all of these non-standard arrangements? This brings up very large questions about the meaning and broader purpose of marital arrangements. Marital institutions in all societies have been concerned, above all, with procreation. They have also been concerned, perhaps to a lesser extent, with social harmony. Marriages *settle* things. Once she or he is "taken," then aspiring lovers are no longer welcome to apply. But if you are one of those disappointed aspirants, you could well take the view that the case *shouldn't* be closed, that the person in question would be better off with you, as well as you with her, and that she or he deserves you, rather than the individual who has somehow wound up in those desirable arms. And to make things really difficult, the aspirant in question could possibly be right about that, too. Then what?

Is there an interest here that society ought to protect? Suppose that in perfectly good faith both parties have promised to love, honour, and obey each other till death do them part—but shortly after, one of the parties has a change of mind. Even if they did make that promise in good faith, is it one that we can reasonably insist on them adhering to thereafter? Perhaps; but then if we have a standardized institution in the course of which people ritually make such "promises," is it reasonable to think that they *were* made in good faith? Arguably not. And if this is the only condition on which one is permitted to live with a person of the opposite sex, then the conditions under which the promise is made seem unfair. We undertake long-term commitments because we think they are a good thing. If, after some time, it has become perfectly clear that such a commitment is not a good thing after all, shouldn't we be able to back out before it's too late? There is more than a little wrong with an institution that makes this impossible.

Often there will be children to consider, and that crucial dimension of the subject will get more attention in the last part of this chapter; but first we have to ask about the parties immediately concerned, for if marriage isn't good for *them*, then the whole idea lies under a cloud of suspicion. And in fact, it very often does seem to be good: there are plenty of happily married people around—people who are glad they got married, glad to have married the particular people they did, and, especially, happier to have done that than to have remained unmarried. The fact that there are also plenty of marriages that are working badly shouldn't blind us to the real merits of the many good cases. What it should do, though, is assure us that much is unforeseeable and that we ought not to frame an institution of marriage that effectively locks people, irretrievably, into unhappy situations. Having marriages that are undoable at the insistence of both parties seems the minimum condition for a reasonable marital institution.

What about dissolvability by just one party? This, too, seems reasonable, for one person surely should not be able to keep another in unhappiness, any more than she or he should be able to keep another in involuntary servitude. Indeed, the difference between the two seems rather slim.

Still, if they have been together for some time, the party wanting to leave may owe something to the party who would have preferred to continue the marriage. How much, though? This is not an easy thing to say. Sometimes it will have been clear that one partner's contribution to the other was such-and-such, and it will even be reasonable to put a monetary value on it. But often it won't. When people differ about that, reasonable ways to settle the issue will be urgently needed. A great deal of emotional energy and grief are often expended on such things and no easy formula exists. It is obviously not a matter we can settle in the abstract. The current practice of splitting assets 50-50, for example, is obviously a very rough rule of thumb and will often be unfair.

We should also recognize that to talk in terms of marital breakup as being "unhappy" is also potentially misleading. Why shouldn't a marriage be good *for awhile*? The famous anthropologist Margaret Mead said, "I have been married three times, and not one of them was a failure!" While divorces are often accompanied by turmoil, some are not: the parties amicably go their separate ways. An acquaintance tells me that he and his ex-wife now have a better relationship than they ever had when they were married: divorce, apparently, has been the occasion for real friendship between them.

What about plural or same-sex marriages? We may not understand why people want to enter into such arrangements and may suspect that they are unlikely to work very well. Yet there are cultures in which polygamy is frequent, and many same-sex couples have been together for a very long time. Here again, we must look before we condemn. Women in polygamous situations have sometimes professed themselves entirely satisfied, finding valuable possibilities in those relationships that are not easily otherwise available. It seems arbitrary to forbid such arrangements in an otherwise predominantly monogamous society. What's the point? If it is to assuage the feelings of those who think monogamy is right, then I need hardly remind the reader that that begs the question: the monogamist's attitude is that monogamy should rule, but he must have good reason for this if it is to be given credence. And the point is that it appears that he does not.

Monogamy is the inevitable standard in any society, when one thinks about it, so long as the ratio of males to females is about even, as it is. A society with a lot of young unmarried men "on the loose" is a notoriously bad idea, socially speaking; but if most are married, then it is impossible that most should have more than one wife—unless the wives also share husbands, of course. And while that, too, is conceivable, it is remarkably unlikely.[3]

Here, in fact, is another crucial test case for liberalism. Some might feel discomfort at the prospect of a neighbour in a nonstandard marital situation. Should we say that the latter is "harming" the former on that account? We should not: one person's sheer dislike of another or his or her ways is not an acceptable basis for moral criticism.

A further consideration commends the acceptance of polygamy in contemporary Western societies. It has been a demographic fact about those societies for quite some time that women outlive men. At birth, the ratio of men to women is more than unity, but by the time they reach adulthood the difference disappears, and soon after it is reversed. By late middle age, women outnumber men by an appreciable margin; in old age, the margin becomes lopsided. It is not possible for everyone to marry one and only one member of the opposite sex with a reasonable expectation of living with that person for the duration of both their lives; the male will in the normal case die very much sooner than the female. Perhaps, if it were a familiar option, polygamy in later age would be preferred by many to a spouse-free condition. Of course, many would not. But the point is, why should society exclude an option potentially beneficial to the others?

Macro Considerations

The questions whether a society should have an institution of marriage and, if so, of what type may strike one as unreal. After all, nobody can just "decide" to change this institution. Legislators, for example, cannot. If they are legislators in a democratic society, the reason why they cannot is obvious: their constituents, most of whom are married, are unlikely to support any radical change in that domain. And in a dictatorial society, any dictated changes will be unsuccessful because unenforceable, and probably will produce widespread misery as well.

However, it could become less abstract if we could introduce it as a consideration in favour of or against marrying in one's own particular case. Can it so function? Suppose that you think your society in general would have certain desirable properties if it had a marriage institution of such-and-such a type. Would that be a good reason why *you* should get married? The answer is: not necessarily, but possibly.

Suppose that the society would be more stable if most people were married along the lines of a marital institution of such-and-such a type. Very well: but then, what *most* people will do, such as get married in that institution or not, is independent of whatever *you* do—whether or not you in particular get married in that way. However good a thing it might be if all were, one or a handful doing things differently will make essentially no difference to the general character of your society. So clearly, considerations of this type are not necessarily decisive. Within the limits of what is feasible, you should do what is best for you whether or not that would also be good for society at large—though not, of course, whether or not it would be bad for it.

But what others do could tip the balance. Suppose that there is a person you could see yourself marrying. And suppose that in addition, you like the kind of society that you would become a part of by marrying that person. That just might be enough to make you decide in favour of doing it.

Are there such factors, though? Is the scenario I have just described possible? This would seem to be a question of sociology, and factual evidence is essential. My impression, formed from some decades' experience and not at all from sociology textbooks, is that a society in which almost everybody is married and has a family, with strong and generally well-observed commitments, is going to be a stable and prosperous society with a low crime rate and many flourishing associations and community activities. It may also be pretty dull, frankly; or at least it will strike clever young people that way, and not unreasonably.

Can we have it both ways? That's a nice question, about which reasonable people may differ and on which, to put it mildly, not all the information is in. But it is not unfair to say that the clever young people in question are probably wrong, in the end. It all depends on what sort of people you have in your community and how much in the way of interesting activity they create. Unmarried couples and assorted single persons can have a good time in social interaction in such a society without necessarily destabilizing the institutions of marriage and the family. Not necessarily, to be sure—but in fact there is some tendency for the stably marrieds to close ranks against such people, and part of our question is whether it is a tendency one should be disposed to resist.

As one example of the possible costs entailed by such resistance, consider the small community of stably married people into which a single person descends. That individual is likely to have a tough time of it socially. He or she will not be invited to parties attended only by couples or families who know each other well, and will tend to be isolated by others and be treated as something of an outcast. The people who treat him or her this way are, on the model we are considering, just doing their job, as they see it—defending a stable institution of marriage and family. But the single individual ends up miserable, while those who treat such individuals that way lose out on some valuable company and probably some interesting ideas.

The Individual Question: Should You Marry?

Should one marry? The obvious answer is in the affirmative if one would be happier on the whole if one does. But, as Aristotle said so long ago, it is also not very helpful. What may be helpful here is merely emphasizing that it is the right question to ask: Will *I* be happier? Not, is it my social duty? Or, will the *other* person be happier? But, will *I* be? Marrying someone out of pure altruism is a tragic mistake, especially because it is self-defeating. When she finds out that you don't really love *her* and that she doesn't really make you happy, then that will make her miserable rather than grateful for your generosity. And she will soon become so, for marriage is a close personal relationship in which facts of that sort are unlikely to remain in the dark.

Why would marriage make you happier? One major reason is that it will enable you to have a family and you will find that interesting and fulfilling, despite all the expected headaches. That is indeed an excellent reason, but we must appreciate that it works independently of others. She may be a perfectly wonderful mother, and you may admire and support her for this; but what if you nevertheless don't really *love* her in her own right? When the children leave and the two of you have another thirty years to stare at each other across the breakfast table, it may dawn on you that this wasn't such a good idea. That is one of the spectres haunting the institution of marriage as we know it. To avert it, you have to marry someone you really like, whose company you enjoy, whom you get on with, and the basis of your doing so must be enduring qualities—in both of you. The institution of courtship, where people spend a fair amount of time together before getting married, is intended to help out in this respect, but its track record in North American society is spotty and often said to be no better than in societies where arranged marriages are the norm. For all that, few would want to surrender the freedom to choose. So one must choose wisely and hope for the best. (And it is, after all, quite possible to surrender that freedom. You could join an association that would embrace the idea of assigned marriage, with a system for so assigning, and so on. Why not? Presumably this is almost what happens, for instance, in some Sikh communities in North America.)

But basically, we have a choice. What should be the basis of that choice, then? We'll concentrate on the personal factors alone here, leaving the family for later. These can be divided into three sorts, I think: romance; company; and suitability in respect of general life goals and circumstances. They interact with each other so much that the division is inevitably somewhat artificial. Still, the fact is that people can be romantically involved with each other and yet not really be all that good companions, once they get out of bed; and people who are terrific fun to be with, in or out of bed, may be so unsuitable in other respects that prospects of a successful liaison are dim; and some might make excellent partners for many purposes, yet have no romantic attraction for each other. Which of the three has priority?

Actually, the answer is pretty easy: they go in reverse order. That B would make a suitable long-term mate for A in various circumstantial respects is the most important general type of consideration. If you and he are going in the same direction in life, other things more readily fall into place. If you aren't, no amount of romance or personal pleasure in each other's company will keep you together. Or rather, romance and companionship won't endure if you are very much at odds in other respects.

These are pieces of prudential advice, of course, and do not lead directly to a moral rule. Morality concerns how we are to treat people in general. In that sense, it also tells us how we are to treat friends and loved ones. Of course, so long as A and B *are* friends, acting towards each other in the ways that define friendship, then morality has virtually nothing to say to them regarding their mutual relations. The same should be true of marriage: in detail, they will differ greatly, and it is strictly the business of the partners to it to make such arrangements as are mutually satisfactory. It is when one partner is tempted to treat the other in a less than friendly way that morality becomes relevant. And what it will then say is that, given that this individual has behaved as a true and good companion, you owe it to him or her not to engage in mean treatment. If you wish no longer to be friends, then you should not break off in an unnecessarily painful, cowardly or underhanded way. We shouldn't betray anyone, of course, but the advice is more important in the case of friends, for persons to whom we have no connections are persons we aren't ordinarily in a position to betray, whereas friends are highly vulnerable. And the same is true, but in greater degree, in the case of a spouse, who has been, or is to be, not just a friend but much more than that.

In this connection, we should note, and express agreement with, the sensitivity of society at present towards physical abuse in marriage. Such abuse is assumed by today's pundits to be against women, but it is by no means confined to the male partner—it is not much less frequent, perhaps surprisingly, in the other direction. The point is that it is obviously, in general, to be condemned. If one or the other partner is not living up to his or her commitments, as seen by both, then the aggrieved spouse can, and probably should, leave rather than resort to violence to try to fix things up. Violence, indeed, doesn't "fix things up." It makes them worse.

Two aspects of "suitability" may be distinguished here. One concerns *character*, the other specific life goals, background, and circumstances such as "material" prospects, by which is usually meant income. The romantic in us tends especially to downgrade the latter factors, but it can also easily lead us to disregard the first of them, character. And that is a serious error. Nothing can be more important than being of basically good character. To marry an evil person is to become, in effect, an accessory to an enemy of humankind, and of course it is also to walk into a trap. It is, one might say, to betray the social contract; for in undertaking to love and support evil, we abet it when we ought to be doing our best to correct it. Moreover, an evil character makes a person untrustworthy, unreliable. Prospects for long-term happiness with such a person are nil.

One facet of character is *fidelity*. But when people talk of fidelity in marriage, they almost always have in mind only fidelity of the specifically sexual kind. But that is a mistake. Whether sexual fidelity is part of the arrangement between you and your spouse is a variable, even a negotiable matter. What matters, though, is that both fulfil whatever terms they do commit themselves to—and that they understand each other to have some commitments, absent which we are not talking about marriage any more.

A good character is necessary but, of course, far from sufficient for a good partnership: persons of admirable character can make each other thoroughly miserable. And in the case of marriage, the bloom of happiness is imparted by the romantic dimension, despite its being the least important of the listed factors. To be sure, this is misleading, for if romance can last, then nothing else matters. But if the other things aren't in place, romance is virtually certain not to last, and when it goes, everything will be that much more painful. What is needed is a setting in which romance can endure. Even if it won't—as it very likely won't—companionship, pleasure in each other's company, and opportunities for common enjoyments provide very satisfactory substitutes. Indeed, some would say that though the flame of romance will surely burn down, yet if there is real companionship, accompanied by reasonable health and material stability, those sources of happiness will soon prove better: romance may even be seen as something of a bother, an upsetting, chaotic factor that is better left behind. Or it may solidify into something different but still warm and endearing.

Which view is right? Fortunately, we needn't try to settle it, for romance is a gift of fortune. The couple who remain not merely in a loving and friendly relationship but actually "in love" are, we may reasonably say, quite exceptionally fortunate, but the rest of us needn't be very upset about not being so favoured, for there is nothing much we can do about it, and there are plenty of satisfactions to take its place. Or rather, some of the things we may be tempted to do instead, such as to take up with some charming person we scarcely know and have a "fling," are likely—though not certain, as we must add—to have high personal costs that we will see in retrospect not to have been worth paying; while becoming morose and bitter, cold and despairing, will make life itself worthless. We should aim at what we can achieve, and for most people, what we can achieve is stability, good nature, tolerance, and a fair degree of steady care about our partner. With any luck, those will make much more than just a very good start towards a satisfying personal life.

The Family

Last but not least we turn to the family. Indeed, we might well have turned to it first, for from the biological point of view, reproduction and therefore the family are the fundamental point of a society's marital institution: its marital institution just *is* its reproductive institution. Differing sorts of marriage institutions are differing ways of handling the need to keep society staffed.

The family as we have known it for centuries is under fire in many quarters. Radical feminists allege that the family is the root of much evil, in particular as a prime vehicle for and root cause of male dominance. No one is against reproduction as such,[4] but some think that it ought to be handled very differently from the family as we know it. And that, if true, is surely very important.

What is "the family as we know it"? Roughly, it is the arrangement in which children are produced by one couple and are nurtured in a household occupied exclusively by that couple and its own children. Anyone else in the domestic establishment is either a near relative or hired, not equal in perceived domestic status to members of the family. Some deviations from this pattern due to death, infertility, and perhaps economic limitations are inevitable; but intentional deviations, such as breakup of the parents' marriage, are not acceptable and are strongly discouraged or simply forbidden.

What are the alternatives? There are many. Many people of both sexes could live communally and rear their children collectively; a very few primitive societies seem to be organized in some such way, or nearly so, and one hears of the occasional sophisticated example in industrialized societies. Or one woman could normally produce her children by two or more different fathers, and those fathers typically engender their offspring by different mothers. It would also be possible for children typically to be brought up in single-parent households. And an indefinite number of variants are possible, many of which are instantiated occasionally, somewhere.

But in all but a very tiny handful of primitive societies, there has been a standard paradigm for families: monogamy or, much more rarely, polygamy has been the rule; and almost everyone got married, had at least two children, and nurtured those children to maturity in their own homes. With recent divorce rates, among other things, there has been appreciable deviation from this paradigm in North America. Although it is still statistically normal to marry before having children, many do not, and of those who do, many divorce before the children mature; thus we have a high incidence of single-parent families, many of which are so from the start. Some few women obtain sperm from sperm-banks and become artificially inseminated; their children grow up from the beginning with only a female parent on hand and no notion who their biological fathers may be. Homosexual couples acquire children by similar methods or by adoption, and those children grow up with two same-sexed parent figures.

Those who participate in these arrangements sometimes view them not as unfortunate compromises but as genuine improvements over the standard arrangements. Are they right about that? Should society hold up a different paradigm as its ideal? If we retain a favourable attitude towards the hitherto standard system, is this just bias? Are proponents of the hitherto standard system mere fuddy-duddies, irrationally fearing the unknown? That is the general question to ponder here.

We may tackle these questions from two different directions. We can ask whether there's anything really *wrong* with the standard arrangements: are there serious criticisms of the system as such that we have overlooked or failed to come to grips with? And we can consider proposed new systems for possible advantages. Even if what we have is generally acceptable, and even if we have a perfect right to remain in our "rut," if that's what we decide it is, should we think that we are missing something important—that our lives would be better were we to strike out in one of the new directions? Let's consider, starting with the first option.

Critiques of the Standard Family

Probably the most important criticism at present stems from radical feminism (other feminists hold that the present system is merely in need of improvement, not replacement.)[5] They contend, especially, that the present system is one that maintains dominance of the female by the male—"patriarchy." These criticisms are often advanced in passionate tones and sometimes by means of arguments that pay little heed to the canons of reason. For example, the author of this set of notes being himself a male, some of these critics will hold that there is simply no point in reading further, since I belong to the class that is the problem. If that reasoning were sound, then the reply would be simple: females stand, on the view of the feminists, to gain from the allegedly needed reforms. Thus they, too, are interested parties. Therefore, *they* should not be listened to either. And who does this leave to carry on the argument?

But both arguments are unacceptable, for they both beg the question, as well as committing one or both of two common fallacies—the fallacy of *argumentum ad hominem* ("against the man") and the *genetic* fallacy (that of confusing an idea's origin with its conceptual merits). We should reject all such tactics here, appealing only to what stands up to good evidence, if it's a matter in regard to which evidence is possible; and if not then we must be careful in our analysis so that we can see what is required and whether or not we can get it. Whether we can reach a rational conclusion is not known in advance. All we can do is try, and hope that something satisfactory emerges.

Emotional arguments are to be avoided. Whether Q follows from P is not an emotional matter, even when P and Q themselves are about emotional matters. But that certainly does not mean that we must reject emotion as being irrelevant to our subject. That would be absurd! Emotion is the stuff of life, and an ideal of life that proposes to dispense with it altogether is certainly not rational, but quite the reverse: the person proposing to do this is proposing to live the life of a cold, unfeeling bore. In the case of marriage and family, we are dealing with long-standing, deep-rooted emotions, ones that won't just go away with the flick of an ideological whisk-broom. That is something to be taken into account as completely germane to the matter before us.

Is traditional marriage inherently a relation of domination? Is it inherently unequal in some importantly pejorative sense? One main problem, I think, is that these are ambiguous claims. Indeed, it is probably *the* main problem. They are also vague, and in some cases unavoidably so. We must try to arrive at reasonable clarity about them.

(1) Right at the outset, we must be careful to distinguish between the claim we are discussing, namely that marriage is *inherently* a relation of domination, from the claim that most marriages involve domination by one or the other partner. Most contemporary

feminist critiques claim that marriage involves domination by the male. That claim may be advanced in a way that can be empirically assessed. For example, does "wife-battering" occur? Obviously that is objectionable, as is husband-battering (understandably a much less discussed and less frequently admitted problem). But equally obviously, there is nothing about the marital relationship as such that calls for this, and if in the past wife-beating was explicitly permitted by the law, we should agree with feminists of all persuasions that that is an outrageous provision—and of course that it has long since disappeared, along with the disparity regarding the right to vote, to own businesses, and all sorts of other obvious inequities. The present discussion assumes that such things simply aren't issues any more.

(2) Does inequality consist in *difference*? If so, of course, then the case may be cheerfully conceded. Women can bear children; men cannot. But both are necessary for reproduction. If that were enough to establish "domination," then who would it show to be the dominators? No man can bear a child, but a community with a tiny number of men and a large number of women could reproduce indefinitely. Should we take this to show that women dominate men when it comes to reproduction? You may if you like, no doubt. But why do so?

(3) Is the argument that if people could just *choose* their roles, then everyone would obviously prefer the man's role? Again, it is hard to evaluate this clearly, since the most basic point about the whole situation is precisely the impossibility of choosing these roles. If you could choose to be Beethoven, would you do so? But what can this question mean? If you were Beethoven, you would not be *you*, after all: "you" would be Beethoven instead—a completely distinct individual. But if, given that you *are* you, you ask whether you should try to do all sorts of things that Beethoven did, then that is a question of detail with any number of answers—mostly negative. For Beethoven was a musical genius of transcendent order, and only a handful of other people in the history of the world could reasonably judge themselves to be like that. And even they were of very different temper and personality from Beethoven and/or lived in very different circumstances. To try to emulate Beethoven either in general or in detail might be completely misguided, even for one possessed of boundless admiration for Beethoven's music. In like manner, women are admirable, but it does not follow that men should try to be as much like them as pos-

sible. A large-scale counterfactual of the kind this question puts to us is, in a word, *silly*. There is no sense to it, and therefore, no good argument can be founded on some answer to it. Anyone who appeals to such an argument is either trying to "con" us or is the victim of a major conceptual error.

(4) Should men do more of the dishes, the diaper changing, etc., etc.? Should the woman be ready to go wherever the man wants to go in the interests of the best job? If these are central to our main question about marriage as a relation of dominance, then these and a thousand others are certainly rationally discussable. And there is every reason to expect them to have answers that reasonably vary. Consider the division of labour in ordinary life, for comparison. Should professors take turns milking the cows, delivering the mail, playing the concertos, adjusting the printing presses? The short and sensible answer is: of course not! It might be fun, or educational, but to suppose that life would generally be improved thereby is to engage in a romantic fallacy. If people generally specialize in what they are good at, leaving what they are merely ordinary or worse at to others, then we shall all do better. That is the obvious truth on which the division of labour is founded. When I reject the idea that abandonment of this division would improve things as an instance of the "romantic fallacy," my point is that to uphold any such conclusion you have to look not at people as they are but as you might *like* them to be. To do that is to adopt the romantic view of things.

Even in moral matters, the romantic fallacy *is* a fallacy. People are not as you or I or some particular theorist would like them to be: they are as they are; and "as they are" is tremendously variable! Yet as rational beings they reason from their existing interests and desires, not from the ones some ivory-tower theorist thinks they should have. Once we do this, then the fact that the division of labour is, generally speaking, efficient at producing the things people actually want is decisive. The support it provides for the principle of division of labour is not just tentative or ambiguous: it is, for all practical purposes, conclusive. For real-life people with things to do, interests to pursue, lives to live, it *settles* the matter. Is traditional marriage a case in point? Is it based on efficient division of labour or is its division counter-productive, like the rigid class systems of pre-revolutionary France?

We must begin by clearly appreciating the difference between division in respect of the fundamental functions of reproduction, which are set by biology, and many other differences that are clearly not set by biology. Males *can* change diapers—as the author's own case attests. But it doesn't follow that it makes sense to lay down a hard-and-fast rule that all males are to change, say, 50 per cent of all diapers. People differ in temperament with respect to all of these variables, and temperament quite definitely matters in such things—far more than ideology. Temperament affects performance, and performance matters, to *both* parties, indeed, to all concerned parties—especially to the children whose care we are concerned with here and who gain or lose in the end. In addition, it obviously affects general well-being. The person who tries to perform a job for which she or he is temperamentally unsuited is likely to be miserable, as well as to do that job badly; if another person is quite willing to do it instead, and does it well into the bargain, then what is the point of insisting on the other one's being put in that place?

Some might reply that the point is to achieve equality. My question about that response is whether it is a genuine reply, or only a failure to think? When people are different, what does it even mean to speak of equalization and what could be the *point* of trying to "equalize" them? But there is one very general way in which equality does indeed come to the fore. Certainly the weight of society should not be brought down on one side or the other in any of these matters. Couples are to work those questions out between themselves, with no imposed requirements for one or the other. The bottom line is agreement. Each person tries to get the best general situation possible, given her interests, abilities, resources, and capacities. If both do as well as possible, then there is nothing more to be said, whatever the proportions in which tasks are done. Any change would merely make somebody worse off without producing gains for anybody. To enforce equality in such cases is worse than useless.

Consider, for instance, the formerly typical arrangement in which the woman does domestic work while the man works outside the home at paid jobs, supporting wife and children with his earnings. She has virtually total security while he is alive. If he dies without leaving behind savings or insurance, then she and their children may be in very bad shape; but then, knowing that, he typically does save and buy insurance. Let us suppose that he has done this well. Is this, then, a good deal or a bad deal? There simply *is no general answer*. There can't be, for it depends on things that can't be known in the abstract. For example, the level of insurance that would relieve one party of insecurity may be beyond the family's means. Trying to achieve it, by investing a large part of the family earnings in insurance, may be very unwise—too much else may be sacrificed. Meanwhile, it is perfectly possible that the woman would not see it as any sort of improvement at all that she, too, should go forth and earn money at paid jobs, leaving a semi-competent husband, or no one at all, to do the domestic chores, or leaving a hired domestic servant to do them. All of these things are possible, and there is ample evidence that people vary extensively in their possession of the attitudes, temperaments, and incomes that would make good sense of one or another particular arrangement. The general claim that one party dominates just because the two do different things is groundless.

In the context of discussion of these issues, we must remember, domination is supposed to be a concept with moral significance. Most people do not think that they are "dominated" by their elected politicians—though I suspect they're wrong about that, but that's another matter. Marxists thought that workers were dominated by their bosses. They're wrong about that, too, and that isn't just another unrelated instance: it's of the essence here. In agreeing to do that job and work under that boss, the worker has *accepted* the general situation—sometimes unwisely, no doubt, but very often with good reason. And in the home, if one spouse tends to direct the other, that is the other's business. He or she may leave if dissatisfied, and in the meanwhile can negotiate anew or object. But the objection will be pointless unless reasons that make sense to the other party are forthcoming.

Many will raise an eyebrow at this, for sometimes it would be expensive or otherwise difficult to leave. In the cases where it would be expensive, we can point a finger at the law, which ought to award assets and income fairly to divorcing parties. In the cases where it is otherwise difficult, we must distinguish those in which the perceived coercion is essentially psychological from those in which it is due to physical threat. The latter should be and is illegal—enforcement of the law is the problem, not the moral principle behind it. But where coercion is emotional or in some other way psychological, there is a very great problem in attempting to bring the law to bear on it, and we, the people of the community, have to decide whom to support and how to help.

But the fundamental question is, what are the right principles to invoke? When has someone done his or her spouse a wrong in a relationship? Where physical violence has been resorted to, we will of course object. Where a pattern of clear psychological harassment exists, we will likewise object. But our objection ceases to be reasonable from the general point of view and becomes merely partisan if instead we object just because *we* wouldn't accept such an allocation of domestic labour or such an allocation of disposable income, or whatever. The first question is whether *they* accept it, with clear knowledge of what they are accepting and on the basis of their own interests.

There is, to be sure, a second and immensely more difficult question we can raise: whether they would still accept it if they understood all of the critic's arguments. And here things get very difficult indeed, for the arguments in question may be subtle and may be loaded with fallacious reasoning, innuendo, and all manner of irrelevant appeals, as well as solid facts or plausible conjectures. In any case, even if the arguments are well taken, they may be beyond the comprehension of those concerned. But the very difficulty of this suggests a partial solution: that we ought never to intervene, without their acceptance, in a situation actually accepted by parties who are reasonably well aware of the publicly knowable facts about their situation—unless, to make our usual condition, the couple's situation is also producing definitely harmful consequences for others. Of these others, children are the most likely victims.

Children

Families, from the macro social perspective, are institutions for producing and nurturing children. There are two large sets of issues here. The first is, how does this affect the marital institution? And the second concerns the ethics of child-raising: what are our duties towards children, and why?

There are some fairly obvious answers to the first of these. For one thing, children require a large amount of care by somebody; for another, is the woman who is going to bear the children, and during the period immediately before and for some time after childbirth she is likely to need a good deal of help. Moreover, we are mammals, and women's breasts are a natural source of highly nutritious food for newborns. Whoever is taking care of the child is going to need the support, ordinarily, of the other partner who will be out earning a living a good deal of the time. If breast-feeding is used, it will impose appreciable inconvenience on the mother if she is also working outside the home during the time when she does this.

In addition, there are many familiar differences between men and women, such as their physiques, the pitch and timbre of their voices, and various instinctive tendencies which in almost every case make a woman instantly recognizable as a woman, a man instantly recognizable as a man, that matter in relating to children. There is nothing the least bit surprising about the fact that early-age child-care activities are overwhelmingly performed by women, everywhere. Proposing "equality" along these lines is proposing to impose what are typically radical changes on one or the other sex. When the whole point of doing this is equality for its own sake— ideology, in short—it must be asked, why should that be a point thought worthy of pursuit? There is, I think, no good answer to that question.

On the other hand, many women nowadays either enjoy working outside the home or feel economically compelled to do so. This undoubtedly complicates family life, but it need not make it impossible or unfulfilling. It does, though, offer many challenges. Children will inevitably spend a lot of time outside the home, except in rare cases where externally hired child care can be afforded, and those children will inevitably derive a great deal of their acculturation from peers, teachers and the like rather than, almost exclusively, parents and siblings, as so often was the case in the past.

The question that will bring up for the parents, practically speaking, is how much and in what ways they will exert influence on the development of their children. Our question, philosophically, is, who has the right to exert that influence, and what kind of influence they ought to exert. So our other large question is, what is the proper way of treating such children, and why?

An obvious way to go on this would be to argue that children, after all, are fellow people and have the same rights as everyone else. The trouble with this argument is that it has a false premise. Children are *not* simply "fellow people," and it is therefore an open question whether they have the same rights as adults. In fact, it is clear that, especially in the case of very young ones, they obviously cannot and do not. Most people think that parents have rights over their children that they quite plainly do not have in relation to other adults or to other people's children; I side with "most people" on this point. Conversely, some enthusiasts want to say that children have *more* rights than the rest of us. But whether or not that is so, there is certainly a question of the basis for a sound view, since young children, at least, are decidedly not full-standing members of any social contract and, indeed, are not full moral agents at all in their earliest stages.

One of the main points in this subject, of course, is that children grow—how they grow!—and they change, markedly and more or less steadily from birth, when they have about the same intrinsic capabilities as nine-month fetuses, through to maturity, when they join the ranks of fellow adults. Obviously their moral capabilities change along with so many other things during this lengthy period, and slippery slope arguments will abound if there is a serious need to make major distinctions regarding their proper treatment in different phases within this period. Ideally, from the pure theorist's point of view, we would have a nice continuous function concerning proper treatment to match the continuous variables of the child's growth and development. Then we would be able to say, "Well, the child is precisely *here*, so you should be treating him in accordance with the principles appropriate to that, which are precisely *these*." Unfortunately, we don't have any of these nice neat formulae and must, for better or worse, rough it.

Regarding the early end of the spectrum of childhood, we have already discussed infanticide. Whatever the moral status of that option, the project of the family entails that it has been rejected. From early infancy and for some time thereafter, I have argued, we must look to considerations of the public interest. Which interests? The answer is pretty easy, in fact: the public's interest is that any given infant should become an adult who won't threaten people's lives and properties, won't be a large net draw on its resources, and will add, preferably a lot, to the value of the community by increasing its range of desirable options in the way of life activities. Insofar as childhood upbringing affects these matters, then it is obviously of public concern. Do we know enough to make such considerations the foundation of any important moral result?

Indeed we do. There is good evidence, for example, that hardened criminals come almost exclusively from homes in which there was unaffectionate, erratic, and violent parenting. By contrast, a warmly affectionate home environment with clear, reasonable, nonviolent, and consistent discipline all but ensures that children will grow into non-violent, pleasant, and productive people. It is eminently reasonable to support social institutions known to have such results.

Parental warmth and kindly discipline are not confined to the paradigmatic Western family, to be sure—and indeed, have too often been more or less lacking in it; yet it is an institution well suited for the purpose. Strong support and vivid warmth aren't readily available for dozens of little strangers. Nor are they as readily available from the one person who has to do *all* the work in the home as from one or both of the two persons who between them do it all, leaving time for rest and disengagement for the other parent every so often. As Wilson and Herrnstein report, "Apparently, mothers can make up for whatever loss in child-rearing capacity is caused by the absence of the father.... But if the mother must try harder, we should expect some to fail; ... if one parent must do the work of two, then, at the margin, less of that work will get done." And they add in a footnote, "It is because of the greater costs of being a single parent, among other reasons, that the mother-father-child triad is the universal family unit."[6]

Considerations of efficiency sound unromantic, and even when emotional efficiency is in question such talk may seem unromantic. And so it is. Replenishing a population is a serious business that matters enormously to everyone. Romance is a wonderful and great thing, without which life would be far less worth living; but even so, it is no substitute for the sober concerns of securing a human environment of individuals who will be an asset rather than a liability to you, me, and themselves.

My thesis, then, is that our rights *against each other*, as adults, are the proper sources of rights for children. Children are potential adults. To treat them well is to set them on the road to being the sort of adults we want to have around; to treat them badly is virtually to invite them to become the sort of people we don't want around. Parents who fail towards their children are parents who fail their neighbours and fellow humans, as well, of course, as the adults those children become when they grow up.

Marriage, Children, and Divorce

The most striking change in the marital ways of the West over the past several decades has been in the area of divorce. We have gone from a society in which divorce was very rare to one in which it is familiar to everyone—one hears that some 50 per cent of marriages will end in divorce.[7] This is certainly in part due to the loosening of the legal restrictions that formerly made divorce difficult and expensive; it is now much easier and much less expensive. Should it be so? Or should we re-erect substantial barriers to divorce?

A recent writer[8] broaches this question in a thought-provoking way. The loosening of marital bonds was ardently sought by feminists as well as by males, she observes; it was thought to strike a blow for liberty and equality: neither party to a marriage could keep the other one in a marriage against her or his will. So far, so good. When the woman is liberated from her marriage, she is now free to live what was formerly a man's life—and to compete in the job market with males on equal terms, or rather, on what *would* be equal terms but for one thing: children. In most cases, after all, the woman is the one who gets the kids, and with them she takes what used to be a full-time job, leaving her with a much less than equal capability of competing with males, who are used to working overtime for the top spots, applying 100 per cent of their energies to success in the workplace. No one with a small child to take care of can do this, and women are usually the ones in that position. Thus, if a marriage breaks up leaving the woman only "equality," she actually emerges worse off. And so do the children. For no broken marriage, from the child's point of view, is likely to equal what the family provides when two reliable parents are around, offering security, help, entertainment, instruction, and love. The woman who claims to be able to equal that package by herself is very likely deluding herself. She is perhaps thinking of the package the child would have with her horrible ex-husband for a father and supposing that she by herself is better than *that*. And she may, to be sure, be right about that; but also, she may have forgotten what it was like to be a child—or may herself have come from a broken home.

From the child's point of view, the reliable two-parent home is a luxury, and the two-parent home where one of the parents is a full-time parent, having no major time-consuming commitments outside the home, is absolutely plush. If you want to have children and to do as well as possible by them, this should be borne in mind. No amount of money, even, can make up for that missing extra adult who is always around, or not far away, and who provides another voice, another court of appeal, another point of view, while he's at it. And it is surely useful for children of either sex to have extensive experience with adults of both sexes by the time they are on their own. A still larger set of adults, of course, could do that, too. But there is a problem of focus if many adults have equal status as providers of attention and love: those are goods that do not divide well. The love that one person can provide another when that other is one of a great many others cannot, however genuine, equal the love provided by one for whom the subject is unique or at most one of a handful of claimants, as in the typical monogamous household.

Should we think that children have equal rights with adults? If we must put it in those terms, then the answer is that they should not, and during a fair amount of their early lives it is in any case impossible for them to do so. But we need to keep rights in the proper perspective. They should not be our foremost consideration here, should they? If one is going to be a parent at all, one should want to be a good one. And there is no way that you can be so good a *one* as to equal, from the child's point of view, *two*, if both are good ones. That's something that you, the parent, have a lot of control over.

Divorces, we must remember, don't just happen, like diseases. Your love and concern for your children, quite natural and wholly admirable, motivates you to do your best to make their home as supportive as possible. For the reasons given, that includes making your marriage work if it possibly can. And if it can't, it means, if you are the male, taking your full share of responsibility for the children. Divorce should be expensive for the partner who doesn't get the child, for it *will* be very expensive for the other one. Again, we must not forget: it's the child who inevitably pays. Only in the most extreme cases—probably not yours—is the child likely to find the post-divorce situation better than the way things were before. Children, of course, do not know best about everything. But who can possibly be better qualified than they about a matter like *that*? And what, after all, is the point of having children if one isn't ready to bring them up well? Our duty, in the strictest sense, is to bring up children who are not going to be a nuisance to others. But every parent wants, surely, to do much better than that. We want to raise our children to the best lives possible for them. Or at least the best lives for them, compatible with having a reasonably good life ourselves, though those two goals are often identical anyway.

Intrinsic Rewards

Our experiences with children are, from common experience, among the most valuable and delightful we can have. Watching children grow is fascinating; interacting with them, observing their spontaneous, uninhibited, and wonderfully plastic and creative dealings with their surroundings is a source of great pleasure and instruction to any adult who takes the time to do so. It is understandable that people can be annoyed with children—their own as well as others—and on those occasions the need to resist impulses towards excessively restrictive or even violent behaviour is great. But one's general disposition should be one of kindness, sympathy, understanding, and love. Those are the dispositions that will pay off in the longer run, or sooner - and not those of cruelty, malice, authoritarianism, and the rest of the more vicious tendencies in our nature.

None of the preceding, of course, is intended to support any claim that it is our duty to *have* children. Just the opposite, actually: for the point of the preceding paragraph was to call attention to a familiar fact that explains why people will have children without pressuring them to do so. Leaving people free to do what they want will leave us with plenty of children. Our question here is addressed only to those who are ready to engage, willingly, on this important and challenging life project.

In former times, people inclined towards the view embodied in the maxim, "Spare the rod and spoil the child." Of course, if it were true that the child would otherwise be "spoiled," then applying the rod would quite possibly be justified. Experience, however, suggests that it is not. And if it is not, then one can also appeal to the rule that one should treat people of all ages as decently as possible: if nothing legitimate is gained by bad treatment, then good treatment is in order. In fact, as suggested above, it may well be just the opposite: using the rod, and especially using it inconsistently, spoils the child, by turning him or her into a hard-hearted, angry, resentful, and malicious person. In extreme cases, it turns him into a murderer or a rapist, or perhaps into someone with mental health problems. Actually, it is becoming increasingly clear that corporal punishment is never necessary, and thus never justified, as a method of dealing with children. Recognizing that they are people, with their own thought processes and wills, and that their points of view, though often under informed, are nevertheless reasonable, goes far toward heading off the sort of disciplinary problems that many parents believe they have with their children.

But another fascinating question is whether we should, as nearly as possible from the beginning, treat children as we would adults; that is, as being entitled to liberty of action in the most general sense compatible with recognizing similar liberty for all others.

Here the big question is whether we are right to think that we know better than the child what is good for it. The point of view of this book in regard to adults has been, unrelentingly, that people are their own bosses and that whatever we think is good for them, it must be checked out with the intended recipient of our instruction or correction before it passes moral muster. Should we take the same point of view towards children?

There is much that small children don't know, and some of it will, quite possibly, hurt them. But children do learn rapidly, for one thing. For another, they very soon begin to have a pretty good idea what they want; which quite possibly differs a good deal from what we think is good for them. Parents have the upper hand over children, for a long time. Not only are they more competent at a great many things, but they also earn the wherewithal to make life possible for the child, and certainly to make it comfortable and pleasant. But how do we play all these cards? A plausible suggestion is that from very early on, children should be brought up as responsible people with lives and interests of their own. The parent who tries to run her child's life is likely to discover that she's done a bad job of it, and certainly that the child would have been happier doing it *his* way.

The topic of what makes a good life for children, including especially a good preparation for later life, is close to all-consuming in practice for many parents. But prominent on the list of questions is that of education. There is a paradigm, provided by the public school systems, and another, provided by the prospect of university or college education, to which most unthinkingly adhere, or perhaps adhere because they think they have no choice. But there are choices all along. For example, the option of home-schooling one's children is one to be taken very seriously indeed. It is, of course, vigorously opposed by the educational establishment, but the concerned parent will do well to look into it—especially when she discovers that home-schooled children typically do much better at academic subjects than their institutionally educated counterparts.[9] Family life provides vistas for living that we do well to think about.

Summing up

This long chapter has delved into a large group of important matters: sex, love, marriage, and family. There has been considerable change on all of those fronts in the past generation or two, and I

have tried both to insist that we should not heavy-handedly suppress most of this and, at the same time, to present a sympathetic
account of the considerable virtues of the traditional arrangements.
There should be all of these things in a life, but getting them all to
fit comfortably together is not easy. From the broader perspective,
though, our focus must be especially on family and whatever is
required to make it work, for the future of civilized society depends
on that. We want to produce the best new people, meaning those
better for all of us, especially, non-violent and productive ones.
Considerations of characteristic human differences and requirements, as well as the familiar biological facts about people, strongly point to the more or less traditional family as the most nearly
optimal arrangement towards this end, not least because it enables
the best emotional accommodation for most people. This certainly
does not mean that male heads of households are to have complete
authority about everything; the primacy of mutual accommodation
and acceptance remains in place. Nor does it mean that we may
require people to participate in it or harass those who elect non-
standard options such as same-sex partnerships. What it does mean
is that traditional arrangements have enough going for them to be
deserving of careful consideration. We are unlikely to do better.

Chapter Twelve

Pornography, Prostitution, and Sexual Harassment

In this chapter, we consider three loosely related subjects. What they have in common is that they are ways of dealing with our sexual instincts that have been widely disapproved of and widely practised, and they raise issues about relating to others that make them eligible for treatment in this book.

Pornography

Pornography is the depiction, by visual, literary, or aural means, of subject-matter intended to be sexually stimulating, when that depiction is for the *purpose* of such stimulation. Pornography is a sort of depictional aphrodisiac. Or at least, that was once the idea. Recently, the depiction of non-sexual violence against people has also come to be described as pornographic. Although we will in general have the sexual type in mind in the following discussion, the connection, or a supposed connection, between violence and sex is a major part of the conceptual concern with this matter, as we will see.

Official suppression, censorship, and/or strict control over the circulation of pornography has been commonplace in our society for a long time and remains the principal form of current censorship. Movies are rated, some are suppressed, and others altered by their makers to avoid the censor's hand. The same has been true of books, at various times, though currently "hate literature" is a more likely target than pornography. The question that concerns us here is whether such interventions are justified.

Liberal vs. Conservative

Standing against censorship is the *liberal* principle: that people should be able to live the sort of life they choose, exercising their own taste (or lack of it), not being subject to the rule of others. In political terms, the liberal holds that the purpose of a commonwealth is the advancement of the several goods of its members, a point that the conservative agrees with. *But* the liberal adds that the goods in question must be good in the view of the individual members of society, rather than in the view of some self-appointed or state-appointed authority. It is in this full sense that the liberal holds that the state exists for the sake of the citizen, and not the other way around. The conservative, by contrast, holds that in some or a lot of cases, certain people—namely those in power or hoping to be in power—know what is good for *us*, the people. "We are out for your good!" say they—but it is *they* who will decide what that good is. The same distinction is applicable to morality. A liberal morality attributes to individuals the right to live as they please, free of interference from others, subject only to such controls as are necessary to uphold the same freedom for all. A conservative morality, by contrast, holds that there are right or wrong ways of life, that it is our duty to steer people, by force if necessary, into the right ones and away from the wrong ones—*and* that what is right and wrong is known independently of the values and interests that people actually see themselves as having. Of course, which values are the right ones is a subject on which views will vary greatly from one conservative to another.

My characterization of conservatism is broader than that prevalent in ordinary usage—if there is any such usage. If a society were to force its subjects to read pornography or engage in non-standard sex acts, on the ground that those were part of the ideal way of life that all should adhere to, then few would call this "conservative," although it would, in my usage, be precisely that—and objectionable to the liberal for the same kind of reasons as would be the prohibition of such things on a similar ground. For present purposes, however, we needn't worry about that. In this discussion, we will simply take the conservative to hold that the depiction of sexual acts with a view to stimulating sexual sensations may properly be suppressed.

Harm

Everyone agrees that we may insist on someone's not doing x if his doing x would be *harmful* to others. The question is, what constitutes harm? The liberal version of the harm principle is that harm consists in physical damage to the body, to one's property, or to one's civil and political rights. This is the version of the harm principle that leaves us maximally free to live our lives as we see fit, with all that that entails, for better or worse. It does not allow mere "damage" to one's beliefs, for instance, to count as a reason for restricting the offending person's liberty.

We will explore the subject of censorship in the light of this principle, asking what kind of restrictions, if any, it would approve and whether there is any justification for principles more congenial to would-be censors.

Disgust

It is obvious enough that there can be a rationale for censorship in *conservative* terms: that someone else's activity in some respect is "abhorrent" or "disgusting" is taken by the conservative to be a sufficient basis for action to prevent the alleged miscreant from carrying on in the offending manner. How would the conservative try to argue for his claims? Presumably, he hopes to persuade you that the sort of life you live if you view pornography, say, is one from which you would recoil if you could just view it properly. But what if his audience does not recoil? That the consumer of pornography doesn't see it that way is taken by the conservative as evidence of his base nature: question-begging arguments are the conservative's stock in trade. They are appeals to our aesthetic sense, or our sense of propriety, but not appeals that can be backed up with further reasons; we must either take it or leave it. In the case of pornography, for instance, what we must either just take or leave is that the pleasures people might get from viewing pictures of genitalia or of people engaged in sex acts are "bad" pleasures. But if they really are pleasures, it is going to be difficult to convince the pornographer that they are also bad ones, for he reckons all pleasures to be good, insofar as that's what they are.

Public/Private

If someone professing to be liberal in his views wants to support any censorship, he must search for an argument of a different kind. He must show that use of the materials in question visits some genuine harm on someone. But the only "harm" he is usually able to demonstrate is *offence*: some people, such as himself, are offended by the prospect of other people viewing this kind of material. But offence is surely not enough for this purpose. If it were, we would all be at the mercy of everyone else's whims and tastes. In fact, though, there is a tacit assumption at work here that needs to be brought out. No one could seriously think that offence can't *ever* be sufficient cause to justify restrictive activity on the part of the offended person. If you offend me in my living room, for example, then I might well be justified in showing you the door. You might think me unreasonable, and for that matter you might be right; still, I surely have the right to do that. What makes all the difference is whether the space in which the expression takes place is privately owned or not. If it is, then the owner has the authority to decide what will and won't be said or done or shown on the premises. But if it is not, then we have a problem, for non-private property is either just unowned (which is rare) or *public*, in which case the familiar problems of politics set in.

Our question, then, must concern conduct in *public* areas, those where we encounter each other routinely. The general idea concerning such areas is that everyone has the right to be there, going to and fro as they please. Nobody can "show the door" to anyone, for no individual or small group of individuals owns the place. That, indeed, is just the trouble. If no one has any more right than any other, on what rational principle can we govern interactions? How do we decide who has to give way in a public space, when presumably both have the right to be there?

It's easy enough to give a partial answer to this, for not everything in a public area is public. You and I are not public property. The perimeters of our bodies, at least, define a frontier beyond which other members of the public may not go even if the area we respectively occupy is a public area. Physical attacks against each other's bodies, or unwanted touchings, are prohibited on the same ground that verbal attacks within our houses may be prohibited by the owner. But what about verbal attacks in public places?

We can also usefully distinguish between, say, a verbal attack at a volume that is physically painful and one that is only "painful" in some other sense. But that will take us back to the subject of offence. And here it seems we can again hardly deny its relevance in some cases: offensive verbal attacks are not routinely allowable in public, either. Our discourse ought to be peaceable, not intended to offend. The same can be true regarding our appearance, perhaps. To go forth topless in public, as one woman did in a small Canadian city one hot summer's day, is to try unilaterally to impose a standard of dress (or undress) that is likely to offend many. Are we justified in coercively prohibiting such exhibitions? May we say that those who are offended are merely prudish and have no real reason for their being offended? I'm inclined to agree with that, in fact, but it is surely a matter on which opinions may legitimately differ. Thus, there is a question whether we would merely be imposing another standard if we insisted that citizens must put up with displays of public nudity. It seems uncomfortably comparable to an earlier example: *requiring* people to engage in sexually deviant behaviour.

That it is impossible to please everyone here is illustrated by the case of the devout Muslim woman, who goes forth in public dressed in heavy veil and robes. She is presumably offended by the carefree attire of most of those around her. But one can easily imagine that some women would actually be offended at the Muslim woman's dress, holding that her costume shows a submission to male domination that is beneath human dignity. The Muslim woman and the feminist are then in a zero-sum game: a given kind of attire will offend one of them only if it won't offend the other. In fact, we are inclined to award both of them the right to dress as they please, requiring both to restrain any offence they might feel, this being the price they pay for going forth in public at all. Yet the would-be nudist is required to wear something in the interests of not offending others, and there is a problem drawing the line. Why should we cater to the offence of the "prude" when we do not do so regarding the Muslim or the feminist?

Privacy and Porn

Actually, pornographic viewing doesn't take place in public either. All that happens in public is that enough information is made available to the public, in the form of advertising (which, in turn, can be discreetly displayed), to enable some of its members to seek out the private locations in which they can pursue their interests. So long as those locations are clearly identifiable, they can also be avoided by those of differing taste. Privatization enables all parties to be satisfied, it seems. And the liberal does not defend the *public* display of pornography.

Or does she? Here we have to distinguish between what the privatization idea would do if it were thoroughly carried out and what would happen in the real world if we tried to approximate it— that is, between what philosophers call "ideal" or "perfect compliance" theory and "partial compliance theory." Total privatization means that all costs and benefits of an act are borne by the agent. No costs are imposed on anyone, and no one benefits at the expense of anyone else.

Now let us return to our problem. Suppose that all acts of reading or viewing satisfy our privacy requirement. Nobody sees anything that she doesn't want to see, nobody reads anything that she doesn't want to read; and nobody reads or sees anything without the consent of whoever provides it (authors, booksellers, movie-house operators, and so on). Is everything just fine, then? The liberal says yes. But many think not, and we must look carefully at their proposed reasons.

There are two types of objection to be concerned with here. First, there is the view that some material *inherently demeans* certain people. This, some hold, harms those people sufficiently to justify restriction even on liberal terms. And second, there is a concern with the effects of such material on the consumer's subsequent behaviour. His viewing of pornography, for instance, stimulates him to go out and rape people.

These two objections are important, because they are addressed by people who at least claim to be sympathetic with liberalism. We must look closely at them.

Demeaning Depictions

The first objection is advanced, for instance, by many feminists against pornography. Women, they say, are demeaned in such material. They are portrayed as inferior, or as slaves of men, or as mere "sex objects" to be used as men wish. Probably some pornographic literature does not do this, but let us suppose that some does. The interesting question is whether this would provide ground for suppression.

Here's an example to think about: in the Old Testament, a good many groups of people in the Middle East were portrayed as a pretty bad lot. The Philistines, for instance, were depicted as a bunch of yahoos who went around beating up on people until at last courageous little David came along and laid their main champion low with a deft application of high (for the times) technology. Are the people who make this charge proposing, then, that we should outlaw reading of the Old Testament? That book is not a "sacred cow," to be sure; yet very few of those who favour suppression of other literature would take kindly to the thought that it should be on the list. Obviously, evil can be portrayed without implying approval.

Falsity

It might be said that the depiction of women in pornography nevertheless does imply approval, and that its depiction is false and thereby creates a false image of women in general. Would this be a ground for objection even if true? I find it difficult to see how any other construal can be put on it than this: that what are claimed to be demeaning portrayals, say of women or of Palestinians, are false. Women are not slavish, passive, and mere sex objects; Palestinians aren't cruel and warlike. After all, if these claims were actually true, then there is at least some question why it would be held wrong to depict them in those ways.

But if that's the claim about pornography, then the trouble is that we are back to the old arguments for censorship so successfully refuted by John Stuart Mill in his famous *Essay on Liberty*. The fact that statement p is false cannot be used as a ground for suppression of those who would say it, though it does provide an excellent occasion for *refuting* it.

This isn't the end of the matter, however. There are truths about people that nevertheless may not be broadcast. Your sex life, for example, is not something the details of which I am entitled to know. We suppose, and for excellent reason, that there is a right of privacy that should not be invaded even if the result would be the publication of any number of true statements. However, this charge would not be sustainable against pornography, provided that it was produced within the confines of our privatization restrictions. After all, the actors in those films are required by our principles to have participated voluntarily in their production, for example, by accepting payment large enough to make it worth their while. On the face of it, we don't as yet have a clear case against pornographic portrayals, however demeaning we may think them to be.

Voluntariness

Proponents of the objection we are considering might well respond to this by claiming that the actresses in question did *not* participate voluntarily. But to make good this claim—which is superficially implausible, after all—they have to stretch the notion of voluntariness well beyond its normal usage. The soldiers from an all-volunteer army who were unfortunate enough to have been killed in battle nevertheless did volunteer. They signed up in full knowledge that their work entailed a risk of death. The actress in a pornographic movie knows what sort of customers will leer at the results; it is up to her to consider whether she is willing to assume all sorts of undignified positions, with that expected result, in return for the proffered fee.

It might be complained that it isn't really up to the actress to decide whether to act in a scene that depicts women in that way: if she acts in it, then that is how they are depicted, whether she intends that or not. But is this a valid complaint? No one can *make* women that way, just by so depicting them. Nor can anyone plausibly claim to know all women; our actress is, after all, just one woman among others, and women differ. And in any case, the porn actress would surely disclaim any such intention, insisting that she is only portraying one particular character of that kind—not women in general. Anyone who thinks that any character in any artistic representation *must* represent *everybody* is surely going far beyond the intentions of typical artists, as well as supposing something that is quite obviously untrue.

Truth, Falsity, and Harm

Is truth good in itself? Is truth any kind of value at all? And is it a value *for* all? *Is* society just one big clone of Plato's Academy, after all? Opinions may vary on the first one, but to the third, it is hard to see how the answer could be affirmative. Aristotle claimed that "all men by nature desire to know," but as any elementary school teacher will tell you, this is not at all obvious, especially if it means that everyone's goal in life is to maximize her supply of information about the universe, as compared with other possible goals. That relatively clear conjecture we may pretty confidently dismiss. Moreover, those who don't go in for such exotic amusements are guilty of no moral error.

On the other hand, we might mean that *falsehood*, or more precisely, the provision of false "information" in response to requests for information, is a *disvalue* for anyone. That is indeed plausible. One cannot act well *on the basis of* falsehoods. If my doing x successfully is contingent on some supposed fact, p, and p is false, then my action to that extent, and in that respect, misfires. How and why action might thus be contingent varies and may sometimes need explaining. But in typical cases, there's no problem at all: if you want to accomplish goal G by performing some act, x, then you are assuming that x is connected to G. If someone tells you this and what he says is false, he has put you out, at very least by motivating you to perform a useless action. Or worse, for you might instead get something you really don't want. In some cases, the point of not being in error is less clear. Certainly it could be in someone's short-run interest, at least, to deceive someone else, and even perhaps himself, about some limited matter. (Yet even the self-deceiver needs to know what is true in order to persuade himself of what is false; if what he wants to believe were actually true, he could spare himself the trouble of deceiving himself about it!) That truth, in the sense of not being in error about things that matter to you, is generally clear enough.

The question of how falsehoods might harm is rather complex. Here are several pointers and queries.

(1) To say, sincerely, what is in fact false is to stand in need of correction, for to be in possession of what is false is likely to be unfortunate or worse. One does better to be refuted. And one has the moral duty to entertain proposed refutations rather than ignore them. To what extent must one do so? That's not easy to estimate; my point is that they shouldn't just be shunted aside, unless one has good antecedent reason for believing them false without further examination.

(2) To say what one *knows* is false is to make oneself liable for consequences. When one's misinformation reasonably motivates others to act badly, with results unfortunate for them or others, then one bears liability for the misfortune and may in principle be sued for damages.

(3) What if A impugns the reputation of B on grounds that are either meaningless or logically insulated from refutation? For example, suppose A claims that B is "evil" but that his supposed evil consists in having a certain mysterious, unique, and inexplicable but suitably sinister-sounding property? That seems pretty nearly equivalent to falsehood, especially if propagated among gullible people. (Consider the claim that someone is a "witch," for example, as in Salem, Massachusetts in the seventeenth Century.) At any rate, it is not a rational ground of action. Its equivalence to falsehood lies in this: that for any given action, x, by some person, C, that has certain effects on person B, C's doing x to B *for the reason* that B is F (where x is evil in our defined sense) is based on a *necessarily irrelevant* ground. If 'F' is indefinable, then the "fact" that B is F couldn't be a good reason for treating B in any one way as opposed to any other.[1] There is also the problem of assessing responsibility of those who act badly on the basis of this drivel. If B assassinates C because B has been told by A that "God ordered it," how do we apportion blame between B and A? A difficult question, but surely both are to blame.

(4) The fact that one dislikes person B is, of course, a putatively good reason for having as little as possible to do with him. It can also seem to be a reason, so far as it goes, for performing acts that would violate his rights; but there are then independent reasons against it, overriding mere dislike—that, indeed, is part of the point of calling those things "rights." Nor, of course, is the fact that I dislike B any reason, so far as it goes, why *you* should dislike B. We do not have a general, basic duty to like each other, but we do have a general interest in good relations with all people, so we should not easily indulge in ill-considered dislikings. Still, it does not violate someone's rights if you ultimately dislike that person.

(5) Do we harm someone *by* disliking him? We must be careful to distinguish this from the question whether you might come to harm someone *as a result of* disliking him. That, of course, is common enough, and wrong. But in those cases, we typically have in mind someone's really harming someone in various familiar ways, such as by striking him; we don't mean that the very fact of dislike is itself harmful to the other person.

But could it not sometimes be so? We might first point out that one could keep one's dislike to oneself rather than manifesting it in readily observable ways. It's difficult to see how one could regard the sheer *fact* of someone's dislike, independently of any outward manifestations, as constituting "harm." True, we can easily enough imagine someone having a desire that everyone like him, and who would be wounded if they do not. But we cannot credit supposed harms of this type. To do so is to court disaster: everyone is really enslaved to everyone else if we can blame Jones merely for disliking Smith.

Does the allegation that pornography demeans women identify a genuine ground of moral objection to it? We have noted that portrayals of some person mistreating others may not be false for clearly this sometimes actually happens. It is the "message"—that this is a good way to treat those others—that we may be concerned about. We certainly don't want anyone believing it. But whether this is a ground for suppressing the message is another question. If we think it is, we must be assuming that the audience for the message is gullible and incapable of properly evaluating claims of that kind, or else that it is evil, in which case the video or picture isn't "convincing" them, but is instead just pandering to or reinforcing a base tendency of character that is already present.

We must in any case distinguish those pornographic materials that are, in effect, "hate literature" from those that are not. Most are surely in the latter category: they depict people sexually carrying on in various ways that plenty of possible viewers would find distasteful, but that the buying audience clearly does not. Nor, characteristically, did the participants. But there is a question about inferring intentions from what one sees on a screen, hears on a soundtrack, or reads in a text. Those who depict evil are not necessarily advocating it: indeed, one must describe something to condemn it. Many fine movies are devoted almost wholly to depicting evils. The message of those movies, usually, is precisely that they *are* evils.

Now, it is clear that normal people can witness depictions of evil, and even advocacy of it, without being in any way corrupted by this. Cinema buffs have long been keen on certain cinema classics, such as *Birth of a Nation* and Leni Riefenstahl's depiction of the Third Reich, which are and were intended to be out-and-out exercises in propaganda, without being converted to the KKK or the Nazism. To suppress such movies on the ground that their message is evil would be absurd, if those audiences are typical. And to assume, in general, that those witnessing pornography *must* be in fact corrupted by it is to make an assumption that we ought not generally to make about people. People must be generally presumed to have minds of their own, as well as to be responsible for their actions—which brings us to the other major question, concerning pornography's effects on the consumer's behaviour.

Motivation To Do Evil

This objection to pornography is that exposure to it induces people to engage in harmful behaviour, such as rape. That objection cannot be dismissed along the lines we have just been considering. If it is true that reading x will *cause* A to go out and commit murder, rape or something comparably evil, then obviously we have reason to be concerned.

Some reason, yes—but how much? When, if ever, do we have a case for outright censorship arising from possibilities like this? It is importantly true that murder and rape, among various other forms of interpersonal assault, are things that no person should do to anyone, under almost any conceivable circumstances. Someone who does this is rightly considered liable for criminal proceedings. And if we knew of any actual *causes* of any of these kinds of activity, such that we could know in advance, and for certain, that person A was going to do an act of such a kind, then we would certainly be entitled to prevent A from carrying out his evil plans. But the trouble is, we do *not* know of any such causes.

We do know that certain ways of treating young people, especially very young ones, drastically reduce the probability that they will end up performing such deeds, while certain others greatly increase it. For example, hardened recidivistic criminals, the ones who commit another major crime almost right away upon their release from prison for the last one, have invariably been brought up in domestic environments characterized by frequent violence, verbal and otherwise, by wildly inconsistent disciplinary practices, and with a pronounced shortage of parental (especially maternal) affection. Readers of this book have probably been fortunate enough to have been brought up in good homes. Even so, not nearly 100 per cent of children from bad homes will end up hardened criminals— merely a lot of them. Virtually 100 per cent of those brought up in "good" homes will not end up like that—but not *quite* 100 per cent. Should we try legally requiring parents to provide good homes for their children? If this could possibly be successful, it would have a drastic effect on the crime rate—virtually eliminating it, it seems. But it is clear that massive failure awaits any legal initiative of this kind.

Now apply that result, from an area where the evidence is strong, to the present one, where it is extremely weak. Is there a connection between witnessing pornographic materials and the likelihood of committing rape? Nobody would claim that there is anything remotely approximating a necessary condition here: millions of people view pornography without being rapists. It is certain that eliminating pornography entirely while leaving other things the same would leave us with plenty of rapists. In some cases, I gather, it might even increase the number: pornography in those cases acts as a substitute for the real thing, satisfying the would-be rapist before he gets out the door. It is very clear that this is an empirical question, and one that is decidedly *not* easy to answer; the evidence, such as it is, is overwhelmingly inconclusive.[2]

All this requires us to address a further issue: what standards of evidence are we to use? Let us suppose that on the whole, people being exposed to pornography slightly increases the probability that they will later commit rape (and we do not even know that as yet). Now consider a figure we shall call P: the probability that a given individual will be a rapist given that he is a pornographer, less the probability that he would have been a rapist even if he hadn't been a pornographer. P, in other words, represent the marginal increment in this probability for members of the class of consumers of pornography. Then our question is, what value of P would justify depriving the *entire* class of consumers of pornography of opportunities to view it? The likely answer is that wherever we might want to put it, the real value of that probability in the population we have is far, far lower than that.

Consider another comparison. Alcohol is a causative factor in a good many murders and a great many automobile accidents. We may be quite certain that the incidence of murder or criminal negligence among drinkers as compared with what it would be for those same people if they didn't drink is significant—far higher, given what we do know, than P. Yet prohibition in the U.S. was agreed to be a massive failure, and there is a genuine issue whether it would have been justified even if it hadn't been. Depriving everyone of alcohol when only some are induced by its consumption to commit criminal acts punishes the innocent in order to get at the guilty. Is this just?

Most readers will probably feel that the joys of alcohol consumption greatly outweigh those of pornography consumption. Perhaps so—but then, the joys of listening to a Mozart string quintet far outweigh either. Yet I don't think we are justified in requiring people to listen to Mozart; and this is not only because our efforts would no doubt prove a total failure. It is instead because how we shall run our lives is up to those whose lives they are, not to others—even if those others have terrific taste.

Zero Risk?

Some may insist that crimes like rape are so serious a matter that if we can do anything at all to make it less probable, then we should do it. That is a common attitude towards many other things as well. But it is wrong—profoundly wrong in one direction and absurdly so in another.

To see its absurdity, consider your own case and the risks you will quite reasonably take in order to gain modest pleasures. The most obvious and spectacular case is presented by smokers, who take a statistically very significant risk of contracting cancer in return for a modest amount of pleasure. But their conduct is perfectly rational (and I say this as a moderately fanatical non-smoker). Given the choice between a probably longer but smoke-free life and a probably shorter and smoke-filled one, they prefer the latter. It's their choice, so long as they keep the smoke out of the lungs of the non-smokers. For another example: there are people who voluntarily move to places like New York City from amazingly safe places like Selma, North Dakota, despite the vastly greater likelihood of being killed, mugged, or raped if they do so. They reckon that the more interesting things they can do in New York more than compensate for the increased risks of life in the big city. And they are not irrational to reason this way.

Given all this, if we imposed total censorship of pornography, who would lose and what would they lose? Presumably the consumers of porn would lose, and what they would lose are the various pleasures they take in such literature. The overwhelming majority of these people will never rape anybody, and of the tiny minority who would, most would do so whether or not they watched pornography. Thus the innocent consumers of pornography would be penalized for the behaviour of the others. And that isn't fair, just as it is not fair that the alcohol consumers among us who do not drive when drunk and do not knife people in heated arguments while inebriated should be deprived of their pleasures in order to protect the world from the others who do.

It is perfectly clear that nothing in life is perfectly safe, once one considers the matter carefully. What walk of life has not produced its monsters, its aberrations? Academics convinced of some bizarre theory go forth to assassinate innocent people; accountants, preachers, secretaries—you name it: who can sincerely claim to know for sure that no persons in that walk of life will as a consequence of following it go out and do major harm to someone? To prohibit these activities on that account would be to commit palpable wrongs now in the interests of preventing vague and remote possible wrongs in the future.

On the Theory of Social Risk

I will now suggest a social cost-benefit assessment for proposals like abolition of pornography. First, assign some definite negative value to the actual committing of one of the acts whose prevention we aim at. Then assign an equal positive value to each case in which the act in question didn't occur, though it otherwise would have. Society has paid itself that much in each successful case. Now assign another value, to the costs of the interferences we make in the interest of preventing the larger disvalues. And now suppose that society pays a compensation to each innocent person whose life is interfered with in this way. Then ask whether this was a good investment of society's time and energy.

Let's admit that it is very difficult to estimate the gains of such a policy. The best one can do would be to compare incidences of rape before and after the massive regime of censorship is installed. Nobody knows what the result would be, but if it is only a tiny diminution of the rate of rape—which is the worst we currently have reason to believe—then we have our result: we will have paid an astronomical amount in the way of lost liberty for a tiny gain in personal security—ten kilos of prevention for one gram of cure. This is not a rational way to run a society.

All in all, we do better to continue our liberal maxim. Every individual person is presumed innocent until proven guilty, and guilt will be proved only by deeds, not by the suspect's choice of reading or viewing matter. Other methods, such as argument or moral suasion, especially in early childhood, will have to be employed to protect the public.

Paternalism

Should we perhaps control what gets exposed to the *immature* eye? It does seem rather difficult to suppose that no sort of "censorship" is admissible in such cases, to be sure. But there are at least three angles from which to view this matter. One focuses on parental control and consent. Some parents will not wish their children to be exposed to certain of what they consider subversive influences—religious or moral, for instance. Another concerns the proper extent of community involvement in the nurturing of children. Particular parents may wish *their* children not to be exposed to certain material, but what if other parents are happy to expose theirs to it? The community may not arbitrarily rule in favour of one parent and against another.

Finally, there is the possibly distinct question of developmental psychology. Is it possible to know what is truly good for children, ignoring what their parents or other people *want* for them? These are difficult matters, and it is impossible to deny that what they are exposed to will likely have influence on them. But also, I think, what influences them will depend heavily on context. In a home where there is an extremely repressive atmosphere about sexual matters, a child's exposure to certain kinds of pornographic literature might help to turn him into the Montreal mass murderer;[3] and yet, the same literature read by the child of tolerant and supportive parents might produce nothing but wry amusement. Indeed, there is probably little if anything that normal children can read or view in such an atmosphere that would produce serious harm to them in later years.

But here again, a major effort to intervene in the home is likely to be hugely counter-productive. What is likely to be much less so, I think, is a policy of holding parents responsible for the behaviour of their children, at the same time encouraging the distribution of advice and information about child care. Behind almost every teenager committing a violent crime is a parent who did a lot of things very wrong. It might greatly encourage parents to seek advice on what it was, and how to correct it, if when a teenager does go wrong, those parental influences were allowed to be exposed. Parents are not acting primarily as agents for the community when they take charge of their children's upbringing. They are, instead, making their own diverse judgements about what makes life good or bad. If that is how things stand even with the case of children, they must stand yet worse with the case of adults.

Prostitution

Prostitution has famously been said to be the "oldest profession"— a claim close enough to the truth that we would do well to ponder the fact. Prostitution is putting sex on the market, in a case-by-case way. The professional purveyor of sex regards men as customers and sells her services by the service: one act of sexual intercourse, or some other specified sexual activity, for such-and-such a number of dollars. This is widely thought to be immoral, and it is usually legally regulated in some way, including, in many countries, by outright legal prohibition. The question is whether these restrictions are justified.

It's easy enough to see why there is a market for sexual services. People have sex drives, and the prostitute is willing to satisfy the urge for sexual experience in the most straightforward way. Prostitutes do not demand love or commitment or involvement with children: all they want is the customer's cash and a minimal degree of respect.

Is Marriage a Form of Prostitution?

The suggestion has been advanced, both by feminist critiques of the institution of marriage and by others, that marriage is really a sort of prostitution anyway. The difference is that the price is a lot higher in the case of marriage. Is that a reasonable comparison? Certainly most defenders of marriage would be offended by it, but we must consider the suggestion on its merits, whatever people may say. The question is what, if any, its merits are.

At the most general level, certainly, the point must be conceded outright. Commitment and love are costs in the classic economist's sense of requiring the forgoing of other goods. Those costs, both in monetary and, especially, other terms, can be very high. The person undertaking to marry is ready to pay those costs, and may not even see them as such. If the way you would most prefer to spend your time is x, then the fact that in doing so you forgo the opportunity to do y or z may not strike you as important. But anyone who has undertaken such commitments is aware that there will be times when the fact that they are costs becomes apparent.

If the costs of marriage are higher, why do people so frequently get married? The short answer is that they are, in their view, getting a better product. Spouses are not just, and not even primarily, sexual playmates: in addition, they help with all aspects of life, provide very valuable child care, emotional support, and ongoing companionship. Not surprisingly, these things "cost more," especially in the non-monetary sense. Even in financial terms, however, marriage is likely to be quite a lot more expensive than might be the services of a prostitute.

One way to put the moral question about prostitution, then, is whether cheap sex is, as such, immoral. When people demean the prostitute, it is often in terms reflecting that: the "cheap whore" is a familiar category of abuse. Yet economy is reckoned a virtue in refrigerators and an indefinitely wide range of other purchasable services. When a kind of goods is described as "cheap," that may be either a compliment or a condemnation. When it is a condemnation, it usually implies inferior performance. But whether the latter holds of prostitutes is questionable. A successful prostitute builds up a clientele of repeat business. These men must have been reasonably satisfied with their purchases. The claim that prostitutes' services are generally of inferior quality in some way is not credible as a generalization. As with any consumer items, performance will vary a good deal from one case to another; some will be outstanding, some inferior, and a lot will, by definition, be approximately average. And as to prices, there is a lot of variation there as well: the $1,000-a-night call-girl is not literally cheap!

Marriage and Monopoly

Again in economists' terms that may offend, the effect of making prostitution illegal, or for that matter of making it the object of general abuse, is to make marriage a sort of monopoly, or more precisely an oligopoly. Society increases the costs of prostitution to the point, hopefully, where the prostitute is put out of business. In the case of other goods and services, monopolization is inefficient and normally immoral: if Jones wants to get into the widget-selling business, his competitors have no right to use force to induce him to desist. Is the same true of prostitution? On the face of it, it certainly is. The prostitute is subject to police harassment, occasional jail terms, and perhaps denial of protection and medical services of a kind that she is likely to be more than ordinarily in need of. Of course, it will be said that the life of the prostitute is bound to be miserable in any case: but even if true, that is hardly justification for going out of our way to make it even more so.

The general point of view of this book is that we are not justified in prohibiting actions unless they do other people some definite harm, as measured by the actual, self-recognized interests of those to whom it is done. Prostitution is, on the face of it, a harmless activity to those immediately involved. The claim that either the customers or the suppliers are harming themselves is moral conservatism at work. When services are highly desired by people and taken advantage of, repeatedly, when offered, the claim that those who indulge in them are harming themselves requires a kind of assessment of ways of life that are, in our view, properly left to the persons concerned. The illegalization of prostitution must, then, be compared with the imposition of duties on imported goods or the seizing by governments of monopolies in certain areas. It is, in short, the arbitrary imposition of other people's values on the persons involved, and as such those impositions are wrong.

Does the sheer existence of prostitution, as a no-commitment, for-cash alternative in the sexual marketplace, render marriage less likely or less eligible? That is difficult to say. However, we should note that in many European countries prostitution is quite legal, and though it is regulated, this is not done in such a way as to make it effectively unavailable. It has flourished in those countries for many centuries. Even so, marriage shows no sign of going out of fashion or being driven off the market by competition from prostitution. If the claim that prostitution drives out marriage is meant as an empirical one, then it seems to be false.

If marriage is, as I have generally claimed, a superior product, its superiority has to be proved in the market-place, not in smoke-filled rooms of dictators or even democratic politicians. And of course, it is: happy marriages are numerous, highly prized, much sought after, and have an extremely high survival value. The problem is that for many people this way of life is not available. Either the right other person is just too difficult to find or their temperaments do not fit them for such a relationship. Those for whom temperament is the problem are people who will have to avail themselves of either prostitution or casual sex, if possible, or nothing. Why deny them these pleasures in the futile hope of persuading them to do what they probably cannot do—assume normal married life?

It has also been argued, with considerable empirical support, that the availability of prostitution or of mistresses has saved some marriages. A and B might be doing very well in most ways, but not sexually; A solves the problem by going to prostitutes. This is less efficient, no doubt, but quite possibly a genuine improvement over the status quo and possibly, even, the only realistic alternative short of a dissolution that neither party wants.

Obviously prostitution presents a public health risk. But it is a risk that can be faced and dealt with. A well-known brothel in the state of Nevada—the only state of the United States in which prostitution is legal—claimed that its women had no incidence of AIDS or of any of the major venereal diseases. Needless to say, that was a major selling point—a fact that those who drive prostitution underground, where effective controls over potential disease are far less likely ought to bear in mind.

Are Prostitutes Coerced?

Probably the most fashionable objection to prostitution from intellectual critics has been along the lines of the claim that the prostitute is "forced" into her profession by economic necessity. And there have been and continue to be a few places in the world where such a claim has plausibility. But in contemporary North America and Europe, it has essentially none. Women are as employable at ordinary work as men, and have been for some time. The professional prostitute characteristically makes an income twice or more than what she could get from waitressing or other unskilled jobs. No doubt she goes into prostitution for the money, but it's not because she has no alternatives; rather, it's that this one is better, at least in narrowly economic terms.

Pimps and the Law

Prostitution is, however, very frequently connected with the presence of males (almost always) who offer protection and clientele in return for, usually, a very high proportion of the prostitute's gross income. This is due almost entirely to laws against prostitution, making her much more vulnerable to assault from the unscrupulous and inducing the woman to put herself in the care of a male.

He, too, of course, is engaging in criminal activity, but it is more readily disguised, and he is likely to be armed, unlike the prostitute herself.

Another feature of the law, especially here in Canada but operative in many places, is very strong restriction on their ability to advertise. In Canada, prostitution itself is technically legal—but communicating for the purpose of getting business is not. This is a beautiful example of hypocrisy in the law. No business can be pursued in the absence of communication, since sales cannot be made without it; so making it illegal is equivalent to making prostitution itself illegal. Such laws enable the police to make life miserable for the prostitute, as do laws prohibiting brothels and other establishments where prostitution could be pursued in the considerable safety made possible by numbers and organization.

Sexual Harassment

In recent times, the identification and enforcement of prohibitions on sexual harassment have become a familiar feature of public life, especially at universities and in large workplaces. It is an interesting subject, because if we are to have sexual unions, we must have some sort of sexual overtures and approaches. Yet it is perfectly understandable that women can find some of these unwelcome or frightening. The question is how we can identify the undesirable ones and subject them to suitable controls without, as it were, throwing out the proverbial baby with the bath water.

When, then, does person A "harass" person B? First, harassment is *unwelcome*. You cannot harass somebody in a way that he or she likes. Second, harassment does not involve literal assault, which is basically another matter; rather, it is verbal or confrontational. And third, harassment is repeated and persistent: one-time harassment is normally a contradiction in terms. If we look carefully at each of these dimensions, we should have a pretty good handle on harassment—and will likely find that most of the current to-do about it is not at all what it seems. It is, instead of a means of dealing with a real problem in a rational way, mainly a way of enhancing the powers of bureaucrats, officials, and seekers after political power.

(1) Suppose a young man is highly attracted to a certain young woman who is not at first inclined to reciprocate his interest. What should he do? He may, of course, simply give up; and if whatever he

does is regarded as "harassment" by authorities and others, then he quite likely will give up. But that may not be in the young woman's interest. It is perfectly possible, and even fairly likely, that on closer acquaintance she would find him a desirable and interesting person. His very persistence, if he persists may be an indication of a virtue: a tendency not to give up in the pursuit of worthy goals is surely not something to be taken lightly in, for instance, a potential husband or in many sorts of companions.

The problem here is that we don't simply know whether a given overture is welcome or not. Obviously a lot depends on his approach. Is he polite? Is he crude? Is he brash? Is he silly? But an initial indication of disinterest by the girl is not necessarily to be taken as definitive from his point of view. (I speak here to the standard case, but much of what is said here can easily enough apply to women trying to arouse the attentions of men, or even to same-sex cases.) What should be our rule here? This brings up the other two features mentioned above.

When an overture is essentially verbal, it could be objectionable in various ways: by being intrusive, too loud, ill-tempered, presumptuous, blatant, and so on. All of these are fairly familiar to civilized people, and we can reasonably insist that people not exemplify any of these uncivil features. And we also all know that what is too loud in one context is not so in another, what is presumptuous at one time and place is only reasonable in another, and so on. The rule of civility, as we may call it, is built on our sense of what is normally acceptable. We can think of a case in which saying a certain thing at a certain volume in a certain tone of voice would be, uncontroversially and definitively, uncivil. But lots of cases won't be like that. A considerable part of our daily discourse with acquaintances, in fact, consists in making assessments of this kind. But the idea of making civility into a strict rule that can be the basis of prosecution and serious punishment is itself the antithesis of civility. It is essentially certain that any such rule is going to inflict much more unjust damage on the innocent than deserved punishment on the guilty.

(2) In some cultures, many men readily behave in ways that we, in our much more reserved milieus, find very offensive. Males feel free to "feel up" women on public transport, street corners, and just about anyplace where they routinely are at close quarters. In those respects, women are, we would say, unsafe in public places. We regard an unwanted touching as a minor assault;

indeed, the upholders of strong moral attitudes about sexual harassment tend to talk as if these were major assaults. But what would make them so? A quite aggressive male thinking he was engaging in a quite minor indication of his interest might unthinkingly inflict a bruise, say. At anything beyond that level, his foray clearly should be actionable. But should it be at that level or below? If A touches B in a way that leaves no marks and causes no pain, but is clearly not sought by B, what are the damages? The obvious suggestion is that the man owes the girl in question an apology, at the least. And if he persists? That would bring us to our third characteristic.

(3) The most nearly defining feature of harassment is its persistent nature. Of course, this is not a completely independent feature. I persistently say "hello" to colleagues and secretaries as I arrive at work or walk about campus. This is not regarded as harassment, despite its persistence. If I knew that a certain familiar person hated my guts, I would be less likely to try to greet that person, to be sure, but it would be difficult for him or her to make a case for harassment even so, so long as the encounters were normal.

What is needed, then, is persistent behaviour that is also unwelcome to its object. Going back to our opening case of young man A pursuing young woman B, we may suggest that no matter how civil his overtures, there comes a point when he really ought to give it up—the girl just doesn't want him and that's that. But how many instances is that? Who can say? Common sense and the experience of ordinary life are all we have to go by; but between three and a half-dozen sounds as if it's in the right ballpark.

The problem with real harassment is that beyond some low number the marginal unwelcomeness of the overture increases. The young woman understands that a first try can hardly be objected to, unless she wants to create a reputation as a prude; but after the first few, none of which have warmed her heart to the gentleman in question, the next one gets more annoying. She may begin to be uncomfortable and wonder whether he has darker motives in store.

A relevant factor here is the amount of trouble the harasser goes to in order to make his intrusion. Consider "stalking," for example. If A regularly goes over to B's home, quite out of the way from his regular route, and stands for hours near her door, observing every coming and going, B reasonably becomes afraid and uncomfortable. Here harassment takes on an ominous quality. If A has no plausible and legitimate motive for his locational habits, it is reasonable to insist that he desist.

Enter the Behaviour Police

Contemplation of genuine and serious cases of these kinds is enough to assure us that the attempt to find a definitive, simple, out-and-out feature of behaviour that marks it as "harassment" in a sense justifying severe controls is impossible. Some cases of harassment involve assault; when that is so, there is no problem about a separate charge of harassment—assault is obviously wrong. Others move toward the stalking model. Here the offender needs to be made aware of his behaviour and its effect on the victim, and if he persists, then action can be taken. Minor harassment can be met with voiced and displayed rejection by its object, and a modest number of such is enough so that normal offenders will get the message and desist. But to frame rules that would identify as harassment a single case that includes no assault beyond the trivial is to cry for the moon, conceptually speaking.

Because it is so, when codes of conduct are drawn up couched in vague and nebulous terms, as they inevitably will be, then we should be suspicious of those who draw them up. We should be even more suspicious if, for example, the rules enable persons to claim to be victims without real evidence and without the possibility of the accused's being able even to supply evidence against the charges. That is fully characteristic of these rules, and just what we should expect. Indeed, to guard against that, we should make those who charge others with violation liable, themselves, if their charges are shown to be fruitless. After all, established agencies of enforcement are taken seriously by most of us. If they declare someone to be guilty of something, it inevitably affects his reputation or could have worse consequences. A considerable number of academics have lost their jobs as a result of what turned out to be trumped-up charges of "harassment," and doubtless the same is true in any sizeable organization that attempts to create and enforce such rules.

Down through the centuries, one standard recourse of aspiring politicians is to accuse their political enemies of immorality, especially in their sexual or financial lives. As I write this, the President of the United States has been impeached for perjury, but perjury regarding minor sexual incidents that were fully voluntary, so far as the public knows, on the part of both participants. That is an outstanding example of the use of this device for getting back at political enemies. In more local cases, the consequences are similarly severe to those found guilty, though of less interest to the general public.

But we must persist in holding that *all* people have rights in and to their persons that are not to be assaulted by intrusive officials any more than by their fellow citizens in unofficial capacities. Sexual harassment is mostly a method by the self-righteous to exert power over the innocent or, at best, the marginally guilty. We have much more need to be on the watch for officiousness than for enthusiasm on the part of ordinary people trying to promote their sexual well-being.

Summing Up

It is easy to be offended at what we are told is a frequent theme of much pornographic literature—that it depicts women as slaves or willing victims of assorted kinds of mistreatment. Even so, the case for outrightly preventing people from creating and seeing such materials is very weak. Normally, all participants have acted voluntarily. And there is considerable room for divergent taste as accounting for much of the denunciation. Finally, we would need good evidence of a very strong causal connection between viewing pornography and being moved to commit actual violence before a case for suppression could become strong. In fact, there is at best extremely weak evidence of any such connection. Society would be wisest to leave intact the right of free speech and expression, and to expect its parents to avert evil tendencies by proper attention and training in their family life rather than by trusting the censor to nip such tendencies in the bud.

The case for regarding prostitution as a legitimate activity is even more straightforward. It is inherently a voluntary kind of activity, though the danger of its turning into an involuntary one obviously exists. But so long as it is what it claims to be—a commercial transaction involving sexual favours—the case for putting it in a special category of moral condemnation is extremely weak.

Finally, the attention given to a supposed problem of sexual harassment seems to be essentially political and bureaucratic. Once we look carefully at the phenomenon in question, it is obvious that we cannot make easy rule-like pronouncements about it. Unlike with pornography and prostitution, here harm to victims is undoubtedly possible. But the problem of the harms being subjective and extremely difficult to assess is at its most serious here, and solving these problems by heavy-handed criminalizing interpretations of what may be and usually are perfectly normal activities, necessary to the process of sexual mate- and partner-selection, is a cure that is potentially far worse than the disease.

Chapter Thirteen

Non-Discrimination and Affirmative Action

These subjects are among the most conspicuous areas for legislation at present, and are closely linked. Both raise serious questions, and the prevailing orthodoxies regarding each are subject to major objections. Non-discrimination is the more basic one, since affirmative action is usually invoked as a kind of antidote for what has claimed to be discrimination in the past. Hence, we will discuss it first.

We must begin by asking a question about discrimination that is not asked often enough: what is it? There is, by now, a satisfactory short definition: discrimination is *treating some people less favourably than others for morally irrelevant reasons*. (The word 'arbitrary' can be used equivalently to 'irrelevant.') The notion thus defined calls for considerable comment.

To begin with, the phrase 'less favourably' must be taken very literally. You cannot substitute 'worse,' for example, without being dangerously misleading. Once we start talking about treating people *badly*, strictly speaking, then we are no longer talking about discrimination, but instead about simple evil or injustice. For example, we may not torture, beat, or kill people; but the supposed evil of discrimination is not like that. Discrimination in hiring, to take the single most important contemporary context, consists in *not hiring* people, though for putatively arbitrary or irrelevant reasons. It involves treating one person *less well* than another, then, but not treating the latter *badly*. To *harm* someone is to make him or her worse off than they would have been if you had done nothing to them. But when you don't hire someone, you are, precisely, doing nothing to them: discrimination in hiring consists in passing people over for a certain kind of *good* treatment—giving them a desired job. Thus it consists in *not doing a good* rather than *doing a harm.* Those you don't hire may have expected you to and be disappointed when you did not, but that doesn't mean you have actually harmed them, unless they had a right that you not disappoint them in that respect. Yet the normal case is that they have no such right. Giving people a job is not ordinarily something we are required to do; and not giving them a job is absolutely normal. Just now, for instance, I have failed to give you, the reader, a job—any job. I have also failed to give you two-thirds of my current salary, just as I have not done any number of other nice things I conceivably could have done for you. Perhaps you deserve some of those, and the reasons I have failed to give it to you are probably quite irrelevant, morally speaking. Still, as I am sure you will agree, I have done you no harm, no wrong, in all these non-doings. If discrimination is claimed to be wrong, then, it will have to be shown why it is basically different from any of these things. But no one has shown this.

The term 'treat' in our definition brings up the question *in what respects* considerations of discrimination become applicable. Here again there are major pitfalls to avoid. What if I am literally treating? If I walk along the bar, offering a drink at my expense to this person or that one, picking at random from the dozen present, or perhaps picking them on the basis of the colour of their ties, am I now to be accused of discrimination? Surely not. Again, we see the need for a good explanation of which types of treatment could merit the term "discrimination," as opposed to the types that do not. In countries like Canada, the law identifies housing, education, health, and employment as areas in which discrimination is prohibited or limited. Why those and not others? Evidently we need to know how such things differ from the example about the bar.

Let us take an arguably more important context than drinks at a bar—marriage. Do we have duties of non-discrimination here? Should the state require us to randomize our selection among potential marital partners in the interests of equal opportunity? After all, almost everyone discriminates uninhibitedly in that context. They marry whom they *like,* and they like people for reasons that are remarkably irrelevant morally, such as the colour of their eyes or their taste in movies.

Here an important potential snag in our deliberations arises from the fact that, in our time and place, the provision of many services is required by law. When it is, then the people who provide those services have a *legal duty* to do so. We have seen, however, that law is not the same thing as morality. We can ask whether the law creating that legal duty in certain cases is doing the right thing. Nevertheless, once law has been brought into the act, it is clear that we may not use it for personal advantage, or to play political favourites. If our government is going to provide services, then clearly it has a duty to provide them impartially. But that does not prove that morality requires impartiality of us all in everything we do. It may be a purely political fact, rather than a reflection of a moral requirement, that so many services are now in the "public sector," where impartiality is, one hopes, a *sine qua non*.

Even in the public sector, we should note, the ambit of impartiality is strictly limited. Notice that all of the public services in Canada are offered only to Canadian residents, and in other countries only to the citizens or residents of those countries. If non-discrimination were a *human right*, though, they should be offered without regard to nationality or country of residence. Yet, in fact, all governments discriminate sharply against non-citizens, and insist that their citizens do so, too. If you are a private Canadian employer, you are not allowed to hire an American or a Hungarian on equal terms with your fellow Canadians, whether or not being Canadian constitutes any kind of qualification for it. In all those innumerable cases in which it does not, how is it relevant to hiring people for *my* job that the person in question should be Canadian?

The point here is that if there is a duty stemming from the employer's professional obligations, for example as a civil servant, then that provides a reason why she should be impartial in that respect. But that has no tendency to show that everybody owes everybody a duty of impartiality. And it also, of course, raises the question whether that public service is one that people really have the right to expect from their governments.

We now see that the all-important word in the definition of discrimination is the word 'irrelevant' (or 'arbitrary'). Nobody questions that we may treat some people more favourably than others. The question is what restrictions to place on such differential treatment: which distinctions are such that we treat people wrongly by treating them less well than others in those respects?

We act towards others on the basis of our interests, which are of two kinds: affections—loves and hatreds, likes and dislikes—and other interests—how useful or the reverse they are to us, as in business transactions. These are not sharply distinct, of course. We love children, spouses, friends, and we also derive many benefits from our interactions with them. Clearly, our affections will prompt us to treat people we like better than ones we don't; similarly, our other interests will prompt us to extend more opportunities and benefits to those who benefit us in turn. One would expect, then, that a person's bestowal of favours would be roughly proportionate to his degree of favourable inclination and the amount they benefit him.

People who think that there is something inherently unjust about discrimination might think that we shouldn't be dealing with people on a basis of self-interest *at all*. Some religions, and most notably the Christian, have been thought to imply some such thing. That is certainly a misperception in the case of Christianity, which teaches people that if they love others, God, at least, will love them, even if no one else does, and will reward them in Paradise, if not before. That plainly is an appeal to long-range self-interest. Nor, I think, will examination of other religions reveal anything markedly different. How could it? Total, uncompensated self-abnegation is absurd, and we should be extremely suspicious of the motives of those who claim to teach it; characteristically, our unselfishness turns out to redound to our advantage. Be that as it may, the point of view of this book is that self-interest is wholly legitimate, that curbs on our pursuit of our interests are curbs on short-sighted, narrow, ill-judged pursuit of those interests, but nevertheless based on our real, long-run interests. Morality, in particular, bids us take account of others, who think much as we do and are similarly self-interested, and to adjust our actions accordingly.

At some ultimate level, perhaps, fundamentally arbitrary distinctions in our treatment of others may be irrational. If there is literally *no* difference between B and C, how could I treat B and C differently? But even that has a good answer in any case: I might deal with B rather than C because I simply can't deal with both, I must choose, and yet have no reason to prefer one to the other. So I simply choose, by chance or whim. Walking along the street in Cairo or New York, one might impulsively give a dollar to this beggar rather than that one, for no other reason than that one happens to have one dollar and not two, and doesn't think it worth bothering to make change so as to give them each fifty cents. But isn't that perfectly reasonable? Of course it is, and people do this constantly. The man you end up marrying, if any, may well be one whom there is no more and no less reason to choose than some other; but you choose him because you want to marry, and he happens to qualify and be available. That is a perfectly reasonable thing to do. By contrast, it would be unreasonable to insist that you marry only the Perfect Man—by the time *he* comes into view, you will have been long in the grave, and will have endured a lonely existence in the meantime.

On the other hand, you, of course, choose the *best* man from among those available. If you think that Jones would make a better husband than Smith, you will marry Jones, in the absence of very special reasons to the contrary. The same goes for employing someone. Choosing genuinely arbitrarily, with absolutely no reason for choosing as you do, is virtually unintelligible. So if the point of denouncing "discrimination" were in order to be sure that we don't engage in such activities, then the denouncers would be wasting their time. People always have *some* reasons for what they do, even if only that they must do something and lack time, inclination, or resources to make fine distinctions. And if they act for ill-considered reasons, then they may act unwisely—but no charge of injustice applies merely on that account; we cannot be free without being free to make mistakes. There is, then, no clear foundation for principles of non-discrimination merely in the structure of practical reason.

Comparative Advantage

However, we do need to pay attention to an interesting and treacherous set of motives: jealousy and envy. People are often sensitive not only to how well they themselves are doing, in various respects, but also to how they stack up against others. The runner who sets out to be the fastest human alive is not interested merely in how fast he himself runs, but in whether he is faster than others. If we are dealing with a number of people who are motivated to a significant degree by these comparative interests, then if we do not treat one person "the same" as that person's associates in the respects they are interested in, we are likely to be in for trouble. There will be complaints, bad tempers, whisperings, and the like.

Suppose you have a business and must decide how much you should pay your various employees. What principle will you use?

Well, first, you will surely want to pay your good workers enough to keep them from moving somewhere else. It would be imprudent not to, for if they leave, you will have to find new employees who may be less capable, and in any case it may be quite awhile before they can perform as well as the veteran you have let go. Secondly, you will want to pay more to those who are worth more, as measured by their contribution to the success of your business. Obviously, this interacts with the first factor, for if you offer less to someone who does more, then he or she will be motivated to go elsewhere; but if you over-pay someone, you are losing money— you could have hired some equally productive person for less money and pocketed the difference. Since the point of the enterprise is to make money, such practices are self-defeating.

So far, so good. But suppose that some employees insist on getting just as much as others, even though, in your judgement, they don't do as much for you. Do you pay them more, thus making your operation less efficient? Or do you pay them less, thus risking their disaffection? The latter might lead to poor performance, even sabotage, on their part; the former might lead to financial ruin. So you have a problem. There is no simple solution to it. But there *is* a relatively simple abstract principle to invoke: you solve the problem by finding the compromise between the two contrary forces that will make your firm maximally profitable over the longer run. You will likely pay some people a little more than you think they really deserve, for the sake of keeping harmonious relations among your employees and thus sustaining morale and, consequently, output.

Now, there may also be some among your employees whom you would like to pay more because you simply like them more, and not because they are worth more. This, too, will cost you profits— but perhaps you are willing to spend the money anyway. Is this something to be prohibited? If it is, could anything but envy or jealousy be the reason for the prohibition? The question about discrimination comes into sharper focus when we consider such examples.

The Puzzle about Non-Discrimination

We don't *owe* people jobs—they aren't among the things we have a basic duty to provide for others. Those who are in a position to distribute jobs are, mostly, in business, and their companies *create* the jobs in question; jobs don't grow on trees for the picking. Those companies were usually established for the purpose of making money by the sale of goods or services. Nobody may require anyone to do that: whether we want to go into any sort of business or offer anyone a valuable service is up to us, not anyone else.

But if it is up to us, then can we be thought to have a *duty* to offer the jobs in our business to A only on equal terms with B? Again, consider our earlier comparison with marriage. Do we have a duty to treat candidates for spousehood equally? Am I supposed to give Agatha and Belinda equal chances, an equal opportunity, for my hand in marriage? Surely not. Similarly, if I am inviting people over for dinner, or getting a bunch of people together to play ball or to help me build my summer cottage, plainly I have no moral duty to invite the general public, randomizing over friends and total strangers alike.

Similarly, then, if I have no duty to go into business, and it's *my* business, then why must I randomize over women and men, whites and blacks, or whatever, when it comes to handing out jobs? Why can't I hire whomever I please? It is useless to respond by saying, "because you have a duty to treat people equally," for whether that is so is exactly what's in question here. Moreover, the examples of hands in marriage, handouts to arbitrarily chosen beggars, and any number of others one could readily produce strongly suggest that it is false. We do *not* have to treat people equally. We may and should treat people we like and people who do more for us better than others.

Perhaps it will be said that the fact that person B is my friend is what makes it *relevant* to treat him better than some unknown. But *why* is it relevant? Those many people who think we have a duty not to discriminate against others think that the fact that B is a friend of mine is *not* a good reason why I should be able to hire B instead of C: that, they insist, is "irrelevant." And in fact, what is called discrimination, generally speaking, consists in preferring some groups of people over other groups just because you like them better. But why should we think that wrong? *What's* wrong with it?

The fact that the ones you have preferred will end up slightly better off than those you haven't is perfectly true—indeed, that was the point of your treating them better. But then, did the unpreferred ones have any right over you, to end up equally well off from your choices? There is no obvious reason to suppose that there is any such right. Indeed, there seem to be clear and compelling reasons to suppose that there is not.

Competence

Most people who talk about discrimination in hiring think that what is relevant to hiring is competence, the ability to do the job. Indeed, they go on to insist that people from the groups allegedly "discriminated against" are just as good at the task in question as people in the group allegedly favoured: black people just as competent as whites, and women as men, for instance.

There is an oddity, indeed a basic paradox, about this claim, taken as a reason why we have a *duty* to refrain from discrimination. Duties normally curtail action from motives of self-interest. If you have a business, it is *in your interest* to hire competent people, or more precisely, to hire the most competent person you can get at a given wage. If B is better than C at the job, and you can get B for the same wages as C, then it's in your interest to hire B, and as a good business person, that's exactly what you will do. For if you don't— if, for instance, you insist on hiring your incompetent friends instead—then your costs of doing business will be higher than they need be. If you do enough of that, you'll be uncompetitive against your more rational rival business people who don't care about the race, sex, national origin, religion, or other characteristics of the people they hire, so long as they get the best worker at the lowest cost.

Discrimination is, therefore, inherently inefficient. It costs money. If your sole motive is to make money, then, you will not discriminate. Yet, letters to the editor, political speeches, and any number of laws passed by legislatures are designed to get people, and in the latter case to *force* people, not to discriminate. But why would all the pressure, and the use of force, be necessary if the aim was to get them to do precisely *what they want to do anyway*—namely, what makes them more money? It doesn't make sense!

On the other hand, suppose that their aim wasn't to make money? Suppose the organization you are hiring for is devoted to something else, such as the welfare of some particular group—your school, say, or a church or club? Would we still have to hire the "most competent," even if those competent people weren't interested in the purposes of the club or the church in question? Does the Presbyterian Church down the street have to consider Catholic and Presbyterian applicants for the position of janitor on equal terms? Why? What the manager of a club, church, or other non-business group wants is to promote the purposes of the club, and from that point of view also, the enforcement of so-called "non-discrimination" is arbitrary and wrong. It is interesting, and ironic, that the very thing discrimination was supposed to essentially consist in—namely arbitrary treatment—is precisely what an anti-discrimination principle seems to require.

To tell an interest group that they must ignore their interest when it comes to hiring would be to do what governments have no business in doing: namely, to tell people how to live their lives, rather than letting them live the life that *they* choose. If the interest is in making money, then to tell a business whom to hire and whom not, is either to tell it to do what is most efficient and hence makes it the most money—which is absurd because redundant—or to force it to engage in inefficient practices, thus denying it the right to do what it exists to do. Either way, the intervention is wrong. People do not have a duty to make money; we have no business *forcing* people to maximize their incomes or profits. And on the other hand, so long as the business or other activity they are engaged in is inherently legitimate, providing people with goods and services that do not, of themselves, involve the doing of evil to anyone, then we also have no right to curtail their pursuit of this in the interests of some other cause.

In recent years, non-discrimination theorists have changed course. Instead of merely insisting that people not discriminate on the basis of supposedly irrelevant characteristics, enthusiasts for equality now insist that workers in employment X must be half male and half female, and that the fraction of those employees who are of one race or ethnic group, or whatever is the currently fashionable alleged discriminandum, be equal to that group's fraction in the whole surrounding population. Plainly, this is entirely arbitrary from the point of view of those who create and sustain those businesses. What the business person wants is to hire the people who will make the most money for the business, be those people male or female, black or white, or whatever. If those who can contribute the most should happen to be of one colour, sex, or ethnic background rather than another, then employees in that business will tend to be predominantly of that kind. Here again, to require that people pay heed to such structural characteristics of their workforce is arbitrary and invasive.

Forced Affirmative Action

There is a problem, then, explaining why what is called "discrimination" should be considered evil or immoral at all. But let us suppose, for the sake of argument, that there is such a duty to treat people "equally." Let's also assume that in the past some people have not been treated equally in those respects. Should we now try to help matters out by actively promoting the prospects of the formerly discriminated-against group, such as by requiring employers to employ some larger proportion of that group than they would otherwise do, or have done in the past?

Notice that the question before us is not whether any such programs, by anyone, are ever allowable. In fact, what makes it obvious that they can be is the very argument we have just been constructing regarding discrimination. Affirmative action discriminates; but if discrimination is morally permissible anyway, then that would not be a fatal objection to it. However, the question is not whether it's inherently all right to *practice* it. Rather, our question is whether it's all right to *impose* such a program, by the coercive powers of government. The question, in other words, is whether justice ever requires such a program.

A Fallacious Argument for Affirmative Action

Those who think that affirmative action is required by justice often use fallacious arguments. One especially popular one is that affirmative action will help to correct the past injustices that allegedly occasion it. But that is not so. The only way to do that would be to find the *particular* people who lost whatever they didn't get by virtue of discrimination and then see to it that they get it after all, or are suitably compensated for their loss. But a lot of those victims are dead and beyond compensation, while in many other cases, other difficulties would stand in the way. In any case, the problem with expecting a program of "affirmative action" to help out is that it doesn't do that. Instead, it rewards *new* people, people who in most cases have never been discriminated against. And it rewards them excessively. If the problem was that they weren't treated equally, then the right thing to do by way of "compensation" would simply be to treat them equally. But affirmative action treats them *unequally*. Instead of ensuring that they get the same chance as others, it gives them a greater chance than those others. If in the past men got the jobs instead of deserving women, clearly the cure would be to open the doors so that the deserving women now may get them as well—rather than shutting the door on the men, deserving or not, thereby giving women greater chances than men for such employment .

Moreover, a program of forced affirmative action penalizes employers who have never discriminated against anybody, by forcing them to consider more favourably people they might not otherwise have hired. This is often obscured by claiming that the program only requires employers to hire the "equally best qualified," rather than to lower their standard. But what if the non-discriminating employer hires more women than men? Suppose that he has done so because more of the best candidates were women? But no program of affirmative action is going to rest content with that. It's going to insist that the employer is "subtly" discriminating after all. It may, and probably will, impose a quota, regardless of any evidence about the proportions of males and females among the most-competent individuals. If the reason for the program was a belief that competence is equally distributed between the group favoured by the affirmative action program and the other groups not so favoured, then the basis of that belief is no longer the experience of employers but an a priori belief by the government that it is so distributed. It will end up forcing employers to take people whom *they* didn't believe were as desirable as the ones they would otherwise have hired if they'd had their choice. And there will be no market test imposed on the government to see whether its wisdom on this matter has proven correct. That test will be imposed exclusively on the employer, and since it is the test he faces daily in business, the imposition of an a priori criterion of this kind is highly likely to be wrong from the start. The businessman will be forced to pay the cost. Or his customers will. And, in the end, his other employees will do so, too, for they will share in diminished income or bear the brunt of plant closures and contractions if the result is disastrous.

Affirmative action programs also require administration. If we're going to force people in businesses X, Y, and Z to be egalitarian in their hiring, then overseers will have to be appointed to see to it that they do so. The people sent out for that purpose will not, of course, know as much about the business as its managers and owners—after all, they've never been in that business. Nevertheless, they will presume to instruct the actual managers and owners, deciding who is and who is not "equally qualified"! Inevitably, this will have adverse effects on efficiency. The numerous administrators required to superintend the program have to be paid by somebody, and the less-efficient employees hired because the employer was forced to hire them will produce less. Both of these factors conspire to reduce the amount of goods and services available for people who would have liked to have them, and to raise the price of the ones that are produced.

Equal Pay for Equal Work

A similar idea to affirmative action is the enforcing of a principle of "equal pay for equal work." There is, again, an oddity about the whole idea, for paying equal amounts to people who are equally profitable is precisely what the market situation of a business induces it to do anyway. It already is paying "equal pay for equal work," as far as it is concerned. But the business firm uses the *right* criterion—marginal effect on profitability—rather than the irrelevant criterion imposed by the rule, such as hiring on the basis of who expends the most calories. But the administrator, or the lobbyist, or the member of the group that is supporting the allegedly discriminated-against people doesn't think that marginal profitability is the appropriate criterion. He or she will come along with some *new* ideas about who is better than whom at that job—ideas engendered in the political climate of the time, not by any rational assessment of the needs of the business.

So again, what will happen is that the business will become less efficient. It will either have to pay the costs of the administrators, in which case its customers will pay, or else the taxpayer will. But if the taxpayer does, then that will leave him with less money to buy the products of this company, or of any other. The effect is the same: higher prices, and thus a lower standard of living, for the people served by those businesses.

In addition, the people who have now lost out on jobs they otherwise would have gotten will hardly be very happy with the new state of affairs. They will resent the beneficiaries. Meanwhile, the people now hired, who are perceived as having been hired for reasons of affirmative action rather than because they are the most able people available, are likely to be looked upon with suspicion or condescension by their new colleagues. In general, everyone loses, except perhaps the special group that it is the aim of the legislation to benefit—for awhile.

Why should the government have the right to do any such thing? Why should it benefit one group in the population at the expense of the rest? These are not trivial or merely academic questions. Wars have been caused by just such measures.[1] When you draw a line dividing a group into two and force people to treat one of those groups more favourably than the other, the losers become resentful and the winners self-righteous and protective. Both resort to politics and coercion instead of peaceful production. None of this makes for smooth human relations.

Determining The Distribution of Competence

To make any assessment of discrimination on a group basis, one has to know two things: first, the proportion of those in the allegedly discriminated-against group who were in fact hired, and, second, the proportion who *should have been* hired. How are we to know the latter?

Sometimes one can have what is called "anecdotal evidence": first-hand observation by someone of a case in which an allegedly less competent individual was preferred over another individual who was presumably superior. Anecdotal evidence has two major disadvantages. First, it is necessarily far too limited to afford any secure generalizations about the large classes affected by any affirmative action program. Second, those who tell the anecdotes are very likely to have their own axes to grind. How does the teller of the anecdote know that the successful applicant *wasn't* better than the rejected one? And if it is disputable, why should we believe the narrator of the anecdote rather than the employer, who, after all, has an interest in hiring the person who will produce the most profit?

Those who support coercively imposed affirmative action, while of course influenced by anecdotal evidence, are primarily moved by their perception of structural disparities. They note, for example, that more men than women are hired in a certain line of work. Since the numbers of men and women in the population are about equal, they infer that something is wrong. But the inference doesn't follow directly. From "The population is x% Fs" and "The percentage of persons employed in work W is less than x," we cannot infer that Fs were discriminated against *unless* we have reason to believe that the percentage of F's in the class of most desirable candidates for W is the *same* as it is in the general population. And there is often excellent reason for expecting that *not* to be true.

Indeed, in the special case of men and women, there is one extremely important reason for expecting it not to be true, for we are not counting marriage as a case of "hiring"—even though there is really very good reason for so counting it in some respects. But if we don't, then all of those women who marry and have families instead of "going to "work"—that is, joining the paid labour force—reduce the size of the female hiring pool available for all other occupations.[2] So long as more women do that than men, the result must be that we cannot assume that any other given occupation should show an equal distribution by sex among its employees, absent which we can impute discrimination.

Nor is that all. What if the F's are typically not very *interested* in making their living at that particular job? Suppose that women typically just don't like to work in coal mines, while men typically just aren't much interested in secretarial work? Doesn't that matter? It need have nothing to do with anything as abstract as "native ability." Whatever the reason for these differences in interest, they will affect the structure of the available pool for that kind of work. And whenever this is so, it will be wrong to force employers, in the supposed interests of "equality," to hire a similar percentage of males and female for that employment. Of course, the same holds for any other groups as well: groups of different ethnic background, race, or any other arbitrarily selected characteristic can be expected to have different patterns of preference, as well as different specific skills.

There are innumerable differences between various groups besides the defining differences, and there is no reason why some of those should not be relevant to occupational choice and suitability. The number of black males on American professional basketball and football teams is vastly greater than the proportion of blacks in the general populace, while the number of Orientals is vastly smaller. Is this due to discrimination? Certainly not. The difference in height and other physical attributes alone would account for it. In hockey, many professional players on American teams are Canadians, to the surprise of no one who knows anything about the climates in the two countries. On the other hand, the number of women employed in the hand-assembly branches of the electronics industry, or in sewing, is vastly greater than their 50 per cent incidence in the general populace. Is this due to discrimination? Again, the sheer physical differences of the two groups is enough to account for it: the typically smaller and more delicate hands of women are obviously better for manipulating tiny physical objects. Examples could be multiplied indefinitely.

This problem is so enormous as to be, in all likelihood, insoluble—that is, insoluble in any way that is favourable to the argument for affirmative action programs. That is why those who argue for them just assume, without argument, that certain proportions "obviously" ought to be equal and let it go at that. This a priori attitude is hardly appropriate to real life, where everything depends on the facts. It is absurd to make such claims in this field; philosophers have long been aware that the human intellect is simply not the tool to rely on, exclusively, when what is at issue is how things are out there in the world. For that we also need observation of the world, which is often very different from the way pure intellect might like it to be.

Achieving Other Goals by Affirmative Action

One major source of support for affirmative action, very likely, consists in employing it as a device for achieving some *other* social goals. Someone may support the imposition of a quota of 50 per cent women in a certain area because he thinks that in the ideal society, that's how that area would be served. Never mind that there are not nearly enough women interested in or available for that kind of job, as things are, to staff 50 per cent of the available positions, or that there is no reason to expect that there ever will be, so far as our best current information is concerned: our theorist has the Ideal Society all figured out, and he's jolly well going to make us all go along with it if he can. But we shouldn't allow that kind of Utopian planning. We must deal with people as they are, and not with people as we or any particular group think they ought to be. Realistically, it makes all the difference that the positions in question may not be popular with women. It's not our business to revise human nature to suit our theories.

Summing Up

It is, all in all, *very* difficult to justify either forced anti-discrimination or forced affirmative action in the sense in which they are now popular. Our leading principle in this book has been that people in general should, in the absence of good reason, have the right to do as they want, work at or produce what they wish, and associate with their fellows on terms of agreement rather than by force. Those who don't accept this general account of morals should be asked on what they propose to base their visions, and why they should be allowed to impose those visions on ordinary people trying to make the best lives they can for themselves. The arguments typically employed in those directions are either riddled with outright fallacies, vague at crucial points, or just arbitrary, high-flown pronouncements. The rule of liberty stands, in business contexts as in the others we have explored.

Chapter Fourteen

Obeying the Law

I conclude this set of essays with a consideration of a subject that is not on the front pages, though it was as recently as the years of the Vietnam War. It is very widely thought that one of the principles of morals is that we ought to obey the law—where, of course we mean 'law' in its *legal* sense. That one ought to obey the *moral* law is self-evident. However, it is not in the same sense self-evident that one ought to obey the civil law—the law of the state, the province, the municipality, or whatever level of government is in point. We live in an age when legislation and politics are ubiquitous. The moral status of all these enactments is thus a matter of general importance. Indeed, there is so much law that few could claim to be sure that they have not disobeyed at least some laws. Should we feel guilty about that and try to make amends? That is our question here.

Four Views

It is not very clear just what the principle of obedience to the law means. Here are four possible accounts:

1. That we ought *always* to obey the law, no matter what it says we are to do.
2. That we should *prima facie* obey the law—that is, obey it, *other moral considerations being equal.*
3. That we should obey *just* laws.

4. That we should presume that any given law is reasonable or just, in the absence of special reason to suppose otherwise.

The first of these interpretations amounts to fascism. No matter how evil the law may be, we are to obey it: turn our Jewish neighbours in to the Gestapo, denounce the racially mixed couple down the block for violating the anti-miscegenation laws, and so on. We need only state this to reject it.

The second asserts that there is what philosophers call a "prima facie obligation" to obey the law. (See the short explanation of this in Chapter One.) The fact that x is against the law is, on this view, in itself *some* reason why we morally should refrain from doing x. If the law is evil enough, that could outweigh this obligation, but in the absence of a quite strong defect in the law, morality requires us to obey it. This is probably the standard view among students of moral philosophy today, and the view we will examine carefully here. It will come as no surprise by this time that I propose to dissent from it.

The third view has the merit of being obvious and the disadvantage of being useless. What is a just law, after all? If it is a law requiring us to do what is just anyway, then of course we ought to do it, and the fact that it is also against the law is neither here nor there. If, on the other hand, the intention was to claim that *all* laws are just, or that they are just simply because they are laws, then we would be back to view (1). If it was to claim that laws are prima facie just, then that is what view (2) says. Thus (3) may be set aside as true but unhelpful.

The fourth view, which I shall be defending, is to be distinguished sharply from the second even though it may have a rather similar effect. A *presumption* that a law is a good law is always rebuttable on a closer look. This fourth view doesn't accept any general, inherent obligation to obey laws. Instead it supposes that there is reason to give the law the benefit of the doubt. Of course, we can imagine regimes that are bad enough so that this presumption is reversed. Whether we live in such a regime here and now is an interesting question, but if we do, then this fourth view will simply imply that we should reverse the presumption, since it is empirically based.

Let's look at the general idea of law, then, to see which view is most reasonable.

The Purpose of Law

To discuss this matter at all, we need a view of what law is all about—a philosophy of law. That is a subject with a long history of heated disagreement, to be sure. However, I don't think the areas of disagreement put the view I am going to suggest here in serious doubt. At any rate, I shall put it forward in the hope that the reader will find it compelling.

First, and most generally, law is *for the good of the people*. That is, the whole and only purpose of the law is to promote the good of those subject to it, as distinct from the good of those who make the law. Law is *not* for enhancing the incomes of MPs, cabinet ministers, civil servants, or any other employees of the State. The standard modern theory of government has it that governments ought to be democratic. In such countries, government is broadly by majority rule. Then the point that government is for the good of the governed also entails that government is not for the purpose of lining the pockets *of the majority*. The liberal view of the state, which I presume is now universally accepted, implies this—although it is hardly ever lived up to in practice.

Second, the "good" being promoted has to be a *common* good, not a special one. Government has no business promoting the well-being of one group at the expense of the rest. The previous point was that it is not to promote the interests of the majority at the expense of the minority, but this principle extends the idea universally: government must not be to the benefit of *any* group at the expense of any other. This point has serious implications when we consider that the costs of anything a government does are always borne by the citizenry, since they pay the taxes that are the only source of income governments can have. (That continues to be true, though less obvious, even when governments run businesses; for when they are monopolies, then those businesses are run at the expense of others who might want to compete, and of the customers who might have had a better deal from others if they'd been allowed to offer their wares.) What has to justify such impositions is a greater benefit, one that outweighs the costs of taxation *even* from the point of view of those who are taxed.

Third, it follows from the preceding that all laws must be for the sake of some or other *publicly acceptable* good, a good that everyone understands and, however grudgingly, approves. Let's call this good G. Now consider a law, L, requiring people to do something that promotes G or refrain from something that would tend to defeat G. Let's let x stand for whatever the law requires of the individual citizens. For example, suppose they are required to drive no faster than 100 km/h (60 mph), the purpose being to promote safety: x is not exceeding that velocity, G is safety.

But now we come up against a familiar fact of life: for almost all values of G, there is no way to identify any set of actions, x, such that x will *always* promote G. Whether it does will *always* depend on circumstances. The qualification 'almost' is important. We can distinguish a subclass of cases where x is wrong in itself, such as murder. Murder, of course, will by definition always bring about the death of some innocent person; non-murder will always promote the safety of potential victims. But the relation between driving below 100 km/hr and not having an accident isn't anything like the relation between non-murdering and the non-murdered people who benefit from the avoidance of murder by others. Often it will be perfectly safe to drive faster than the speed limit; sometimes it may be dangerous even to drive considerably slower than it. If the speed limit were strictly enforced, safety would not be enhanced by comparison with careful non-enforcement.

Now, theorists of the law have long held to a certain theme on this matter. This is the theme that a rule of justice might call for actions that, in particular cases not only do no good *to the agent*—which, of course, will often be true—but no good to *anybody*. Requiring you to keep your promise may be hard on you at the time, but it does good for the person you promised to do something for, and almost always results in some good for you as well. But requiring you not to cross the street in the middle of the block when there are no cars around, or to drive at less than a certain speed in perfectly safe conditions, does neither you nor anyone else any good at all. On the contrary: it makes you worse off, for it would have saved you time and trouble to cross the street at that place or to drive rather faster.

The claim that legal rules ought to be obeyed *even when they do no one any good* is held by many well-meaning people. It is, I suggest, an illusion; and the power of illusion is strong in the human frame. The illusion consists in looking myopically at the possible good to be gained, while ignoring the crucial question of the likelihood that it actually will be attained by the law in question and then ignoring its real costs. Here's an example: to enjoy the benefits of highway travel on two-lane roads, we need a rule of the road, such as that one is to keep to the right; otherwise, people would be hard put to avoid smashing into each other. But we also need exceptions, as when a faster car can pass safely, or when the right lane has a big hole in it. Such exceptions make things much better than rigid adherence to a keep-right rule, for it allows people to travel at different speeds as suits their temperaments, automobiles, and transportational requirements. But there will be places where it won't be obvious whether passing is safely possible, so in those places we hire people to paint yellow lines on one side of the centre line, prohibiting passing by persons in that lane. Now suppose that the vehicle in front of you is going far below the customary speed, and you clearly can pass safely, despite the yellow line. Does justice require that we stay in the right lane, despite the loss of a considerable benefit for one party, while doing the other no good at all? Is justice like that? Of course not! Those who answer in the affirmative, talking of "sacred obligations" and the like, would seem to be engaging in prattle. To think that way is just a mistake.

Or it might not be prattle. It might be worse. Laws doing no citizen any good may yet serve the interests of the regime. Regimes whose purposes systematically diverge from those of their citizens are tyrannical. Such regimes certainly ought not to be upheld or encouraged. The life expectancy of such governments should be as short as possible. Democracy is praised as a way of getting rid of evil regimes. It doesn't do that very well, but it does do it sometimes. When the democratic regime is itself evil, of course, that's another matter. But we are no friends of democracy if we say that the citizen ought to obey the bad laws of democratic regimes any more than those of any other regime. The only reasons there could possibly be for enforcing any rules in particular cases that work out to *no one's* benefit are two, that I can see: first, worries about citizens' knowledge of the relevant conditions, and second, ease of administration. Both deserve comment.

Citizen Ignorance

Sticking rigidly inside the yellow line might be argued to be safer on the ground that it avoids reliance on the imperfect judgements of motorists. Is this a good argument? It is widely accepted, especially by persons in positions of superior power. But the argument overlooks a fundamental point: it is impossible to have *any* observance of *any* law without judgement, and it is easy to find cases in which obeying the law would be clearly dangerous and in which not allowing citizens to use their own judgement would be disastrous.

Sometimes the reason for disallowing some act is that ordinary citizens can hardly be expected to know the relevant facts. If some product is claimed to be dangerous, owing to chemical facts, then that may be something that only trained scientists could have discerned. But does the law necessarily know better than we? Unfortunately, there is no certainty here, either. The Canadian government banned over-the-counter sales of saccharine on the scantiest "evidence" imaginable. The citizen who supposed the substance was actually dangerous was being seriously misled in this case. Nor are such cases atypical.

Administrators: Whose Side Are They On?

The second argument in support of rigid adherence to the law proposes that it promotes ease of administration. That can be a legitimate factor in a few cases, no doubt. It might sometimes be just too difficult for the policeman on the beat to draw the fine distinction between what is genuinely dangerous and what is merely a bit out of line. But this argument subtly slides from cases of genuine doubt, where it makes sense to let the officers rule, to the great majority where there is no such problem, but where the law's agents might have to resist the temptation to enforce rigidly the law on the books. In those many cases, the principle of administrative ease ends up appealing to the *benefit* of the administrator, who gets a cushy and possibly exciting job arresting people who are in fact acting with complete rationality. This is the downside of the state: the guardians appointed to oversee efficient cooperation end up reinforcing rules in ways that aren't for the good of people after all, instead enforcing *inefficient* "co-operation": "I'll do this stupid thing in order that you can do *that* stupid thing." Clearly, this, too, is not the point of law.

The same considerations can apply to conscience, that sublime moral sentiment that drives fanatics like Robespierre to compulsive meddling for the "public good" when he would have done better for all of us by staying home and, as one writer suggested, "cultivating his taste for roses and sentimental verse."[1] As with the law, this is a major problem in the moral life: how to harness the moral sentiments, which can be directed at almost anything, no matter how lunatic, in such a way as to serve their only rational function, that of overseeing reasonable co-operation. Conscience can indeed be very useful when it is inducing us to keep our side of a bargain at the moment when we'd really much rather do something else. But it becomes a great liability when it sends people off to the guillotine because they haven't recited the official prayer of public virtue.

I hope that the suggestion that we ought to obey the law just because it is the law now looks unreasonable. Of course, it is most unreasonable in the spectacular cases where the law is itself evil: racist laws, laws requiring people to turn their Jewish neighbours over to the Gestapo, and many others in history have been spectacular cases in point. But my claim here is that quite ordinary laws and their administration quite typically involve ordinary, modest evils, and that they, too, are laws we should not think that we have a genuine duty to obey. Law *as such* is not morally obligatory but morally indifferent. Whether it deserves to be obeyed, either in general or in a particular case, is always an open question.

Civil Disobedience

During the Vietnam War, when many young Americans were evading the draft, fleeing to Canada, burning their draft cards, or going to jail rather than serve in the army, many articles were written by philosophers about civil disobedience. Most of them assumed that there is a heavy obligation to obey the law and tended to agonize over what to do about patently unjust laws. They tended to conclude that one has to make a very large scene about it: get arrested, get your picture in the papers, spend half of your life going to lawmakers, or to jail, or whatever it takes to get the law changed. I suggest that they went much too far.

Ordinary folks may not have time for such heroics. What we will do is evade pointless or bad laws whenever possible. Almost all drivers on Ontario's busy Highway 401 exceed the posted speed limit at any given time. Should they have qualms of conscience about this? Indeed not. No doubt it would be terrific if thousands of people would clamour for a change in the laws. But to think that they have a moral obligation to do this is simply a mistake. Ordinary people with things to do will disregard the law whenever it's a nuisance and there is no obvious reason to respect it. Far from being something that should occasion conscientious pangs on their part, I suggest that they are doing precisely what they should do. Lawmakers, in turn, should be moved to alter the laws when they see that they are very widely and very reasonably disobeyed. And to arrest as many people as they can under the old ones first would not constitute an exercise in justice but rather an exercise in Draconian arrogance.

In many cases it is, to be sure, a difficult empirical question whether the law will promote its object effectively. Speed laws are a good case in point: statistically, speeding is the least important cause of accidents, but speed laws are by far the most strenuously enforced. There are innumerable other examples. When there is contention, many people think, we should err on the side of conservatism or we ought to accept the authorities' view and not rely on our own judgement. But there is no good general argument for either of those views, and there is a very good general argument against. Authorities, after all, are biased in favour of legalism—that's how they make their living. There is no good reason to expect them to be impartial and scrupulously accurate. And there is no real alternative to relying on one's own judgement.

Should we obey the law, then? This question does not admit of a simple answer, but these points seem reasonable.

(1) Many laws require us to do what we ought to do anyway—not kill each other, for instance. Obviously we should do what those laws tell us to, not because the law requires it but because it's right.

(2) Many laws help to sort out situations where there would otherwise be confusion: telling us to keep right, for instance. Here following the law is generally advisable. But even in such cases there can be exceptions, and in those cases we should not take the fact that what we would be doing is illegal as any real reason not to do it.

(3) Many laws ask us to do things it is *usually* a good idea to do. We should usually do those things, of course. But in the unusual cases, we should not, or at least should not feel that we must.

(4) Bad laws, finally, should, if possible, be disobeyed, either by evading them or, in extreme cases, by putting up a fuss in hopes of getting them changed.

The Presumption

It is an important principle of law that we are to presume that accused persons are innocent until proven guilty. We can suggest a somewhat analogous presumption regarding the law: in the absence of special information showing otherwise, we should presume that the law deserves our acquiescence. This is a weak presumption, which can be rebutted and often will be. But it puts the law in the right perspective, making it out to be the product of imperfect people working within a highly imperfect system but trying to make their rulings in the public interest. The law, then, deserves a modest respect along the lines indicated—neither more nor less.

Summing Up

The right view, then, is the fourth of my four identified general views about this matter. In a decent country, most laws presumably have at least some basis. If we don't know what that is, and there's no obvious reason not to obey them, then we should obey them for the time being. The fact that something is a law, if you live in a decent country, is some reason to suppose that there's a fairly good reason for it. There is, then, a *presumption* that we should obey the law. This is different from the much more popular view that laws have a prima facie claim on our obedience. They do not. When laws ask us to do things that there is no independent reason to do, in terms of the interests of those concerned, then those laws are unreasonable and do not deserve our obedience. And to determine which it is requires using our heads.

Afterword

On Moral Matters

We have heads to use, and we need to use them, for our own good and the good of others. Nobody else can do our thinking for us, ultimately, and those who presume to do so should be viewed with suspicion. The view of morality maintained in this book is that moral principles should provide the conditions on which we may all live the best lives we can. Just what that best life for you will turn out to be is something I have not tried to tell you—especially because I can't. Only you can do that! The many conclusions I have tried to justify on the basis of extensive argument are not things I or anyone can *tell* you. They are, instead, suggestions, based on argument, to be considered carefully and to be accepted only if they pass the test of reasoned consideration. Of course, I think that they are right and will pass that test. And I certainly think that there are right and wrong answers, and better and worse answers, to these questions. But you must, inevitably, judge my proposed answers for yourself—which does *not* mean that whatever you think is right *is* right, nor even that it is right *for you*. It means, rather, that a responsible person simply has to think these things through for himself—or, of course, herself. I hope that this book has provided food for thought, especially for the many people who probably held rather different views on many of these questions before picking it up.

Notes

I hope to set down my thoughts on the history of moral theory, similarly stimulated by classroom experience.

Preface

1. Jan Narveson, ed., *Moral Issues* (Oxford: Oxford University Press, 1983); Eldon Soifer, ed., *Ethical Issues* 2nd ed. (Peterborough, Ont.: Broadview Press, 1996).

Chapter One

1. Above all by Charles Stevenson. See the excellent collection of his papers, *Facts and Values* (New Haven, Conn.: Yale University Press, 1963).
2. As in the case of Robert Latimer, a Saskatchewan farmer who out of sympathy killed his twelve year-old daughter Tracy, afflicted with cerebral palsy, who had a mental age of three months and weighed 40 pounds. Reported in *Kitchener-Waterloo Record*, November 6, 1997, 1, on the occasion of his second trial for murder.
3. The now classic exposition of this view is found in W.D. Ross "What Makes Right Acts Right?" It is widely anthologized, but originally appeared in Ross's *The Right and the Good* (Oxford: Clarendon Press, 1930).
4. This is a good place to express my debt to the work of Kurt Baier, whose formulation of a moral rule this essentially is. See his influential *The Moral Point of View* (Ithaca, N.Y.: Cornell University Press, 1958).
5. Hobbes. *Leviathan*, Everyman Library ed. (New York: Dutton, 1950), ch. 13, 101.

6. I made this point in "Formalism and Utilitarianism," *Australasian Journal of Philosophy* (May 1965): 58-71.

Chapter Two

1. See Epicurus, *Principal Doctrines*. A.I. Melden, *Ethical Theories* (Englewood Cliffs, N.J.: Prentice Hall, 1968)
2. See Robert Martin, "Suicide and False Desires," in Narveson, ed., *Moral Issues*.

Chapter Three

1. Philippa Foot, "Euthanasia,"in Narveson, ed., *Moral Issues*, 7.
2. This estimate of the matter was confirmed, in private conversation, by Professor Ronald Melzak of McGill University, one of the world's foremost experts on pain. At some level, there is an epistemological question here that no amount of expertise could answer, perhaps. But it surely helps that people with a *lot* of experience are fully confident of this view.

Chapter Four

1. See Locke's "Second Treatise of Civil Government," sect. 7. (Among many editions: John Locke, *Two Treatises of Civil Government* (Cambridge: Cambridge University Press, 1960), p. 271.
2. At least one journal, *Criminal Justice Ethics* (published by John Jay College of Criminal Justice, City University of New York), is devoted to precisely these questions.
3. The general line taken in this paragraph is reminiscent of Immanuel Kant's views on morals. See his *Foundations of the Metaphysic of Morals*, and his *Metaphysical Elements of Justice* (variously translated; these are the English translations employed in the Bobbs-Merrill editions).
4. I am grateful to Jennifer O'Rourke for pointing out that the law in Canada on this matter has recently been altered.
5. See, for example, Hugo Adam Bodau, ed., *Death Is different: Studies in the Morality, Law, and Politics of Capital Punishment,* (Boston : Northeastern University Press, 1987). A useful set of tables on pp. 326-27 of this book compares murder rates in states in the United States with the death penalty and states

that have abolished it. The murder rate is invariably higher in the death penalty states, typically two to three times as high. There are many reasons why such statistics can't be taken to be conclusive, and the study in question (by William C. Bailey) reanalyzes the data in illuminating ways.

6. See Isabel Lebourdais, *The Trial of Steven Truscott* (Toronto: McClelland & Stewart, 1966), for a careful study of a famous trial leading to the conviction, with sentence of death (fortunately commuted), of a fourteen-year-old boy for the murder of a twelve-year-old girl. See especially the statements of jurors at the trial, pp. 220-21. See also the later book, *Who killed Lynne Harper?*, by Bill Trent with Steven Truscott (Montreal: Optimum, 1979.) It is not easy to read such studies and retain much faith in the jury system for murder trials.

7. For more, see Randy Barnett, "The Justice of Restitution," in Narveson, ed., *Moral Issues*; Barnett, "Restitution: A New Form of Criminal Justice," *Ethics* 87 (July 1977): 279-301; and especially, Barnett, *The Structure of Liberty* (New York: Oxford University Press, 1998). See also Jan Narveson, "Moving from Punishment to Compensation," *Canadian Journal of Law and Jurisprudence* 5,1 (January 1992): 57-68; Mane Hajdin, "Criminals as Gamblers: A Modified Theory of Pure Restitution," *Dialogue* 26 (1987): 77-86.

Chapter Five

1. The entire depressing story is superbly told in Barbara Tuchman's *The March of Folly* (New York: Ballantine Books, 1984), Ch. 5.

2. This argument was worked out in the author's "Pacifism: A Philosophical Analysis," *Ethics* (1965).

3. Detailed in William L. Shirer, *The Fall of the Third Republic* (New York: Harper & Row, 1969), 251-84.

4. A current example: the city of New York has experienced a marked decline in most kinds of violence over the past few years. This decline is attributed by all observers to the increased surveillance and readiness to respond to incidents of its police force.

5. The classic source is a brief exposition by St. Thomas Aquinas, in *Summa Theologica* II, II, Question 40. For a readily available edition, see William P. Baumgarth and Richard J. Regan, *St.*

Thomas Aquinas on Law, Morality and Politics (Indianapolis: Hacket Publishing, 1988), pp. 220-222.

6. William Earle, "In Defense of War," in Narveson, ed., *Moral Issues*, 43-58. My discussion of Earle follows it.
7. Life is not simple. The oil wells of Kuwait are on Kuwaiti territory, indeed, and this makes it reasonable to suppose that they are the proper owners of those resources. Yet they were discovered by Western oil companies' geologists, and later typically expropriated by the local governments. Never mind: let us assume that the oil in question did "belong" to the Kuwaitis — certainly it didn't belong to the Iraqis!
8. James Bacque, Other Losses (Don Mills, Ont.: Stoddard, 1989).
9. See Jan Narveson, "Getting on the Road to Peace," *Ethics*, (April 1985).
10. United Nations General Assembly Declaration on the Inadmissibility of Intervention in the Domestic Affairs of States and the protection of Their Independence and Sovereignty, 1965.
11. Kant, *Perpetual Peace*, trans. Lewis White Beck (New York: Liberal Arts Press, 1957), 11.
12. See Michael Doyle, "Kant, Liberal Legacies, and Foreign Affairs," *Philosophy and Public Affairs* 12, 3-4, (Summer-Fall 1983).

Chapter Six

1. See Tom Regan, *The Case for Animal Rights* (Berkeley: University of California Press, 1983). An issue of *The Monist* 70, 1 (January, 1987) contains articles by many of the major figures in the philosophical debate on animal rights—but not, regrettably, Regan, whose shorter essay, "The Case for Animal Rights," may be found in *Advances in Animal Welfare Science* 1986/87 (The Hague: Martinus Nijhoff), with a companion piece by myself, "The Case Against Animal Rights," as well as many useful more empirical pieces by a variety of scholars and practitioners. The Institute for the Study of Animal Problems, which sponsors and edits these volumes, is to be complimented for including papers such as mine, so antithetical to their own point of view.
2. For one particularly good contribution to my side of this controversy, see Michael Bayles, "Intuitions in Ethics," *Dialogue* 23, 3(September, 1984): 439-55.

3. Stephen Satris, ed., *Taking Sides*, 3rd Ed., has a pair of articles (pp. 128-47) by Regan and Philip Devine, arguing respectively for and against a vegetarian way of life.

4. Jan Narveson, *Morality and Utility* (Baltimore: Johns Hopkins University Press, 1967). See pp. 86-87 for a brief discussion of animals.

5. I denied it, though, in Jan Narveson, "Utilitarianism and New Generations," *Mind* 76, 301 (January 1967): 62-72, reprinted in S. Gorovitz, *Mill's Utilitarianism, Text and Commentary* (Indianapolis: Bobbs-Merrill, 1971); and in Narveson, "Future People and Us," R.I. Sikora and Brian Barry, eds., *Obligations to Future Generations* (Philadelphia: Temple University Press, 1978), reprinted in A.R. Gini, David Ozar, and Patricia Werhane, *Philosophical Issues in Human Rights* (New York: Random House, 1985). The subject is a difficult and intriguing one. See, especially, Derek Parfit, "Future Generations," in Narveson, ed., *Moral Issues*, 414-44.

6. See also the point made by Julian Simon in *The Ultimate Resource* II (Princeton, N.J.: Princeton University Press, 1996), 288. Demand for meat in the U.S. has expanded rather than diminished grain-producing capability, so that "there will be no discernible improvement in the food supply of people in poor countries if you do not eat meat."

Chapter Seven

1. See James Rachels, "Killing and Starving to Death," in Narveson, ed., *Moral Issues*.

2. See Garrett Hardin, "Living on a Lifeboat," in Narveson, ed., *Moral Issues*.

3. In my late utilitarian days, I addressed this problem in "Aesthetics, Charity, Utility, and Distributive Justice," *The Monist* 36, 4 (Autumn, 1972): 527-51. Compare with Peter Singer's famous article, "Famine, Affluence, and Morality," *Philosophy and Public Affairs* 1, 3 (Spring 1972): 229-43. Of closely related interest is his "Rich and Poor," in Soifer, *Ethical Issues*, 60-76.

4. Lest this be thought a caricature, it is just about the conclusion that Singer comes to: "it does follow from my argument that we ought to be working full-time to relieve great suffering of the sort that occurs as a result of famine and other disasters." Singer, "Famine, Affluence, and Morality," 238.

5. See Onora O'Neill, "Lifeboat Earth," in Narveson, ed., *Moral Issues*, 179-93.
6. For example see Jack Powelson, *Facing Social Revolution* (Boulder, Colo: Horizon Society, 1987); Julian Simon, *Population Matters* (Rutgers, N.J.: Transaction Press, 1991).
7. Dervla Murphy, *Muddling Through in Madagascar* (London, 1985).

Chapter Eight

1. I will, in general, indiscriminately refer to biological humans at all phases after conception and before birth as "fetuses," though that term isn't used so broadly by medical people. I am assuming in this that distinctions between, say, the zygote (the two-celled entity immediately following conception), the embryo, and the fully developed fetus are of little philosophical interest. My discussion will not rule out any such arguments, but will argue that they are irrelevant to the abortion issue.
2. See Don Ross, "Abortion and the Death of the Fetus," in Narveson, ed., *Moral Issues*.
3. Joel Feinberg, "A Question about Potentiality," in Narvson, ed., *Moral Issues*.

Chapter Nine

1. See Derek Parfit, "Future Generations" in Narveson, ed., *Moral Issues*, 414-44.
2. One of the most important books on the subject is Charles Murray, *In Pursuit of Happiness (and Good Government)* (New York: Simon & Schuster, 1990).
3. My colleague Rolf George has superbly set forth this point of view in "Who Should Bear the Cost of Children?" *Public Affairs Quarterly* 1, 1(1990).

Chapter Ten

1. For the figures and original sources, see Ronald Bailey, ed., *The True State of the Planet* (New York: Free Press, 1995), specifically the articles by Nicholas Eberstadt (pp. 7-48) and Dennis Avery (pp. 49-82).

2. Paul R. Ehrlich, *The Population Bomb* (New York: Ballantine Books, 1970).
3. See the article by Sejo in Bailey, ed., *The True State of the Planet*, 177-210.
4. While the Amazon is decreasing, this is not due to rational use by people; it is because the Brazilian government is subsidizing its destruction. As with starvation, this is a political problem, not a problem of economics.
5. See Julian Simon, *The Ultimate Resource II* (Princeton, N.J.: Princeton University Press, 1996), 277.
6. The best single source for relevant information is Bailey. ed., *The True State of the Planet*, which includes essays written by ten of the top experts in each field.
7. See Bernard Cohen, "The Hazards of Nuclear Power," in Julian L. Simon, ed., *The State of Humanity* (Oxford: Basil Blackwell, 1995), 576-87.
8. See Robert Balling, Jr., "Global Warming: Messy Models, Decent Data, and Pointless Policy," Simon, ed., *The State of Humanity*, 83-108. See also Robert Balling, Jr., *The Heated Debate* (San Francisco: Pacific Research Institute for Public Policy, 1992); Patrick J. Michaels, *Sound and Fury: The Science and Politics of Global Warming* (Washington: Cato Institute, 1992).
9. See S. Fred Singer, "Stratospheric Ozone: Science and Policy," in Simon, ed., *The State of Humanity*, 536-43.

Chapter Eleven

1. For a fascinating (and charmingly written) account of Inuit (then known as "Eskimo") practices in these matters, see Duncan Pryde, *Nunaga* (New York: Bantam Books,1973), esp. chs. 9-11.
2. P.J. O'Rourke, *Eat the Rich* (New York: Atlantic Monthly Press, 1998), 2.
3. According to anthropologist Helen E. Fisher, "In fact, no Western experiment in group marriage has managed to thrive for more than a few years....The human animal seems to be psychologically built to form a pair-bond with a single mate." Fisher, *Anatomy of Love* (New York: Norton, 1992), 72.
4. The Shakers, a religious sect that prohibited sex, didn't exactly "flourish" but did have some sway in part of the U.S. in the nineteenth century. Needless to say, there are now extremely few Shakers!

5. A good example of radical feminism is found in Marilyn French, *The War against Women* (New York: Simon & Schuster, 1992). For the "liberal" type of feminism, see Janet Radcliffe Richards, *The Skeptical Feminist: A Philosophical Inquiry* (Hamondsworth: Penguin Books, 1980). Christina Hoff Sommers, *Who Stole Feminism?* (New York: Touchstone Books, 1994), is excoriated by some feminists as a betrayal and hailed by many as a fair, balanced, and reasonable assessment. Whatever else, Professor Sommers convicts several feminists of some egregious statistical howlers (see pp. 14-17, for several examples).The British writer Patricia Morgan has been investigating family issues for many years. See her *Farewell to the Family?* (London: IEA Health and Welfare Unit, Choice in Welfare No. 21, 1995).

6. See James Q. Wilson and Richard Herrnstein, *Crime and Human Nature* (New York: Simon & Schuster, 1985), esp. 245-63. See also Wilson's *Thinking about Crime* (New York: Vintage, 1983), 48. Wilson and Hernstein write: "McCord and McCord...draw the lesson...that the true causes of delinquency are found in the absence of parental affection coupled with family conflict, inconsistent discipline, and rebellious parents."

7. This doesn't mean that 50 per cent of *first* marriages end in divorce, for many of the marriages ending in divorce were themselves second or third marriages. Correcting for that error leaves, even now, a familiarly high percentage of first marriages that continue until the death of one partner.

8. Mary Ann Mason, *The Equality Trap* (New York: Simon and Schuster, 1988).

9. See the Web site <hslda.org/central/statsandreports/ray1997/ind> in which it is said that an extensive survey in the U.S. showed that home-schooled children, including those of parents who had not themselves completed high school, scored typically in the eightieth percentile on standardized academic tests.

Chapter Twelve

1. For the philosophically inclined, what this illustrates is the total independence of meta-ethics and ethics. Theories of that sort were popular in the first half of the twentieth century. The classic source is G.E. Moore's *Principia Ethica* (Cambridge: Cambridge University Press, 1903), which proposed that 'good'

designates a "unique, indefinable property." Would you be turned on at the thought of having one of those?

2. The essential book on this matter, and indeed for almost all empirical questions about this subject, is F.M Christensen *Pornography: The Other Side* (New York: Praeger, 1990).

3. In 1989, a young man armed with automatic weapons walked into a classroom full of young women at the Montreal Polytechnique Institute, and proceeded to spray them with bullets, killing fourteen before he killed himself. He professed to be objecting to feminism. His early childhood was heavily repressive. See Ivor Shapiro, "Did Marc Lepine Murder 14 Women?" *Chatelaine*. 63 (June 1990).

Chapter Thirteen

1. See the sobering study by Thomas Sowell, *Preferential Policies* (New York: William Morrow, 1990), esp. 76-87 concerning the war in Sri Lanka.

2. Walter Block and Michael Walker, eds., *Discrimination, Affirmative Action, and Equal Opportunity*, (Vancouver: Fraser Institute, 1982). See also the especially instructive chapter on "Affirmative Action in Faculty Hiring" in Thomas Sowell *Education: Passions Versus History* (Stanford, Calif.: Hoover Institution Press, 1986). Enthusiasts for affirmative action, in the author's experience, are rarely interested in facts, despite the strong empirical requirement of demonstrating past discrimination in the areas concerned. The reader is unlikely to encounter any case in which the argument for affirmative action has not engaged in the fallacious reasoning described above.

Chapter Fourteen

1. P.H. Nowell-Smith, *Ethics* (Harmondsworth: Penguin Books, 1954), 247.